PROTEST, REFORM AND
IN KHRUSHCHEV'S SOV

CW01084929

Protest, Reform and Repression in Khrushchev's Soviet Union explores the nature of political protest in the USSR during the decade following the death of Stalin. Using sources drawn from the archives of the Soviet Procurator's office, the Communist Party, the Komsomol and elsewhere, Hornsby examines the emergence of underground groups, mass riots and public attacks on authority as well as the ways in which the Soviet regime under Khrushchev viewed and responded to these challenges, including deeper KGB penetration of society and the use of labour camps and psychiatric repression. He sheds important new light on the progress and implications of deStalinization, the relationship between citizens and authority and the emergence of an increasingly materialistic social order inside the USSR. This is a fascinating study, which significantly revises our understanding of the nature of Soviet power following the abandonment of mass terror.

ROBERT HORNSBY is Honorary Research Fellow, Centre for Russian and East European Studies, University of Birmingham. He is also a Teaching Fellow in Russian History at the University of Leeds and, from May 2013, a Leverhulme Early Career Research Fellow in the School of History at the University of Kent.

NEW STUDIES IN EUROPEAN HISTORY

Edited by

The aim of this series in early modern and modern European history is to publish outstanding works of research, addressed to important themes across a wide geographical range, from southern and central Europe, to Scandinavia and Russia, from the time of the Renaissance to the Second World War. As it develops, the series will comprise focused works of wide contextual range and intellectual ambition.

A full list of titles published in the series can be found at:
www.cambridge.org/newstudiesineuropeanhistory

PROTEST, REFORM AND REPRESSION IN KHRUSHCHEV'S SOVIET UNION

ROBERT HORNSBY

CAMBRIDGE
UNIVERSITY PRESS

CAMBRIDGE
UNIVERSITY PRESS

University Printing House, Cambridge CB2 8BS, United Kingdom

Cambridge University Press is part of the University of Cambridge.

It furthers the University's mission by disseminating knowledge in the pursuit of education, learning and research at the highest international levels of excellence.

www.cambridge.org
Information on this title: www.cambridge.org/9781107521247

© Robert Hornsby 2013

First published 2013
First paperback edition 2015

A catalogue record for this publication is available from the British Library

ISBN 978-1-107-03092-3 Hardback
ISBN 978-1-107-52124-7 Paperback

For Kevin

Contents

Tables

Acknowledgements

I have been fortunate enough to benefit from the advice and encouragement of many fine scholars as I worked on this book. Jeremy Smith, Melanie Ilič and Alex Titov in particular saved me from numerous blind alleys and instead pushed my thinking in much more interesting and productive directions. Others who have read part or all of the manuscript and provided all manner of useful suggestions include Philip Boobbyer, Yoram Gorlizki, Ed Kline, Arfon Rees, Mark Smith and Gleb Tsipursky. Two anonymous reviewers at Cambridge University Press also helped sharpen my thoughts on a number of key issues.

Conversations with Vladimir Bukovsky, Aleksandr Daniel, Aleksandr Esenin-Volpin, Andrei Grigorenko, Zhores Medvedev and Yuri Orlov proved particularly illuminating. Those who have kindly sent me useful documents or granted me access to their own unpublished research include Krista Berglund, Mike Berry, Ed Cohn and Jeff Hardy. During stays in Russia I have enjoyed the hospitality of Mila and Galina Petrovna Kosterina, and the friendship and support of Bob Henderson, Pia Koivunen, Siobhan Peeling, Sean Roberts, Ulrike Ziemer and Stephen Taylor.

Lastly, by some way the largest debt of gratitude is owed to my parents, John and Norma Hornsby. Without their support this book would most likely not exist.

Transliteration

The British Standard system of transliteration has been used throughout this work, but with some exceptions in regard to places and the names of well-known individuals which already have an 'accepted' English spelling, such as Ludmilla Alexeyeva (as opposed to Lyudmila Alekseeva) and Joseph Brodsky (rather than Iosif Brodskii). Some of the scholars cited in this book have published works in both English and Russian. Where their English-language works do not use the British Standard system, the existing transliteration conventions have been followed. When Russian-language works are cited, the British Standard system of transliteration has been employed.

Introduction

It is certainly well known that the decade which followed Stalin's death was a time when the USSR underwent a series of major upheavals as the Soviet system began to turn away from the stifling and repressive grip of late Stalinism. What is less well known, since the subject rarely came to public attention in the USSR or the West at the time, is just how far this was a period when elements of Soviet society refused to accept their lot and, for one reason or another, openly clashed with the authorities. Questions of ideology, culture, economic distress, nationalism and religion all stirred popular emotions and evoked an array of dissenting responses from the masses. Of course, the system held firm and the vast majority of citizens remained compliant, but the stories of those who did not do so give us many valuable insights into the nature of the Khrushchev period and the later Soviet system.

There was no 'dissident movement' during the Khrushchev era, but a great number of people – hundreds of thousands according to some estimates – unambiguously expressed varying degrees of frustration, anger and opposition towards the political authorities.[1] These expressions could take many forms, including public outbursts against government policies, mass riots, anonymous letters, abuse aimed at members of the Party leadership, leaflets calling on workers to take strike action and underground groups threatening to incite revolution. For their part, the authorities consistently refused to accept the legitimacy of almost any political complaint rising up 'from below' and sought to ensure that dissonant voices were stifled as far as possible. Thousands of those who protested were packed off to labour camps and prisons for 'anti-Soviet activity' and some

---

[1] For example, Ludmilla Alexeyeva and Valery Chalidze – both highly authoritative voices on the history of Soviet dissent – estimated that over 500,000 Soviet citizens participated in mass disorders, disturbances, demonstrations, protest meetings and strikes between 1953 and 1964. See L. Alexeyeva and V. Chalidze, *Mass Unrest in the USSR*, Washington, DC: Department of Defense Office of Net Assessments, 1985.

were detained in psychiatric institutions. Many more were dismissed from jobs or expelled from universities, while others found themselves ejected from the Communist Party and Komsomol or were given warnings of dire consequences if they did not step back into line at once.

Unlike the Brezhnev era, when Soviet dissidents were often the focus of attention from the global media and Western academics and politicians, relatively little was written during the Cold-War period about political protest during Khrushchev's time at the helm.[2] In those works that did appear, commentators tended to suggest that dissent under Khrushchev had been predominantly restricted to a handful of literary works and to simmering intellectual ferment among members of the intelligentsia.[3] With the opening up of former Soviet archives we can now see that although challenging liberal literature by the likes of Il'ya Ehrenburg and Aleksandr Solzhenitsyn was the most widely accessible medium for criticism – by virtue of the fact that such stories, poems and essays could be bought in shops and read in libraries by Soviet citizens and Westerners alike – it was not the only means of expression for negative political attitudes. In fact, thanks to the combined effects of both self-censorship and state censorship, the famous liberal literary works of the 'Thaw era' generally expressed some of the very mildest criticism that was aimed at the authorities.

In her classic study on Soviet dissent Ludmilla Alexeyeva described the Khrushchev era as 'an incubation period when people began to learn to talk about the problems of Soviet life'. Focusing her attention primarily on the liberal intelligentsia who would go on to dominate the Brezhnev-era dissident movement,[4] Alexeyeva was undoubtedly correct to assert that the Khrushchev years were a time when the foundations were being laid for future struggles, yet they were also much more besides. The era witnessed unprecedented spells of dissension within the Communist Party and Komsomol and mass disturbances on a scale that was unheard of in later years. Large volumes of critical and oppositional leaflets were distributed in

---

[2] The most notable exception to this trend was an article by Albert Boiter on popular unrest in the early 1960s. See A. Boiter, 'When the Kettle Boils Over', *Problems of Communism*, No. 1 (1964), 33–43. Vladimir Kozlov has rightly pointed out that parts of Boiter's material were based upon rumours and other unsubstantiated sources that have since proved to be inaccurate. See V. Kozlov, *Mass Uprisings in the USSR: Protest and Rebellion in the Post-Stalin Years*, London: M.E. Sharpe, 2002, pp. 6–7. Nonetheless, Boiter drew a number of useful analytical points and his work remains a valuable, if flawed, early source on Khrushchev-era dissent.

[3] For example, in 1972 Cornelia Gerstenmaier wrote that 'for about a decade, during the mid-50s and early 60s, hostile political currents found expression almost exclusively in literary works'. C. Gerstenmaier, *The Voices of the Silent*, New York: Hart Publishing Company, 1972, p. 32.

[4] L. Alexeyeva, *Soviet Dissent: Contemporary Movements for National, Religious and Human Rights*, Middletown, CT: Wesleyan University Press, 1987, p. 269.

public spaces. People also formed underground political groups and even a few would-be terrorist cells. In other words, dissent under Khrushchev was not simply about liberal intellectuals in Moscow 'awakening' and beginning to question the regime's moral authority. It was also about Gulag returnees and workers hurling political abuse at the police, miners forming underground groups in Rostov, Party and Komsomol members both attacking and defending Stalin after the Secret Speech, forestry workers distributing anti-Khrushchev leaflets in Arkhangel' and students all over the USSR protesting against the bloody suppression of the Hungarian rising.

While the somewhat teleological view of the Khrushchev era as a time of 'incubation' or 'underdeveloped dissidence' made sense for those looking backwards from the perspective of the Brezhnev-era dissident movement, it also provides only a narrow view of – or else overlooks – a whole host of events and trends that had far-reaching implications for the Soviet system as a whole, not just for the dissenting activity of later years.[5] As I show throughout the book, and particularly in Chapter 9, there were all manner of important connections between Khrushchev-era political dissent and the dissident movement of the Brezhnev years. Nonetheless, with high levels of underground activity, huge public disorders and extensive worker protest taking place between the mid 1950s and mid 60s, there were too many significant points of distinction for us to regard Khrushchev-era dissent as simply an embryonic form of the subsequent human-rights movement.

One of the most distinctive aspects of dissent in the Khrushchev era was its diversity, both in the social origins of protesters and the behaviours they engaged in. Under Stalin, those acts of protest that have since been documented were largely spontaneous and volatile, and were often centred upon angry workers and peasants.[6] The Brezhnev years, on the other hand, were characterised by far more legalistic and sober criticism that saw dissent primarily restricted to the metropolitan intelligentsia, albeit a fairly small proportion of that body.[7] Fittingly for its chronological position between the two eras, the Khrushchev period was a time that featured enraged acts of protest by workers and peasants as well as more cerebral criticisms made by members of the intelligentsia. Consequently, dissent could be crude and

---

[5] In regard to earlier historiography on Khrushchev-era dissent, see V. Kozlov and S. Mironenko eds., *Kramola: inakomyslie v SSSR pri Khrushcheve i Brezhneve 1953–1982*, Moskva: Materik, 2005.

[6] See, for example, L. Viola ed., *Contending with Stalinism: Soviet Power and Popular Resistance in the 1930s*, London: Cornell University Press, 2002.

[7] The literature on the Brezhnev-era dissident movement is particularly rich. See, for example, J. Rubenstein, *Soviet Dissidents: Their Struggle for Human Rights*, Boston, MA: Beacon Press, 1980 and R. Tökes ed., *Dissent in the USSR: Politics, Ideology, and People*, Baltimore, MD: Johns Hopkins University Press, 1975.

explosive at some points, and then more sophisticated and considered at others, depending on the issues at hand. In practice, there was often minimal convergence between these different types of dissent. Working-class protest, which changed only a little following Stalin's death, generally still flared up on the spur of the moment and centred upon quite personal-ised and material issues such as poor living standards and specific abuses of power, whilst members of the intelligentsia were likely to show their frustration at slightly more nebulous problems, like the uneven progress of deStalinization or the Party's dogmatic restrictions upon cultural affairs.

Even though outbursts of worker and peasant anger tended to originate in material discontent, they could quickly become politicised in their language and gestures. Because this was such a large sector of society – and one in whose interests the regime purported to rule – working-class discontent in particular had the potential to be very dangerous for the authorities, especially in an era when people's aspirations were rising fast. An increasingly consumerist social contract meant that living standards clearly fed into social stability. After a major flaring of worker discontent during the summer of 1962 – and a particularly brutal government response at Novocherkassk – the dynamics of dissenting behaviour began to shift and protest activity among workers declined in both frequency and scale. This was not necessarily because would-be protesters became any more afraid to voice criticism of the authorities, but because the regime began to take ever greater care to prevent mass discontent from again reaching such a danger-ous level. First and foremost, this meant alleviating the more acute material frustrations within society, such as growing desires for consumer goods and better housing. Although it demanded a certain re-orienting of economic priorities, this was a price worth paying in order to help head off large-scale dissent.

The situation in regard to the liberal intelligentsia was somewhat differ-ent. For them, the major turning point came when Khrushchev first exposed Stalin's failures and cruelty in the Secret Speech, on 25 February 1956. In denouncing Stalin, the Secret Speech implicitly also denounced rule by terror, thus providing an assurance that there would be no return to full-blooded Stalinism, under which the voicing of political criticism was liable to end in unmitigated disaster. Responses to protest remained harsh by any other standard, but they were no longer murderous. The realisation that one could now speak up without ultimately facing physical destruction thus loosened slightly the shackles of self-censorship on those who consid-ered the consequences of their actions before protesting. The main chal-lenge for the authorities in handling the frustrations of intelligentsia dissenters lay in the fact that their complaints were often of a more fundamentally politicised nature than those of workers and could not so easily be 'bought off' with material improvements, but instead required genuine reform. As such, their grievances were mostly ignored or suppressed while those of Soviet workers met with a more sympathetic response.

Many of the behaviours examined herein would have been entirely acceptable under less authoritarian regimes or would have simply constituted regular political interchange, rather than dangerous acts of protest. Soviet domestic priorities dictated a wider conception of subversive behaviour which encapsulated a range of acts that one generally would not recognise today as being subversive. Perhaps most notably, this included a fierce protection of the official public sphere from any sign of ideological heterodoxy, whether originating in the West or the East, from neo-Bolshevik underground groups or from drunkards in the street. However, as I show at several points, there were also plenty of protest behaviours taking place that would have been unacceptable or else would have attracted close interest from the state under any political system, either then or now. Khrushchev-era dissent often centred upon people, causes and behaviours that bore limited resemblance to the broadly liberal and legalistic protests of Andrei Sakharov et al. from the late 1960s onwards.

Whilst acknowledging the deep significance of the regime's abandonment of mass terror, a growing number of scholars have emphasised that the well-established characterisation of the Khrushchev era as a time of relative liberality, or 'thaw', is problematic in a number of important ways. This is especially evident when one looks at policies and attitudes toward dissenting behaviour.[8] In fact, the trend was not for the Khrushchev regime to show significantly greater acceptance of discordant political expressions from among the masses. Those who kept quiet were no longer in danger of facing groundless repression, and those who did fall foul of the authorities would not face such severe punishment, yet there was still to be no compromise or meaningful dialogue with citizens deemed 'anti-Soviet', including those who ultimately considered themselves loyal critics. While there was greater scope for disagreement among political elites and some toleration of nonconformist thought in the cultural sphere, things had changed relatively

[8] See, for example, M. Dobson, *Khrushchev's Cold Summer: Gulag Returnees, Crime and the Fate of Reform after Stalin*, Ithaca, NY: Cornell University Press, 2009 and B. Firsov, *Raznomyslie v SSSR 1940–1960 gody: istoriya, teoriya i praktika*, Sankt Peterburg: Izdatel'stvo Evropeiskogo universiteta v Sankt Peterburge, 2008.

little for the ordinary citizen in terms of what they could legitimately do or say about political issues.

Naked coercion of dissenters never disappeared entirely, but the authorities in the post-Stalin era did become considerably more sophisticated – and were often remarkably effective – in the way that they dealt with their detractors. Once mass repression had been abandoned with Stalin's passing, the Khrushchev regime had to find new ways of keeping protest and non-conformity at a minimum. By lambasting the late dictator after years of adulation, the Secret Speech created uncertainty for a time as to where the new boundaries of acceptable and unacceptable comment lay. By failing to prescribe discourse on the matter, the authorities also inadvertently prompted citizens to search for their own conclusions about what the attack on Stalin said about the Soviet past, present and future. As a result, many of those most earnest in taking up Khrushchev's call to overcome the consequences of the Cult of Personality soon faced censure for 'overstepping the mark'. By proclaiming a vaguely defined 'return to Leninism' it also facilitated a wider ideological discourse that quickly proved threatening within a political system that was essentially focused on consolidating and preserving gains already acquired by the revolution, rather than launching a genuine revolution of its own.[9] Though there was never any question of tolerating entirely unfettered comment, the authorities were initially ill prepared for taking on critics so soon after proffering a new and less repressive style of government.

When the Hungarian rising and the subsequent Soviet response compounded and amplified tensions already arising more widely from the Secret Speech and the post-war years, the authorities considered it necessary to reassert their prerogative to tackle dissent with alacrity. For over a year there was a small-scale reversion to the 'bad old days', as the number of citizens jailed on political charges shot up during 1957 and 1958. Thereafter, social control again became less heavily reliant upon such direct and draconian measures. Instead, new mechanisms for policing proliferated and were honed as the boundaries between state and society were deliberately blurred. Popular opinion was carefully shaped to leave non-conformists isolated and unpopular. Public involvement in the work of the authorities and intrusion into citizens' everyday lives became an increasing feature of the Soviet system, as new layers of social control and peer-policing were employed to stifle the expression of political doubts and discontent. In

---

[9] On the subject of the post-war Soviet regime's focus on consolidating gains already won, see J. Fürst, *Stalin's Last Generation: Soviet Post-War Youth and the Emergence of Mature Socialism*, Oxford University Press, 2010.

many ways, the post-Stalin decline in repression was ultimately compensated for by an increase in the scope and effectiveness of policing.

Mass conformity was not maintained solely by punishment and intimidation, however. For the majority of the population, Soviet rule was widely accepted as legitimate, even if it was not always embraced in all its forms. Communist notions of social fairness and collectivism had taken root and in fact proved to be recurrent themes on which the authorities were criticised for failing to deliver. As the limits to which the masses were willing to be pushed by their political leaders narrowed following the Second World War, and then narrowed further following Stalin's death, the authorities began to make less exacting demands, in terms of both material sacrifices and ideological zeal. Living standards rose and positive incentives for compliance proliferated, such as growing access to consumer goods, new apartments and university places or the occasional granting of permission to travel abroad. Alongside changes to policing and intermittent appeals to communist idealism, this helped to make possible the maintenance of a social order in which an increasingly educated and informed public, with rising aspirations for the future, would remain overwhelmingly compliant without either deep political reforms, such as democratisation or freedom of expression, or reversion to mass state violence.

Looking at the range of measures that the Soviet leadership put in place to combat dissent, we can see that many of them were based upon eminently rational (though that is not to say 'fair') assessments of the domestic situation, yet often they were implemented in a heavy-handed and unhelpful manner that exacerbated, rather than alleviated, existing problems. For example, they were fundamentally correct in the belief that foreign powers – most notably the US – were conducting propaganda warfare with the aim of undermining the Soviet system in the eyes of its people. Nonetheless, the spectre of foreign subversion was consistently overstated, to the point where it became counter-productive and masked entirely organic and broadly apolitical reasons for citizens' discontent, such as low wages or poor housing. They were also correct to view the younger generation as a potentially fertile breeding ground for non-conformist views and behaviour, but they often diagnosed inappropriate or unhelpful reasons for this, such as 'insufficient respect for physical labour', rather than accepting that in reality students struggled on pitifully low stipends and post-war youths held different ambitions and interests to their parents' generation. This did not make them 'anti-Soviet'. Dogmatic thinking prompted a perception of even mild political non-conformity which could heighten those tensions that did come to the surface. As a result, even those who had desired to help repair the system through loyal and constructive criticism tended to find themselves increasingly alienated and marginalised. Conversely, private doubts and frustrations were no longer such a major concern for the authorities, provided that they remain unvoiced. Although the point was never made absolutely explicit, efforts at shaping and transforming the masses increasingly came to centre upon inducing obedience rather than upon instilling communist values as the vitality of the Soviet project waned.

Formerly classified archival materials have helped to turn research on the Khrushchev era and Late Socialism more widely into a particularly active field since around the turn of the millennium, as historians are now increasingly taking over from where contemporary political scientists and journalists left off. With a wealth of new archival material now available to the researcher, the last few years have seen emerge a much more detailed and nuanced picture of the period in question. Monographs by the likes of William Taubman (on Khrushchev himself), Miriam Dobson (on the release of Gulag inmates), Thomas Wolfe (on journalism), Vladislav Zubok (on the post-Stalin intelligentsia) and Stephen Bittner (a micro-history of the Khrushchev-era Arbat district in Moscow), along with edited volumes by Polly Jones (on deStalinization) and Melanie Ilič and Jeremy Smith (on state and society under Khrushchev), have provided a wealth of new information on the era and posed significant challenges to a range of long-standing assumptions and interpretations of the period.[10]

Notions of the Khrushchev period as a time of 'liberal communism' are rightly being questioned, though this questioning tends to centre upon comparisons with the succeeding Brezhnev era, rather than the preceding Stalin years.[11] Ideas of the Khrushchev era as a time when high politics was predominantly characterised by struggle between 'liberals' and 'conservatives' (or 'reformists' and 'Stalinists') within the elite are also being further

---

[10] It is also worth noting that a number of excellent Ph.D. theses have been produced in this area recently. See, for example, B. Tromly, 'Re-Imagining the Soviet Intelligentsia: Student Politics and University Life, 1948–1964', Ph.D. Dissertation, Harvard University, 2007; E. Cohn, 'Disciplining the Party: The Expulsion and Censure of Communists in the Post-War Soviet Union, 1945–1961', Ph.D. Dissertation, University of Chicago, 2007; G. Tsipursky, 'Pleasure, Power and the Pursuit of Communism: Soviet Youth and State-Sponsored Popular Culture during the Early Cold War Period, 1945–1968', Ph.D. Dissertation, University of North Carolina at Chapel Hill, 2011; J. Hardy, 'Khrushchev's Gulag: The Evolution of Punishment in the Post-Stalin Soviet Union, 1953–1964', Ph.D. Dissertation, Princeton University, 2011.

[11] See, for example, B. Firsov, *Raznomyslie.*

refined.[12] Similarly, notions of a mass retreat from meaningful participation in public life and withdrawal into a world of private concerns are being challenged by new models that highlight extensive interaction between public and private activities and relationships.[13] In terms of periodisation, assumptions of a relatively liberal early period and a more conservative later period have been found to hold true in some important respects but not in others. The worst excesses of Stalinism were quickly abandoned forever but key pillars of the Brezhnev-era political system were firmly established by the time that Khrushchev was removed from office. Citizens' increased awareness of and interaction with the outside world was an important catalyst for social change but it was often much more slow-burning and less overtly ideological in nature than was first assumed when Soviet young people began scrambling for blue jeans, jazz records and Western youth slang.[14]

The ups and downs of deStalinization have rightly been the focus of much academic attention but they by no means defined the everyday lives of Soviet citizens throughout the period. Nor were they always at the heart of dissenting activity – something which a long-standing focus on intelligentsia protest has tended to obscure. While Khrushchev's denunciation of Stalin at the XX CPSU Congress in February 1956 either sparked or facilitated much of the intelligentsia dissent that subsequently followed, it was generally not such an important catalyst for expressions of political discontent among other sections of the population. The catalysts for dissenting behaviour were myriad: only a portion of them related to questions of liberalisation. As Nikolai Mitrokhin points out, for example, for millions in the armed forces it was not the Secret Speech but the swingeing military cuts of the late 1950s that were key to their experience of the era.[15] For Soviet Jews, it was often the authorities' anti-Semitism that generated most resentment. For workers and peasants, issues such as increases in the price of foodstuffs and restrictions on private plots engendered far greater discontent than did questions of political reform.

---

[12] The more traditional 'conflict model' can be seen in works such as Carl Linden's *Khrushchev and the Soviet Leadership*, Baltimore, MD: Johns Hopkins University Press, 1990. One of the most notable challenges to this approach in recent scholarship has been in Miriam Dobson's *Khrushchev's Cold Summer*.

[13] See, for example, L. Siegelbaum ed., *Borders of Socialism: Private Spheres of Soviet Russia*, Basingstoke: Palgrave Macmillan, 2006.

[14] See, for example, S. Zhuk, *Rock and Roll in the Rocket City: The West, Identity, and Ideology in Soviet Dnepropetrovsk, 1960–1985*, Washington, DC: Woodrow Wilson Center Press, 2010.

[15] See N. Mitrokhin, *Russkaya partiya: dvizhenie russkikh natsionalistov v SSSR , 1953–1985*, Moskva: Novoe literaturnoe obozrenie, 2003, p. 6.

Much attention has been paid to Soviet dissent over the years, firstly in the West during the Cold War, and then during *glasnost'* and the immediate post-Soviet period inside what was the USSR. In both cases one can point to a whole range of factors driving interest in Soviet dissidents, such as humanitarian concern, political expediency and simple curiosity about what really lay beneath the Soviet regime's monolithic façade. Some looked for evidence that the classical liberal values of Western civilisation had been able to survive in the face of a decades-long attempt to produce a new, Soviet man.[16] Doubtless there were also many who hoped that in monitoring dissent they were picking up on early signals of an impending mass rejection of communism. With the Soviet Union now long since collapsed, more than a few of these earlier reasons for studying dissent have also expired. Nonetheless, there is still much to be learned from this theme.

Dissenting behaviour cannot be used as an always-reliable and straight-forward prism through which to view the state of the Soviet system. In some cases protesters quite possibly were voicing the concerns and frustrations of silent millions but one could never be entirely sure of that. In many cases protesters almost certainly represented no one but themselves. Questions of motivation and intent often remain a matter of interpretation, rather than fact. Nonetheless, in aggregate form acts of protest and criticism do give an insight into what particularly aggrieved certain sections of society at any given time and allow us to interpret some of the on-going political and social changes for which the Khrushchev period became known, whilst also providing tantalising glimpses of deeper-lying troubles, such as declining faith in the integrity and ability of the Soviet regime's political leadership. The forms and themes of protest activity can also help us to gain an idea of how deep the roots of the Soviet system had penetrated by the 1950s and 1960s. Many critics during the early part of the Khrushchev period, for example, assailed the authorities from distinctly communist ideological positions. More often than not, the language and protest behaviours that dissenters deployed bore the hallmarks of a profound identification with, or at least an acceptance of, the system rather than its rejection.

Responding to dissent was only a part of the regime's workload, and a reasonably small part at that, but it was nonetheless an important facet of the state's domestic activity and one that tells us much about the period in question. In terms of the authorities' responses to dissenting behaviour, we learn about what factors shaped attitudes toward critics, how policy-making

---

[16] On this broad theme see A. Krylova, 'The Tenacious Liberal Subject in Soviet Studies', *Kritika: Explorations in Russian and Eurasian History*, Vol. 1, No. 1 (Winter 2000), 119–46.

was conducted, the way that policies were implemented and how different elements of the Soviet state apparatus functioned in tandem with each other, or failed to do so, as the case may have been. Just as the policies and pronouncements of the authorities gradually demonstrated to the man and woman on the street how political life had and had not changed since the death of Stalin, so instances of protest and expressions of anger showed the authorities what had and had not changed in terms of popular attitudes and aspirations. Out of this interchange, new rules of the game were established.[17]

Although my focus lies primarily on tracing broad trends of dissenting behaviour and regime responses, where the evidence is sufficiently rich I have also tried to say something about the values, attitudes and goals of the individuals involved, as well as the reasons why their discontent was manifested in the way that it was. For the most part, these were not quite the 'islands of separateness' that Carl Joachim Friedrich and Zbigniew Brzezinski envisaged in their totalitarian model.[18] Similarly, dichotomies of 'belief' and 'unbelief' are of relatively limited value. Most often the evidence shows a degree of interaction between the two. In many cases acts of protest were prompted by unique circumstances and were themselves the exception rather than the rule within a person's wider lifespan. Dissenters did not stand apart from the system but were a product of it, sometimes in a very direct way. The early Khrushchev years in particular often saw critics' frustrations rooted in an idealistic belief in communism, combined with the desire to correct a system that was deemed to be failing in some way but not beyond hope. There was no hard and fast dichotomy between positions of dissent and conformity: those who protested volubly over one issue might just as easily accept or embrace the authorities' position on others. Furthermore, there is no need to assume a permanence of attitude among those who spoke out: even otherwise wholly obedient communists could turn vitriolic for a time as personal circumstances fluctuated and political sensibilities were either offended or aroused (both of which proved to be the case following Khrushchev's February 1956 attack on Stalin).

Many acts of protest resulted from anger at very specific events or individuals rather than rejection of the Soviet system as a whole, yet the ubiquity of the political sphere – in the form of language, symbols, rituals

[17] See V. Kozlov, *Mass Uprisings*.
[18] See C. Friedrich and Z. Brzezinski, *Totalitarian Dictatorship and Autocracy*, Cambridge, MA: Harvard University Press, 1965.

and much else besides – and the authorities' dogmatic attitude toward critics quickly helped to give almost all discontent some political colouring. Often those who started out hoping to help the Soviet system recover from the effects of a quarter-century of Stalinism found themselves attacked and alienated, some of them subsequently becoming particularly strident critics. As the era progressed, the idealism of the mid 1950s faded among dissenters. By the early 1960s a growing proportion of critics advocated major political change and even violent resistance. Many others came to shun the world of politics entirely wherever they could, showing interest neither in protest nor in ideological engagement beyond a perfunctory level.

While the flow of literature on Soviet dissent has slowed considerably since the fall of the communist regime, a handful of recent volumes have made major advances in the field.[19] Most notably for the present work, the Russian historian Vladimir Kozlov has produced two particularly important works on protest behaviour in the post-Stalin USSR.[20] In looking at subjects such as mass riots and demonstrations, Kozlov has already done much to map the contours of sub-intelligentsia dissent, a process to which I seek to add further details and argument throughout this book. Where the present work differs most notably from that of Kozlov is in examining both dissent and government policy against dissent within the same analytical field, as opposed to looking at dissenting behaviour in isolation. This has, I feel, helped me to draw a number of wider conclusions about the nature and relationship of protest and social control. Also, while Kozlov and Mironenko's *Kramola* (*Sedition*) consists principally of reproduced documents from the files of the Soviet Procurator's office, I have sought to add a little more analytical flesh to the bones of such documents and to draw on a number of additional sources, such as records from the Central Committee's General Department, from the Party Control Commission, the Department of Komsomol Organs and from Radio Liberty's monitoring of the Soviet media. This has allowed me to tease out a number of wider conclusions about the nature of the post-Stalin political system in the USSR.

It is also important briefly to revisit what we mean by 'dissent' in the Soviet context. This study does not seek to address the whole spectrum of

---

[19] Examples of excellent English-language works on dissent in recent years include P. Boobbyer, *Conscience, Dissent and Reform in Soviet Russia*, London: Routledge, 2005 and R. Horvath, *The Legacy of Soviet Dissent: Dissidents, Democratisation and Radical Nationalism in Russia*, London: Routledge, 2005. Most recently, see V. Kozlov, S. Fitzpatrick and S. Mironenko eds., *Sedition: Everyday Resistance in the Soviet Union under Khrushchev and Brezhnev*, New Haven, CT: Yale University Press, 2011.

[20] See V. Kozlov, *Massovye besporyadki v SSSR pri Khrushcheve i Brezhneve, 1953–1980gg*, Novosibirsk: Sibirskii khronograf, 1999 and V. Kozlov and S. Mironenko eds., *Kramola*.

non-conformity in the Khrushchev years, nor does it focus upon issues such as intra-elite political debate, labour indiscipline or what could be termed 'passive dissent', such as listening to foreign radio broadcasts in the privacy of one's own home or criticising the authorities in conversations with friends and family. This is not at all because such matters are unworthy of study, but because, as Michael David-Fox has pointed out, one quickly finds there are practically no boundaries to what constitutes 'dissent' when one begins to incorporate such behaviours.[21] With this in mind, one is inclined to use as a base for our understanding of dissent Roy Medvedev's argument that, in the Soviet context, a dissenter '. . . does more than simply disagree and think differently; he openly proclaims his dissent and demonstrates it in one way or another to his compatriots and the state'.[22] This element of interaction between protest and authority lies at the heart of the present study.

Aurel Braun's typology of dissenting behaviour as being essentially religious, nationalist, economic or political is a good place from which to compartmentalise acts of protest.[23] The focus here lies on what Braun defined as political issues, though the boundaries of the term are necessarily somewhat inconsistent at times and in fact economic issues often fed into political statements. Perhaps the most useful connection to draw in the Soviet context is with the dissident movement of the Brezhnev era, which has generally been categorised into three principal fields of protest activity: nationalist, religious and human rights.[24] In the Khrushchev period one can clearly see nationalist and religious dissent taking place across the USSR as well as a third, more nebulous, genre of protest activity which was neither nationalist nor religious, though it was not primarily concerned with defending human rights either.[25] The kinds of protest that I have termed

[21] M. David-Fox, 'Whither Resistance?', in M. David-Fox, P. Holquist and M. Poe eds., *The Resistance Debate in Russian and Soviet History: Kritika Historical Studies 1*, Bloomington, IN: Slavica, 2003, p. 233.
[22] R. Medvedev, *On Soviet Dissent: Interviews with Piero Ostellino*, New York: Columbia University Press, 1977, p. 1. This is a point that has been echoed by Sheila Fitzpatrick in the English-language edition of Vladimir Kozlov's *Sedition*, and one that largely takes us out of the realm of James C. Scott's 'hidden transcripts' approach to dissenting behaviour. See J. Scott, *Domination and the Arts of Resistance: Hidden Transcripts*, New Haven, CT: Yale University Press, 1990.
[23] A. Braun, 'Dissent and the State in Eastern Europe', in C. E. S. Franks ed., *Dissent and the State*, Toronto: Oxford University Press, 1989, p. 116.
[24] The best example of this classification can be seen in the title of Alexeyeva's major work on the subject: *Soviet Dissent: Contemporary Movements for National, Religious and Human Rights*.
[25] The Western tendency to label the Brezhnev-era *pravozashchitniki* as human-rights activists has the advantage of linguistic clarity but is somewhat inaccurate. As Robert Horvath has pointed out, they were interested in the defence of rights and the rule of law as a whole, rather than just human rights. R. Horvath, *The Legacy of Soviet Dissent*, p. 84.

political dissent instead tended to include a wider array of contemporary political matters, such as criticism of government policies, officials and attitudes. As a term, 'political dissent' has only fleetingly been applied to the USSR before now, though it has been used in the context of numerous other authoritarian regimes.[26] In this case, 'political dissent' describes a range of behaviours that have thus far largely remained without classification in the English language. Russian sources that touch on this theme have used several terms, including: *inakomyslie* (otherwise-thinking), *kramola* (subversion or sedition), *raznomyslie* (different-thinking) and *protivostoyanie* (confrontation), none of which quite carries the right connotation in the English language.[27] I have also opted to forego use of the term 'dissident'. In part this is because the word is so deeply intertwined with the dissent of the Brezhnev era that it would blur the specificity of Khrushchev-era dissent. More importantly, many of the acts of dissent that I describe were isolated and exceptional instances in people's lives that in no measure defined who that person was in a political sense.

Of course, the Khrushchev era was a time of burgeoning nationalism in the Baltic republics, Ukraine, Russia and the Caucasus.[28] This was also a period in which believers from many religious faiths, such as Jews, Baptists and Jehovah's Witnesses, all had their own struggles with the Soviet authorities.[29] Nationalist and religious protests were undoubtedly important phenomena that helped to shape the era, but they fall beyond the scope of this study. While there are clearly advantages to be drawn from looking at all forms of dissenting behaviour collectively, there are also benefits in studying each individually, not least because this allows one to examine and discuss largely unexplored matters in greater depth. With such a profusion of nationalities and religions in the USSR one could say only a little – and perhaps nothing new – about each in a single work. All three broad strands of dissent – nationalist, religious and political – had a

---

[26] See, for example, Ian Kershaw's *Popular Opinion and Political Dissent in the Third Reich: Bavaria 1933–1945*, Oxford University Press, 2002; J. Maravall, *Dictatorship and Political Dissent: Workers and Students in Franco's Spain*, London: Palgrave Macmillan, 1979; R. Zuzowski, *Political Dissent and Opposition in Poland: Workers' Defence Committee 'KOR'*, London: Greenwood, 1992.

[27] See V. Kozlov and S. Mironenko eds., *Kramola*; B. Firsov, *Raznomyslie* and V. Kozlov, *Neizvestnyi SSSR: protivostoyanie naroda i vlasti 1953–1985*, Moskva: Olma-Press, 2006. State-generated documents from the period in question often used the term *antisovet* (anti-Soviet).

[28] On nationalist dissent see, for example, A. Alexeyeva, *Soviet Dissent*; B. Nahaylo and W. Swoboda, *Soviet Disunion: A History of the Nationalities Problem in the USSR*, New York: The Free Press, 1990 and A. Weiner, 'The Empires Pay a Visit: Gulag Returnees, East European Rebellions, and Soviet Frontier Politics', *The Journal of Modern History*, Vol. 78, No. 2 (June 2006), 333–76.

[29] On religious dissent during the period see, for example, W. Fletcher, 'Religious Dissent in the USSR in the 1960s', *Slavic Review*, Vol. 30, No. 2 (June 1971), 298–316.

commonality of conflict with the authorities but they also differed from each other notably in their themes, forms and aims, and it was not until well into the Brezhnev era that there was any significant degree of interaction between dissenters of such different stripes.[30] In fact, the Soviet authorities, too, implicitly differentiated between religious, nationalist and political dissent, hardly ever clamping down on more than one of the three at any given time and often employing distinct methods to deal with each of them.[31]

None of this is to suggest that nationalist and religious protest were, by definition, apolitical. On the contrary, both were subjects loaded with political meaning and consequence. For the most part, though, they did not centre upon contemporary political affairs or questions of ideological interpretation.[32] Dedication to a 'terminal community', whether that be one's nation or one's religion, provided a framework for protest that was often lacking among those responding negatively to contemporary political stimuli, such as policies and political personalities. Even so, nationalist and political dissent (and in some republics, nationalist and religious dissent) both overlapped and intertwined at times, especially in the non-Russian republics. Vociferous reactions to the Hungarian crisis across the USSR's western borderlands – in Ukraine and the Baltic republics – were a perfect example of this.[33]

The literary output of the Khrushchev period, of course, was heavily shaped by the political developments of the era and itself helped to shape those years, both as they played out at the time and in the way in which they have subsequently been remembered. However, where previous discussions of dissent under Khrushchev have generally focused upon cultural hetero-doxy and the fluctuating limits of creative freedom, the present study does not do so. Key works, such as Vladimir Dudintsev's *Not by Bread Alone* and Aleksandr Solzhenitsyn's *One Day in the Life of Ivan Denisovich*, are still raised as important moments in the history of Soviet dissent, and as factors which helped shape the discourse of political discontent, but they are no

---

[30] There were exceptions to this trend, such as Petro Grigorenko's long-standing interest in the fate of the Crimean Tatars, but the overall pattern holds true. Extensive interaction only really began with the creation of the Moscow Helsinki Group in 1976.

[31] For example, Amir Weiner shows that in late 1956 and 1957, authorities in the Western borderlands were trialling new, more inclusive methods of dealing with the problem of returning nationalists. At the same time, the number of people being arrested elsewhere for criticism and abuse of political figures and policies was increasing rapidly. See A. Weiner, 'The Empires Pay a Visit'.

[32] There were, of course, exceptions to this rule, such as protests at official anti-religious campaigns and at the 1959 education reforms.

[33] See A. Weiner, 'The Empires Pay a Visit'.

longer placed at the very heart of Khrushchev-era dissenting behaviour. This is firstly because previous authors have already covered the literary thaw in detail and with great skill.[34] Perhaps more importantly, my aim is to go beyond the relatively narrow bounds of intelligentsia dissent with which the ups and downs of cultural liberalisation were most intimately linked, placing the genre within the wider picture of dissenting activity.

One of the principal reasons it has been possible to produce a work that differs from earlier studies on dissent is primarily through evidence contained in Soviet archives that have become accessible only in more recent years. Many materials, such as KGB reports on public disturbances, minutes of Central Committee meetings and records of criminal investigations into dissenting behaviour, are now open to researchers and are reasonably plentiful. Some important sources have either disappeared or else remain inaccessible, yet sufficient evidence has become available for us to paint a far more detailed picture of events than was previously possible. Of course, important question marks remain as to the strengths and weaknesses of such state-generated sources.[35] Hiroaki Kuromiya, for example, has provided valuable insights into the staggering extent to which Stalin-era sources like these featured manipulated evidence, fabricated conspiracies and false confessions extracted through torture.[36] Although by no means entirely eradicated, such problems are drastically reduced when using analogous documents from the Khrushchev era.

The Soviet law-enforcement apparatus hardly became a model of fairness and transparency after Stalin's death, but in terms of the reliability of the sources that it generated, the system improved greatly during the 1950s and 1960s. Crucial evidence could still be presented out of context, defendants pressured or witnesses intimidated and key details omitted at trial, but cases were very rarely created entirely out of thin air, in order to satisfy campaigns against whole social and national groups or simply to sate the Gulag's

---

[34] On the cultural thaw, see, for example, D. Spechler, *Permitted Dissent in the USSR: Novy Mir and the Soviet Regime*, New York: Praeger, 1982; P. Johnson, *Khrushchev and the Arts: The Politics of Soviet Culture, 1962–1964*, Cambridge, MA: MIT Press, 1965; M. Zezina, *Sovetskaya khudozhestvennaya intelligentsiya i vlast' v 1950e–60e gody*, Moskva: Dialog MGU, 1999. The best work of recent times is Vladislav Zubok's *Zhivago's Children: The Last Russian Intelligentsia*, Cambridge, MA: Harvard University Press, 2009.

[35] The best works on the subject of documents created by the security organs are by Peter Holquist and Cristina Vatulescu. See P. Holquist, '"Information is the Alpha and Omega of Our Work": Bolshevik Surveillance in its Pan-European Context', *The Journal of Modern History*, Vol. 69, No. 3 (September 1997), 415–50 and C. Vatulescu, 'Arresting Biographies: The Secret Police File in the Soviet Union and Romania', *Comparative Literature*, Vol. 56, No. 3 (Summer 2004), 243–61.

[36] See H. Kuromiya, *The Voices of the Dead: Stalin's Terror in the 1930s*, London: Yale University Press, 2007.

appetite for manpower. For the most part, Khrushchev-era KGB reports and investigation records were a concise and reasonably sober record of events, and one that the political leadership wished to be fundamentally accurate in detail, though this is not to say impartial. Because they were overwhelmingly classified, most of the sources used in this study did not have any overtly propagandistic function. They were not intended to fool the public or the outside world, but to relay information and to help officials and members of the Party leadership make decisions and take action. Although successive heads of the KGB were inclined to overstate the challenge that dissent posed for the authorities (thus increasing the resources and prestige allocated them to fight dissent), and Party officials could overstate or understate evidence of unrest, depending on which best suited their purposes at the time, it was not in their interests seriously to mislead Khrushchev and his colleagues.[37] As Moshe Lewin pointed out, '... the regime, especially in the post-Stalinist period, often had at its disposal a mass of good material and, in addition, rigorous analyses of the country and of the outside world'.[38] Much can be drawn from that good material which has come to light.

The problem still remains that official documents often only allow us to see what the authorities saw – and they cannot have seen everything. Even so, the KGB and Soviet political elite were certainly better informed on matters relating to dissenting behaviour than anybody else either inside or outside of the USSR, thus making their materials on the subject especially useful when evaluated with care and supplemented by a wide array of additional sources. One must still remain alive to the fact that official accounts such as investigation records were shaped by the intentions, aims and assumptions of the observer, rather than the observed.[39] For example, official reports often branded comments made by even loyal Communist Party and Komsomol members as 'anti-Soviet' simply because they had voiced disagreement with the prevailing ideological orthodoxy, not because those responsible actually were opposed to the Soviet regime. The value judgements contained in such documents, therefore, often tell us much more about their authors than they do about their subjects. Furthermore,

---

[37] In particular I have in mind Ivan Serov, Vladimir Semichastnyi and Yuri Andropov as KGB chairmen who were considered to have habitually exaggerated the threat posed by dissenters. Vladimir Shlapentokh argues that the KGB was generally a source of reliable information for the leadership. See V. Shlapentokh, *A Normal Totalitarian Society: How the Soviet Union Functioned and How it Collapsed*, New York: Oxford University Press, 2001, p. 56.

[38] M. Lewin, *The Soviet Century*, London: Verso, 2005, p. ix.

[39] On this theme, see L. Viola, 'Popular Resistance in the Stalinist 1930s – Soliloquy of a Devil's Advocate', in L. Viola ed., *Contending with Stalinism*, pp. 17–43.

such documents were created according to a pre-determined structure. They relied heavily upon a small range of set phrases, and were subject to considerable editing as they moved up the political ladder. Put simply, they lacked nuance and presented matters from the viewpoint of a suspicious and intolerant regime, rather than from the viewpoint of the individual or individuals on whom they focused. Nonetheless, key information such as biographical details and descriptions of physical events were for the most part reliable, since the Party leadership wished that to be the case.

This book is divided into two sections. The first part focuses on the period from 1953 to 1958, while the second looks at the years 1959 to 1964.[40] The early part of the era was characterised by a sense of great change and uncertainty as the Soviet system adapted to the new social and political environment that followed Stalin's death. Of those who protested around this time, most showed a desire to correct the communist regime's failings, though they could nonetheless be vociferous in their criticism. The authorities were rarely proactive in tackling their critics at this point and instead relied upon what could be termed a 'fire-fighting' approach to dissent. The later part of the Khrushchev era, on the other hand, was characterised by both greater stability and growing cynicism, as the outlines of the long-term post-Stalin Soviet system became more solidly established. The authorities' actions against dissent started to become more sophisticated and increasingly effective, while those who continued to criticise often displayed a growing sense of alienation from the Soviet system, even though many of them had at one time been proud communists and still shared many of the regime's purported values.

This division of the Khrushchev period is reflected in the way that Parts I and II of the book have been conceptualised. Chapters 1 to 4 take a fairly rigorously chronological approach, tackling in parallel the major events and themes of dissenting activity and regime response between Stalin's death and the end of 1958. The first two focus upon events surrounding the Secret Speech of February 1956, firstly looking at acts of dissent arising from the Speech and then at the way the authorities responded to those acts.

[40] Aleksandr Pyzhikov also bisected the Khrushchev era at about this point in *Khrushchevskaya ottepel'*, Moskva: Olma-Press, 2002. It is also notable that the KGB, too, later divided the Khrushchev era at this same point. See V. Chebrikov et al., *Istoriya sovetskikh organov gosudarstvennoi bezopasnosti: uchebnik*, Moskva: Vysshaya krasnoznamenskaya shkola komiteta gosudarstvennoi bezopasnosti pri sovete ministerov SSSR, 1977. In this case the KGB used the periods 1953–8 and 1959–71. The fact that the later period extends well into the Brezhnev era can be taken as a reflection of the continuities between the regime's responses to dissent under Khrushchev and Brezhnev.

Chapter 3 then examines the explosive burst of dissenting behaviour that accompanied the Hungarian uprising in the autumn of 1956, while Chapter 4 looks at how the authorities attempted to rein in this burgeoning protest and criticism by resorting to an eighteen-month spell of legal repression that saw more citizens jailed for political crimes than at any other time during the post-Stalin era.

Chapters 5 to 9 employ a slightly looser chronological framework in examining a number of major trends and themes in dissenting behaviour and state policy against dissent during the remainder of the Khrushchev years. Chapters 5 and 6 focus upon underground activity and public disorders in the first half of the 1960s. This is followed in Chapters 7 and 8 by an examination of the policies for preventing and punishing dissent that the regime came to rely upon from the end of the 1950s. Lastly, Chapter 9 outlines the Khrushchev-era roots of the Soviet human-rights movement that subsequently emerged in the early years of the Brezhnev period and brought to the attention of the wider world the confrontation between critics and authority inside the USSR.

PART I

CHAPTER I

An end to silence

The first half of the Khrushchev era saw protest and political criticism on a scale that had not been witnessed for many years inside the USSR. Events such as Khrushchev's denunciation of Stalin and the Soviet invasion of Hungary in autumn 1956 prompted widespread and occasionally vociferous dissent. Thousands were jailed for 'anti-Soviet activity' and many others were reprimanded by the Party and Komsomol, or else fired from their jobs, expelled from university and otherwise persecuted by the authorities. Overt dissenting behaviour was not restricted to a small section of the metropolitan intelligentsia, as later tended to be the case in the Brezhnev era, but could be seen at practically all levels of society and in every region of the country. This was, however, a period in which the majority of political criticism remained essentially loyal to the regime and its ideology, with most dissenters tending to focus on 'correcting' rather than directly assailing the existing system. For a time, the mid to late 1950s was a period of great ideological energy and renewed idealism – though this could generate its own problems for the authorities.

In many ways, Khrushchev's denunciation of Stalin in February 1956 can be viewed as the epicentre of much of the dissent that followed over the next three decades. It was by no means the start of protest activity in the USSR, however. Earlier periods had also featured countless instances of protest and criticism aimed at the authorities – quite probably on a greater scale at several points in the early Stalin years, such as during collectivisation – but the Secret Speech did mark the beginning of a new stage in the evolution of dissenting behaviour inside the Soviet Union, particularly for the intelligentsia who would subsequently go on to play such a prominent role among critics of the regime. For a short period of time the system at least seemed to be less immutable, and people were quick to explore its new boundaries and to work out what had and had not changed since Stalin's death and subsequent disgrace. Public forums such as Communist Party meetings and debates briefly became the setting for penetrating questions and outspoken political remarks before the authorities again managed to rein in even fundamentally loyal and constructive criticism. Hopes of thorough-going liberalisation would overwhelmingly be dashed and, as the decade wore on, initially loyal criticism would grow increasingly alienated and eventually turned into deeper cynicism and disenchantment.

It is possible to discern two broad streams of political protest that existed during the Khrushchev era: worker dissent and intelligentsia dissent. Although workers and members of the intelligentsia shared numerous common interests – such as the desire to avoid a return to arbitrary state repression – they were also distinct from each other in many ways and naturally placed different values on different questions. It should therefore come as no great surprise that they often had quite distinct grievances and generally also expressed them in different forms of protest.[1] This is not to say that there was no blurring of the two, however, or that there was never an element of convergence on any given point. Perhaps most notably, we can see that even among most dissenters of both groups there was not only a general acceptance of the regime's right to exercise power, but a distinct sense of identification with the purported aims and principles of the October Revolution, if not always with the way that those beliefs and goals were being implemented in the present.

Worker dissent had practically always existed inside the USSR and pri-marily involved spontaneous and occasionally explosive forms of protest which, although often manifested in political language and imagery, tended to be rooted in material discontent and a sense of resentment at overbearing and insensitive officialdom rather than outright ideological hostility.[2] As with the peasant rebellions of Tsarist times, outbursts of worker dissent did not necessarily represent any kind of fundamental opposition to the existing political system, though by their sheer weight of numbers and the occasional volatility of their protests, they represented a danger that could not be permanently ignored. Fortunately for the authorities, their grievances as a group were usually relatively simple to remedy by economic means. Intelligentsia dissent, on the other hand, tended to result in planned and calculated acts of criticism that more accurately reflected a genuine degree of

---

[1] Geoffrey Hosking, for example, has argued that '. . . there was no contact whatsoever between workers and intellectuals: they lived in different intellectual and moral universes'. G. Hosking, *Rulers and Victims: The Russians in the Soviet Union*, Cambridge, MA: The Belknap Press of Harvard University Press, 2006, p. 297.

[2] For purposes of clarity it is worthwhile to point out that here the term 'intelligentsia dissent' also encompasses the student body, though they often fell somewhere in between the intelligentsia and the workers in terms of dissenting behaviour. Peasant protest, what there was of it, is included under the umbrella of 'worker dissent'.

dissatisfaction at aspects of the contemporary political environment. As with workers, it was only ever a small minority of the intelligentsia who protested, while the majority remained outwardly passive – whether afraid to speak out, broadly content with their lot or else actively supportive of the regime. Although rarely outright oppositional at this point, intelligentsia dissent often centred upon frustrations at specific state policies and practices, rather than material questions. Even though intelligentsia dissent proved far less explosive than worker dissent, it was to prove more enduring and in many ways was more difficult for the authorities to manage. Under Stalin, there had been plenty of sporadic outbursts of worker protest throughout the country, while dissenting activity in the Brezhnev era (especially that of the Soviet human-rights movement) would be very much dominated by the open and politically liberal protests of the intelligentsia. Uniquely, the political dissent of the Khrushchev years featured a combination of both, albeit without any notable fusion of the two. Roughly speaking, the period saw the decline of worker dissent and the rise of intelligentsia dissent. Nonetheless, both were to have their own impact on the era in question.[3]

Although outside of the main chronological focus of this study, it is worthwhile for purposes of context briefly to raise the issue of dissenting activity in the years immediately prior to Khrushchev's rise to power. The sheer volume of repression under the umbrella of 'counter-revolutionary activity' during the Stalin years has surely meant that many or perhaps most genuine acts of protest and criticism from that time have been buried under a great mass of entirely or partly fabricated cases. Even so, this is a field in which plenty of excellent research has been carried out since the fall of the USSR and the subsequent opening up of Soviet archives.[4] We know that the collectivisation process, for example, provoked widespread protest. In Ryazan, there were cases of arson, physical violence, threats and calls for mass resistance.[5] Jeffrey Rossman has recounted how low living standards

---

[3] This categorisation also helps to solve a dilemma posed by Vladimir Kozlov, who has rightly pointed to a certain incongruity in trying to accommodate some very diverse acts within the same analytical field, such as political graffiti and crude abuse aimed at Party leaders on the one hand and the legalistic defence of human rights on the other. In short, we can deal with this problem by looking at worker and intelligentsia protest as close relatives in the bigger picture of dissenting responses to the regime, but not quite one and the same thing. See V. Kozlov and S. Mironenko eds., *Kramola: inakomyslie v SSSR pri Khrushcheve i Brezhneve 1953–1982*, Moskva: Materik, 2005, p. 6.

[4] See, for example, L. Viola ed., *Contending with Stalinism: Soviet Power and Resistance in the 1930s*, London: Cornell University Press, 2002; J. Rossman, *Worker Resistance under Stalin: Class and Revolution on the Shop Floor*, London: Harvard University Press, 2005; and S. Davies, *Popular Opinion in Stalin's Russia: Terror, Propaganda and Dissent 1934–1941*, Cambridge University Press, 1997.

[5] T. McDonald, 'A Peasant Rebellion in Stalin's Russia: The Pitelinksii Uprising, Ryazan, 1930', in L. Viola ed., *Contending with Stalinism*, p. 99.

prompted a strike in Ivanovo *oblast'* during 1932 in which around 16,000 workers participated.[6] Sarah Davies has used declassified NKVD files to show that a diverse range of themes, such as the assassination of Sergei Kirov in December 1934, subscription campaigns to fund the Soviet contribution to the Republican effort in the Spanish Civil War and the swingeing 1940 Labour Decrees, all provoked a flurry of critical and hostile outbursts among the public. Reports spoke of election ballots filled out in the name of 'Trotsky' or 'the Tsar' and recounted instances of swastikas daubed onto walls in paint.[7] Evidently, as stifling and dangerous as the Stalin years were for the expression of discontent, there were still cases of violent protest and sharp, though primitive, criticism.

What Jochen Hellbeck in particular has added to scholarship on this theme is the importance of ideology, raising the point that many of those who spoke out under Stalin did so from a position of profound identification with the goals and values of the Soviet system. They were not detached from the communist project, but a part of it.[8] The point is a relevant one for Khrushchev-era dissent, though it is also rather easily overstretched. All acts of protest were at least shaped by their contemporary environment (in terms of language, subjects of discontent and more besides). Some were actually prompted by what we might call 'communist values', though others were not. Some of the issues on which the authorities were criticised (such as privileges enjoyed by elites) and the ways in which dissenters behaved (often inspired by tales of the Bolsheviks' 'heroic' struggle prior to the revolution or consciously modelling their behaviour on that of their revolutionary forebears) could be telling.[9]

With the price to be paid for disobedience and non-conformism set prohibitively high in the Stalin years, and the reach of the security organs often perceived as near-universal, it should come as little surprise that the kinds of reasoned and persistent criticism of policies, practices and political figures that began to occur in later years still remained very rare at this point. Even so, the late-Stalin-era USSR was by no means free of frustration and

---

[6] J. Rossman, 'A Workers' Strike in Stalin's Russia: The Vichuga Uprising of April 1932', in L. Viola ed., *Contending with Stalinism*, p. 45.

[7] See S. Davies, *Popular Opinion in Stalin's Russia*.

[8] On this theme, see J. Hellbeck, *Revolution on my Mind: Writing a Diary under Stalin*, London: Harvard University Press, 2006.

[9] Indeed, Elina Zavadskaya and Olga Edelman rightly point out that there was more than an element of role-playing among underground groups in particular. E. Zavadskaya and O. Edelman, 'Underground Groups and Organisations', in V. Kozlov, S. Fitzpatrick and S. Mironenko eds., *Sedition: Everyday Resistance in the Soviet Union under Khrushchev and Brezhnev*, New Haven, CT: Yale University Press, 2011, p. 294.

unrest. Veniamin Iofe, for example, has shown that a handful of genuine underground groups were uncovered in Taishet, Moscow, Saratov and Voronezh.[10] Social tensions were also rising closer to the surface, not least of which were widespread desires for better living standards and a slackening of political controls.[11] The eight years between the end of the Second World War and 1953 had done little or nothing to satisfy hopes and aspirations for a more just and responsive system. For some, such as the Jews of the Soviet Union, things grew appreciably worse.

The vast labour-camp network in particular was becoming much more combustible by the late 1940s, as increasingly hardened inmates began to stage occasional protests and work refusals.[12] Life on the outside was less volatile, though still surprisingly unruly at times. The mass brawls, hooligan disorders and all manner of criminal activity that had flourished in the immediate post-war years were mostly in abeyance by the end of the 1940s, though they still remained an occasional fixture of Soviet life. The post-war years had also started to see the coming to maturity of a generation who through their dress, their cultural tastes and much more would begin to challenge the staid behavioural and cultural norms that governed everyday life in the late Stalin era.[13] Already by the mid 1950s Komsomol officials were reporting signs of members' disenchantment at the organisation's ideological stagnation, and students in Moscow showed a willingness to organise themselves in protest at unpopular education policies.[14] In a number of ways, then, Stalin's death at the start of March 1953 was not quite the watershed moment that some sources have suggested. Some of the key behaviours and attitudes that would characterise the 'Thaw era' had already begun to emerge in the aftermath of the war.[15] In terms of government policy, however, the change was much more decisive, a fact made plain by the almost immediate cessation (later that same month) of the anti-Semitic, and entirely fabricated, Doctors' Plot, in which a (predominantly Jewish) group of Kremlin doctors had been arrested in January 1953 on concocted

---

[10] See V. Iofe, *Granitsy smysla: stat'i, vystupleniya, esse*, Sankt Peterburg: Nauchno-informatsionnyi tsentr 'Memorial', 2002, p. 119.

[11] See E. Zubkova, *Obshchestvo i reformy 1945–1964*, Moskva: Izdatel'skii tsentr 'Rossiya molodaya', 1993.

[12] See, for example, V. Kozlov, *Neizvestnyi SSSR: protivostoyanie naroda i vlasti 1953–1985*, Moskva: Olma-Press, 2006.

[13] See in particular J. Fürst, *Stalin's Last Generation: Soviet Post-War Youth and the Emergence of Mature Socialism*, Oxford University Press, 2010.

[14] J. Fürst, *Stalin's Last Generation*, pp. 352–3.

[15] As Juliane Fürst has argued, 'the life and culture of the years 1953–56 made visible what had been growing under the heavy blanket of late Stalinist rule for many years'. J. Fürst, *Stalin's Last Generation*, p. 31.

charges of poisoning members of the Soviet leadership. Naturally enough, post-Stalin changes in government policy would subsequently start to show an impact upon the lives of Soviet citizens.

Sporadic strikes and risings in the Gulag intensified following Stalin's death in March 1953, particularly once the post-Stalin amnesties began to reduce the population of the camps, leaving a hard core of prisoners increasingly embittered by their own continued incarceration. Two of these early post-Stalin camp disturbances in particular stood out as omens of a growing refusal to submit. In July 1953 a spontaneous strike at the Vorkuta camp complex in the far north of Russia quickly spread to include around 18,000 inmates, with prisoners managing to take control of the camp inside the perimeter fence for over a week before the authorities responded with devastating force. At Kengir, in Kazakhstan, prisoners rose up and were able to expel the camp authorities in May 1954, ruling as a 'Provisional Government' for almost six weeks before the state sent in tanks and soldiers to bring the situation back under control, again at the expense of many prisoners' lives.[16]

Reviewing the case files of individuals convicted under article 58-10 of the criminal code during the three years of collective leadership that followed Stalin's death, one can quickly see that nationalist and religious activity made up the considerable bulk of convictions for 'anti-Soviet activity' at that time.[17] The former largely represented the conclusion of repressions against citizens of Ukraine and the Baltic states that had been on-going since the Second World War, and the latter was primarily a result of the brief but widespread anti-religious campaign that was initiated by Khrushchev in 1954.[18]

In regard to those sentenced for behaviours that can be categorised as political dissent during the period of collective leadership, the general tone of protest activity had changed only a little since the 1930s and 1940s. Dissenting behaviour was often still spontaneous and fairly crude. Typical examples included the twenty-five-year-old prisoner I.N. Pisarev's December 1953 conviction after drawing swastikas on the wall of a labour camp in Chelyabinsk *oblast'* and writing 'Down with the Soviet regime! Long live

[16] Although it presents a somewhat romanticised image of the events in question, Aleksandr Solzhenitsyn's account of the '40 Days of Kengir' is nonetheless illuminating. See A. Solzhenitsyn, *The Gulag Archipelago*, Vol. 3, London: Collins/Fontana, 1978, pp. 290–331.

[17] To speak of a Soviet criminal code is useful for reasons of linguistic clarity, though it is not entirely accurate. In fact, each of the fifteen union republics had its own criminal code with differing code numbers used to denote much the same crimes.

[18] See J. Delaney-Grossman, 'Khrushchev's Anti-Religious Policy and the Campaign of 1954', *Soviet Studies*, Vol. 24, No. 3 (January 1973), 374–86.

Truman!"[19] Similarly, I.N. Rodin, a thirty-five-year-old war veteran and invalid, was jailed in June 1955 after drunkenly cursing and abusing members of the Communist Party leadership while riding a trolleybus in Moscow.[20] These kinds of outbursts continued to predominate in the case files of those who were jailed for dissent. Where the relevant documentation is available, it shows that those arrested and sentenced for such acts were for the most part poorly educated males from the Slavic republics of the USSR.[21] Quite frequently they were also intoxicated at the time of the offence in question, or were actually already serving sentences in camps and prisons. Such behaviours certainly did not disappear after the Secret Speech, but they were supplemented by more deliberate and cerebral criticisms that saw Soviet dissent enter a fundamentally new stage.

For young people and members of the intelligentsia, green shoots of liberalisation first began to emerge soon after Stalin's death. Among the most significant literary works published in the period before Khrushchev rose to sole power were Vladimir Pomerantsev's 1953 essay *On Sincerity in Literature* and Il'ya Ehrenburg's 1954 novella *The Thaw*, whose title would soon become an appellation for the era as a whole. Both were notable primarily because they challenged the highly conservative Zhdanov Decrees on culture, placing personal and moral questions ahead of previously all-important political matters, something that was to become a particularly notable trend of intelligentsia dissent in subsequent years.

While Pomerantsev, Ehrenburg and others like them were necessarily restrained in their criticism, since they still had to get past an eagle-eyed censorship regime, their works did represent a vital cultural–political milestone and an important forerunner of the kind of intelligentsia dissent that was soon to become more frequent and more pronounced in the wake of Khrushchev's attack on Stalin.[22] Furthermore, the physical permanence and

---

[19] GARF, f. 8131, op. 31, d. 77681, ll. 1–3, in V. Kozlov and S. Mironenko eds., *58-10 Nadzornye proizvodstva prokuratury SSSR po delam ob antisovetskoi agitatsii i propaganda: annotirovannyi katalog Mart 1953 – 1991*, Moskva: Mezhdunarodnyi Fond 'Demokratiya', 1999, p. 207.

[20] GARF, f. 8131, op. 31, d. 67444, in V. Kozlov and S. Mironenko eds., *58–10 Nadzornye proizvodstva*, p. 241.

[21] Procurator files on individuals sentenced for anti-Soviet activity included a survey of basic biographical data such as age, profession, nationality and place of residence. Education levels were also recorded in many files, though this was not always the case.

[22] The traditionally accepted account of Khrushchev-era cultural liberalisation tells us it was essentially a tool with which to win over and re-energise the liberal intelligentsia. More recently, though, Gleb Tsipursky has added to this by arguing that increased cultural consumption was part and parcel of the wider increases in consumption that were already beginning to define the emerging post-Stalin social contract. See, for example, M. Zezina, *Sovetskaya khudozhestvennaya intelligentsiya i vlast' v 1950–60e gody*, Moskva: Dialog MGU, 1999; P. Johnson, *Khrushchev and the Arts: The Politics of Soviet Culture*,

geographic spread of the printed word – in the form of books, articles and essays – ensured that even isolated instances of cultural liberalisation left a lingering mark that could never be completely erased, giving the 'thaw' literature a status that other forms of criticism simply could not rival. Nonetheless, the predominant historiographical focus on the intelligentsia as a locus of dissenting activity has perhaps overstated the popular impact of such works. While many young intellectuals and professionals had their minds fired by this new literature, there were also plenty of others whom it passed by, yet they too would go on to make their grievances known during the 1950s and beyond. Still, the extent to which even this nascent cultural liberalisation – which today looks rather feeble at times – was seen as potentially dangerous to the political status quo can be inferred from the fact that almost every challenging literary work of the era was followed soon after by aggressive retrenchment and recrimination from those individuals and institutions opposed to thorough-going liberalisation. As with the intermittent literary thaws of the period, the turn against Stalin originated 'from above'. Unlike the brief instances of cultural liberalisation that had already taken place, however, its implications were so wide-ranging and combustible that the pressures and hopes it brought to the surface could not be so effectively controlled or quashed by those who had set the ball rolling.

Khrushchev's five-hour long indictment of Stalin, delivered to a closed session of the XX CPSU Congress late at night on 24 February 1956, has long been recognised as one of the pivotal moments in Soviet history. After years of veneration, Stalin's record as war leader, his stifling of democracy within the Communist Party, his split with Lenin and his role in engineering the vast cult surrounding his person were all lambasted by the new First Secretary. The mass imprisonment, exile and execution of countless Party members during the Great Terror were traced back to the late *vozhd*. Nonetheless, Khrushchev declared the system fundamentally sound, and insisted that those who had succeeded Stalin were themselves victims, rather than accomplices: aided by the malign influence of his fellow Georgian Lavrenty Beria, the blame lay exclusively with Stalin. Khrushchev then promised a 'return to Leninism', putting the Soviet project back onto the proper path toward communism from which Stalin had deviated so badly. Even though it was highly selective in terms of its content, this attack on what Khrushchev labelled the 'Cult of Personality' proved to be one of the most significant factors underpinning dissenting behaviour throughout the

1962–1964, Cambridge, MA: MIT Press, 1965; and G. Tsipursky, 'Pleasure, Power and the Pursuit of Communism: Soviet Youth and State-Sponsored Popular Culture during the Early Cold War Period, 1945–1968', Ph.D. Dissertation, University of North Carolina at Chapel Hill, 2011.

entire post-Stalin era, and many dissenters of even much later periods subsequently cited the speech as a key factor in changing their view of the regime.[23]

News of Stalin's crimes undoubtedly came as a shattering blow for many people. Indeed, a number of earlier accounts have argued that it fatally undermined the regime's claim to infallibility and thus did grave damage to the prestige and credibility of the entire Soviet system.[24] This was certainly how some people reacted to the Secret Speech, but there was no monolithic response from society as a whole. Reactions were naturally shaped by a whole range of personal and political factors. Huge numbers of people had had their lives ruined or else lost friends and loved ones under Stalin but many others had much invested in the era and could justifiably look on it as a time of great personal advancement. For some, the Speech seemed to raise the spectre of being called to account for what they had done in the recent past; for others it offered absolution. Not everyone was shocked by the revelations that Khrushchev presented. There were millions who had been imprisoned themselves or else had seen family and friends fall into the Gulag. Others had personal recollections of times before Stalin's rise to power or had heard from relatives and friends of how Lenin's revolution had been distorted under Stalin's rule. More than a few people had developed doubts about Stalin and Stalinism already before the late dictator's death and certainly prior to the XX Congress.[25]

Owing to the fact that the Secret Speech was neither published in the Soviet media nor officially acknowledged by the CPSU leadership until the late 1980s, there remains something of a question mark as to how many people actually knew that Khrushchev's denunciation of Stalin had even taken place.[26] However, Lev Lur'e and Irina Malyarova have recently produced figures indicating that somewhere in the region of 34,000,000 people attended meetings around the country in which the report was read

---

[23] Examples include Petro Grigorenko and Leonid Plyushch. See P. Grigorenko, *Memoirs*, New York: W.W. Norton, 1982, p. 222; L. Plyushch, *History's Carnival: A Dissident's Autobiography*, London: Harvill Press, 1979, p. 12.

[24] See, for example, F. Barghoorn, *Détente and the Democratic Movement in the USSR*, London: Collier Macmillan, 1976.

[25] See, for example, 'Len Karpinsky: The Autobiography of a Half-Dissident', in S. Cohen and K. vanden Heuvel eds., *Voices of Glasnost: Interviews with Gorbachev's Reformers*, New York: W.W Norton, 1989, p. 285 and L. Alexeyeva and P. Goldberg, *The Thaw Generation: Coming of Age in the Post-Stalin Era*, Boston, MA: Little, Brown and Company, 1990.

[26] Aleksandr Pyzhikov, for example, has suggested that although the Secret Speech soon became widely known abroad, this was not the case inside the USSR. See A. Pyzhikov, *Opyt modernizatsii sovetskogo obshchestva v 1953–1964 godakh: obshchestvenno-politicheskii aspekt*, Moskva: Izdatel'skii dom 'Gamma', 1998, p. 9.

out and later discussed after its initial airing at the XX Congress in Moscow.[27] With the population of the USSR standing at a little under 210,000,000, this would indicate that around one-sixth of the country heard the details first-hand. When one considers that many of those attendees – mainly CPSU and Komsomol members but also some non-Party students and workers – would have spoken to friends and relatives about such a shocking turn of events, it seems highly likely that a great many citizens would have quickly heard at least an outline of what had taken place at the end of the XX Congress.

With the exception of riots that flared across Georgia between 5 and 10 March 1956, the exposure of Stalin's crimes generally did not provoke an immediately volatile response. What one sees on reading accounts of individuals' initial reactions to hearing the Speech is that the feeling was often one of stunned silence, whether through shock at the content of Khrushchev's remarks or amazement at the fact that such news had even been voiced at all.[28] Although in many cases the Secret Speech would prompt longer-term re-evaluations of the system which proved overwhelmingly negative, there is also plenty of evidence to show that, in the short term at least, Khrushchev's attack on Stalin and his promise of a 'return to Leninism' sparked genuine and widespread enthusiasm for reinvigorating and 're-launching' the faltering communist project, especially among young people and members of the intelligentsia.[29]

Fedor Burlatsky, for example, described a 'rush of young blood' into the Party and a heightened sense of idealism among young people.[30] Revolt Pimenov, who had resigned from the Komsomol several years earlier and would be jailed for anti-Soviet activity less than eighteen months after the Secret Speech, wrote that upon hearing of Khrushchev's remarks on Stalin he had been sufficiently moved to consider applying to join the Communist Party.[31] Raisa Orlova described the atmosphere of the post-XX Congress period as 'echoing the mass-meeting type of democracy' that had followed

---

[27] L. Lur'e and I. Malyarova eds., *1956 god. Seredina veka*, Sankt Peterburg: Neva, 2007, p. 170.
[28] See, for example, L. Lur'e and I. Malyarova eds., *1956 god.*
[29] On the theme of long-term reassessments following the Secret Speech, see numerous interviews with former dissidents in V. Pimonov ed., *Govoryat 'osobo opasnyye'*, Moskva: Detektiv-Press, 1999.
[30] F. Burlatsky, *Khrushchev and the First Russian Spring: The Era of Khrushchev through the Eyes of his Adviser*, London: Weidenfeld & Nicolson, 1991, p. 13. Burlatsky himself was no 'ordinary' chronicler of this surge of idealistic youth, but a keen ally of Khrushchev and a representative of what could be termed the Communist Party's liberal wing. Nonetheless, other recollections from the time support his assertion.
[31] R. Pimenov, *Vospominaniya*, Moskva: Informatsionno-ekspertnaya gruppa 'Panorama', 1996, p. 19. Pimenov recalled that in his case this sense of optimism began to fade within a couple of months.

October 1917.[32] One ought to be cautious about accepting too readily Orlova's analogy with the Lenin era, not least since she herself was not born until 1918. Nonetheless, it does raise the important point that this was one of only a few times (and certainly one of the last times before the arrival of Mikhail Gorbachev) when the Soviet system looked to be on the verge of significant change – when those with an idealistic desire to help reshape their country felt that it might be possible to do so.

A much more enduring legacy of the XX Congress – since this wave of renewed idealism largely failed to see out 1956 – was the realisation that it had become possible to give an honest and critical opinion on the situation in the country without facing absolute disaster for oneself, one's family and one's friends. The price to be paid for speaking out had lowered sufficiently that it need not be entirely prohibitive for those who anticipated the consequences of their behaviour. As Moshe Lewin wrote: 'When in 1956, Nikita Khrushchev launched his sensational attack on Stalin at the Twentieth Party Congress, Soviet society, and especially the intelligentsia, understood that the days of Stalinist show trials and arbitrary arrests and executions had gone for good.'[33] Thereafter, a clear strand of intelligentsia dissent began emerging alongside the kinds of spontaneous and crude worker protest that had always existed. Although it was generally charac-terised by essentially constructive criticism of specific flaws in the contem-porary regime, and an ethos of 'fulfilling the goals of the XX Congress', this loyal criticism was consistently frustrated, suppressed and punished by the authorities, eventually leading to more fundamental critiques of the wider system. It is worth adding two initial caveats to Lewin's analysis of the Secret Speech, however. Firstly, the element of intimidation that remained even after terror had been abandoned was undoubtedly still a powerful disincen-tive to dissenting activity. Secondly, there was also a generational issue at play: young people found it much easier to accept that the 'dark days' had gone for good than did those who were old enough to have been touched by those events in some way.

Overlaying this tumultuous political change was an initial atmosphere of confusion and misapprehension at the exact meaning of these new anti-Stalin pronouncements, a phenomenon Michael Scammell labelled a 'chasm of uncertainty'.[34] For many years inside the Soviet Union there had been practically no ambiguity about what could and could not be said,

---

[32] R. Orlova, *An End to Silence: Memoirs*, New York: Random House, 1983, p. 112.
[33] M. Lewin, *The Soviet Century*, London: Verso, 2005, p. 156.
[34] See M. Scammell, *Solzhenitsyn: A Biography*, New York: W.W. Norton and Company, 1984, p. 404.

yet the XX Congress suddenly muddied the waters. It was made clear not just by the Speech but also by articles in the national and regional press that the official attitude to Stalin and Stalinism had shifted, but there was little indication as to exactly where the new boundaries of acceptable and unacceptable comment and behaviour had settled.[35]

As was customary, official meetings were organised up and down the country to discuss the results of the latest CPSU congress. First came the task of informing rank-and-file Party and Komsomol members of the contents of Khrushchev's remarks. The report on Stalin's crimes was often read verbatim and no questions were to be asked.[36] In many cases, audiences – sometimes up to a thousand strong and often numbering several hundred – were barred from taking notes during the meetings, though there were certainly some who managed to do so furtively. When further sessions were subsequently held for those same groups to discuss the contents of the report, people began to have their say and to ask their questions.

For the first time in a long while, the unanimous backing that the Party leadership had long expected of its members was not forthcoming. The tone of the ensuing discussions differed from one location to the next. In most places this was dictated by the attitude of the local Party leadership, many of whom were far from overjoyed at the attack on Stalin and consequently tried to keep things as brief and as superficial as possible.[37] After all, many of them had more to lose than to gain from an unfettered discussion of what had taken place during the Stalin years. Even so, there were plenty of instances where citizens criticised, questioned and cast doubt on vital aspects of the recent past and the present state of the Soviet system, often receiving voluble support from members of their audience as they did so.

These discussions of the Secret Speech in spring 1956 witnessed a wave of criticism, 'truth-telling' and questioning on a scale that had not been seen in Soviet public spaces for many years. Naturally enough, Stalin was the most frequent target for criticism. In meetings of both the Communist Party and the Komsomol there were also sharp attacks on individual leaders and on the climate of subservience and hypocrisy that had developed in the country. At Moscow State University (MGU), a student meeting demanded that the Komsomol be freed from the 'corrupting influence' of

---

[35] The most widely circulated of these articles was 'Why the Cult of the Individual is Alien to the Spirit of Marxism-Leninism', *Pravda*, 28 March 1956. Lenin's Testament was also published in *Kommunist* during June 1956 in a further attempt at undermining Stalin's reputation.

[36] L. Lur'e and I. Malyarova eds., *1956 god*, p. 92.

[37] See M. Dobson, *Khrushchev's Cold Summer: Gulag Returnees, Crime and the Fate of Reform after Stalin*, Ithaca, NY: Cornell University Press, 2009.

Communist Party control.[38] Elsewhere, there were calls to re-examine the positions of the entire leadership and proposals that Stalin be posthumously expelled from the Party.[39] Anastas Mikoyan – one of the most long-standing and senior members of the CPSU leadership – was branded a hypocrite after audience members compared his fawning remarks on Stalin at the XIX CPSU Congress in 1952 with his criticism of the same man at the XX CPSU Congress, four years later.[40] US reports from the period spoke of Central Committee member Dmitri Shepilov having been 'given a hard time' by an auditorium full of students when he addressed them on the subject of the XX Congress.[41] Some likened members of the leadership who had survived the Stalin years to wartime deserters who had fled under fire, since they had been in a position to help others and had not done so.[42] Letters flowed in to the Central Committee demanding that Stalin be removed from the mausoleum he shared with Lenin on Red Square.[43] Although individuals in the provinces and the non-Russian republics tended to be rather more circumspect on the Stalin question than those in Moscow – since political change could be even more fleeting outside of the capital – official documents show that critical remarks were being presented in all parts of the USSR.[44]

One of the most interesting aspects of this short period was the brief emergence of something approaching public opinion, in the Habermasian sense of the term. Because the authorities would not officially acknowledge that the Secret Speech had even taken place – since that meant exposing to the outside world the issues it contained – they could not properly prescribe how to interpret what it said about the past and what its implications were for the present and future.[45] Those implications, however, were potentially huge. Consequently, people began to raise these very issues in public spaces like Party and Komsomol meetings, as well as in university dorms, cafés and workplaces, often clamouring for more information on the abuses that

---

[38] L. Silina, *Nastroeniya sovetskogo studenchestva 1945–1964*, Moskva: Russkii mir, 2004, p. 108.

[39] RGANI, f. 5, op. 32, d. 39, ll. 135–6.

[40] See A. Pyzhikov, *Opyt modernizatsii*, p. 57. Although nothing like the extent of Khrushchev's revelations in the Secret Speech, Mikoyan had actually been the first to offer muted criticism of Stalin during his own speech to the XX Congress.

[41] Telegram from US embassy in Moscow to US Department of State, 23 April 1956. Budapest, HU OSA 299.

[42] Mikoyan was one such leader. C. Hooper, 'What Can and Cannot Be Said: Between the Stalinist Past and New Soviet Future', *Slavonic and East European Review*, Vol. 86, No. 2 (April 2008), 315.

[43] B. Firsov, *Raznomyslie v SSSR 1940–1960 gody: istoriya, teoriya i praktika*, Sankt Peterburg: Izdatel'stvo Evropeiskogo Universiteta v Sankt Peterburge, 2008, p. 258.

[44] See, for example, K. Aimermakher et al. eds., *Doklad N.S. Khrushcheva o kul'te lichnosti Stalina na XX s"ezde KPSS: dokumenty*, Moskva: Rosspen, 2002.

[45] K. Loewenstein, 'Re-Emergence of Public Opinion in the Soviet Union: Khrushchev and Responses to the Secret Speech', *Europe–Asia Studies*, Vol. 58, No. 8 (December 2006), 1329–45.

Khrushchev had spoken about and pushing to expand the scope of his revelations. The lack of guidance on how it was to be interpreted allowed, even forced, ordinary citizens to begin their own assessments of what Khrushchev's report meant, often reaching conclusions that were at best politically troubling. There was thus real potential around this point for the emergence of what Polly Jones called a 'de-Sovietized' public opinion.[46] This was a deeply problematic situation for a regime that placed great value on its ability to dictate popular discourse, especially when the subject matter was so potentially explosive. The results were naturally unpredictable, and the Soviet system was hardly geared up for unpredictability like this. In the future, much more care would be taken over how to present and to manage even far less controversial issues than the exposure of Stalin.

Some of the most fascinating evidence on these discussions can be seen in a memorandum sent to the Central Committee's General Department from the Department of Party Organs, which provided a summary of questions submitted at the thousands of meetings held to discuss the Secret Speech. According to the memorandum, the three most commonly asked questions were: 'Why was Khrushchev's report so limited in its contents?', 'Why was there no self-criticism or open discussion of the report?' and 'What guarantees are there that there will not be another cult?' Among other frequently asked questions were: 'Are not other Presidium members also guilty? They must have known [what was happening under Stalin] but will not admit it'; 'Is there not also a cult around Lenin?' and 'How could the newspapers lie for so long and now change track so easily?'[47] These were exactly the kinds of questions that the authorities could not afford to abandon to independent public assessment, yet this is ultimately what happened for a time after the XX Congress.

At the Academy of Sciences' Oriental Studies Institute in Moscow there were demands for wider discussion of Khrushchev's report and calls for a special Party congress to be held on the matter. Speakers branded elections in the USSR 'a farce' and the soviets 'powerless' and 'ineffective'. When votes were held over whether to censure those who had just spoken out, the motions were comprehensively defeated.[48] The difficult questions continued to come from all across the USSR. In Estonia, Party members asked whether the condemnation of long-standing 'enemies' such as Trotsky and

[46] See P. Jones, 'From the Secret Speech to the Burial of Stalin: Real and Ideal Responses to De-Stalinization', in P. Jones ed., *The Dilemmas of De-Stalinization: Negotiating Cultural and Social Change in the Khrushchev Era*, London: Routledge, 2006, p. 42.

[47] RGANI, f. 5, op. 30, d. 139, l. 5.

[48] RGANI, f. 5, op. 32, d. 46, ll. 82–7, in K. Aimermakher et al. eds., *Doklad N.S. Khrushcheva*.

Bukharin would now be reconsidered and whether Stalin's *Short Course* textbook on the history of the Communist Party should still be used for teaching purposes.[49] In Ukraine, Party members wanted to know if the 1941 pact with Nazi Germany had been a mistake, and whether those people who had been deported would now be allowed to return.[50] In Uzbekistan, one member asked why the Party would not set term limits on top government and Party posts, or else reform the electoral system so that such abuses could not be repeated.[51] More prosaically, Party members in Kazakhstan enquired as to what they were now supposed to do with all their portraits of Stalin.[52]

For some people, these meetings were taken up as a chance to let fly with all manner of personal and professional grievances that bore limited relation to the direct content of the Secret Speech. At Yerevan State University, for example, speakers complained about the Party leadership's unwillingness to pursue Armenia's territorial claims against Turkey and its failure to protect the half-million Armenians living on the other side of the Turkish border. At Moscow's Institute of Law, speakers took issue with the failings of the country's legal system and with the Ministry of Justice.[53] At the Gorky Institute of World Literature, discussions on the Secret Speech quickly saw members of the audience criticising the deleterious effects of tight bureaucratic control over culture.[54] At one meeting in Stanislav *oblast'* a speaker announced he had grown so exasperated in waiting to be allocated a new apartment that he was 'ready to resort to terrorism'.[55] Countless people lamented their poor standard of living and the unavailability of various goods. In short, these discussions of the Secret Speech opened a small window into which could rush all manner of complaints, some overtly political, and some less so. Presumably, this seemingly dramatic change of political direction made it appear for a time as if there were an increased chance of having one's frustrations remedied, whatever they were.

Even a few of those who were intimately linked with enforcing the will of the authorities in the Soviet system overstepped the mark. The Department of Party Organs noted that during a meeting of Communist Party members at the Armenian MVD a certain Karapetyan made a statement which was described only as 'malicious slander aimed at a number of Presidium

[49] RGANI, f. 5, op. 31, d. 53, l. 25–2, in K. Aimermakher et al. eds., *Doklad N.S. Khrushcheva.*
[50] RGANI, f. 5, op. 31, d. 54, ll. 43–7, in K. Aimermakher et al. eds., *Doklad N.S. Khrushcheva.*
[51] RGANI, f. 5, op. 31, d. 54, ll. 113–19.
[52] RGANI, f. 5, op. 31, d. 52, l. 54, in K. Aimermakher et al. eds., *Doklad N.S. Khrushcheva.*
[53] RGANI, f. 5, op. 35, d. 24, ll. 78–81, in K. Aimermakher et al. eds., *Doklad N.S. Khrushcheva.*
[54] See RGANI, f. 5, op. 32, d. 46, ll. 2–5.
[55] K. Aimermakher et al. eds., *Doklad N.S. Khrushcheva*, p. 550.

members' and had called for those same individuals to be held responsible for what had happened under Stalin.[56] In Latvia, a meeting of the KGB's primary party organisation in Riga saw members Kukushkin and Lobanov rile officials with their 'incorrect assessment' of Khrushchev's report. With vocal support from Lobanov, Kukushkin declared that he was unconvinced by Khrushchev's simplistic explanation of the origins of the Cult of Personality and insisted that blame should also be directed at the members of the Central Committee and Politburo (sic).[57] Both men were quick to retract their remarks when the spectre of punishment loomed, however.

The best-known of these controversial discussions on the Secret Speech took place during a Party meeting at Moscow's Thermo-Technical Institute. This was the second most prestigious scientific institute in the entire Soviet Union and the Party cell involved was attached to the USSR Academy of Sciences. Like a number of others around the country, the young physicist Yuri Orlov and three colleagues (R.G. Arvalov, V.E. Nesterov and G.I. Shedrin) took it upon themselves to give their unexpurgated views on the matters that Khrushchev had addressed. Arvalov questioned why the Congress had not been allowed to discuss Khrushchev's report. He cast doubt on the explanation of the roots of the Cult and even suggested that the workers ought to be armed in order to prevent such abuses of power in the future. Nesterov lambasted the fact that nothing had been said about the Stalin cult while the dictator was alive and pointed out that more communists had been killed during the 1930s than had died during the October Revolution, in what he scathingly said was 'supposed to be the most democratic country in the world'. Shedrin supported the sentiments of Arvalov and Nesterov before asking why it was that in the French parliament a communist could criticise the government without facing jail, yet in the Soviet Union even the Supreme Soviet would not criticise the government.[58]

Orlov began his own remarks by noting that Khrushchev's condemnation of the Cult of Personality was undoubtedly a positive and progressive step that would aid the cause of peaceful co-existence.[59] He then spoke of a sense of moral decay within the Communist Party and society at large. He

---

[56] RGANI, f. 5, op. 31, d. 52, l. 2.

[57] Both Kukushkin and Lobanov were expelled from the Party but subsequently reinstated after acknowledging that their views had been mistaken. K. Aimermakher et al. eds., *Doklad N.S. Khrushcheva*, p. 493. The Politburo had been renamed 'the Presidium' soon after Stalin's death.

[58] RGANI, f. 4, op. 16, d. 24, ll. 18–54.

[59] I am particularly grateful to Professor Yuri Orlov for sending me the stenographic report of this speech, from which much of the present paragraph is drawn.

announced that Marxism-Leninism was not a truly scientific ideology (as official discourse proclaimed it to be) and insisted that even three years after Stalin's death, people were still forced to 'hold their fingers in the wind' in order to judge the political atmosphere, and adjust their behaviour accordingly.[60] Only a few minutes after he had begun speaking, Orlov concluded by suggesting that every communist should think seriously about what had taken place within their own lives and the life of the Party, adding that 'some of us were mistaken, but some adapted ... we cannot allow it to happen again'. This emphasis on the prevention of future abuses, rather than punishment for the abuses that had taken place, was fairly common. Even so, as Orlov's remarks implied, Khrushchev's insistence that the Stalin cult and its attendant abuses did not reflect any kind of deeper malady within the Soviet system was far from universally accepted.

Soon after the meeting in question, the head of the institute, Abram Alikhanov, informed the quartet that he had received orders to fire them and reportedly remarked that 'you are either heroes or fools for what you did'. Echoing this sentiment, Erik Kulavig recently surmised that 'it is highly probable to suggest that only the bravest, or the most naïve, dared to come out with their criticisms' at this time.[61] Although appealing in its common-sense approach, this assessment of events is ultimately somewhat unsatisfactory, not least because it leaves us with an overly simplistic paradigm of dissent as essentially either 'heroic' or 'mistaken'. In fact, in those who spoke out at this time we can discern a plethora of motivations, from confusion, anger and disappointment through to idealism, curiosity and a simple desire to 'tell the truth'. To suggest that those who made controversial remarks did so only out of bravery or naïvety runs the risk of understating both the unique nature of the situation in question and the complexity of citizens' relationships with the Soviet system. As the present chapter shows, few really knew what had changed at first, neither the authorities nor ordinary citizens.

Unsurprisingly, there were consequences of the meeting at the Thermo-Technical Institute. When the cell re-convened the following day, a motion was put forward to condemn the quartet's remarks as 'politically immature' and 'mistaken'. The majority of those present, however, either chose to abstain from voting or rejected the proposal, another clear sign that the traditional order of things had been shaken. When the four were attacked in

[60] Interview with Yuri Orlov, Ithaca, NY, December 2006.
[61] E. Kulavig, *Dissent in the Years of Khrushchev: Nine Stories about Disobedient Russians*, Basingstoke: Palgrave Macmillan, 2002, p. 26.

the press a few days later, their case became known nationally and aroused considerable sympathy in some quarters, with their remarks being cited as a source of inspiration by numerous subsequent dissidents.[62] Aggrieved at the way their junior colleagues were being lambasted, a number of fellow scientists from across the USSR collected money to support the dismissed physicists until they were able to find work again. Effectively blacklisted and unable to find a scientific post any closer than Yerevan, where he was hired by Alikhanov's brother, Orlov arrived in Armenia a year later to discover that many Armenians' had been greatly impressed by his comments at the Thermo-Technical Institute.[63] One need only contrast this situation with accounts of people who did not dare to speak of jailed family and friends during the height of the Stalin era to see that major changes were under way.

People who came forth with controversial remarks like those described above rarely fit the bill as 'anti-Soviet' or 'bourgeois elements', as the Soviet authorities and some hopeful Western observers proclaimed them to be. As Yuri Orlov pointed out fifty years after his own comments on the Secret Speech, 'it would probably look good for me now to say that I really was an anti-communist then [as the newspaper attacks on him and his three colleagues implied], but that is not true at all. I was still very much a communist.'[64] Igor Volgin captured the sentiments of many of those who spoke out at the time when he stated that 'all of my generation of students were anti-Stalinists, but they were not anti-Soviet'.[65] Or, as Leonid Borodin recalled of the time: 'I considered the system my own, but my opponents considered it theirs.'[66] This kind of optimism at the possibility of 'reclaiming' the Soviet system from Stalinism may have been short-lived but it does appear to have been widespread in the spring of 1956.

A number of recent scholars have pointed out that acts such as speaking up at Party or Komsomol meetings were not simply about the content of what one said, but can actually be seen in terms of participation in the Soviet political system – a process that could be central to one's identity as a 'good communist'.[67] This is an approach that has particular relevance for

[62] Petro Grigorenko was one such individual. See P. Grigorenko, *V podpol'e mozhno vstretit' tol'ko krys*, New York: Letinets, 1981. The memoirs of Revolt Pimenov show him to have been similarly influenced by Orlov's speech and the resulting press condemnation. R. Pimenov, *Vospominaniya*, p. 25.

[63] Interview with Yuri Orlov, Ithaca, NY, December 2006.

[64] Interview with Yuri Orlov, Ithaca, NY, December 2006.

[65] Interview with Igor Volgin in L. Polikovskaya ed., *'My predchuvstvie … predtecha': ploshchad Mayakovskogo 1958–1965*, Moskva: Obshchestvo 'Memorial', 1997, p. 44.

[66] V. Pimonov ed., *Govoryat 'osobo opasnye'*, p. 20.

[67] See, for example, A. Yurchak, *Everything was Forever Until it Was No More: The Last Soviet Generation*, Oxford: Princeton University Press, 2006.

the period in question, since the discussions following the XX Congress were not only a chance to participate in the system but seemingly also to help reshape that system. The trend was by no means a universal one, but many Party and Komsomol members in particular who questioned and criticised were seeking to be of assistance in the drive to overcome the 'Cult of Personality'. Cynthia Hooper rightly argues that Khrushchev's approach to the Stalin question seemed to announce not just the authorities' obligation to tell the truth to those beneath them, but also for those at the bottom to tell the truth to those at the top.[68] As such, uncovering and presenting 'the truth', however inconvenient, was seen as a way of rendering a service to the system: helping to heal the wounds of the past and to overcome the problems of the present, not just releasing bottled-up frustrations and disappointments.[69]

Most often for young people and members of the intelligentsia this entailed the kind of ideological self-image presented above by Igor Volgin: 'anti-Stalin but not anti-Soviet'. This was a conception that tended to be centred upon a romanticised view of Leninism and the revolutionary period that we can perhaps consider an 'imaginary past', in much the same way that many Soviet citizens would later picture an 'imaginary West': a vaguely defined zone in which reposed all manner of inaccurate or unrealistic hopes and assumptions.[70] There were a whole host of factors feeding into this sense of nostalgia for an era that most of those who spoke up had never witnessed. Importantly, this was a phenomenon bolstered – if not actually created – by the way in which Khrushchev had framed his attack on Stalin as a juncture at which the Soviet system would 'return to Leninism' and the idealism of the 1920s. This created the space for the likes of Orlov, Volgin and Borodin to participate in the existing discourse on changes to the system and to do so from a steadfastly loyal position of identification with both the Revolution and the XX Congress, even whilst offering occasionally sharp criticism of the contemporary regime. As the growth of neo-Bolshevik dissent soon showed, until the authorities more effectively dictated their own conception of the 'Leninism' that was being returned

---

[68] C. Hooper, 'What Can and Cannot Be Said', 321.

[69] In this connection it is also worth pointing to Benjamin Tromly's argument that support for the Secret Speech helped create the conditions for the emergence of Ukrainian cultural nationalism, since it encouraged idealistic young Ukrainians to think about national questions as they sought to overcome 'Stalinist perversions of Marxism-Leninism' in nationalities policy. Presumably, this did not only apply to Ukraine. B. Tromly, 'An Unlikely National Revival: Soviet Higher Learning and the Ukrainian "Sixtiers", 1953–65', *Russian Review*, Vol. 68, No. 4 (October 2009), 615.

[70] On the topic of the 'imaginary West', see A. Yurchak, *Everything Was Forever*, p. 161.

to, reasserting the primacy of this revolutionary ideology was to prove unsettling.

Over the weeks and months that followed the XX Congress, the initial sense of uncertainty that the Secret Speech had triggered began to ebb away. It was, however, intermittently revived by Khrushchev's occasional backtracking on the Stalin issue. This could be seen in a letter sent to the Central Committee Presidium by M. Petrygin, an engineer from Tuaps, after Khrushchev had spoken about Stalin in glowing terms during a function at the Chinese embassy in January 1957. On the occasion in question, Khrushchev declared that 'being a communist is inseparable from being a Stalinist' and stated: 'may god grant that every communist will be able to fight for the interests of the working class as Stalin fought'. He had also praised Stalin at an official event to celebrate New Year's Eve a few weeks earlier, when he declared that he and all his colleagues were 'Stalinists in our uncompromising fight against the class enemy'.[71] While the first two remarks can in part be put down to the First Secretary playing to the sensibilities of his audience – since the Chinese regime had been both taken aback and angered by the attack on Stalin at the XX Congress – all three comments were broadly representative of both his contradictory attitudes toward the late *vozhd* and his proclivity to change political direction dramatically and without warning.

Petrygin's letter to the Presidium members began sarcastically: 'Dear Comrades! It appears that there are two Khrushchevs: one who defends Stalin and one who attacks him.' He then went on to ask, 'Who can believe in a Party that so naïvely explains the criminal activities of Stalin?' He wrote that Khrushchev's speeches were 'causing disorder in our minds and creating uncertainty about whether the consequences of the cult will be overcome'. Tellingly, Petrygin ended the letter by signing off: 'sorry for being so direct but I think that this is the best way'.[72] The pointed but ultimately respectful tone of these remarks was characteristic of much dissent at the time and, as in many other cases, it represented something akin to loyal criticism. As with speeches at Party and Komsomol meetings, letters like Petrygin's can be considered not just in terms of their direct content. Writing to political bodies, newspapers and official organisations was a relatively common practice inside the Soviet Union and, as Alexei Yurchak points out, it was another important means of integrating oneself within the system, since it offered a way of communicating with an

---

[71] W. Taubman, *Khrushchev: The Man and His Era*, London: The Free Press, 2003, p. 301.
[72] RGANI, f. 5, op. 30, d. 189, ll. 29–32.

otherwise inaccessible authority.[73] Letters like this were not just a way to vent one's frustration, but could also be an attempt to participate in a political system that offered precious few avenues for input from below.

Not all of those who vented doubts and frustrations at this point did so in either a constructive or an idealistic and loyal manner, however. In Arkhangel' *oblast'*, for example, the twenty-five-year-old mechanic Boris Generozov was arrested in April 1956 after producing six political leaflets and reading them to fellow workers at a forestry plant. Calling for the Communist Party to be disbanded and members of the Central Committee to be jailed, he insisted that the people had to take power into their own hands. Excerpts from the leaflets in question give a useful indication of Generozov's arguments:

> The Stalinist Communist Party has nothing to do with Lenin's Party. It is criminal and against the people. The Party hides Stalin's crimes from the country and is now run by cowards and degenerates. The soviets and trade unions are used only to terrorise the people.
> Do the people need such a Party? Or a Party at all? No! It is not needed!
> All of the country is striving for communism, we do not need exploiters. The Party is not creating the conditions for this transition.
> Is it possible to believe in this government? No! Never!
> For three years the Party has hidden Stalin's crimes and now exposes them only because they are under pressure from public opinion.[74]

Like many others who pictured the revolutionary-era Soviet system as the ideal, Generozov was not old enough to have seen those days himself, but it was abundantly clear that Leninism represented an ideological benchmark by which subsequent years were to be measured, and would always come up wanting. In contrasting 'Stalin's Party' (by which he quite clearly also meant the party that Khrushchev now presided over) with that of Lenin, Generozov was both aping the discourse of the Secret Speech and demonstrating just how easily that same discourse could be turned against the authorities. The promise of a 'return to Leninism' not only enabled people to adopt sharply critical ideological positions that nonetheless displayed a genuine sense of loyalty to the wider Soviet system and to the message of the XX Congress, but also aroused an array of hopes and passions that would always be difficult to contain within the fairly narrow political framework of deStalinization that the authorities envisioned. Furthermore, unceasing idealisation of Lenin and the revolutionary era also made it

---

[73] A. Yurchak, *Everything was Forever*, p. 60.   [74] RGANI, f. 5, op. 30, d. 141, l. 13.

virtually impossible for Khrushchev's 'return to Leninism' to match up to expectations.

While the sharpness of his tone can hardly be labelled 'constructive criticism', even Generozov had quite clearly come to terms with the meta-narrative of the communist project. Even though he showed such disregard for the contemporary leadership and for the Secret Speech, he was explicitly not rejecting the revolution as a whole: quite the contrary, he was eager to build the communist paradise. His accusation that the Party was actually holding back the drive toward communism and was an 'exploiter' of the people provided a further demonstration of the tendency of more openly confrontational or hostile criticism simply to invert official rhetoric: most likely an indication that vocabularies and conceptual frameworks for expressing political discontent were not always sophisticated enough to depart significantly from established discourse at this stage.[75]

Even in the wake of the Secret Speech, not all dissenting remarks expressed opposition to Stalin and Stalinism, however. Khrushchev's attack on the 'Cult of Personality' also gave rise to a sharply contrasting theme of dissenting behaviour: that of protest and criticism in defence of Stalin. This was a response that could be found among at least some people in practically all sectors of society, from the Party *aktiv* and the military down to ordinary workers and students. Even though they were to a large extent the product of specific national circumstances, the mass disorders in Georgia during March 1956 were proof enough that the Party leadership risked a serious backlash on this front. Aleksandr Gidoni, for example, recalled that the vast majority of his fellow students at MGU had been genuinely distraught at Stalin's death in 1953 and suggested that the Secret Speech had actually aroused pro- and anti-Stalin sentiments on a comparable scale among his classmates.[76] That the attitudes of these people have been largely absent from the historiography on Soviet dissent is perhaps telling of the extent to which the focus of commentators has fallen on seeking out 'liberal' resistance to the regime, rather than the reasons for the enduring appeal (or, perhaps, grip) of Stalinism.

It ought to be borne in mind that one should not simply view those less willing recipients of Khrushchev's remarks on Stalin as cynics, dupes or brutes. They did not revel in the human carnage that Stalinism had wrought, but basically either refused to accept Stalin's culpability in mass

---

[75] See, for example, J. Hellbeck, 'Fashioning the Stalinist Soul: The Diary of Stepan Pudlubnyi', in S. Fitzpatrick ed., *Stalinism: New Directions*, London: Routledge, 2000, pp. 77–116.

[76] A. Gidoni, *Solntse idet s zapada: kniga vospominanii*, Toronto: Sovremennik, 1980.

repression or saw his achievements as significantly greater than his failings. For many older people in particular, it was nigh on impossible to separate loyalty to Stalin from loyalty to the whole communist project. As Stephen Cohen has argued, for many people 'ending the terror and making limited restitutions was one thing; desecration of the past and radical reforms in the Soviet order, for which they had sacrificed so much, was quite another'.[77] Supporters of Stalin did not always accept the new line meekly. Plenty spoke out at Party and Komsomol meetings, some wrote to newspapers and journals reaffirming their support for the Georgian, and others more quietly continued to resist any assault on his reputation.

Yuri Aksyutin has presented some striking cases of Soviet citizens either questioning or rejecting the attack on Stalin. A retired colonel named Chursin, for example, insisted that '. . . I somehow do not trust all the facts that are laid out . . . Stalin raised me on his ideas from my childhood and I will not reject those ideas now. I had and will [continue to] have the highest opinion of Stalin.'[78] Reference to the length of time ('from my childhood') that one had been a follower of Stalin and to the formative impact of the Stalin years were common among the remarks of those who defended the late dictator, but this was not an apologia for being 'set in one's ways'. It not only sought to demand respect for the views of the speaker but also pitted the traditional and proven against the new and potentially dangerous path set out by Khrushchev. A letter from Antonina Mikhailovna Peterson – apparently a Party member of fifty years' standing and a veteran of the revolution as well as of the wars with the Whites and with Nazi Germany – doubtless summed up the mood of many fellow veterans: 'These attacks on Stalin do not sit well. His name should be restored. We *frontoviki* will never forget him.'[79]

In Gori, the birthplace of Stalin, discussions about the Secret Speech were probably always going to be fraught with contention after the town's greatest son had been unceremoniously knocked off his pedestal. At a meeting of almost 300 communists there on 19 March 1956 a slew of speakers disapproved of the attack on Stalin and the majority of the local *aktiv* refused to condemn those who had been involved in pro-Stalin riots that had broken out in the town earlier that same month.[80] Another

[77] S. Cohen, 'The Stalin Question after Stalin', in S. Cohen ed., *An End to Silence: Uncensored Opinion in the Soviet Union, from Roy Medvedev's Magazine 'Political Diary'*, New York: W.W. Norton, 1982, p. 41.

[78] See Iu. Aksiutin, 'Popular Responses to Khrushchev', in W. Taubman, S. Khrushchev and A. Gleason eds., *Nikita Khrushchev*, London: Yale University Press, 2000, p. 185.

[79] RGANI, f. 5, op. 31, d. 189, ll. 1–2, in K. Aimermakher et al. eds., *Doklad N.S. Khrushcheva*.

[80] RGANI, f. 5, op. 31, d. 52, ll. 2–4, in K. Aimermakher et al. eds., *Doklad N.S. Khrushcheva*.

interesting example of a dissenting voice raised in defence of Stalin can be found in a report sent from Vladimir *obkom* to the Department of Party Organs on 19 April 1956. At one of the meetings held to discuss the Secret Speech there, the long-standing CPSU member G.M. Vozzhanikov declared that Khrushchev had unfairly 'blackened Stalin's character' and had 'belittled his achievements', insisting that he (Vozzhanikov) would oppose any resolution on the condemnation of Stalin, before adding 'I am for Stalin and fought alongside him for thirty years, I do not know Khrushchev, he is a newcomer and he is a long way behind Stalin.' Vozzhanikov's anger did not subside. He returned to his attack on Khrushchev several times over the next few days, until he was thrown out of the Party the following month.[81]

In some ways it is surprising that there was not a truly major backlash of support for Stalin, since many clearly still held a great deal of genuine regard for the late dictator. There were undoubtedly plenty among the public and within the Party who resented the message presented in the Secret Speech, yet for the most part they seem to have remained silent at this point. Perhaps, as Yuri Orlov had suggested, they were 'holding their fingers in the wind'. Ironically, the likelihood is that the legacy of state violence and intimidation of society that Stalin had bequeathed his successors was also a major reason why more people did not dare to defend him openly against Khrushchev's attack. Still, in this connection it is worth noting that there were plenty in the Party and state machinery, and within the KGB in particular, who had little enthusiasm for Khrushchev's deStalinization. As such, those who sought to defend Stalin may well have found it easier to evade formal repercussions than did those who had embraced the Secret Speech a little too fulsomely for the authorities' liking.

The pro-Stalin dissent that began with the Secret Speech later proved resurgent following the so-called 'anti-Party affair' in June 1957, when prominent Stalinists such as Vyacheslav Molotov and Lazar Kaganovich were removed from the Party leadership and disgraced after their failed attempt to oust Khrushchev. A number of cases have been unearthed where Soviet citizens protested the ejection from the leadership of these long-standing 'comrades in arms' of Stalin. An anonymous letter to *Pravda* in July 1957, later traced back to one G.G. Logunov, began as follows: 'Respected editor, is it really possible that you accept such a disgraceful thing as the sacking of Molotov, Malenkov, Kaganovich and Shepilov? Bear in mind that the people's sympathy is with them and not with Khrushchev

---

[81] RGANI, f. 5, op. 32, d. 54, ll. 53–5, in K. Aimermakher et al. eds., *Doklad N.S. Khrushcheva*.

et al. If the people are silent then that is only because they are extremely intimidated.'[82] In Kuibyshev, a meeting held to discuss the anti-Party affair produced so much opposition to the official line that it had to be abandoned.[83] Others pointed out that, like Molotov and Malenkov, Khrushchev too had been involved in repressions during the Stalin era.[84] In Dagestan ASSR there were demands for the members of the anti-Party group to be given a platform to explain their policies over the radio so that the people could make their own decision.[85] The subsequent renaming of enterprises and towns that had been named in honour of those now in disgrace also saw sporadic outbursts of public complaint, especially when Stalingrad later became Volgograd in 1961.[86]

One of the most interesting aspects of the above comments is the apparent sense of naïvety among some of the pro-Stalin dissenters about the true nature of the Soviet system; this was notably displayed in the remarks made in Dagestan calling for Molotov and his fellow plotters to be granted a platform. Quite possibly there was an element of wilful misunderstanding at work – consciously playing upon Khrushchev's own rhetoric of 'trust in society' – but this was not necessarily the case. After all, those who had most keenly embraced the Stalinist system presumably had until that point shown least inclination to look beyond the official (and deeply misleading) discourse on subjects such as freedoms, rights and Soviet democracy. Evidently, strident opposition to the official line could induce a strikingly different perspective on the nature of the Soviet system.

Those least likely to reject the message of the Secret Speech, on the other hand, were the millions who had lost relatives and friends in the mass repressions or else had passed through the camps themselves, and especially the three-quarters of a million prisoners who were still incarcerated by February 1956.[87] One of the major consequences of Khrushchev's attack

---

[82] GARF, f. 8131, op. 31, d. 85762, l. 13, in V. Kozlov and S. Mironenko eds., *Kramola*, pp. 147–8.

[83] M. Dobson, *Khrushchev's Cold Summer*, p. 191.

[84] Being located outside of Moscow during the worst of the repression, Khrushchev was not so deeply complicit in the crimes of the era. Nonetheless, he was sufficiently vigorous at 'uncovering enemies' during his time as head of the Ukrainian SSR to earn himself the nickname 'the Butcher of the Ukraine'.

[85] A. Pyzhikov, 'XX s''ezd i obshchestvennoe mnenie', *Svobodnaya mysl'*, No. 8 (2000), 83.

[86] The government legislated in 1957 to prohibit the future naming of places in honour of those still alive. Thus, towns and cities named after the likes of Molotov and Voroshilov either reverted to their previous names or took on entirely new ones. It was not until 1961 that Stalin's name was systematically removed from buildings, streets, towns and geographical features. See G. R. F. Bursa, 'Political Changes of Names of Soviet Towns', *Slavonic and East European Review*, Vol. 63, No. 2 (April 1985), 161–93.

[87] Dobson cites a figure of 781,630 camp inmates in January 1956. M. Dobson, *Khrushchev's Cold Summer*, p. 51.

on Stalin was that it gave the final impetus toward the release, and some-times also rehabilitation, of most of those political prisoners who remained confined in the country's network of labour camps and prisons.[88] This process of draining the Gulag had already begun soon after Stalin's death, in the first instance focusing on 'criminal' prisoners rather than 'politicals', but even as of May 1956 there were still well over 110,000 'counter-revolutionaries' incarcerated.[89] Almost eighteen months later, that total had dropped to less than 14,000.[90] The camp network was by no means completely disbanded, but the sheer volume of prisoners who flowed out of the Gulag and back into society during the early to mid 1950s made this a highly significant socio-political development, particularly in regard to dissent.

In the most western regions of the Soviet Union, in the Baltic states and western Ukraine in particular, the release and return of thousands of former nationalist prisoners posed a real challenge for the authorities there. After displaying fierce resistance to their countries' forced incorporation into the USSR during the mid 1940s, there was little doubt that plenty of those being released from camps had by no means reconciled themselves to Soviet power in the meantime: this is seen in the fact that nationalists from these areas tended to be at the forefront of camp uprisings and demonstrations throughout the post-war era.[91] Even before events in Hungary further crystallised unrest, there was considerable tension in the area, with hun-dreds of citizens having illegal weapons confiscated from them in western Ukraine and a number of officials being physically attacked or murdered.[92]

The effect that the mass prisoner releases had upon dissent across the USSR as a whole was somewhat varied and unpredictable. Quite a few of the freed inmates were all too soon back in the camps for one reason or another. There were numerous instances following the 1953 amnesties when former prisoners wrote hostile leaflets and engaged in political outbursts apparently with the sole intention of being sent back to the Gulag as a result

---

[88] Jeffrey Hardy shows that Nikita Khrushchev personally played a significant role in speeding up the rate at which these reviews were carried out and prisoners released. See J. Hardy, 'Khrushchev's Gulag: The Evolution of Punishment in the Post-Stalin Soviet Union, 1953–1964', Ph.D. Dissertation, Princeton University, 2011, p. 58.

[89] The exact figure provided in a report from the KGB to the Central Committee was 113,735 'counter-revolutionary criminals'. RGANI, f. 89, op. 18, d. 36, l. 2.

[90] As of September 1957 the exact figure was 13,765, according to the MVD. Of those, 856 were due for release at the end of 1957. GARF, f. 9401, op. 2, d. 492, l. 143.

[91] See A. Weiner, 'The Empires Pay a Visit: Gulag Returnees, East European Rebellions, and Soviet Frontier Politics', *The Journal of Modern History*, Vol. 78, No. 2 (June 2006), 333–76. See also V. Kozlov, *Neizvestnyi SSSR*.

[92] A. Weiner, 'The Empires Pay a Visit', 357.

of their limited prospects 'on the outside'.[93] The same thing happened at times in the amnesties that followed the Secret Speech. A considerable number of those who were sentenced under article 58-10 around this time were apprehended as a result of making hostile political statements at train stations or on trains, shortly after being released.[94] One example of this can be seen in the case of the Ukrainian P.N. Sobolev, of Kirovskaya *oblast'*, who was sentenced under article 58-10 after making what his case file referred to only as 'anti-Soviet remarks' on a train to Perm on his way home from camp.[95] Similarly, on 25 March 1957 the just-released prisoners I.A. Bodinkov and S.A. Kuznetsov were both sentenced under article 58-10: the former after making threats against communists in Smolensk and 'approving of life in the US'; the latter after engaging in what the KGB investigation labelled 'anti-Soviet hooligan behaviour' at a train station in Khar'kov.[96]

Biographical details on these three men show that they had all been sentenced more than once, and two of them (Bodinkov and Kuznetsov) were classed as being 'without defined occupation'. While no details on the education levels of Sobolev or Bodinkov appear to have been recorded, Kuznetsov's rather meagre four classes of schooling fit comfortably within the wider demographic trend of minimal formal education among those who engaged in this kind of hooligan-type dissent. 'Marginals' such as these were to feature heavily in the cruder and more volatile dissent of the Khrushchev era.[97]

Occasional hooligan-type outbursts aside, it seems that in most cases release and rehabilitation tended to be effective at buying a former prisoner's silence, even if it did not always ensure their support.[98] Felix Serebrov, for example, recalled that even though he did not engage in dissenting activity upon his release from the Gulag in the amnesties that followed Stalin's death, he was filled with 'hatred toward communists'.[99] Although they were

[93] See M. Dobson, 'Show the Bandit Enemies no Mercy! Amnesty, Criminality and Public Response in 1953', in P. Jones ed., *The Dilemmas of De-Stalinization*.

[94] As Juliane Fürst shows, train stations were also a recurring site for such clashes during the late Stalin years. See J. Fürst, *Stalin's Last Generation*, p. 171.

[95] GARF, f.8131, op. 31, d. 81493, in V. Kozlov and S. Mironenko eds., *58–10 Nadzornye proizvodstva*.

[96] GARF, f. 8131, op. 31, d. 78019, ll. 1–3 and f. 8131, op. 31, d. 81617, ll. 1–3. See V. Kozlov and S. Mironenko eds., *58–10 Nadzornye proizvodstva*.

[97] See E. Zubkova and T. Zhukova eds., *Na 'krayu' sovetskogo obshchestva: sotsial'nye marginaly kak ob''ekt gosudarstvennoi politiki, 1945–1960-e gg.*, Moskva: Rosspen, 2010.

[98] See N. Adler, 'Life in the "Big Zone": The Fate of Returnees in the Aftermath of Stalinist Repression', *Europe–Asia Studies*, Vol. 51, No. 1 (January 1999), 15.

[99] 'Interv'yu s Feliksom Serebrovym', in V. Abramkin and V. Chesnokova, *Tyurmennyi mir glazami politzaklyuchennykh*, Moskva: Sodeistvie, 1993, p. 44.

relatively few in number, there were still some released prisoners who demonstrated a more purposive type of dissenting behaviour. One example of a former inmate apparently left deeply politicised by his time in the Gulag was the thirty-six-year-old Georgian Kh.A. Asadulin, who had been sentenced for 'betrayal of the motherland' in 1945 and was released in February 1955. Between that time and his arrest in 1960, Asadulin produced over 10,000 political leaflets that were secretly distributed in Baku, Tbilisi and Kirovabad. According to the subsequent investigation, the leaflets in question consisted of calls for citizens to struggle against the Soviet regime, slander of the CPSU's domestic and foreign policy, and praise for the American way of life.[100] Under interrogation, Asadulin stated that he had decided to struggle against the regime whilst in prison and had promptly done so upon his release.[101]

While they may have been broadly realistic, confessions such as this should not simply be taken at face value. Although widespread torture and other brutal methods of interrogation were no longer part and parcel of police investigations by this stage, abuse of detainees had not disappeared entirely and there was always scope for the manipulation or outright misreporting of evidence. The fact that Asadulin's confession fitted so neatly with the authorities' concerns about former political prisoners, and was so formulaic in its language, instils a sense of caution. Nonetheless, the volume of leaflets produced over several years clearly shows that the author went to some serious effort to get his point across, and that this was no 'moment of madness'.

Most significant in some respects was the impact that coming face to face with Gulag survivors had upon members of the younger generation. Like many others, Mikhail Aksenov recalled that it was the influence of encountering returnees that destroyed the last of his faith in the regime and turned him into an ardent critic of the Soviet system.[102] Vladimir Bukovsky, too, spoke about the important influence that meeting released prisoners and hearing their stories had had upon his own growing sense of distaste toward the regime.[103] They were, after all, living testament to the system's capacity for inhumanity. Others,

---

[100] It is worth restating here that what the authorities considered 'slander' may well have been entirely balanced or justifiable criticism. Unfortunately, the case file in question does not contain copies of Asadulin's leaflets.

[101] Asadulin was jailed for seven years in December 1960. RGANI, f. 5, op. 30, d. 320, ll. 60–1.

[102] Interview with M. Aksenov in I. Kirk, *Profiles in Russian Resistance*, New York: Quadrangle, 1975, p. 209. Sergei Kovalev was another Brezhnev-era dissident who recalled that meeting former Gulag inmates had a strong influence on his attitude toward the regime. See E. Gilligan, *Defending Human Rights in Russia: Sergei Kovalyov, Dissident and Human Rights Commissioner, 1969–2003*, London: RoutledgeCurzon, 2004.

[103] Interview with Vladimir Bukovsky, Cambridge, March 2007.

of course, had lost friends and family and were thereafter permanently embittered.[104] In short, the subject of the Stalin-era camps was not one that could be easily brushed under the carpet by freeing those who had survived them.[105]

It is also instructive to look at the kinds of dissenting behaviour that were taking place within the remaining camps and prisons at the time. This is particularly important since approximately one in ten of those who were sentenced for anti-Soviet activity during the early Khrushchev years were already in prison when they committed the offences which would subsequently see them branded as anti-Soviet. For the most part, those serving inmates who were sentenced for anti-Soviet activity were not originally 'politicals' but had been initially convicted, and in some cases repeatedly convicted, for 'criminal' acts like theft and assault, or worse.[106]

The kinds of dissenting acts that such prisoners engaged in generally represented little more than hooliganism or anti-state protest under a political façade: a lashing out at authority by targeting what was held dear. An example of this kind of behaviour could be seen in the case of the twenty-six-year-old Chuvash I.E. Kryshkin. Already serving a criminal sentence in Chelyabinsk *oblast'*, Kryshkin was convicted of counter-revolutionary activity in May 1957 after being caught drawing swastikas on a wall in the camp compound.[107] Later that same month, the Russian N.A. Saparov, who had been jailed twice already by the age of twenty-six, was sentenced again in Kemerova *oblast'* after writing slogans calling for resistance to the regime on walls and on his clothes.[108] Another case file, on V.A. Vasil'ev, in the Mordova camp network, stated only that the prisoner had been convicted under article 58-10 for etching an 'anti-Soviet tattoo' across his own face.[109] The investigation protocol did not deign it proper to

---

[104] The evidence of a causal link between the repression of family members (particularly parents) and dissenting activity has perhaps been overstated in the past, though it surely existed for some people. The Medvedev brothers, Roy and Zhores, are the most widely cited 'proof' of this link. Zhores Medvedev, however, stated that professional matters (relating to Trofim Lysenko) were key to his emergence as a dissident, rather than the repression suffered by family members.

[105] On this theme see in particular M. Dobson, *Khrushchev's Cold Summer*, and N. Adler, *Trudnoe vozvrashchenie: sud'by sovetskikh politzaklyuchennykh v 1950–1990 gody*, Moskva: Zven'ya, 2005.

[106] This was generally not the case with nationalist prisoners from Ukraine and the Baltic republics, who were often at the forefront of protests, underground groups and demonstrations in the camps throughout the post-war years.

[107] GARF, f. 8131, op. 31, d. 80497, ll.1–2. In fact, swastikas were the most common item of camp graffiti, according to Vladimir Kozlov. See V. Kozlov, *Neizvestnyi SSSR*, p. 119.

[108] GARF, f. 8131, op. 31, d. 83874, ll. 1–2.

[109] GARF, f. 8131, op. 36, d. 1015, ll. 1–3. This case file reveals that Vasil'ev was sentenced again for the same offence in 1966. The almost complete absence of detail in Vasil'ev's file suggests that this was not a case into which either the KGB or courts were prepared to conduct anything more than a cursory investigation and trial.

state exactly what Vasil'ev had inscribed on himself, but Anatoly Marchenko's eyewitness account of the Khrushchev-era camps cited some of the most frequent slogans of self-made tattoos as 'Khrushchev's whore' and 'Slave of the CPSU'.[110]

One of the most common avenues for political attacks on authority among prisoners was the age-old principle of 'the enemy of my enemy is my friend'. As First Secretary of the Communist Party and head of the regime that had seen fit to jail these people in the first place, Khrushchev was an obvious target for prisoners' animosity. Anyone deemed to be his opponent was therefore liable to be championed by inmates on that basis alone. One encounters a diverse cohort of figures such as Eisenhower, Hitler and Stalin all being hailed as heroes among sections of the camp population simply because they were seen as fellow enemies of Khrushchev. The names of those considered to be among his nemeses even kept pace with contemporary political developments as members of the anti-Party group, such as Molotov and Kaganovich, along with John F. Kennedy and Mao Tse-tung, all came to feature in anti-Khrushchev statements and graffiti around the time of their respective altercations with the First Secretary.

At first glance, the aim of these kinds of behaviours was little more than to offend the political sensibilities of the Soviet authorities, and they certainly did just that. In many cases those who remained in the post-Stalin camps and prisons essentially had nothing more to lose and nothing to gain from submission, since they were unlikely ever to be reintegrated into 'decent' society. While many of those on the outside who came forth with critical remarks and controversial questions at this stage tended to do so with the best interests of the communist project at heart, most of the outbursts and acts of defiance among inmates were primarily driven by a desire for confrontation with authority.[111] However, there were also other motivations at work, too. For some, there were tactical reasons for these acts of self-mutilation, vandalism and abuse of authority. Believing rumours that political prisoners were held in better conditions and subject to lower work norms, or else hoping to avoid enemies and debts among fellow prisoners in their existing place of incarceration, many 'criminals' attempted to have themselves reclassified as 'politicals' by making anti-Soviet statements and drawing political slogans around the camp complex.[112] This was a classic

---

[110] A. Marchenko, *My Testimony*, Harmondsworth: Penguin Books, 1969, p. 141.

[111] See V. Kozlov, *Neizvestnyi SSSR*, p. 116.

[112] GARF, f. 8131, op. 30, d. 5080, l. 8. As Chapters 4 and 8 show, the prisoners in question were badly wrong in believing that 'politicals' had it easy in the camps.

scenario of inmates trying to play the system to their own benefit and one that could easily paint an exaggerated picture of ideological ferment in the camps and prisons. Eventually, a 1958 Supreme Court resolution warned prosecutors as to what was happening, advising that such individuals should no longer be sentenced under article 58-10 but dealt with in a more appropriate manner.[113] From then onwards the frequency with which serving prisoners were among those convicted of political offences dropped markedly, a point which aptly demonstrated that it was the authorities who retained the prerogative to define both 'Soviet' and 'anti-Soviet'.

[113] GARF, f. 8131, op. 32, d. 5080, l. 33.

CHAPTER 2

Putting out fires

Responses to dissenting behaviour undoubtedly became far less draconian than they had been during the Stalin years, but the scope for criticism remained narrow and punishment could still be harsh. Along with entirely invented plots and swingeing repressive campaigns directed at whole social and national groups, twenty-five-year labour-camp sentences and executions for counter-revolutionary activity were quickly reined in. For those who did not transgress the boundaries of acceptable comment and behaviour, the post-Stalin years saw growing security from arbitrary persecution as well as an improving standard of living. Dissenters, however, were still in a decidedly precarious position, since the changes wrought upon the system following Stalin's death were primarily for the benefit of those who 'toed the line'. William Henry Chamberlain's assessment that the Soviet Union had changed 'from a terror state to a strict police state' is perhaps the most useful place from which to start.[1]

Policy against dissent was a dynamic field of activity in the first half of the Khrushchev era. Solutions were being sought for behaviours that, to a large extent, constituted fundamentally new challenges as the Soviet regime adapted to the post-Stalin, post-terror environment. The new leadership wanted to revive and re-energise society but they were not prepared to grant the public significantly greater political liberties as they did so. This was to be one of the key dilemmas of the mid to late 1950s, and policy against dissent lay right at its heart. As popular reactions to the Secret Speech demonstrated, things did not always run smoothly at first. What one can see in the authorities' responses to dissent during this early stage of the Khrushchev period is essentially a process of development by trial and error as they attempted to reconfigure effective policing of protest and criticism in the absence of mass violence. Different approaches were

[1] W. Chamberlain, 'USSR: How Much Change since Stalin?', *Russian Review*, Vol. 22, No. 3 (July 1963), 228.

employed and lessons were learned, before a more effective and efficient body of policy began to crystallise towards the end of the decade. With the Secret Speech providing the first truly seismic political shock since the death of Stalin, it was at that point that the collective leadership's abandonment of mass repression first began to come under sustained pressure, was found wanting, and soon had to evolve in order to combat more effectively the rising tide of dissent.

Many of the basic assumptions that the leadership made in regard to dissent were either essentially sound or can at least be viewed as eminently logical, though that is not to say 'fair'. However, they were frequently unsophisticated and inappropriate in their application, often pushing the authorities into exaggerated and entirely unhelpful responses to dissenting behaviour. Nonetheless, the policies against dissent that were pursued under Khrushchev ultimately paid dividends by minimising the vast majority of open dissent among both the intelligentsia and the workers. What this often meant, though, was that many of the doubts and frustrations that existed within society were suppressed rather than remedied. Of course, some grew ever more alienated in the process.

Policy against dissent was generally not a field in which one finds the kind of clear-cut divisions between 'conservatives' and 'liberals' that studies on certain aspects of Khrushchev-era politics have emphasised.[2] There were definitely divergent views within the leadership, and between key institutions such as the Procuracy and KGB, on all manner of policy issues, however. Perhaps most significantly, Khrushchev himself tended not to pursue anything like a consistently 'liberal' or 'conservative' line.[3] Even so, preserving domestic stability remained the one priority that stood inviolable for the entire political elite, and all were ultimately prepared to take whatever measures necessary to see that any challenge to the existing order might be quickly snuffed out. In regard to deStalinization, the most important task in the eyes of the leadership was to maintain control of the process: preventing pressures for change from growing and ultimately taking on a

[2] Miriam Dobson has also pointed to the lack of a clear dichotomy between 'conservatives' and 'liberals' on the subject of policy towards Gulag returnees. See M. Dobson, *Khrushchev's Cold Summer: Gulag Returnees, Crime and the Fate of Reform after Stalin*, Ithaca, NY: Cornell University Press, 2009. However, this is not to say that there were no fields in which this paradigm is applicable. See, for example, Gleb Tsipursky's 'Pleasure, Power and the Pursuit of Communism: Soviet Youth and State-Sponsored Popular Culture during the Early Cold War Period, 1945–1968', Ph.D. Dissertation, University of North Carolina at Chapel Hill, 2011, in which the author clearly shows divisions between hard- and soft-liners in the field of youth policy.
[3] See, for example, C. Linden, *Khrushchev and the Soviet Leadership*, Baltimore, MD: Johns Hopkins University Press, 1990.

momentum of their own.[4] This was exactly what the atmosphere following the XX Congress threatened.

Stalin's successors were from the very beginning aware that the dynamics of the Soviet system had changed forever following his death. While 'scared' would be too strong a word, one could certainly say that members of the new collective leadership were apprehensive about society's mood on coming to power. As Leonard Schapiro pointed out: 'the leaders of the Party . . . graphically summed up their own view on the state of popular feeling towards the Party when, immediately after Stalin's death, they spoke of the need for measures to prevent disorder and panic'.[5] While Schapiro's remark perhaps gives an exaggerated picture of animosity toward the Party, it does reflect the concerns of the leadership with some accuracy. For much of the 1950s Khrushchev would repeatedly call for the regime to show 'trust in society': this trust was certainly not in evidence as the military and security organs were placed on full alert at the start of March 1953 in case the announcement of Stalin's death should trigger popular disturbances.[6] The fact that Georgy Malenkov – the initial frontrunner in the race to succeed Stalin – quickly announced that the regime would devote more energy and resources to the production of consumer goods did not just represent the opening salvo of the succession struggle, it also represented an awareness among the collective leadership that a new kind of social contract might be necessary.

Even during Stalin's last years, it was becoming obvious to his inner circle that things would have to change quickly once he left the stage.[7] Senior members of the post-war leadership were well aware of the threat posed by looming economic and social crises arising from the mass repression and stifling atmosphere of the late 1940s and early 1950s. In private, the collective leadership began to reassess Stalin's position almost immediately after his death on 5 March 1953. In public, too, the grandiose celebration of the late *vozhd* soon diminished somewhat, though a multitude of statues, state prizes and enterprises named in his honour still remained for the time being. Other changes were taking place away from the public gaze. The three years of collective leadership that followed Stalin's death in 1953 showed a consistent and marked decrease in convictions for counter-revolutionary

---

[4] See P. Jones, 'Introduction', in P. Jones ed., *The Dilemmas of De-Stalinization: Negotiating Cultural and Social Change in the Khrushchev Era*, London: Routledge, 2006, p. 5.

[5] L. Schapiro, *The Communist Party of the Soviet Union*, London: Methuen, 1970, p. 608.

[6] See L. Schapiro, *The Communist Party*.

[7] See, for example, Y. Gorlizki and O. Khlevniuk, *Cold Peace: Stalin and the Soviet Ruling Circle, 1945–1953*, Oxford University Press, 2004.

crimes: from an average of over 40,000 per year in 1950–2, they dropped to 2,124 sentences in 1954, to 1,069 in 1955 and then to 623 sentences in 1956.[8] Clearly, then, the most significant change in the state's repressive activity – arguably the most important achievement of the immediate post-Stalin era – had already taken place some time before the XX Congress and Khrushchev's rise to sole power.

The volume of on-going repression immediately slackened, but political prisoners were largely overlooked in the first amnesties that began to shrink the Gulag population.[9] In fact, many political prisoners were not even being freed upon completion of their sentence. A March 1955 report stated that over 54,000 released prisoners were summarily directed into internal exile by the MVD without any legal basis.[10] Figures compiled by the MVD showed that by January 1956 there were still some 113,735 'counter-revolutionary criminals' languishing in corrective labour camps.[11] Bearing in mind the huge numbers of thieves and violent criminals who were allowed to return to normal society around this time, it is entirely evident that political prisoners were still eyed with a particular distrust by the authorities, even after the ending of mass repression had implicitly recognised that there was often little or no basis for such convictions. Final confirmation of the arbitrary nature of Stalin-era repression came at the end of February 1956.

Somewhat surprisingly, no concrete plans were established either before or immediately after the Secret Speech in regard of how to police popular responses to it. Ekaterina Furtseva – at the time a member of the Central Committee Secretariat and later a full Presidium member – subsequently wrote that: 'after the XX Congress we were not ready to give a response when the remarks began to come'.[12] A wealth of documents and reports coming in from across the country show this to have been true. In all likelihood this lack of pre-planning was primarily a result of the short timeframe that existed between the decision for Khrushchev to deliver his report on Stalin to the XX Congress and the actual event itself taking place.[13]

---

[8] GARF, f. 8131, op. 32, d. 5080, l. 3.
[9] Aleksandr Solzhenitsyn claimed that political prisoners had been completely overlooked in the amnesties that began to drain the Gulag after Stalin's death. Both Miriam Dobson and Jeffrey Hardy have subsequently shown that this was not the case.
[10] RGANI, f. 89, op. 60, d. 11, l. 2.   [11] RGANI, f. 89, op. 16, d. 1, l. 3.
[12] E. Zubkova, *Obshchestvo i reformy 1945–1964*, Moskva: Izdatel'skii tsentr 'Rossiya molodaya', 1993, p. 136.
[13] Various conflicting accounts have been put forward as to exactly when key decisions were made regarding what would become known as the Secret Speech. Nonetheless, there is general consensus that the time gap between decision and speech was a matter of days, at most. See, for example, A. Pyzhikov, *Opyt modernizatsii sovetskogo obshchestva v 1953–1964 godakh: obshchestvenno-politicheskii aspekt*, Moskva: Izdatel'skii dom 'Gamma', 1998.

However, as significant a political shock as the Secret Speech undoubtedly was, perhaps the Party rank and file had been so quiescent for so many years that one can appreciate why the matter was not ascribed the very highest priority. By their inconsistent and uncertain handling of the critical remarks that followed the Speech, the authorities demonstrated one of the central characteristics of policy regarding dissent in the early Khrushchev years: they were rarely proactive in seeking to forestall outbursts of criticism, but instead responded to them afterwards in an ad hoc manner which showed that punitive policy had moved away from unadulterated Stalinism but had not yet emerged in any kind of long-term, post-Stalin form. In later years it would be inconceivable that such a major political announcement would be made without extensive planning and preparation to deal with public responses. Ruling without terror would require much more care and attention to such details than the authorities showed in the spring of 1956.

With at least a few of its members already in a state of some trepidation over the potential consequences of Khrushchev's remarks on Stalin, it was entirely natural that the top leadership should take an active interest in monitoring closely the comments that arose at the meetings held in its aftermath. The reports coming in almost always began by stating that Khrushchev's speech had met with widespread approval – which was not entirely inaccurate – but many of them soon made clear just what a can of worms he had opened. Khrushchev and his colleagues cannot have been unconcerned by some of the news reaching them from the Department of Party Organs. A letter from Tuvinskii *obkom* on 10 April, for example, stated quite explicitly that the Speech had 'activated anti-Soviet elements' in the area.[14] Some commentators have suggested that when these kinds of remarks filtered back to the Kremlin from Party meetings around the country they convinced the leadership that the Secret Speech had shaken the very foundations of the system.[15] With their own positions occasionally looking precarious, there was certainly no shortage of local officials who wished the Central Committee Presidium to believe as much. However, as the autumn of 1956, and later the summer of 1962, were to show, as and when the leadership perceived a potentially serious threat to domestic stability they were far quicker to respond and much more decisive in their actions than had been the case in the spring of 1956.

[14] A. Pyzhikov, *Opyt modernizatsii*, p. 61.
[15] See, for example, E. Kulavig, *Dissent in the Years of Khrushchev: Nine Stories about Disobedient Russians*, Basingstoke: Palgrave Macmillan, 2002, p.16.

This was a particularly testing time for Party officials below the elite level. As Polly Jones has observed, the leadership in Moscow often seemed more angered by local authorities' failure to detect and deal with instances of dissenting behaviour than by the actual outbursts themselves.[16] Again and again, individual Party organisations were upbraided for failing to provide a proper response to those who spoke up. When several CPSU members made critical comments and posed a series of 'inflammatory' questions and remarks at a meeting in Kuibyshev *oblast'* – including a demand to know what was considered the minimum living wage in the USSR and claims that the Soviet regime was holding back the development of poorer *kolkhozes* – the Party organisation's failure to deal with the situation to the Central Committee's satisfaction led the local *obkom* to become involved. The leadership of the Party cell was deemed to have failed in its duty to provide a sufficiently decisive rebuttal to its critics, and Kuibyshev *gorkom* took control of the matter. It handed out expulsions or severe Party reprimands to all of those who had made critical remarks or asked questions that were judged 'provocative'. Because of their weak response to the original incident, the *raikom* leadership in question was disbanded.[17]

In Stanislav *oblast'* a whole series of officials were reprimanded for their failure to respond with sufficient vigour after a meeting there saw staff at a local Higher-Education Institute hold forth with a range of criticisms. One CPSU member present had stopped the discussion on the XX Congress and started to read reports from the XIX Congress in 1952 (at which members of the leadership had been particularly sycophantic in their praise for Stalin), another demanded 'guarantees' that Party members could now safely speak out, and yet another accused the Party of 'toadyism'. After what must have been a rather uproarious session, there was practically no response from the local Party organisation, at least according to the Department of Party Organs in Moscow. When the *buro* of Stanislav *obkom* met to discuss the events in question, the Party secretary who had overseen the meeting was censured; the *obkom* criticised the weak leadership of Stanislav *gorkom* and attacked the low level of ideological education among cadres there, demanding that both be remedied forthwith and insisting that the session be revisited in order to provide a proper response to those who had spoken

---

[16] P. Jones, 'From the Secret Speech to the Burial of Stalin', in P. Jones ed., *The Dilemmas of De-Stalinization*, p. 44.

[17] RGANI, f. 89, op. 6, d. 5, in K. Aimermakher et al. eds., *Doklad N.S. Khrushcheva o kul'te lichnosti Stalina na XX s"ezde KPSS: dokumenty*, Moskva: Rosspen, 2002.

out. A series of expulsions and Party reprimands duly followed, and the head of the institute's Party organisation was fired.[18]

The same pattern could be witnessed in the very farthest reaches of the USSR, in Sakhalin *oblast'*. Workers and academics at a geology institute there raised all kinds of sensitive issues as they discussed the speech, calling for national and regional leaders to be replaced, demanding a special CPSU Congress be held to address Khrushchev's revelations, and criticising the length of time it had taken the leadership to tackle the Stalin question. Although the *raikom* first secretary verbally chastised a number of those who spoke up at the time, this was not considered a sufficiently stern response. Sakhalin *obkom*, too, came under heavy fire from Moscow for adopting too liberal a line in response to those who spoke out. When the Department of Party Organs looked into the matter they also found that an *obkom* instructor named Simonenko had been present at the meeting but had remained silent throughout. This, they said, 'proved his political unreliability'.[19]

Regional officials such as these were repeatedly accused of showing a 'lack of vigilance' in dealing with critics, sometimes justifiably so. A batch of hostile political leaflets was discovered scattered around the site at an aviation plant in Novosibirsk, for example, yet the local *obkom* secretary, Deryagin, did not bother to report their discovery to the KGB for two whole weeks. As a subsequent Central Committee report noted ruefully, by that time it was too late to do anything about them or to track down those responsible.[20] One can well imagine how this kind of lax approach must have exasperated nervous officials back in the capital.

Local Party bosses were not only coming under fire from above. Just as Stalin's placemen across Eastern Europe – most notably Matyas Rakosi in Hungary – were soon to find that Khrushchev's new line badly weakened their positions at home, some of the late dictator's regional potentates inside the USSR also became subject to attack from below. In Tashkent, for example, in-fighting broke out when the Uzbek Central Committee secretary Usman Yusupov faced criticism for propagating his own personality cult in the republic and 'surrounding himself with toadies and yes-men'. More ominously, one of the speakers revealed in a public meeting how Yusupov had been deeply implicated in his arrest and imprisonment back in 1941, whence the speaker in question had not emerged until after Stalin's

[18] RGANI, f. 5, op. 3, d. 54, ll. 14–24, in K. Aimermakher et al. eds., *Doklad N.S. Khrushcheva*.
[19] RGANI, f. 5, op. 32, d. 45, ll. 135–6, in K. Aimermakher et al. eds., *Doklad N.S. Khrushcheva*.
[20] K. Aimermakher et al. eds., *Doklad N.S. Khrushcheva*, p. 493.

death, twelve years later.[21] There were doubtless many others like Yusupov across the USSR, who had clambered to the top over the bodies of their comrades. The fact that most of those in positions of power at varying levels of the Party-state structure by 1956 had risen to their posts during the Stalin years gives a clear idea of how many people within the political apparatus would not have wanted the past to be dug up and examined too closely. With this in mind, it was perhaps not the very top Party leadership in Moscow who were most deeply unsettled by responses to the Secret Speech, but those lower-level officials like Usman Yusupov whose positions were considerably less secure and were liable to come under attack from either above or below.

In this context, communications such as the report sent from Tuvinskii *obkom* to the Department of Party Organs, warning that 'anti-Soviet elements' had been activated by the Speech, gain a new layer of context.[22] At least in part, they were motivated by self-defence: they were an attempt to force Khrushchev into putting the brakes on deStalinization by over-stating the unrest that it had prompted. Rather than simply viewing such resistance to deStalinization as evidence of Party officials' fundamentally Stalinist political outlook, it can also be interpreted in terms of the apparent threats that the new course posed to their authority and potentially even their freedom. As it turned out, the Secret Speech generally did not lead to any serious retribution for officials who had been implicated in Stalin-era repressions, though they cannot have known this at the time.

In fact, Moscow's tendency to lash out at regional apparatchiks' poor performance around this time can be interpreted as the first in a widening circle of moves to normalise the situation across the country after the upheaval of the Secret Speech. Firstly, Party and Komsomol bosses and *aktiv* were whipped back into shape, then the millions of members of those two organisations, and finally, from December 1956, the Soviet population at large. The rationale was eminently logical: start by explaining and imposing the new orthodoxy on those closest to power, and then move outwards.

Below the leadership level there were a number of factors that hamstrung responses to dissent. Firstly, a large number of Party officials, like Usman Yusupov in Tashkent, were themselves too deeply mired in explaining away their own behaviour during the Stalin years to act decisively and promptly against individuals who spoke out at that moment in time.[23] Perhaps more

[21] RGANI, f. 5, op. 31, d. 52, l. 65, 70–3, in K. Aimermakher et al. eds., *Doklad N.S. Khrushcheva*.
[22] RGANI, f. 5, op. 32, d. 46, l. 21.
[23] P. Jones, 'From the Secret Speech', in P. Jones ed., *The Dilemmas of De-Stalinization*, p. 46.

importantly, the sense of uncertainty that had facilitated many of the dissenting remarks that followed the Secret Speech also impacted upon those who were expected to deal with critics. They too had received practically no direction from above, and the Soviet system hardly encouraged its functionaries to use their own initiative. Furthermore, it was evident that the wind at least appeared to be blowing against the Stalinists in the spring of 1956. To engage in anything resembling zealous persecution of Party members without explicit sanction would not have appeared a sensible move. Until clear instructions began to filter down from the top, the situation was ambiguous for all concerned. Like in Sakhalin and Stanislav *oblasti*, fudging the issue of how to respond to critics, or dodging it entirely, most likely seemed the best option for the time being.

Soon enough, instruction did start to come. One of the first attempts to rein in the growth of criticism that followed the Secret Speech involved making an example of the quartet who had spoken up at Moscow's Thermo-Technical Institute. On 5 April 1956, *Pravda* carried an editorial attacking the four young physicists, claiming that they had 'sung with the voices of Mensheviks and Socialist Revolutionaries'.[24] That same day, the Central Committee Presidium issued a resolution entitled 'On the Harmful Attacks at the Meeting of the Thermo-Technical Laboratory of the USSR Academy of Sciences Party Organisation'.[25] It stated that although the majority of meetings had passed off in the desired manner, 'the Central Committee has noted individual cases of harmful speeches by anti-Party elements who have tried to employ criticism and self-criticism for their own aims'. It accused the foursome of trying to use the struggle with the Cult of Personality to discredit the Communist Party and Soviet state, and 'lauding the false freedoms of capitalist countries', before labelling them 'slanderers'. It also announced that all four had been expelled from the CPSU, acknowledged that the majority of those present had refused to condemn their remarks, and specifically criticised the leadership of the Party cell for failing to give a decisive and timely response to the offending speeches.[26]

The authorities' attempt to engineer popular opinion in their newspaper attacks on the quartet at the Thermo-Technical Institute hardly proved a

---

[24] *Pravda*, 5 April 1956.
[25] RGANI, f. 3, op. 14, d. 13, l. 20, in K. Aimermakher et al. eds., *Doklad N.S. Khrushcheva*.
[26] RGANI, f. 3, op. 14, d. 13, ll. 76–9. Again, when the subsequent vote to condemn the dissenters' remarks failed, the entire Party cell was disbanded. Those deemed to be 'harmful elements' were then expelled from the Party and the remaining 'healthy' elements were re-registered with other local groups.

resounding success, and in some respects even made matters worse by giving their critics the 'oxygen of publicity'. However, the media coverage and the 5 April decree did begin to have the desired effect of clarifying for local officials what could and could not be said in the wake of the XX Congress. A report from Chkalov on 9 April 1956, for example, recounted that a CPSU member named Ternovskii had spoken out with improper remarks about the Secret Speech but local Party bosses had failed to provide the necessary rebuttal. Quite possibly stalling for time until they had a clearer idea of what was expected of them, no decision had been made on what to do with Ternovskii. After the events at the Thermo-Technical Institute were raised in the national media, Ternovskii was quickly expelled from the Party.[27] On 14 April Tashkent *obkom* discussed recent media coverage of events at the Thermo-Technical Institute and decided that they, too, ought to hand out additional reprimands to those in their own ranks who had come forth with controversial remarks.[28] CPSU members and lower-level officials hurriedly wrote in to *Pravda* and other newspapers, expressing glowing approval of the hardening stance toward critics and promising to redouble their efforts against those who tried to use the attack on Stalin as 'an excuse to slander the Party'.[29]

Another notable aspect of the response to the meeting at the Thermo-Technical Institute was the fact that the fate of the four speakers was apparently decided at the very top of the political hierarchy. When delivering the news of their dismissal, the head of the institute, Abram Alikhanov, informed the quartet that, 'I telephoned Khrushchev on your behalf but he said that he was not the only member of the Politburo. Other members demanded your arrest. He [Khrushchev] told me "they should be glad that they got off with dismissals".'[30] In fact, when we bear in mind that very few people were actually jailed as a result of comments made following the Secret Speech, the four could have considered themselves very unlucky if they had been imprisoned.

It was true that the wave of critical responses to the Secret Speech left Khrushchev in a weakened position within the leadership for a time. Nuriddin Mukhitdinov – who spent much of the era as a member of the

[27] K. Aimermakher et al. eds., *Doklad N.S. Khrushcheva*, p. 493.
[28] RGANI, f. 5, op. 31, d. 54, l. 17, in K. Aimermakher et al. eds., *Doklad N.S. Khrushcheva*.
[29] RGANI, f. 5, op. 30, d. 140, ll. 85–103.
[30] Yu. Orlov, *Dangerous Thoughts: Memoirs of a Russian Life*, New York: William Morrow and Company, 1991, p. 121. In his memoir of the era Fedor Burlatsky explicitly pointed to Mikhail Suslov as the Presidium member who agitated for a hard line to be taken on this issue. See F. Burlatsky, *Khrushchev and the First Russian Spring: The Era of Khrushchev through the Eyes of his Adviser*, London: Weidenfeld & Nicolson, 1991, p. 72.

Soviet political elite – recalled him coming under significant pressure to slow deStalinization.[31] Nonetheless, assertions such as Khrushchev's claim of powerlessness have sometimes been taken at face value in the historiography on the era, seemingly proving that the period was a time of near-perpetual struggle between 'Stalinists' and 'liberals' at the apex of political power. While differing opinions were certainly voiced on any number of issues, they did not fit consistently into this rather simplistic model. Khrushchev was a leader who adopted positions according to political circumstances, as were most of his colleagues in the Central Committee Presidium. He did not pursue a consistently 'liberal' line, especially when the prevailing conditions within the leadership and the country at large were not conducive. It is entirely likely that Khrushchev – who on a personal level rarely accepted any kind of criticism – fully supported the decision to remove the quartet from their posts but felt it wise to apportion 'blame' for the move to his colleagues. After all, he had only recently laid out his credentials as a moderate among Stalinists. For him openly to have taken on the role of oppressor at this stage would hardly have been an astute political move. While he may not have been the most sophisticated of political leaders, Khrushchev was usually much too canny for such a false step.

There were practical as well as political considerations at play in responding to events at the Thermo-Technical Institute. One of the most important reasons that the four young scientists escaped greater censure was because the government had no wish to antagonise the country's scientific community, something that politically motivated arrests in their midst would have run the danger of doing. This was, after all, a time when the Soviet leadership was reliant upon physicists in particular for the technical and military advancement that would help them fight the Cold War.[32] As the atmosphere in Khrushchev's new academic towns and advanced research institutes like Akademgorodok and Arzamas-16 would show, top Soviet scientists had come to expect, and received, much greater freedom of discussion and debate.[33]

---

[31] N. Mukhitdinov, '12 let s Khrushchevym: vospominaniya byvshego chlena Prezidium TsK', *Argumenty i fakty*, No. 44 (1989), 4.

[32] Even this was not a completely new development. Stalin, too, had shown far more restraint in dealing with his best scientists than was afforded to the general public, since their level of expertise meant they were effectively irreplaceable. Nonetheless, Stalin's tolerance was based entirely on results. On instructing Beria how to deal with the physicists working on the Soviet atom bomb he reportedly advised: 'leave them in peace, [because] we can always shoot them later'. J. Bergman, *Meeting the Demands of Reason: The Life and Thought of Andrei Sakharov*, Ithaca, NY: Cornell University Press, 2009, p. 54.

[33] On Arzamas-16 during the time that Andrei Sakharov worked there, see J. Bergman, *Meeting the Demands of Reason*. As Jay Bergman shows, scientists there were able to engage in fairly wide-ranging political debates and discussions of banned literature, such as Orwell's *1984*, with relative impunity.

In fact, it was one of the hallmarks of the Khrushchev era that those nearer to the top of the political ladder and in key professional fields such as science, culture and law, were allowed a greater degree of latitude for disagreement with the official line than were ordinary citizens, though this increased latitude could always be retracted if and when it posed any kind of challenge to the established order of things.

With initial attempts to curtail critical remarks not yet yielding ideal results, further measures were soon deemed necessary. On 16 June 1956 a secret letter was circulated to all Party organisations with the typically clunky title 'On the Results of Discussions on the Resolutions of the XX Party Congress and Progress toward Fulfilling the Decisions of the Congress'. With this letter the Central Committee intensified its efforts to close the 'chasm of uncertainty' that the XX Congress had opened up almost four months earlier. After beginning with the standard assurances that the work of the XX Congress had been met with great approval at home and abroad, the letter eventually raised the issue of 'individual anti-Party speeches' that had 'cast doubt upon the new line and slandered the Soviet system'. Although they were described as being unreflective of wider opinion in both the Party and society at large, the letter asserted that attention was being drawn to such speeches in order to show how they should be dealt with. It again spoke of individual Party organisations as being 'weak' and 'complacent' in their responses to criticism.[34] Referring specifically to the incident at the Thermo-Technical Institute, it stated: 'The Party cannot be reconciled with those people in its ranks who consider themselves communists but undermine party-mindedness with their views and slander the Soviet system.'[35] In other words, there was to be no scope for even loyal criticism, especially when voiced in public. The Party leadership did not require or welcome members' attempts to define the contours of the 'struggle to overcome the Cult of Personality'.

On 30 June the Central Committee issued a further decree: 'On the Overcoming of the Cult of Personality and its Consequences'. Stirred by the recent disorders in Poland, this time it linked critical remarks with foreign attempts to undermine the stability of the socialist regimes in Eastern Europe and the USSR. It announced the existence of a secret US government fund of $100,000,000, intended for sowing dissension within the socialist bloc, and pointed to the riots in Poznan earlier that same month as proof of foreign involvement in unrest within the socialist camp. It

---

[34] RGANI, f. 1, op. 2, d. 1, l. 125.   [35] RGANI, f. 1, op. 2, d. 1, l. 124.

acknowledged that some people had drawn the wrong conclusions from the Secret Speech but asserted the need for the Party to remain conscious of Western efforts at subversion.[36] While such a US fund may indeed have existed, it was quite clearly not the stimulus for political ferment in spring and summer 1956. By explicitly linking political criticism to foreign subversion, this decree in particular was intended as a warning to those who participated in 'exaggerated' criticism at Party meetings.[37] As Gennady Kuzovkin has argued, the overall purpose of these successive Party letters and decrees was to elucidate the new limits of acceptable criticism and discussion, to distinguish proper from improper in the new environment, and to re-establish that punishment would follow any transgression of these boundaries.[38]

Young people in particular were at the forefront of the regime's attention by the second half of 1956. Ever since the end of the Second World War, Soviet officialdom had fretted over the seemingly declining moral wellbeing of youth.[39] Along with released prisoners and members of the cultural intelligentsia, the young generation was seen as one of the most likely wellsprings of serious domestic strife.[40] Typically the authorities spoke of problems such as 'insufficient respect for the value of labour', pointing to the rebellious children of the burgeoning middle classes as the root of the problem. Again, this was not entirely unfounded but nor was it the most useful approach to the issues of the time. The leadership were not wholly blinded by ideological dogma, however, since they also took steps to reduce students' workloads, occasionally removed unpopular teachers, improved classroom resources and spent money upgrading school and university buildings that were a regular feature of complaint.[41] Of course, these kinds of changes were much easier and safer to implement than was political reform. Desires for greater freedom of expression and association were overwhelmingly ignored while material demands could be 'bought off'.

---

[36] RGANI, f. 3, op. 14, d. 39, ll. 30–4.

[37] See S. Schattenberg, '"Democracy" or "Despotism"? How the Secret Speech Was Translated into Everyday Life', in P. Jones ed., *The Dilemmas of De-Stalinization*, p. 66.

[38] G. Kuzovkin, 'Partiino-Komsomol'skie presledovaniya po politicheskim motivam v period rannei "ottepeli"', in L. Eremina and E. Zhemkova eds., *Korni travy: sbornik statei molodykh istorikov*, Moskva: Zven'ya, 1996, p. 90.

[39] See in particular J. Fürst, *Stalin's Last Generation: Soviet Post-War Youth and the Emergence of Mature Socialism*, Oxford University Press, 2010.

[40] See RGANI, f. 89, op. 6, d. 2, ll. 1–15.

[41] See Voprosy istorii, 'Studencheskoe brozhenie v SSSR (konets 1956g.)', *Voprosy istorii*, No. 0001 (1997), 3–23.

Statistics on the number of young people jailed by Soviet courts during 1956 cannot have helped ease the authorities' concerns. Although no longer so prevalent as it had been in the immediate post-war years, youth criminality was still surprisingly high. Furthermore, this was not just some kind of criminal underclass on the margins of Soviet society. When averaged out across all regions of the RSFSR, between 20% and 25% of youths jailed in 1956 were Komsomol members. In some places the proportion was far higher. Of the 942 people aged under twenty-five jailed in Dagestan ASSR in 1956, almost 40% were Komsomol members. In Moscow *oblast'*, over 1,700 Komsomol members were sentenced to prison in 1956, while Kuibyshev, Novosibirsk, Gorky, Stalingrad and Chkalov *oblasti* all saw over 500 Komsomol members imprisoned during the course of the year.[42] Even though the vast majority of these youths were jailed for non-political offences, the pattern was nonetheless disturbing, especially since any kind of non-conformity or criminality was still inextricably linked to political unreliability in the eyes of the authorities. Bearing in mind that this was a generation entirely raised under Soviet power, the implications of such youth criminality were serious for an ideology and social system that was expected to eradicate crime. Furthermore, law-breaking among Komsomol members was a problem twice over, since they were not only expected to act as an example to their non-Party peers but were also supposed to be the next generation of CPSU members and builders of communism.

Of course, youth unrest was not just a Soviet problem. A degree of generational dislocation existed in countless societies around this same time in both East and West, as the post-war world soon began to look noticeably different from that which had existed only a few years earlier. Fashions, material aspirations, musical tastes and much else changed quickly, often leaving older generations disorientated and alienated. In the Soviet Union, however, there was an additional ingredient to this sense of dislocation. From the very scale of the repressions during the Stalin years, it was entirely obvious to young people that a great many members of the preceding generation were implicated in those abuses, whether by direct personal involvement or through failing to resist both the human and ideological damage that Stalinism had wrought on the Soviet system. Valery Ronkin, at the time a dedicated Komsomol member, recalled that he became bitterly disappointed at his own father's refusal to speak out in the Stalin years, and told him so.[43] Vladimir

---

[42] RGANI, f. 5, op. 30, d. 231, l. 2.
[43] V. Ronkin, *Na smenu dekabryam prikhodit yanvari* ..., Moskva: Obshchestvo 'Memorial', 2003, p. 25.

Bukovsky, too, recounted a deep and general sense of disillusionment at the evident failings of his elders.[44] While such a viewpoint perhaps under-estimated the power of a whole host of impulses that had acted upon Soviet society to facilitate mass terror in the late 1930s, it would be foolhardy to dismiss such a sentiment as youthful naïvety: after all, the events the young people railed against were some of the very worst atrocities of the twentieth century. What this new 'fathers and sons' problem showed most clearly, however, was a refusal by the post-war generation to countenance any return to terror.

Naturally, Khrushchev and the Party leadership did not entertain any notion of generational moral culpability for the abuses of the Stalin years, just as they refused to acknowledge the existence of a wider sense of rupture between generations. They were, however, deeply concerned that young people were becoming disconnected from the values and aims of the revolution. This was linked to the authorities' fear that without the chal-lenges faced by their parents' and grandparents' generations, young people were 'growing soft' and would be an especially susceptible audience for harmful bourgeois propaganda. Again, one can understand the reasoning at work here, and these kinds of assumptions were not restricted to the Soviet Union, but one can also see that it proved flawed in reality. Young people were often among the most zealous and idealistic communists there were at this stage in time. The growing popularity of Western clothes and music – especially jazz – in the USSR during the 1950s has been described by many foreign visitors and Soviet citizens alike, but it very rarely led to outright political non-conformity.[45] Even so, once the government took a hostile stance on any given issue (such as in its occasional condemnations of 'decadent' jazz in the 1950s), defiance of the official line did start to politicise what were otherwise fundamentally apolitical activities.

In a general sense, the authorities were not unjustifiably concerned. Social and political ferment among Soviet youth had the potential to pose a real problem. Almost 2,000,000 students were enrolled in some form of Higher-Education Institute across the USSR at this point. With the student body growing ever larger and apparently more conscious of its traditional status as a locus of intellectual heterodoxy, it was also clear that this was a section of society which would have to be brought to heel if things were

---

[44] See V. Bukovsky, *To Build a Castle: My Life as a Dissenter*, London: Andre Deutsch, 1978.

[45] One of the best works on this broad theme is Sergei Zhuk's *Rock and Roll in the Rocket City: The West, Identity, and Ideology in Soviet Dnepropetrovsk, 1960–1985*, Washington, DC: Woodrow Wilson Center Press, 2010.

to return fully to normal.[46] On 4 November the question of 'cleansing higher-education institutes of unhealthy elements' was discussed by the Central Committee Presidium and saw members of the political elite showing an increasingly belligerent attitude toward criticism and protests taking place among the student body and university staff.[47] Filipp Bobkov, at the time a young KGB officer and later head of the KGB's Fifth Directorate, recalled how the security organs began to come under heavy criticism from Central Committee members for failing to 'take action' against student protests in autumn 1956.[48] Directors of higher-education institutes were empowered to expel students and withhold their stipends if they were involved in any kind of dissenting behaviour. Pressure was increased on teachers to monitor their pupils. Those deemed 'unworthy of the title "student"' were to be expelled, assigned productive labour tasks instead of academic studies and refused the right to re-enrol at another higher-education institute for two to three years.[49]

According to the then Komsomol secretary Aleksandr Shelepin – who was to become KGB chairman only a couple of years later – emphasis was being placed on educating those who were 'misguided' (as opposed to oppositional) in their criticism, rather than simply taking punitive measures against them. Noting that a mood of pessimism and 'apoliticism' had emerged among Soviet youth since the XX Congress, he wrote that political-ideological work with young people was being strengthened across all union republics. Agitators, teachers, workers and veterans of the revolution were being dispatched to workplaces, student dormitories, canteens and classrooms to explain the Party line and to provide a response to bourgeois propaganda.[50] This was another concerted attempt to reassert the approved ideological discourse and to smother the emergence of independent public opinion in the myriad locations, settings and constituencies where it threatened to arise.

Even with this emphasis on 'education' rather than punishment, the number of Komsomol expulsions rose significantly during 1956, after several years of decline. Data from twelve Ukrainian *oblasti* (see Table 2.1) confirm the trend,

---

[46] On the size, composition and attitudes of the Khrushchev-era student body see B. Tromly, 'Re-Imagining the Soviet Intelligentsia: Student Politics and University Life, 1948–1964', Ph.D. Dissertation, Harvard University, 2007.

[47] RGANI, f. 3, op. 12, d. 1006, ll. 31–3.

[48] F. Bobkov, *KGB i vlast': 45 let v organakh gosudarstvennoi bezopasnosti*, Moskva: Veteran MP, 1995, p. 144.

[49] See G. Kuzovkin, 'Partiino-Komsomol'skie presledovaniya', in L. Eremina and E. Zhemkova eds., *Korni travy*.

[50] RGANI, f. 5, op. 30, d. 233, ll. 1–73.

Table 2.1 *Annual expulsions from the Ukrainian Komsomol, 1955–7*

Oblast'	1955	1956	1957
Vinitskaya	494	779	271
Volynskaya	214	330	214
Luganskaya	1,253	2,532	641
Dnepropetrovskaya	1,442	1,298	550
Drogobychskaya	235	242	152
Zhitomirskaya	215	430	362
Zakarpatskaya	155	263	65
Zaporozhskaya	458	539	274
Kievskaya	542	903	–
Kirovogradskaya	244	307	222
Krymskaya	825	978	–
L'vovskaya	368	331	196
Total	6,445	8,932	2,947*

*Data from Kievskaya and Krymskaya *oblasti* missing.
Source: Department of Komsomol Organs, RGASPI, f. 1, op. 33, d. 1722, ll. 1–150.

Table 2.2 *Annual expulsions from the Kazakh and Uzbek
Komsomol organisations, 1955–7*

Union republic	1955	1956	1957
Kazakhstan	2,593	3,001	2,169
Uzbekistan	1,749	1,875	627
Total	4,342	4,876	2,796

Source: Department of Komsomol Organs, RGASPI, f. 1, op. 33, d. 1690,
l. 11 and d. 1722, l. 81.

and a broadly similar pattern is replicated in statistical information on annual expulsions from the Kazakh and Uzbek Komsomol organisations (Table 2.2).

One of the most interesting aspects of these statistics is the quite steep decline in expulsions that can be witnessed from 1956 to 1957. Since the year 1957 was marked by a major crackdown on dissent which saw both the number of CPSU expulsions and the total number of jail sentences for anti-Soviet activity climb dramatically, the situation within the Komsomol presented a notable anomaly. In the first instance we can perhaps look to the Komsomol as a 'testing ground' where policies aimed at inducing greater ideological discipline – effectively meaning the stifling of criticism – were trialled, found effective, and then applied more widely: thus its own spell of increased expulsions both started and finished before that of the Communist Party. We can probably also look to the upcoming 1957 Moscow World Youth Festival, in which Komsomol members were to be trusted to play the most prominent role in interacting with tens of thousands of foreign visitors, as another reason why the regime needed to bring communist youth back into line with the greatest of haste during 1956.[51]

Within the Communist Party itself, the annual rate of expulsions had been in marked decline since Stalin's death, from 143,293 expulsions in 1953 to 82,362 in 1954, and then 38,540 in 1955, all of which took place at a time when total Party membership was actually growing.[52] This decline was, in itself, part of a wider trend within the CPSU. As Edward Cohn demonstrates, ever since the end of the Second World War the Communist Party had been showing decreasing ideological vigilance over its members' thoughts and feelings, focusing instead on shaping their outward behaviours.[53] This trend would continue for many years to come, but the wave of critical reactions to the events of 1956 clearly demanded a robust response. After dropping by more than 40% year on year since 1953, the previously sharp decline in the number of Party expulsions then slowed to less than 10% in 1956, as 35,058 members were expelled that year.[54] Data on appeals against dismissals from the CPSU show that over 150 members attempted to overturn expulsions for 'participation in anti-Party groups'; over 300 for 'anti-Party discussions; over 300 for 'lack of political conviction'; and over 450 for 'violation of Party discipline'.[55]

The first few months after the Secret Speech saw the authorities focus primarily on re-imposing conformity upon dissonant voices among card-carrying communists, whether in the CPSU or Komsomol. Nonetheless, jail sentences were only rarely handed out to those who had spoken up in meetings and debates. This was very much a time when the regime's emphasis lay upon correcting, or 're-educating', those who incurred disfavour. As such, there was no scramble to repress the ideologically wayward. Even so, the threat of expulsion from the Communist Party and the Komsomol were very powerful stimuli that should not be underestimated. The consequences of arousing such official disfavour could easily last a

---

[51] On the 1957 World Youth Festival, see P. Koivunen, 'The 1957 Moscow Youth Festival: Propagating a New Peaceful Image of the Soviet Union', in M. Ilič and J. Smith eds., *Soviet State and Society under Nikita Khrushchev*, London: Routledge, 2009, pp. 46–65.

[52] See E. Cohn, 'Disciplining the Party: The Expulsion and Censure of Communists in the Post-War Soviet Union, 1945–1961', Ph.D. Dissertation, University of Chicago, 2007.

[53] See E. Cohn, 'Disciplining the Party'. [54] E. Cohn, 'Disciplining the Party', p. 58.

[55] See E. Kulavig, *Dissent in the Years of Khrushchev*, pp. 88–9.

lifetime. It meant exclusion from the country's social elite (with its attendant prestige and perks) and could forever ruin one's chances of obtaining a
university place, a good job or one of the era's much sought-after private
apartments. It could also be a hugely traumatic experience for those with a
deep commitment to the communist project – as was often the case among
those who spoke up at this point in time.

Where, then, lay the new boundaries of permitted behaviour? Both
Sergei Mironenko and Boris Firsov have argued that scope for the expression of alternative views actually changed 'not one iota' with the Secret
Speech. They state, instead, that the most significant impact of the XX
Congress was that those who did not transgress the boundaries of acceptable
comment and behaviour were no longer in danger of repression.[56] In other
words, the regime no longer repressed those who had done nothing at all –
and this new clarity in the 'rules of the game' at least felt like liberalisation
for those who experienced it – but it had not become any more tolerant of
active political nonconformity.

In essence, this argument is a sound one. For Khrushchev in particular,
political attacks on Stalin and thorough-going liberalisation did not necessarily go hand in hand, as many people assumed at the time and have often
continued to assume since. There are, however, one or two points worth
adding. Firstly, data on convictions for counter-revolutionary activity show
that political repression had already been in steep decline for three years
prior to the XX Congress. Thus, the Secret Speech itself did not really mark
a radical change of direction on this issue: indeed, the number of convictions for anti-Soviet activity would very soon begin to rise again. It is also
important to note that even though the Party leadership had not become
any more inclined to tolerate criticism 'from below', it had recalibrated what
was deemed an appropriate response to such criticism in the years following
Stalin's death. Essentially, the tyrannical responses to political offences
(both real and fabricated) of the Stalin years were judged unproductive, or
even counter-productive. While the absence of major philosophical change
on the matter of permitted plurality was undoubtedly significant, so was the
fact that dissenters could now protest and fully expect to survive, even if
persecuted, expelled from the Party or jailed.

---

[56] V. Kozlov and S. Mironenko eds., *Kramola: inakomyslie v SSSR pri Khrushcheve i Brezhneve 1953–1982*,
Moskva: 'Materik', 2005, p. 29. This statement is echoed by Boris Firsov in *Raznomyslie v SSSR 1940–
1960 gody: istoriya, teoriya i praktika*, Sankt Peterburg: Izdatel'stvo Evropeiskogo universiteta v Sankt
Peterburge, 2008, p. 262.

In fact, there was some expanded room for criticism, though it was not granted to society as a whole. Those within the mechanisms of power enjoyed considerably greater plurality of discussion and debate than they had previously. Aleksandr Bovin, for example, recalled that there were many vocal anti-Stalinists within the Central Committee apparatus during the Khrushchev period and that in the advisory group in which he worked (for Yuri Andropov), heated arguments would arise among group members on almost every single subject.[57] Even if their views were not acted upon, professionals in fields such as science, law, politics and culture gained much greater leeway for disagreement with the official line and with each other, at least behind the scenes.

Crucially, these were freedoms that the leadership could, and did, expand or contract as and when it suited. This was something that would have been far harder to control if those freedoms were granted to the whole of society. Instead they went to those over whom the Party apparatus held the most sway, through granting or removing all manner of perks and privileges, such as well-located apartments, chauffeur-driven cars and honorific titles. Many of these were members of the intelligentsia. Of course, there were still fairly narrow limits that had to be observed by those who were granted this increased freedom, but where one can speak of tolerated heterodoxy in the Khrushchev years, it was generally to be found close to the top of the regime, not among the ordinary citizenry. The problem with the Secret Speech was that it had seemed to offer greater plurality for all – making that plurality far harder to control.

Broadly speaking, there were two small niches of acceptable complaint that were open to the general public, and these had barely changed since the Stalin years. The first area of permissible criticism was censure of abuses of power by officials at the lower levels of the political spectrum.[58] This could include exposure of all kinds of wrongdoing by insensitive bureaucrats, venal factory bosses or lazy Communist Party and Komsomol officials: this was a freedom to criticise that had long helped the leadership both to keep officials 'on their toes' and to keep the masses on side. The second was mild criticism of proposed policies and documents that had been put out for public consultation. Perhaps the best example of this was the Third Party Programme in 1961, on which millions of citizens offered their thoughts in

[57] A. Bovin, 'Semi-Glasnost', in S. Cohen and K. vanden Heuvel eds., *Voices of Glasnost: Interviews with Gorbachev's Reformers*, New York: W.W. Norton, 1989, p. 215.

[58] See C. Kenney, 'The Twentieth CPSU Congress and the "New" Soviet Union', *The Western Political Quarterly*, Vol. 9, No. 3 (September 1956), 570–606.

newspapers and at public meetings.[59] Once in force, there was to be no further debate on their merits or otherwise, but whilst open for public comment proposals on issues such as the re-introduction of Comrades' Courts, anti-parasite legislation and Gulag reform could all produce a lively exchange of opinions in the media.[60] The most important point was that any criticism was not to be aimed at the top leadership nor seen to be directed at undermining the foundations of the Soviet system – a slippery and unpredictable concept at best – but must be 'business-like in character', according to *Voprosy partiinoi raboty* (*Questions of Party Work*), a 1957 collection of articles and editorials on ideological developments.[61]

The wider political and social order inside the USSR, along with the Soviet economic system, were the most explicitly forbidden themes of criticism.[62] As Vladimir Shlapentokh pointed out, what these subjects immediately implied to the authorities was the presence of deep-seated hostility toward the fundamental principles of Soviet rule: a not entirely unfounded, though undoubtedly extreme, viewpoint. In addition to these subjects, one can also add the broad theme of 'the West' as a subject that could be broached only in a negative manner if one hoped to avoid attracting trouble. Because the authorities saw citizens' attitudes toward the West as a key indicator of their political loyalty, it naturally followed that any kind of dissenting behaviour centred upon the West, such as drawing negative comparisons between the standard of living in the Soviet Union and the US, or attempts to communicate with foreign organisations, raised the spectre of disloyalty and even espionage, thus making any transgression of behavioural norms all the more dangerous.[63] This perceived connection between political criticism and foreign subversion was to make dissenting activity particularly risky, especially during times of heightened international tension. That apparent link was to remain central to policy against dissent right up until the

[59] On the scope and nature of public consultations on the Third Party Programme, see A. Titov, 'The 1961 Party Programme and the Fate of Khrushchev's Reforms', in M. Ilič and J. Smith eds., *Soviet State and Society under Nikita Khrushchev*, London: Routledge, 2009, pp. 8–25; and P. Vail' and A. Genis, *60-e: mir sovetskogo cheloveka*, Ann Arbor, MI: Ardis Publishers, 1989.

[60] See, for example, S. Fitzpatrick, 'Social Parasites: How Tramps, Idle Youth and Busy Entrepreneurs Impeded the Soviet March to Communism', *Cahiers du Monde russe*, Vol. 47, No. 1–2 (janvier–juin 2006), 377–408.

[61] *Voprosy partiinoi raboty*, Moskva: Gosudarstvennoe izdatel'stvo politicheskoi literatury, 1957. See L. Schapiro, *The Communist Party*.

[62] V. Shlapentokh, *Soviet Intellectuals and Political Power: The Post-Stalin Era*, Princeton University Press, 1990, p. 78.

[63] See V. Shlapentokh, *Public and Private Life of the Soviet People: Changing Values in Post-Stalin Russia*, Oxford University Press, 1989, p. 139.

commencement of *glasnost'* in the late 1980s, though no solid evidence connecting the two has thus far come to light.

In regard to the permissibility of criticism, the attitudes that underpinned the Soviet system had not changed anything like as much as the attack on Stalin at the XX Congress seemed to imply. In fact, the Khrushchev regime was often quite successful in putting across an exaggerated image of domestic liberality. There were still some well-publicised attacks on certain nonconformists, most notably Boris Pasternak in 1958, but the leadership became increasingly mindful of the regime's image both at home and on the international stage after Stalin's death and strived to project a picture of relative inclusivity and restraint, so long as this did not clash with other priorities.[64] A handful of Soviet Muslims were allowed to go on the Hajj, foreign experts were invited to see the newly remodelled and 'progressive' Gulag, and more Western literature was published for Soviet audiences. Most notably, Khrushchev declared that there were no longer any political prisoners in the USSR – something that he knew was palpably untrue. Even more strikingly, in January 1964 the Soviet representative to the UN on human-rights issues, Boris Ivanov, voted in favour of two separate motions that proclaimed 'every citizen's right to freedom of expression and opinion; the right to freedom of peaceful assembly and association' and 'every citizen's right to leave any country, including his own, and to return to that country'.[65]

Of course, in practice these commitments were complete fallacies that were not to materialise until decades after Khrushchev's ouster, and few can have had much optimism in the Soviet regime's sincerity at the time. This was entirely in keeping with a long history of disinformation and propaganda on the theme of the regime's attitude toward its citizens' rights and freedoms. Stalin had refused to ratify the 1948 Universal Declaration of Human Rights ostensibly on the grounds that it 'did not go far enough'. Under Brezhnev the Soviet Union signed the 1975 Helsinki Accords with little or no intention of fulfilling its human-rights clauses.[66] Gorbachev, too, initially insisted that there were no longer any political prisoners in the USSR, until Anatoly Marchenko's death at Chistopol prison in December 1986 prompted an international outcry.

---

[64] As a number of scholars have pointed out, this striving to portray a slightly softer image of the Soviet system was primarily aimed not at the West but at the Third World, where the Soviet leadership was seeking out new allies and clients.

[65] Budapest, HU OSA 300-80-1, Box 688.

[66] On this theme, see S. Snyder, *Human Rights Activism and the End of the Cold War: A Transnational History of the Helsinki Network*, Cambridge University Press, 2011.

This gap between the regime's public and private faces has long been acknowledged as a feature of the Soviet system but has perhaps been a little underplayed in regard to the period in question. Khrushchev's own claims to have been buffeted by Stalinists within the leadership, or otherwise misled into taking harsher actions than he should have done, do not always stand up to scrutiny.[67] Set-piece events like speeches denouncing Stalin and the publication of liberal literary works such as Vladimir Pomerantsev's *On Sincerity in Literature* were unquestionably significant in the effect they had on elements of the public but they did not necessarily reflect a major new political direction. The fact that the Khrushchev era even gained the appellation 'the Thaw' from one such liberal literary work demonstrates how signs of liberality emanating from the apex of power have long shaped perceptions of the era, arguably to a considerably greater extent than can be said of either the Stalin or Brezhnev years.[68]

As one of the most prominent organisations in the wider historiography on the Soviet system, the KGB has been conspicuous by its absence so far in the present chapter. In regard to perhaps no other point in Soviet history prior to the Gorbachev era could one progress so far in a discussion of dissent without placing the security organs at the very centre of events. In the immediate aftermath of the Secret Speech, however, they largely remained on the side-lines. That the newly constituted Committee for State Security (KGB) had been given institutional responsibility for leading the struggle against dissent could be seen in the 15 February 1954 Central Committee resolution 'On the Formation of the Committee for State Security under the Council of Ministers', which defined one of the new organisation's principal roles as 'struggle against the hostile activity of any kind of anti-Soviet elements inside the USSR'.[69] The language being used to describe many of the critical remarks following the XX Congress clearly put at least some people squarely in the category of 'anti-Soviet elements'.[70]

---

[67] Khrushchev subsequently apportioned much of the blame for the furore that accompanied the overseas publication of Boris Pasternak's *Dr Zhivago*, for example, to Mikhail Suslov, since he had apparently been the reason why the work was rejected for publication inside the Soviet Union. S. Khrushchev ed., *Memoirs of Nikita Khrushchev*, Vol. 2: *Reformer: 1945–1964*, University Park, PA: Pennsylvania State University Press, 2006, p. 550.

[68] In this respect it is worth raising the point that the Khrushchev era has yet to attract anything like the volume of historical enquiry that has centred upon the Stalin years. Neither was it the subject of quite the same level of contemporary research into Soviet society carried out during the Brezhnev era by Western academics and journalists.

[69] RGANI, f. 3, op. 8, d. 84, l. 18.

[70] The resolution on events at the Thermo-Technical Institute, for example, was entitled 'On the Enemy Attacks . . .' Another began with the heading 'On the anti-Party, slanderous speeches of . . .'

Why, then, were the KGB not leading from the front? In the first instance, they too had been somewhat hobbled by the Secret Speech, since the security organs (albeit rebranded and reorganised since Stalin's death) were inextricably linked to the repressions and abuses of power that Khrushchev had exposed. The resulting decline in the organs' prestige was to be a lingering source of institutional resentment from the KGB, who rarely looked back on the Khrushchev era in a positive light in later years.[71] More importantly, one of the key reasons for remodelling the Stalin-era security apparatus had been to bring it more firmly under the control of the Communist Party, and in this they appear to have been successful. The KGB chairman Ivan Serov was a long-standing associate of Khrushchev – the pair had worked together in Ukraine during the Second World War – but his attitude toward critics was far from liberal. Serov was a *Chekist* through and through: he had been involved in the security organs since the days of the Great Terror and was no supporter of deStalinization.[72] Until the Party gave the order, however, the KGB would now have to watch and wait.

Even when the KGB did eventually swing into action, its remit was substantially different to that of the 1930s NKVD. There were no more mass operations or 'unmasking' of counter-revolutionaries and 'rooting out hidden enemies'. Critical opinions were no longer an immediate concern unless they were manifested in some concrete form. Those who kept their frustrations to themselves were generally safe from harm. In fact, quite a few of those who did speak out at the time were given the opportunity to retract their remarks in order to avoid punishment. Although the Khrushchev era saw the authorities becoming increasingly intrusive into numerous aspects of its citizens' everyday lives, they no longer concerned themselves quite so much with private thoughts if they did not result in protest activity. Even within the Communist Party itself – the vanguard of the drive to construct communism – the level of 'ideological vigilance' was in decline.[73] This was hardly the return to Leninism that Khrushchev had proffered, and was in fact a step on the path toward Brezhnevite stagnation, but it did mark a significant improvement on the Stalin years in humanitarian terms.

That change of emphasis was, according to its own rationale, largely successful. Soon enough there were once again few traces of open criticism

---

[71] See J. Elkner, 'The Changing Face of Repression under Khrushchev', in M. Ilič and J. Smith eds., *Soviet State and Society under Nikita Khrushchev*, pp. 142–61.

[72] See N. Petrov, *Ivan Serov: pervyi predsedatel' KGB*, Moskva: Materik, 2005.

[73] See in particular E. Cohn, 'Disciplining the Party'.

within the ranks of the CPSU and Komsomol. Dissent within the Party was not heard again on any comparable scale for many years to come. The student body and Komsomol, too, would become far less notable sources of criticism and protest once measures were taken to neutralise 'unhealthy elements' in their midst. Of course, this lack of criticism did not mean that ordinary Party and Komsomol members became monolithic in their views, but instead meant that any sources of frustration and disappointment would remain suppressed below the surface.

Before all that happened, however, the problem of dissenting behaviour was to intensify markedly around the end of 1956 and into 1957. The application of punitive measures against dissenters was about to be expanded, as the regime moved from a default position of jailing only the most strident and subversive critics, to launching a wave of political arrests and sentences that sought to re-impose discipline throughout society. With its mass power-bases of the Party and Komsomol already in the process of returning to outward compliance by the end of 1956, the authorities were in a position to turn their attention to the rest of the Soviet population.

CHAPTER 3

After the Hungarian rising

The 'chasm of uncertainty'[1] that had been opened up by the Speech soon began to close as the idealism of spring and summer 1956 ebbed in the face of stalled reform and government retrenchment. It was on the streets of Hungary that autumn, however, where frustrations spilled over most dramatically and culminated in an uprising which was to resonate throughout the Soviet bloc. With the Hungarian authorities in disarray and protestors there demanding freedom of speech, genuine democracy and amnesty for political prisoners, this was a clear test of the Khrushchev regime's liberalising credentials. When, after some considerable vacillation on Khrushchev's part, Soviet troops and tanks brought the Hungarian rising to a bloody end in early November, the reaction of many Soviet citizens stood in sharp contrast to the sense of renewed idealism with which the XX Party Congress had been greeted only a few months earlier.

In Western Europe, many thousands of communists declared their revulsion at the invasion of Hungary and promptly severed their allegiance to Soviet communism. Inside the USSR, many of the same feelings existed, though of course people there could not simply walk away. The sense of hope and enthusiasm that had followed the Secret Speech among idealistic young people and members of the intelligentsia contrasted sharply with the immediate and visceral anger with which many of those same people reacted to events in Hungary. As Vladimir Bukovsky later recalled: 'after all the exposures, denunciations and posthumous rehabilitations, after all the reassurances about the impossibility of repeating the past, we were now presented with corpses, tanks, brute force and lies all over again. Just one more convincing proof that nothing had changed at all.'[2] Lev Krasnopevtsev

---

[1] M. Scammell, *Solzhenitsyn: A Biography*, New York: W.W. Norton and Company, 1984, p. 404.

[2] V. Bukovsky, *To Build a Castle: My Life as a Dissenter*, London: Andre Deutsch, 1978 p. 89. It is important to note that Vladimir Bukovsky was one of the Soviet regime's most outspoken critics and was therefore hardly an impartial commentator, yet his sentiments do seem to have been widely shared among young people in particular.

was even more damning: 'the suppression of the Hungarian rising made it absolutely clear that any restoration of Leninist party norms meant tanks and machine guns, gallows and shootings'.[3] Such strong feelings would be much in evidence around the end of 1956.

Actually, opposition to the military action in Hungary was far from universal across Soviet society, not least because the Second World War – in which Hungary and the USSR had fought one another bitterly – was still so fresh in the memory. Many were also repulsed by the Hungarian rebels' violence and the brutal public lynching of communists. Certainly a sizeable section of the overall Soviet population, and perhaps even the majority, supported the invasion. Doubtless, plenty of people believed state propaganda that depicted the rising there as a bourgeois counter-revolution. Even some of those who opposed the intervention did not do so unambiguously, fearing that the entire socialist bloc would be weakened were the uprising to see Hungary break away. Nonetheless, events in Hungary proved to be the catalyst for a significant wave of popular protest and criticism from late 1956 into 1957. As with the 1968 Prague Spring, those who desired liberalisation inside the USSR tended to view the quicker and deeper reforms being called for across much of Eastern Europe with a sense of excitement and hope for the Soviet system. They believed that if a greater degree of flexibility and plurality were to prove successful elsewhere, then their own regime might eventually accept a similar scenario. As such, the symbolic impact of the invasion of Hungary was especially significant, crushing hopes that had only just been raised by the Secret Speech earlier that same year.

The eighteen months following the Hungarian rising witnessed a notable post-Stalin high-water mark in convictions for anti-Soviet agitation and propaganda. The increased number of arrests that followed partly reflected the priorities of an on-going government crackdown against dissent, but a wealth of anecdotal and archival evidence testifies that there was a genuine swelling of protest activity around the time. KGB reports to the Central Committee and case files from the Procurator's office, for example, indicate a substantial growth in what the authorities referred to as 'anti-Soviet phenomena', such as people sending threatening letters to Party officials, publicly declaring hatred for members of the CPSU leadership, and forming underground political groups.[4]

---

[3] Voprosy istorii, 'Vlast' i intelligentsiya: "delo" molodykh istorikov (1957–58.)', *Voprosy istorii*, No. 004 (1994), 106–35, 111.

[4] See, for example, GARF, f. 8131, op. 32, d. 5080, ll. 1–87.

Cornelia Gerstenmaier gave a tantalising insight into the volume of critical remarks on this theme when she wrote that in Leningrad alone, the Komsomol recommended over 4,000 students be expelled from high school on the basis of comments relating to the Soviet invasion of Hungary.[5] In reality, however, one could probably expect to find that many of those school pupils who commented on events in Hungary did not hold particularly strong opinions about the uprising and subsequent invasion there, but had transgressed the borders of acceptable comment in a relatively innocent fashion, thus telling us as much about the Komsomol's hyper-sensitivity to matters concerning Hungary as anything else. Certainly, the Komsomol, like the Communist Party and the KGB, showed little inclination to provide anything like a balanced judgement of such remarks at this time of apparent crisis.

Interest in events in Hungary was especially prevalent among the Soviet student body. Early stirrings of political non-conformity had been growing in Soviet universities even before the Secret Speech, most famously in the form of *The Literary Bulletin*, an unauthorised wall-newspaper that first appeared towards the end of 1955 in the Mechanical-Mathematical Faculty of Moscow State University. Always leading a precarious existence, with copies being torn down by the university authorities only to be replaced shortly afterward by students, the newspaper was often deliberately provocative, if not outright oppositional in tone. One notable issue even called for Trotsky to be reconsidered and placed alongside Lenin in the country's revolutionary pantheon. Another threatened a student uprising if the paper's editors were expelled from the university. When it came out in opposition to the Soviet invasion of Hungary in late 1956, decisive measures were taken to put a stop to *The Literary Bulletin* and its editors were tracked down and repressed.[6]

Elsewhere, tensions spilled over into more direct action. Universities including Moscow State University, Leningrad State University, Gorky University, Sverdlovsk University, Kuibyshev University and numerous others all witnessed public demonstrations of varying size in opposition to

[5] C. Gerstenmaier, *The Voices of the Silent*, New York: Hart Publishing Company, 1972, p. 92. Unfortunately, Cornelia Gerstenmaier did not give a source for this data. Among those school students who found themselves in trouble over remarks made about the Hungarian rising – in Moscow, rather than Leningrad – were Eduard Kuznetsov and Viktor Khaustov, both of whom went on to be involved in the Brezhnev-era dissident movement.

[6] See Voprosy istorii, 'Studencheskoe brozhenie v SSSR (konets 1956)', *Voprosy istorii*, No. 0001 (1997), 3–23.

the invasion.[7] In Yaroslavl, riot police had to be drafted in to disperse protesters before order was fully restored. Polish and Hungarian students in Moscow, Kiev and Leningrad banded together and formed groups to agitate amongst Soviet students in an attempt to stir further protest.[8] In the capital, a group of over 100 students gathered to hear a Pole named Stefan Troyanovskii who denounced the invasion of Hungary, criticised Soviet media coverage of events there and attacked the inequalities of Soviet socialism.[9] With newspapers from People's Democracies including Czechoslovakia, Yugoslavia and Poland having recently gone on sale in a number of major Soviet cities, it also became possible for those with the necessary foreign language skills to find less heavily censored information on the situation in Hungary, meaning that the Soviet depiction of events there as a 'counter-revolutionary uprising' began to look less and less credible. The regime's virtual monopoly on information about the outside world – always a vital aspect of its social control strategy – was starting to weaken. While the Secret Speech showed that the Soviet regime had consistently lied in the past, the Hungarian rising proved for many that it was still lying in the present.

In Kazakhstan, the KGB reported that after listening to the BBC on short-wave radios students were refusing to accept the Soviet version of events in Hungary and accusing the regime of hiding the truth.[10] A meeting at the USSR MVD club aroused the interest of the security organs when students of the Moscow State Historical Archive Institute raised toasts to the Polish uprising of June 1956, to the Hungarian revolution and to the 'impending fourth Russian revolution'.[11] The Minister of Internal Affairs wrote to the Central Committee on 3 November with the information that the militia had discovered posters pasted up in the centre of Leningrad calling on students of the city's Geophysics Research Institute to launch an

---

[7] M. Kramer, 'The Soviet Union and the 1956 Crises in Hungary and Poland: Reassessments and New Findings', *Journal of Contemporary History*, Vol. 33, No. 2 (April 1998), 196. In addition to the institutes listed above, Kramer also cites protests at the Ural Pedagogical Institute, Moscow Aviation-Technical Institute, Potemkin State Pedagogical Institute, Herzen Pedagogical Institute, the Bashkirian Pedagogical Institute and Smolensk Pedagogical Institute. It is unclear why so many of the universities that witnessed demonstrations were pedagogical institutes.

[8] M. Kramer, 'The Soviet Union and the 1956 Crises', p. 196.

[9] See *Voprosy istorii*, 'Studencheskoe brozhenie', 16. As Benjamin Tromly has shown, many of those students from the People's Democracies who went to study in the Soviet Union at this stage were idealistic believers in socialism but quickly found themselves disenchanted by the failings and injustices they witnessed at the very centre of the world socialist camp.

[10] Zh. Kydyralina, 'Politicheskie nastroeniya v Kazakhstane v 1945–1985gg', *Voprosy istorii*, No. 8 (August 2008), 66.

[11] Iu. Aksiutin, 'Popular Responses to Khrushchev', in W. Taubman, S. Khrushchev and A. Gleason eds., *Nikita Khrushchev*, London: Yale University Press, 2000, p. 193.

uprising.[12] Thousands of miles to the east, in the Tuva Republic, Viktor Vasil'evich Dvortsov was apprehended after circulating a leaflet which read 'Comrade students! Start an uprising like the one in Hungary. Bring more guys to our side. We will be helped by students of other countries, like the USA, England and France. Meet tomorrow at 12 o'clock on the square. Do not think that this is an adventure. No! It is the honest truth.'[13] Of course, Dvortsov's promise of assistance from foreign students was entirely unrealistic on a literal level (there were anyway none in the Tuva Republic at the time) but it did show a certain consciousness of belonging to a body that stretched well beyond the borders of the Soviet Union – emphasising that those whom he appealed to were not just Soviet citizens, but were also students with brethren in universities across the world.[14]

One of the most useful analyses of the situation has been provided by Benjamin Tromly, who argues that Soviet students in the post-war years were attempting to fashion a role for themselves as critical intellectuals in the mould of their pre-revolutionary forebears, believing that such a role was in the wider interests of the system as a whole.[15] As responses to the Secret Speech had already shown, this desire to play a constructive role through loyal criticism clearly existed, though it was by no means restricted to the student body.[16] Not only were these hopes to be denied, but those who harboured them publicly often found themselves vilified as a result. Many of those who moved toward more recognisably oppositionist positions usually did so only when it had become clear that the path of reform which had seemingly been marked out at the XX Congress would not be followed. Tromly's summation of the wider impact of events is particularly compelling: '... by initiating both protest and Soviet retrenchment against it, revolution in Eastern Europe had complicated the loyal and reformist direction of student politics that deStalinization had put in motion'.[17] Not only did Hungary bring a painful end to student hopes of liberalisation, but the point was then to be driven home by the authorities' hard-line responses to those protests which resulted from that very disappointment.

---

[12] GARF, f. 9401, op. 2, d. 482, l. 25.

[13] GARF, f. 8131, op. 32, d. 77481, ll. 1–3. Dvortsov was sentenced to six years' corrective labour in March 1957, though his sentence was subsequently reduced on appeal to three years, on the basis that he had not shown 'genuine counter-revolutionary intent'.

[14] On this theme, see B. Tromly, 'Re-Imagining the Soviet Intelligentsia: Student Politics and University Life, 1948–1964', Ph.D. Dissertation, Harvard University, 2007.

[15] B. Tromly, 'Re-Imagining the Soviet Intelligentsia'.

[16] As Chapter 9 shows, the question of a return to the ideals of the pre-revolutionary intelligentsia, at which Tromly hints, is slightly more problematic.

[17] B. Tromly, 'Re-Imagining the Soviet Intelligentsia', p. 302.

Protests continued around the 7 November Revolution Day holiday in 1956. In Leningrad, a handful of university students joined the main parade in the city, shouting anti-Khrushchev slogans and declaring their opposition to Soviet action in Budapest.[18] In Yaroslavl, Vitaly Lazaryants and two friends interrupted the official rally by marching toward the tribune with a banner demanding the withdrawal of Soviet troops from Hungary.[19] Sculptures of Stalin were vandalised at a park in the Ukrainian city of Kherson and in Sebastopol fourteen posters of Party and government leaders were destroyed. KGB reports noted that a total of over 1,000 hostile political leaflets were discovered in the street or dropped from balloons in Leningrad, Barnaul, Riga and the Transcarpathian *oblast'*.[20]

Bordering on Hungary and including around 50,000 ethnic Hungarians in its population, the Transcarpathian *oblast'* in western Ukraine proved to be one of the most concentrated areas of discontent in late 1956. The Minister of Internal Affairs, N.P. Dudorov, reported on 1 December that the region's Uzhgorodskii and Beregovskii districts in particular had witnessed a 'significant growth of anti-Soviet activity' since the military intervention in Hungary. He stated that there was a great deal of anti-Russian sentiment in the region, that local Communist Party activists had been threatened and beaten and at least sixty people claimed to have banded together to fight against the communist regime, most of whom had only recently returned from the camps.[21] Universities across the Baltic republics of Latvia, Lithuania and Estonia also became the scene of major protests against the Soviet invasion of Hungary.[22] On 27 October a series of gatherings were held in Tallinn, where participants toasted the on-going protests in Hungary and sang the Polish national anthem, while in Lithuania an estimated crowd of 35,000 gathered on 2 November and marched into the centre of Kaunas, where they shouted slogans in support of Hungary and called for Lithuanian independence before clashing with police.[23]

The latter part of 1956 and early 1957 also witnessed some of the last stirrings of open dissent within the Communist Party itself, before iron discipline and conformity were restored for the best part of the next three decades. At a Party meeting in Cherkasskaya *oblast'* in Ukraine, for example,

[18] GARF, f. 8131, op. 31, d. 89522, ll. 1–4.   [19] GARF, f. A-461, op. 2, d. 10996, l. 17.
[20] RGANI, f. 5, op. 30, d. 141, ll. 54–6.   [21] GARF, f. 9402, op. 2, d. 492, l. 121.
[22] A. Weiner, 'Déjà Vu All Over Again: Prague Spring, Romanian Summer and Soviet Autumn on the Soviet Western Frontier', *Contemporary European History*, Vol. 15, No. 2 (2006), 186.
[23] A. Weiner, 'The Empires Pay a Visit: Gulag Returnees, East European Rebellions, and Soviet Frontier Politics', *The Journal of Modern History*, Vol. 78, No. 2 (June 2006), 356.

candidate CPSU member and *kolkhoz* foreman A.I. Zemsha declared that the Party was 'no longer a party of communists but one of fascists' – for which he was subsequently jailed under article 58-10.[24] A report filed by the head of the RSFSR Department of Party Organs, V.M. Churaev, on 21 February 1957 outlined a series of 'anti-Party speeches' around the country. In Yaroslavl a builder named Kiselev had attacked misleading media coverage of events in Hungary and Eastern Europe. Students at a forestry institute in Bryansk proclaimed that the Soviet regime had done nothing to improve the life of ordinary Russians and made scathing comparisons with the standard of living in the US.[25] On being presented with a secret Central Committee letter which effectively announced the beginning of a major clampdown on dissent, one Party member in Kirov *oblast'* surmised that: 'we are now being told either to shut up or face jail'.[26] As the following chapter shows, he was absolutely correct.

Reports from the Department of Komsomol Organs and the Komsomol Department of Agitation and Propaganda showed that open criticism flared again inside the Communist Party's youth wing around this time. A note sent to Vladimir Semichastnyi (at the time, a member of the Komsomol Central Committee but later to become KGB chairman) on 10 December 1956 stated that 'Komsomol organisations have not drawn the correct conclusions from the XX Party Congress and need to strengthen their [propaganda] work amongst young people', before going on to say that 'as a result, in some Komsomol branches an unhealthy atmosphere has appeared, with mistaken views on life, speeches alien to Marxist-Leninist views and a tendency to think in bourgeois terms'.[27] The same report also stated that there had been numerous calls to limit Communist Party control over the Komsomol, and that students were criticising the lack of freedom in the country, attacking the privileges of the political elite and listening to BBC radio broadcasts. Among its concluding remarks the report noted that '. . . as a rule, demagogic speeches receive the necessary rebuff, but some Komsomol members do support them . . .'[28] Quite how many members supported them is impossible to say, but a range of anecdotal evidence and the non-committal language of this last statement suggests it was more than just a handful.

Students around the country questioned the deeper systemic roots of the 'Cult of Personality'; they also resented perceived ideological stagnation and

[24] GARF, f. 8131, op. 31, d. 80330, ll. 1–2.   [25] RGANI, f. 89, op. 6, d. 6, ll. 1–5.
[26] RGANI, f. 89, op. 6, d. 6, l. 1.   [27] RGASPI, f. 1, op. 6, d. 925, l. 17.
[28] RGASPI, f. 1, op. 6, d. 925, l. 9.

conservatism within the Komsomol, criticised patently undemocratic elections and produced journals and wall-newspapers that attacked self-important bureaucrats and politicians.[29] When punishment duly followed, many showed solidarity with their classmates and protested further. Some began to demand that fellow students who had been expelled or repressed in previous years now be rehabilitated, or simply carried out their own unofficial rehabilitations.[30] When the students Vladimir Zlotverov and Ali Kafarov were jailed in December 1956, many of their colleagues at the All-Union State Institute of Cinematography (VGIK) sprang to their defence, holding a meeting of over 300 people in which they condemned the arrests, threatened to write to the CPSU Presidium and demanded an open hearing in which students and university authorities could discuss the matter, though this prospective meeting was ultimately prevented by a wave of disciplinary actions against those involved.[31] When the Leningrad student Boris Vail' was about to be expelled from the Komsomol (which would have also meant being thrown out of university), his course mates threatened to boycott lectures and the case against him was dropped.[32]

The roots of student dissatisfaction were not always purely ideological. Stipends were pitifully low, meaning that the material conditions of those who chose to remain in education were often poor, to say the least.[33] Added to this was a particularly demanding study programme and a raft of unpopular 'Stalinist' teachers as well as the compulsory attendance at political meetings and extensive voluntary work that were expected of Komsomol members.[34] Being a student and a communist meant a lot of hard work. As the Kursk student I. Rykov stated at a public meeting in 1956, 'the Komsomol is boring and if I had the option to join it now, I would refuse. All it expects from us is work and study instead of happiness.'[35] Radio

[29] See, for example, A. Pyzhikov, 'Istoki dissidenstva', *Svobodnaya mysl'* (2003), 77–85.

[30] L. Silina, *Nastroeniya sovetskogo studenchestva 1945–1964*, Moskva: Russkii mir, 2004, p. 110.

[31] For fuller details on what was actually a fairly complex case see K. Smith, 'A New Generation of Political Prisoners: "Anti-Soviet" Students, 1956–1957', *The Soviet and Post-Soviet Review*, Vol. 32, Nos. 2–3 (2005), 191–208.

[32] B. Vail', *Osobo opasnyi*, London: Overseas Publications Interchange, 1980, pp. 170–3.

[33] See, for example, Alexeyeva's account of her own time as a student around this time, in L. Alexeyeva and P. Goldberg, *The Thaw Generation: Coming of Age in the Post-Stalin Era*, Boston, MA: Little, Brown and Company, 1990.

[34] It was not only the students who were showing their discontent and growing harder to manage. Sergei Kovalev, at the time a biology teacher at MGU, petitioned against the teaching of the fraudulent scientific theory of Lysenkoism, which still enjoyed official favour at the time. See E. Gilligan, *Defending Human Rights in Russia: Sergei Kovalyov, Dissident and Human Rights Commissioner, 1969–2003*, London: RoutledgeCurzon, 2004, p. 17.

[35] A. Pyzhikov, *Opyt modernizatsii sovetskogo obshchestva v 1953–1964 godakh: obshchestvenno-politicheskii aspekt*, Moskva: Izdatel'skii dom 'Gamma', 1998, p. 68.

Liberty analyses of articles and letters in the Soviet press suggested that Rykov was voicing a widely held view, and that an increasing number of Komsomol members were voicing disenchantment at the organisation by writing to newspapers, making critical speeches and attempting to evade their Komsomol duties.[36]

In the big cities at least, the popular mood struck some visitors to the USSR as unsettled. After an extended tour of the country in 1957, Zinaida Schakovsky wrote of an 'all-pervading atmosphere of discontent' and an 'immense discontent which is rumbling through the Soviet Union today'.[37] As a White Émigré princess whose family was ruined by the October Revolution, one should not be surprised that Schakovsky gave such a withering assessment of the communist regime's fortunes, but even far less politically coloured accounts by contemporary visitors suggest that her remarks were not completely unrealistic. After spending several months in Russia and Ukraine around the same time, Maurice Hindus wrote that the Soviet people were entirely loyal to the regime and to communism but did concede that the young generation in particular was brimming over with questions and frustrations.[38] The overwhelming weight of primary literature on the Khrushchev period, including even the KGB files of those who were arrested, offers considerably more support for Hindus's assessment than for that of Schakovsky.[39] The Soviet regime was hardly teetering on the brink of mass rebellion. Even so, the scenario that was presented by Hindus constituted a very real challenge for a political system that still sought to keep tight control over public discourse in particular.

Owing to the fact that the regime was engaged in a major clampdown on dissent throughout 1957 and much of 1958, a considerable volume of hard data on the subject was amassed by the authorities. A classified 1958 Procurator review of sentences for anti-Soviet activity gives some useful statistical detail on the prevailing forms of dissenting behaviour around this time. From the 2,498 sentences for counter-revolutionary activity in 1957 (of which 1,964 were for anti-Soviet activity and propaganda), the following statistics were presented: 91.3% of those sentenced had acted alone; 6.1%

[36] Radio Liberty Analysis of Current Developments in the Soviet Press, Budapest, HU OSA 300-80-1, Box 394. That the Soviet press might print discordant views such as these testified to the fact that occasional criticism of the Komsomol leadership was still seen as a useful means of keeping the organisation's elites on their toes.

[37] Z. Schakovsky, *The Privilege Was Mine*, London: Jonathan Cape, 1959, pp. 30, 47.

[38] M. Hindus, *House without a Roof: Russia after Forty-Three Years of Revolution*, London: Victor Gollancz, 1962, p. 58.

[39] See, for example, L. Alexeyeva and P. Goldberg, *The Thaw Generation* and A. Kozlov, *Kozel na sakse: i tak vsyu zhizn*, Moskva: Vagrius, 1998.

had acted in groups of two to three people; a further 2.6% had acted in groups of three or more. Single acts of protest and criticism accounted for 62.6% of all sentences while repeated acts made up 37.4%.[40] The review also discerned four forms of dissenting activity: 'oral expressions of a counter-revolutionary nature' (57.3% of sentences), 'anonymous anti-Soviet letters, diaries and songs' (22%), 'anti-Soviet leaflets' (13%), and 'possession of anti-Soviet literature' (7.7%).[41] By no means all of those who criticised the authorities were jailed, so the picture these statistics paint could never be complete, though they do provide an interesting snapshot of protest activity during the time in question.

The Procurator review also provided a basic demographic breakdown of convictions under article 58-10 for 1957. It showed that workers accounted for 46.8% of all sentences, followed by white-collar workers (18.3%), collective farm workers (9.9%) and miscellaneous – such as pensioners and invalids – (25.0%).[42] With members of the intelligentsia coming under the category of 'white-collar workers', these statistics clearly present a challenge to the traditional historiography of Soviet dissent as a social phenomenon overwhelmingly confined to educated professionals. In regard to age, the review showed that 17.4% of those convicted were less than twenty-four years old, while 67.2% were between twenty-four and forty years of age, with the remaining 15.4% over forty years old.[43] By some way the greatest number of those sentenced were Russians (957 convictions), followed in numerical order by Ukrainians (443), Lithuanians (68) and Belarusians (65).[44]

Although not explicitly mentioned in the Procurator review, it is also worth pointing out that well over 90% of those convicted were men. Whether this reflected that women were less likely to be involved in dissenting behaviour, or were simply less likely to be sent to jail for it, is hard to tell for sure. Both were probably true to some extent. If one looks back to the Stalin era, and particularly at the collectivisation process of the early 1930s, there is evidence to suggest that the latter may well have been the case, with scholars showing that during collectivisation women were actually more likely to be involved in acts of protest than were men because

---

[40] GARF, f. 8131, op. 32, d. 5080, l. 17. An important point to note is that 'counter-revolutionary crimes' (article 58 of the RSFSR criminal code) did not just include 'anti-Soviet activity and propaganda' (article 58, subsection 10 or 58-10) but also included other articles that dealt with crimes, such as espionage (58-6) and terrorism (58-8). Nonetheless, well over three-quarters of convictions for counter-revolutionary crimes around this time were for anti-Soviet activity and propaganda.

[41] GARF, f. 8131, op. 32, d. 5080, ll. 17–18.   [42] GARF, f. 8131, op. 32, d. 5080, l. 6.

[43] GARF, f. 8131, op. 32, d. 5080, l. 6.   [44] GARF, f. 8131, op. 32, d. 5080, l. 5.

they were less likely to face harsh punishment.[45] This quite possibly happened to some degree under Khrushchev too, though it is important to note that the most common offences for which people were jailed during the clampdown – public, and often drunken, clashes with the police – did seem to suggest a somewhat male-dominated sphere of activity. It is also worth drawing attention to Susan Reid's point that discourse on political reform – and implicitly also involvement in political matters more widely – was still overwhelmingly aimed at men under Khrushchev.[46] The much-heralded push to raise the profile of women in public life tended not to result in more substantial political activity, but most often centred upon promotion of material themes such as domesticity and consumer satisfaction.[47]

When one starts to consider the above statistics on convictions a little more closely, it soon becomes apparent that they should not be taken entirely at face value, since they tell us at least as much about the observer (in this case, the KGB and Procuracy) as they do about who and what was being observed. To a considerable extent they reflect the nature of the campaign against dissent that was under way at the time, rather than presenting a wholly reliable image of trends in dissenting behaviour. For example, the breakdown of convictions by age seems to imply that people under twenty-four years old were less inclined toward dissenting behaviour than were other age groups, something the present chapter has already shown was not the case. What it actually shows is that the authorities usually resisted employing custodial sentences against young people in all but the most serious cases.[48] Similarly, the figures provided tell of minimal dissenting activity among the peasantry, yet with far fewer resources for policing in rural areas there was much less chance of the authorities even noticing dissent in the countryside. As such, the data provided do not give

---

[45] See, for example, L. Viola, 'Introduction', in *Contending with Stalinism: Soviet Power and Popular Resistance in the 1930s*, London: Cornell University Press, 2002, p. 5.

[46] See S. Reid, 'Cold War in the Kitchen: Gender and the De-Stalinization of Consumer Taste in the Soviet Union under Khrushchev', *Slavic Review*, Vol. 60, No. 2 (Summer 2002), 211–52.

[47] See M. Ilič, S. Reid and L. Attwood eds., *Women in the Khrushchev Era*, Basingstoke: Palgrave Macmillan, 2004.

[48] See G. Kuzovkin, 'Partiino-Komsomol'skie presledovaniya', in L. Eremina and E. Zhemkova eds., *Korni travy: sbornik statei molodykh istorikov*, Moskva: Zven'ya, 1996. With bald data such as these it is not always practical to think in terms of 'political', 'nationalist' or 'religious' dissent since all are grouped together in the statistics without differentiation. Kozlov's annotated catalogue shows that a large majority of convictions at this stage were for acts that can be classed as political dissent, though by no means all of them were. See V. Kozlov and S. Mironenko eds., *58-10 Nadzornye proizvodstva prokuratury SSSR po delam ob antisovetskoi agitatsii i propaganda: annotirovannyi katalog Mart 1953–1991*, Moskva: Mezhdunarodnyi Fond 'Demokratiya', 1999.

an absolutely accurate representation of protest activity at the time. However, complete statistics on the matter do not and could not exist. With a reasonably large sample of cases, one can certainly put faith in the most basic trend that the report demonstrated: political dissent was a surprisingly diverse social phenomenon. Dissenters, or at least those of them who were caught and jailed, constituted only a small minority within the overall Soviet population – even in 1957, less than 2.5% of all jail sentences passed by Soviet courts were for anti-Soviet activity – yet all areas of the country and all social classes witnessed some degree of protest and criticism.[49]

In the vast majority of cases, the 'oral expressions of a counter-revolutionary nature' on which most convictions were based did not take the form of ideological criticisms at Party meetings, like those that had occurred in the immediate aftermath of the Secret Speech. Instead, the best place to start is with Yuri Aksyutin's description of such acts as 'not so much a manifestation of well-formed attitudes as [they were] a burst of emotion'.[50] They were practically always spontaneous and were usually spurred by confrontations with individual representatives of authority, by difficult personal circumstances, by drunkenness or by any combination of the three. These clashes – some of them undoubtedly provoked or even fabricated by police – often included sharp political expressions, such as threats to beat up communists and kill members of the government, but in fact offered little hard evidence of deep-seated dissatisfaction at the wider political situation. Nor should they be too readily interpreted as people revealing their 'true' attitudes toward Soviet power, since they were so often the product of particularly straitened and adversarial conditions. Such outbursts were essentially a continuation of the kinds of primitive lashing out at officialdom that had always existed: they were primarily about offending the authorities rather than challenging them politically.

In late 1956 and 1957 these spontaneous eruptions of anger often cited the uprising in Hungary as an example to be copied in the USSR. Bearing in mind the severity of the anti-communist violence that briefly swept through Hungary, the Soviet authorities cannot have been entirely unconcerned at this trend, however unrealistic it might be for such a scenario to break out inside the USSR. One case, for example, saw I.V. Yaniv – a thirty-two-year-old metal worker and former prisoner – declare in a Drogobych bus station

---

[49] GARF, f. 8131, op. 32, d. 5080, l. 3.
[50] Iu. Aksiutin, 'Popular Responses to Khrushchev', in W. Taubman, S. Khrushchev and A. Gleason eds., *Nikita Khrushchev*, p. 197.

café that 'communists should be attacked and overthrown as they are being in Hungary'.[51] In Rostov *oblast'* the electrician A.A. Tararin turned up to work drunk and announced that communists were corrupt and self-serving, before adding that they should be 'strung up and shot, like in Hungary'.[52] In many cases like these, the events in Hungary tended to be a timely point of reference rather than the root of deep-seated anger among those who engaged in this kind of public attack on the authorities. More often than not, their statements celebrated mayhem and violence against authority far more than they did the cause of the Hungarian rebels.

Angry public outbursts that did not refer to Hungary around this time often included themes such as threatening to side with the US in the 'forthcoming' war that was widely rumoured to be on the horizon; making unfavourable comparisons between the standard of living in the Soviet Union and the West; shouting slogans such as 'down with the Soviet regime' or 'long live Eisenhower', and calling members of the militia 'fascists' and 'Beriaites'. In fact, the militia was a particular focus for abuse and resentment throughout the era, not least because its members were the most frequently encountered representatives of authority, from whom citizens needed all manner of permits and permissions for their everyday affairs. Perhaps more importantly, though, the country's police had justifiably garnered a reputation for lawlessness and brutality during the Stalin era – a reputation that still persisted in many places.[53] This situation can only have been exacerbated by the fact that the Khrushchev years then saw a swelling number of citizens arrested for all kinds of fairly minor public-order offences, like swearing and spitting, as the militia enthusiastically enforced a government clampdown on petty hooliganism.

An example that was quite typical in terms of the physical scenario and comments that were made involved one Aleksei Lepekhin, an invalid from Astrakhan *oblast'*. Lepekhin was detained by police in August 1957 after robbing a man who had passed out in the street whilst drunk. Upon being confronted by a policeman, and later whilst in detention at the militia station, Lepekhin made a series of angry and highly political statements that led to him being convicted of anti-Soviet activity and sentenced to ten years' corrective labour later that same month. Fellow prisoners, members of the

[51] GARF, f. 8131, op. 31, d. 87486, ll. 1–2.
[52] GARF, f. 8131, op. 31, d. 77378, ll. 1–2, in V. Kozlov and S. Mironenko eds., *58-10 Nadzornye proizvodstva*.
[53] Yoram Gorlizki cites numerous instances in which militia behaviour attracted angry crowds of protesters. See Y. Gorlizki, 'Policing Post-Stalin Society: The Militsiia and Public Order under Khrushchev', *Cahiers du Monde russe*, Vol. 44, Nos. 2–3 (avril–septembre 2003), 465–80.

public and militia staff all testified that Lepekhin had made the following statements: 'I lived better under the (Nazi) occupation', 'Communists do not give us the freedom to live', 'Khrushchev and Bulganin are strangling the working class', and 'Down with the Soviet Union, long live Eisenhower.'[54]

These remarks broached several of the most taboo subjects of the time, simply by inverting official discourse rather than offering any substantive ideological comment. They were unquestionably inflammatory, and Lepekhin knew it. Nonetheless, outbursts like these did not necessarily represent Lepekhin's 'true' thoughts and opinions. It is extremely unlikely that he did actually live better under Nazi occupation, for example. Such remarks primarily reflected a wish to give officialdom a bloody nose. Individuals' relationships with the Soviet system could be complex and changing: to draw overarching conclusions about that relationship on the basis of an outburst that occurred under strained conditions, and which in some cases lasted for only a few seconds, would clearly be pushing the available evidence too far.

Outbursts like these occupied a particularly interesting place in the wider spectrum of dissenting behaviour. They were clearly not the kind of purposive and persistent acts of dissent that would indicate a determination to work toward reforming or overturning the regime. Nor were they anything like the conscious defence of humanitarian principles that characterised human-rights dissent during the Brezhnev era. Nonetheless, declaring a hatred of communists or publicly calling for the overthrow of the Party leadership clearly were serious acts in their own right, whether or not they indicated intent. At the very least these explosions of anger told of a social ferment that could well prove dangerous and unpredictable during turbulent times. Importantly, they also posed a challenge to official dominance of the public sphere. Had the growth of these outbursts against the authorities been allowed to go unchecked, it is entirely possible that they would have begun to erode the still overwhelmingly submissive social order inside the USSR. As the Hungarian rising had shown, demonstrations of discontent could degenerate into chaos very quickly, especially in a country where so many pent-up frustrations had gone unvented for so long.

For people to have made such outspoken and ultimately dangerous remarks apparently in the absence of serious opposition to the regime still seems rather incongruent. While they may not have been 'genuine enemies' of the Soviet system, neither were such people usually among its most active

[54] GARF, f. 8131, op. 31, d. 84518, ll. 4–6.

supporters. Dissenters from the Party and Komsomol, for example, were rarely involved in this type of behaviour. Often those who became embroiled in these kinds of confrontations were 'marginals': habitual criminals, vagrants and others who had not managed or not tried to fit in with 'decent' Soviet society. Even so, plenty of case files showed that citizens with otherwise flawless records could quickly change their opinions and behaviours when personal circumstances and the political environment fluctuated most violently, briefly lashing out with great vitriol before returning to passivity soon after. Yakov Rizoi was a classic example of this. A dedicated CPSU member of twenty years' standing, he was demobilised from the air force in Khrushchev's deep military cuts and began posting 'slanderous' leaflets attacking Party policy, calling on workers to stand up for their rights and to demand an improvement in their standard of living, as well as personally abusing Khrushchev.[55] The fact that socio-economic issues such as living standards could become so sharply politicised indicated firstly that they were increasingly a key aspect of the implicit Soviet social contract and, secondly, the extent to which politics, in the form of language, rituals and symbols, was so entrenched and inescapable in everyday life that it quickly became a target for criticism and abuse in times of frustration.

The frequency with which drunkenness was reported in these kinds of cases was clearly not entirely without significance. Nonetheless, it is also worth stating that drunkenness did not automatically imply that there was or was not any genuine political disenchantment underlying such outbursts. Yuri Glazov's assertion that 'Since vodka loosens the tongue, it should not be surprising that in Russia drunkards blurt out their real thoughts in public' has a certain common-sense appeal but ought to be treated with some considerable caution.[56] One's intuition and experience suggest that there may well be a good deal of truth to this assertion – and Stalin certainly seems to have believed something of the sort if the extent to which he plied underlings with alcohol at his late-night get-togethers is anything to go by – but it should not be taken as a statement of fact. People are not necessarily a reflection of their 'true self' when intoxicated – quite the opposite on occasion – and being more confrontational is not the same thing as being more 'honest'. In fact, the authorities themselves soon came to accept that isolated instances of drunken dissent did not necessarily prove a person was 'truly anti-Soviet'.[57] In a roundabout way, therefore, one who tries rigidly to

---

[55] GARF, f. 8131, op. 31, d. 94020, ll. 1–4.
[56] Yu. Glazov, *The Russian Mind since Stalin's Death*, Boston, MA: D. Reidel, 1985, p. 12.
[57] See, for example, GARF, f. 8131, op. 32, d. 5080, l. 41.

argue Glazov's point takes a more intransigent view of such matters than did the Soviet authorities.

As in Hungary – where a Young Communist literary group known as the Petöfi Circle had played a major role in mobilising protests – even very limited cultural liberalisation in the USSR had already begun to reinvigorate and arouse elements of the intelligentsia. The two literary works from around this time that require particular mention are Vladimir Dudintsev's *Not by Bread Alone* (1956) and Boris Pasternak's *Dr Zhivago* (1957). Like practically all works whose authorship was known to the authorities, the likes of Pasternak and Dudintsev had to take care not to go too far in their remarks but, for the intelligentsia in particular, both transmitted a number of fundamental messages about how one ought to conduct one's life and on the position of the individual in Soviet society and the importance of personal morality.[58]

While Pasternak's offering is accepted to have been of far greater literary merit, it eschewed the overt political comment of *Not by Bread Alone*. To a considerable extent, it was actually its ambiguity and apoliticism that made Pasternak's work so problematic, since the duty of Soviet culture had always been to educate and to rouse the population for the building of the communist future, something that *Zhivago* studiously failed to do. Dudintsev, on the other hand, produced a work that was classically Socialist Realist in form, but one that tapped into a vein of popular resentment by pitching a 'good' Soviet worker (Dimitri Lopatkin) against 'bad' Soviet officials. His attack on obstructive and self-serving bureaucrats struck a chord for many Soviet citizens, especially for the young and educated, many of whom began to refer pejoratively to all Soviet bureaucrats as 'Drozdovs', after the name of Lopatkin's chief tormentor.

Published by instalments in the liberal literary journal *Novy mir* during autumn of 1956, *Not by Bread Alone* proved an instant success. As happened with numerous other works of the period, the discourse which sprang up around Dudintsev's novel soon spread well beyond the matter of its literary merits, touching instead upon wider economic and political problems, along with legacies of the past, cultural change and the ethical dilemmas that the country and its people confronted.[59] One of the best examples that demonstrated how quickly this shift from culture to politics could occur was

[58] See P. Boobbyer, *Conscience, Dissent and Reform in Soviet Russia*, London: Routledge, 2005, p. 69.

[59] D. Kozlov, 'Naming the Social Evil: The Readers of *Novyi Mir* and Vladimir Dudintsev's *Not by Bread Alone*, 1956–59 and Beyond', in P. Jones ed., *The Dilemmas of De-Stalinization: Negotiating Cultural and Social Change in the Khrushchev Era*, London: Routledge, 2006, p. 80.

seen at a packed meeting at Leningrad State University on 10 November 1956, when Dudintsev's work was at the centre of a particularly stormy discussion session in which Revolt Pimenov, a young mathematician, lambasted what he called a 'Drozdovshchina' (the reign of the Drozdovs) – receiving rapturous applause from the crowd as he did so – before facing a stinging rebuke from the rector of the university.[60] The celebrated writer Konstantin Paustovsky was similarly vociferous in his condemnation of the Soviet Union's real-life 'Drozdovs', insisting that they had to be 'mercilessly swept away'.[61] The meeting in Leningrad was not a one-off, either: a British embassy official present at an analogous discussion of Dudintsev's work at MGU described events there as 'a virtual scene of political protest'.[62]

Aside from its lack of ideological conviction, what made Pasternak's work so challenging for the authorities was the global popularity and critical acclaim which met *Dr Zhivago*, especially since it had already been rejected for publication at *Novy mir*. With the relative opacity of the Soviet system in the 1950s a number of informed Western commentators at the time understandably saw the work – which was smuggled out of the Soviet Union in 1957 and published in Italy – as the first sign of political dissent within the USSR.[63] The novel's author and its main protagonist, Yuri Zhivago, certainly fit the bill as symbols of that surviving liberal subjectivity for which many scholars in the West were looking. We can now safely discount the notion of *Dr Zhivago* as the first stirring of post-Stalin political dissent, though the success of the book abroad and the size of the accompanying scandal inside the USSR did make it significant as the first time that cracks in the Soviet monolith became such major international news – a not insignificant development in its own right. The Soviet response to *Dr Zhivago*'s publication abroad was actually rather muted at first, but when its rocketing international popularity became apparent, and Pasternak was subsequently awarded the Nobel Prize for Literature in 1958, it brought down a firestorm of abuse and intimidation against the author – something that served to wreck his health and to undermine the Soviet leadership's

[60] R. Pimenov, *Vospominaniya*, Moskva: Informatsionno-ekspertnaya gruppa 'Panorama', 1996, p. 33. See also D. Kozlov, 'Naming the Social Evil', in P. Jones ed., *The Dilemmas of De-Stalinization*.
[61] H. McLean and W. Vickery eds., *The Year of Protest: 1956*, New York: Vintage Books, 1961, p. 158.
[62] British embassy official cited in telegram from US embassy in Moscow to Department of State, 28 November 1956, Budapest, HU OSA 300-80.
[63] See, for example, A. Rothberg, *The Heirs of Stalin: Dissidence and the Soviet Regime 1953–1970*, Ithaca, NY: Cornell University Press, 1972.

attempts to present a less intolerant image of the system to the outside world.[64]

The year 1956 was to end with a last major controversy in the world of culture, when an exhibition of Pablo Picasso's work was brought to the USSR.[65] With Picasso's later paintings having been consistently lambasted for 'formalism' during the Stalin years, the exhibition was quite clearly another major symbol of the changes Khrushchev was imposing.[66] In both Leningrad and Moscow, however, the exhibition was to become the backdrop to uproarious scenes.[67] From the very outset there was a great sense of expectation as crowds waited impatiently to see the work of such an internationally celebrated artist. As with the earlier discussions on *Not by Bread Alone*, talk soon spread beyond Picasso's artwork. Heated debates and impassioned comments about cultural restrictions inside the USSR quickly began to flare up and were to continue for days and weeks afterward in student dormitories and arts institutes.[68] In Moscow, the militia had to be called to disperse crowds. In Leningrad, dozens of students held a spontaneous and unsanctioned meeting to discuss the exhibition on 14 December. Plans were then made to hold a public meeting at Arts Square in the city the following week. When participants arrived, however, they found that the KGB had cordoned off the square. They headed instead for the building of the Leningrad Artists' Union, where they hijacked a separate discussion and turned it into their own meeting, which again became animated and quickly turned from questions of art to artistic freedom and politics, ending with a number of attendees being hauled off by the militia.

Many of those present have since referred to the Picasso exhibition as a kind of 'awakening', something that has probably been said of more single

---

[64] When dictating his memoirs years later in retirement, Khrushchev conceded that the attack on Pasternak had been a mistake and accepted that *Dr Zhivago* need not have provoked such a furore. S. Khrushchev ed., *Memoirs of Nikita Khrushchev*, Vol. 2: *Reformer: 1945–1964*, University Park, PA: Pennsylvania State University Press, 2006, p. 551.

[65] Eleonory Gilburd has provided by some way the most detailed and convincing analysis of the 1956 Picasso exhibition. See E. Gilburd, 'Picasso in Thaw Culture', *Cahiers du Monde russe*, Vol. 47, No. 1–2 (janvier–juin 2006), 65–108.

[66] Even so, Picasso had still been awarded the Stalin Peace Prize in 1950. As Gilburd points out, Picasso personally insisted on the inclusion of a number of the more challenging works that were exhibited: the Soviet art establishment was not allowed simply to pick and choose what they would exhibit.

[67] See, for example, R. Pimenov, *Vospominaniya*.

[68] The reaction to Picasso's art was by no means uniformly positive. As with many in the Western world, much of the audience found his work incomprehensible and responded with remarks such as 'my children could do better than this'.

events during the Khrushchev era than any other in Soviet history.[69] Anatoly Naiman, who attended the exhibition in Leningrad, recalled that 'We felt a rapture in those Picasso-ed halls; it softened the pain and sadness of understanding how, and for how many years, we had been sitting in a cave, seeing only with the minimum light allowed us.'[70] Eleonory Gilburd's analysis of the events in question is compelling. She writes that 'Picasso's art was not the focus of student unrest ... but he was a convenient and provocative metaphor for expressing far broader discontent and expectations', of which there was no shortage at the end of 1956.[71] As an ideological adherent of the socialist cause, but not an unquestioning supporter of the Soviet regime's activity – most notably, he had spoken out against the invasion of Hungary – Picasso occupied the exact political position that many of those who rushed to see his work wished to be allowed for themselves.

Those who spoke up in official spaces such as Party meetings and scholarly debates, or submitted literary works for publication, were apt to remember that it was still dangerous completely to ignore established ideological norms and conventions. Those who engaged in underground dissenting activity, on the other hand, were not so tightly constrained by such considerations – though their behaviour was of course still shaped by their contemporary environment – since they were clearly already well beyond the bounds of acceptable behaviour and were seemingly protected by their secrecy and anonymity. Nonetheless, while they were able to give much fuller vent to their frustrations and political aspirations, even here the Soviet meta-narrative loomed large, with many underground dissenters disenchanted primarily at the perceived conservatism, careerism and servility of contemporary Soviet political life, rather than the aims and ideals of the revolution.

What the authorities referred to as 'anti-Soviet leaflets' (*listovki*) were perhaps the most consistently widespread manifestations of political dissent in the 1950s and early 1960s. A rudimentary attempt to puncture the Party-state-dominated public sphere, they were an important forerunner of the *samizdat* literature that first began to emerge under Khrushchev before truly flourishing during the Brezhnev era. These leaflets typically included short manifestos written by underground political groups, information on strikes and disorders around the country, appeals for the people to rise up against

---

[69] We also encounter this kind of language in accounts of the Secret Speech, the 1957 World Youth Festival and the publication of Solzhenitsyn's *One Day in the Life of Ivan Denisovich*, to name just three other events.

[70] A. Naiman, 'Picasso in Russia 2.0', *Moscow News*, 15 June 2010.

[71] E. Gilburd, 'Picasso in Thaw Culture', 107.

the regime and transcriptions of foreign radio broadcasts. The total number of *listovki* that were produced and distributed over the course of the period undoubtedly ran into tens of thousands, and quite probably far more. They were discovered by the KGB in practically every large and medium-sized town throughout the Soviet Union, sometimes pasted up on walls and windows of public buildings or scattered on public transport, furtively left in mailboxes, or simply handed out in the street. Like Western radio broadcasts and *samizdat* literature, they sought to undermine the univocal public sphere that the Soviet authorities had relied upon virtually since the revolution. At this early stage of the Khrushchev era, leaflets usually tended to be hand-written and reproduced in quite small quantities of around a dozen or so copies. Although often few in number, the contents of such leaflets could be particularly sharp. Accordingly, the authorities took the distribution of anti-Soviet leaflets very seriously and could mobilise huge resources to track down and remove them from the public domain.

The fortieth anniversary of the October Revolution in 1957 saw hostile leaflets discovered in numerous major cities around the Soviet Union. Batches of varying quantities were uncovered that day in Leningrad, Riga, Kaliningrad, Minsk, Brest, Kiev, Donetsk, Poltava, Vilnius and Stanislav.[72] In Moscow, *listovki* were scattered in the Luzhniki sports stadium, and, more daringly, were left on a police car bonnet and pasted on to the wall of a militia station.

Like major state holidays and anniversaries, elections proved to be a time when popular criticism arose more frequently. Elections for Councils of Workers' Deputies in March 1957 saw *listovki* attacking 'fraudulent' Soviet democracy found attached to buildings in the Ukrainian town of Sumy and in the library of Kiev State University, among other places.[73] MVD reports sometimes spoke of voters openly tearing up and burning ballot cards, refusing to vote and publicly insulting or threatening candidates.[74] KGB files show that elections to People's Courts in December 1957 led to minor disturbances in Moscow, threats against candidates in Kiev and anti-Soviet leaflets found stuffed into a ballot box in Perm.[75] Another protest option available to discontented voters was to reject all the candidates who were listed on the ballot sheet. Although the official data on this matter are limited, and those which do exist should be regarded with a

[72] Iu. Aksiutin, 'Popular Responses to Khrushchev', in W. Taubman, S. Khrushchev and A. Gleason eds., *Nikita Khrushchev*, p. 198.
[73] RGANI, f. 89, op. 18, d. 37, ll. 1–3.   [74] RGANI, f. 89, op. 18, d. 37, ll. 1–3.
[75] RGANI, f. 5, op. 30, d. 231, ll. 122–4.

degree of caution since they cannot be properly verified, the details available are intriguing. The number of negative ballots cast during elections in 1954 was 247,897, climbing to 580,641 in 1958 and 797,000 in 1962.[76] These figures are all the more notable since the practice of casting a 'no' vote involved going to a separate ballot box for 'secret voting', something that would naturally draw attention to those who did so and would most likely have deterred all but the most determined.[77] Although obviously a numerically sizeable negative vote, even the figure for 1962 represented considerably less than 1% of the Soviet voting population at that time. Nonetheless, the rising trajectory of this 'no' vote was not insignificant.

Anonymous letters (*anonimiki*) were another phenomenon central to clandestine dissenting activity during the Khrushchev years. Most frequently these letters were addressed to political bodies such as the Central Committee; to individual representatives of the regime; to editors of newspapers and journals or to managers of industrial enterprises. In later years they were also more frequently sent abroad, either to 'safe' addresses in Germany and Holland that were broadcast by Western radio stations or to foreign political figures, embassies and organisations. Numerous case files of individuals jailed for sending anonymous letters clearly demonstrate that those responsible often sent such letters repeatedly, and sometimes over several years, until they were tracked down by the KGB. In many letters, 'the truth' continued to be a central trope of dissenting activity, just as it had been following the Secret Speech. Letters to political leaders, institutions and private citizens alike consistently demanded 'the truth' or else presented their own 'truth' to the intended recipient on all manner of themes, such as popular moods or poor living standards. The extent to which the Secret Speech had showed the Soviet system to be shot through with lies had clearly not gone unnoticed.

One particularly interesting case involving *anonimiki* was reported to the Central Committee on 12 December 1957. On the staff of the newspaper *Trud*, the forty-five-year-old Communist Party member Dmitrii Kiselev was arrested after sending a series of anonymous letters to readers who had written in to the newspaper supporting several of the authorities' more controversial actions, such as the invasion of Hungary. In his letters Kiselev lambasted correspondents for peddling government lies.[78] According to the

[76] Budapest, HU OSA 300-80-1, Box 127.
[77] J. Gilison, 'Soviet Elections as a Measure of Dissent: The Missing One Per Cent', *The American Political Science Review*, Vol. 62, No. 3 (September 1968), 815.
[78] See Iu. Aksiutin, 'Popular Responses to Khrushchev', in W. Taubman, S. Khrushchev and A. Gleason eds., *Nikita Khrushchev*, p. 198.

KGB, he 'slandered government activity and policy, called for the removal of Party leaders and said the people were starving and the Party does not care'. His police file recorded that Kiselev's letters also called for the entire CPSU leadership to resign and to be expelled from the Party. He had written and sent twenty-two anonymous letters in total between February and August 1957, addressing them to government bodies, industrial enterprises and delegations from capitalist countries at the 1957 Moscow World Youth Festival.[79]

On the whole, one can view critical letters (both anonymous and signed) as an inherently less hostile form of dissent than leaflets. Their contents could, of course, vary considerably: from loyal but critical attempts to communicate with the powers that be, through to anonymous threats and abuse. The fact that letters were intended for communication with private audiences (usually someone in a position of authority), whereas leaflets generally aimed at inciting some kind of public response, is a key distinction. The risks involved in producing and distributing leaflets were also considerably greater than those in writing and posting letters, again suggesting that the former represented a more resolute form of dissenting activity. Nonetheless, the fact that many of those who were jailed for writing *anonimiki* had sent multiple letters, sometimes over a period of several years, highlights the fact that this was still a considered, planned and risky act of protest. As plenty of letter-writers were to find out, the protection seemingly offered by anonymity often proved illusory.

The most taboo form of underground activity involved participating in clandestine political groups. Many of them were little more than discussion circles, though others styled themselves as alternative political parties and even as revolutionary cells. More than any other, this was a form of dissent that was unambiguously forbidden and one that the authorities took extremely seriously, often responding with real ferocity.[80] Nonetheless, underground groups cropped up in all parts of the country during the second half of the 1950s, especially in universities. Frequently at this stage, group members were young and idealistic communists with a real passion for political matters – many of them were either Komsomol or CPSU members – who wanted genuine liberalisation and a return to revolutionary

---

[79] RGANI, f. 5, op. 30, d. 141, ll. 106–7.
[80] As Vladimir Shlapentokh wrote, '. . . the people know from birth that any attempt to create an unofficial organisation is considered by the authorities as a direct threat to the regime . . .' See V. Shlapentokh, *Public and Private Life of the Soviet People: Changing Values in Post-Stalin Russia*, Oxford University Press, 1989, p. 124.

idealism but had grown increasingly frustrated by developments since the XX Congress, and especially by events in Hungary.

The actual deeds of these groups were often very limited, however. Many just talked politics amongst themselves. Often they consisted of only three or four members and were uncovered by the KGB within a few months of being formed, during which time even the most active of them managed only to agree upon a manifesto and to distribute leaflets on a handful of occasions.[81] At this point they did not tend to have formal organisational structures or regulations of membership because of their small size and generally informal nature, as well as the fact that many of these groups were founded on the basis of already existing friendship circles or familial bonds. This is entirely unsurprising when one considers the risks involved in attempting to recruit members for such a dangerous undertaking.

As Juliane Fürst noted in her study on the Stalin-era group 'the Communist Party of Youth', even clandestine organisations such as these highlight the extent to which dissenting behaviour evaded simple dichotomies of support and opposition.[82] This was, after all, the most explicitly outlawed form of dissent but at this stage often involved those who were among the most ideologically committed to the socialist cause. Indeed, as Gabor Rittersporn has argued, sometimes it was paradoxically their loyalty to the overarching Soviet system that impelled such groups to take a stand that would likely be considered 'counter-revolutionary' by the authorities.[83] This sense of political zeal was not uniformly the case, however. While many undoubtedly saw themselves as would-be Lenins, others were somewhat less ideologically driven. Some became involved in underground activity out of a sense of adventure or romance. A strong element of 'role-playing' existed among groups made up of youngsters in particular, often modelling themselves on the heroes of Alexander Fadeyev's massively popular *Molodaya gvardiya* novel about a heroic group of youthful partisans during the Second World War.[84] Similarly, Valery Ronkin recalled the case

---

[81] L. Alexeyeva, *Soviet Dissent: Contemporary Movements for National, Religious and Human Rights*, Middletown, CT: Wesleyan University Press, 1987, p. 295.

[82] See J. Fürst, 'Prisoners of the Soviet Self?: Political Youth Opposition in Late Stalinism', *Europe–Asia Studies*, Vol. 54, No. 3 (May 2002), 353–75.

[83] G. Rittersporn, 'The Great Cause against Bolshevik Practice: High Hopes and Frustrated Loyalties in the Prewar USSR', Paper presented at the 6th World Congress for Central and East European Studies, Tampere, August 2000, p. 2. Cited in J. Fürst, 'Prisoners of the Soviet Self'.

[84] On this, see in particular, J. Fürst, *Stalin's Last Generation: Soviet Post-War Youth and the Emergence of Mature Socialism*, Oxford University Press, 2010, p. 153 and V. Kozlov, S. Fitzpatrick and S. Mironenko eds., *Sedition: Everyday Resistance in the Soviet Union under Khrushchev and Brezhnev*, New Haven, CT: Yale University Press, 2011, pp. 284–94.

of some friends who planned to form their own group in the late 1950s, stating that 'they definitely believed that any kind of anti-Party position would, in the first instance, lead to girls and Western music'.[85] As months passed and the authorities began to clamp down ever harder on critics, the link between dissenting activity and this sense of *joie de vivre* tended to disappear entirely.

Underground activity could seem to young people a way to make their own heroic contribution to the faltering Soviet project, just as previous generations had created the October Revolution, fought the Civil War and defeated Nazism.[86] Many groups argued that the regime had become stagnant and overly bureaucratic. They sought to create, or to recreate, a better form of communism through a return to the values of October 1917 and a degree of political liberalisation. The names of several such groups were a testament to these political leanings, such as 'the Worker-Peasant Underground Party', 'the Socialist Party of the Soviet Union' and 'the Party of Struggle for the Realisation of Leninist Ideas'.[87] For the most part these clandestine organisations were suffused with a deep sense of egalitarianism and distaste for bureaucrats and 'fat-cat' political leaders. These last two were sentiments that would become ever more deeply embedded in society as the perceived gap between elites and masses in the USSR grew more pronounced over the course of the post-Stalin era. They were also distinctly in accord with overarching 'Soviet' notions of social justice. Indeed, the prevalence of underground discourse relating to notions of 'return to Leninism' showed just how deeply the purported values of the system had taken root amongst politically active citizens and how far official ideological discourse pervaded even the most explicitly forbidden forms of activity, particularly among the young and the educated. Lastly, it showed that unless closely directed from above, 'Leninism' could be a dangerous ideology even for the Soviet regime.

Two of the early Khrushchev period's most notable underground groups were based around Revolt Pimenov in Leningrad and Lev Krasnopevtsev in Moscow. Both were formed in the aftermath of the Hungarian rising, demanding a more just and liberal system. Both were uncovered by the KGB within only a few months.

---

[85] V. Ronkin, *Na smenu dekabryam prikhodit yanvari ...*, Moskva: Obshchestvo 'Memorial', 2003, p. 152.

[86] The contrast with the most militant nationalist and religious underground groups on this issue could hardly have been sharper. The former were often interested in bringing an end to the Soviet project on their own territory at least, while the latter were more interested in evading and overcoming its strictures on spiritual activity.

[87] See V. Kozlov and S. Mironenko eds., *Kramola: inakomyslie v SSSR pri Khrushcheve i Brezhneve 1953–1982*, Moskva: Materik, 2005, p. 326.

The Pimenov group came together in December of 1956, primarily driven by mutual opposition to the violent suppression of the Hungarian rising. Revolt Pimenov was a young mathematician at Leningrad State University. He had briefly been incarcerated in a psychiatric unit after resigning from the Komsomol in 1949 and had been expelled from university in 1953 for 'behaviour unbecoming of a Soviet student', until being reinstated after challenging the legality of his expulsion. The Secret Speech had already prompted him to action, holding long evenings discussing politics with friends and secretly producing home-made copies of Khrushchev's report with his own political commentary attached. When Soviet troops went into Hungary he wrote to a number of Supreme Soviet deputies protesting the move and demanding their withdrawal. Boris Vail' had been distributing leaflets since 1955. A youth journal named *Eres'* (lit. 'nonsense' or 'heresy') in which he was involved at the Leningrad Bibliotechnical Institute had come in for attack in the pages of *Leningradskaya pravda*, bringing his name to the attention of Pimenov. At only eighteen years of age, Vail' was almost a decade younger than Pimenov but soon after being introduced the pair decided to form a group that would include several of Vail's student colleagues and Pimenov's common-law wife, Tatyana Verblovskaya. Of those later sentenced for involvement in the group, only Pimenov was beyond his mid-twenties and all but Pimenov were members of either the Communist Party or Komsomol.[88] Typically of the time, they 'boiled with desire for action . . . but did not know how best to act'.[89]

Vail' arranged three group meetings: two at the Leningrad Bibliotechnical Institute in December 1956 and another at Mars Field during January 1957. According to the security organs, at the first meeting Pimenov declared that Stalinist policies were still in effect in the Soviet Union; that there was neither freedom of speech nor freedom of the press; and that the workers were not the true masters in the Soviet system. He then attacked the failings of the *kolkhoz* system and stated that the Yugoslav model of agricultural development was superior to that of the Soviet system.[90] The concluding lines of a November 1956 leaflet produced by the group give a good indication of their ideological standpoint:

---

[88] As mentioned in Chapter 1, Pimenov himself had considered joining the Party in the wake of the Secret Speech.

[89] R. Pimenov, *Vospominaniya*, p. 73.

[90] GARF, f. 8131, op. 31, d. 73957, ll. 32–41. The group's reference to the Yugoslav system of agriculture reflected a phenomenon Benjamin Tromly termed 'Yugoslavophilia', which emerged among Soviet students in particular following the rapprochement between the two countries after Stalin's death. See B. Tromly, 'Re-Imagining the Soviet Intelligentsia', p. 278.

... political power is in the hands of bureaucrats and Party oligarchs who are strengthening the role of the police apparatus and not the Soviets. It is a dictatorship of the Party, not the working class, it relies upon terror in all spheres of life.[91]

Group members paid 25 roubles per month in membership fees, though the money saved was subsequently squandered on alcohol by the individual entrusted to look after it. They also produced several issues of an 'information bulletin' full of officially censored news, mostly taken from foreign newspapers and radio broadcasts. In common with other groups of this time and later, there were disagreements over political direction, practical problems stemming from lack of finances, reliance upon limited and defective information from the outside world and the constant threat of exposure and arrest.[92]

Where this group differed from most others was that they attempted to establish a secondary organisation in Kursk, Boris Vail's hometown. Vail' had visited Kursk in February 1957, taking some of his Leningrad group's literature with him to show to friends there.[93] According to the KGB investigation protocol, subsequent correspondence between Vail' and his friend Konstantin Danilov showed that Vail' had urged his friend to study Marx, to learn 'Bolshevik methods of struggle and conspiracy' and to gather fake documents such as passports, tickets and licenses.[94] Further correspondence included a consignment of leaflets for Danilov's group to distribute, with the slogan 'land to the peasants, factories to the workers and culture to the intelligentsia'. As Vail' later pointed out in his memoirs, the first two of these three demands had actually been slogans from the October Revolution.[95] The advice for Danilov to study 'Bolshevik methods of struggle and conspiracy' was particularly telling. Groups such as this had a ready-made and much celebrated blueprint for subversion right in front of them the whole time. Extensive accounts of the Tsarist-era Bolshevik struggle firstly provided the 'how' of underground activity and also allowed participants to view their activities not as treasonous or counter-revolutionary but, to some extent, in line with media hagiography on the heroism of the pre-revolutionary Bolsheviks.

As it transpired, one of the group's members, Vladimir Vishnyakov, had been trapped by the security organs after he was denounced by a friend named Kobe Kobidze, to whom he had passed illicit leaflets in

[91] GARF, f. 8131, op. 31, d. 73957, l. 45. As Chapter 5 shows, the influence of Milovan Djilas's critique of the Soviet system, on which the group drew here, was to become a major theme of dissenting activity by the end of the 1950s.

[92] R. Pimenov, *Vospominaniya*, p. 72.   [93] B. Vail', *Osobo opasnyi*, p. 164.

[94] GARF, f. 8131, op. 31, d. 73957, l. 65.   [95] B. Vail', *Osobo opasnyi*, p. 163.

March 1957.[96] From Vishnyakov, the trail quickly led to Pimenov and to Vail', who were subjected to covert surveillance for a number of days before their inevitable arrest at the end of that month. Both the Leningrad and Kursk cells were soon uncovered. Eleven participants were jailed for anti-Soviet activity in total, with Pimenov and Vail' sentenced to ten and six years' corrective labour respectively.[97]

The Krasnopevtsev group was centred upon the History Faculty of Moscow State University and had started life as a kind of informal but secretive discussion circle in which participants talked about contemporary political issues and the history of Soviet communism. Most of those involved were teachers, students and recent graduates (six of the nine participants who would be jailed for anti-Soviet activity in February 1958 were Komsomol members and one a full CPSU member).[98] They, too, had hoped that the XX Congress would bring thorough-going political and economic liberalisation but had become disillusioned following the suppression of the Hungarian rising. In March 1957 Krasnopevtsev condemned the damage done to Russia's development by both Tsars and Bolshevik revolutionaries in a thesis entitled 'Important Moments in the Development of the Russian Revolutionary Movement'. In April 1957 he visited Poland as part of a Komsomol delegation and met with a like-minded Pole named Eligiusz Lyasota. The pair soon began to correspond, sending each other political materials that they had prepared. A month later, Krasnopevtsev, Vadim Kozovoi, Vladimir Men'shikov, Leonid Rendel, Nikolai Obushenkov, Marat Cheshkov, Nikolai Pokrovskii and Mark Gol'dman decided to consider themselves an underground group and to move from discussion to action.

In response to the 1957 June Central Committee plenum, when the 'anti-Party affair' had seen the likes of Molotov, Malenkov and Kaganovich fail in an attempt to topple Khrushchev, the Krasnopevtsev group produced 300 leaflets that they scattered around MGU and left on buses. The leaflets demanded that Stalin's accomplices be removed from the leadership and

---

[96] R. Pimenov, *Vospominaniya*, p. 16.

[97] At the original hearing in September 1957 Pimenov was sentenced to six years, but the Procurator's office appealed against the leniency of the sentence and the Supreme Court extended the tariff to ten years in February 1958. GARF. f. 8131, op. 31, d. 73956, l. 304. Vail' was subsequently re-sentenced after continuing his political activity in camp.

[98] Although he was not sufficiently involved in the group to be arrested when it was uncovered by the KGB, Natan Eidel'man – later to become a very successful and popular historian of Imperial Russia – had joined in with some of their initial discussions. See G. Hamburg, 'Writing History and the End of the Soviet Era: the Secret Lives of Natan Eidel'man', *Kritika: Explorations in Russian and Eurasian History*, Vol. 7, No. 1 (Winter 2006), 71–109.

put on trial, that article 58 (counter-revolutionary crimes) be expunged from the criminal code, and that workers be given the right to strike.[99] In August 1957 Kozovoi established contact with an Englishman named Julian Watts – a British intelligence officer according to the KGB – who attended the World Youth Festival in Moscow, and unsuccessfully attempted to pass him 'damaging information' about the USSR.[100] Soon afterward, contact was made with a Frenchman named Lerasno, to whom the group apparently did manage to pass 'sensitive information' about the recent 'anti-Party affair' that had been obtained by Kozovoi, whose father was a Communist Party functionary.[101]

Unbeknownst to the group, the attention of the security organs was roused when they established contact with Watts. Their cover was then blown completely when one of the group accidentally dropped a briefcase full of leaflets in the street and passers-by stopped to help pick up the contents.[102] From there, the KGB began to unravel details of the group throughout late August and early September 1957, before swiftly arresting each of the most active members one after the other. Speaking at his trial in February 1958, Krasnopevtsev admitted that the group had carried out all of the acts they were accused of but denied that they had ever been 'anti-Soviet' in their intent.[103] This was a line of defence that would be employed by many dissenters during the Khrushchev period and after. In Krasnopevtsev's case, and in most others, it proved to be entirely unsuccessful at averting a harsh punitive response.[104] Of all the powers that the authorities reserved exclusively for themselves, the prerogative to decide what was 'Soviet' and what was 'anti-Soviet' was among the most jealously guarded.

This kind of underground activity was by no means restricted to Russia's past and present capitals. At Gorky State University a group referring to itself by the initials OID (meaning either 'Organisation of Thinking

---

[99]   For more complete contents of the leaflets in question, see Voprosy istorii, 'Vlast' i intelligentsiya', 112.

[100] GARF, f. 8131, op. 31, d. 73957, l. 49. The KGB reports do not specify what was in this 'harmful information' though it seems likely that it was the same information on the 'anti-Party group' that was subsequently passed to the Frenchman Lerasno.

[101] GARF, f. 8131, op. 31, d. 79866, ll. 1–110.

[102] Mark Gol'dman also suggested that a number of stool pigeons had managed to penetrate the group as more and more people showed an interest in their theses and leaflets. S. Romanov, '"Ne etomu menya desyat' let v komsomole uchili!": interv'yu s M.S. Gol'dmanom', *Karta: rossiskii nezavisimyi istoricheskii i pravozashchitnyi zhurnal*, Nos. 17–18 (12.06.1997), 46–56.

[103] GARF, f. 8131, op. 31, d. 79865, ll. 1–34.

[104] In February 1958 Krasnopevtsev, Rendel and Men'shikov were sentenced to ten years, while Kozovoi, Semenenko and Cheshkov received seven-year sentences. Gol'dman, Obushenkov and Pokrovskii each received six-year terms.

Friends' or 'From and To') came together towards the end of 1956.[105] A programme was drawn up by three friends, I.R.Gitman, A.Ya. Sadamovskii and V.S. Smyslov, and was circulated around a number of higher-education institutes in the city, quickly drawing the confirmed support of twenty-three local students and the sympathy of many others, according to a report written by the Department of Sciences, Schools and Culture at the end of December.

Unlike those of many of their contemporaries, the group's 'platform' actually called for the break-up of the USSR's fifteen union republics – through peaceful, electoral means rather than violent revolution – yet it still bore the imprint of recognisably socialist thinking. It rejected Marxism, but only in favour of the Populist socialism of Petr Lavrov. It called for the peasantry to be given a free choice between collective or private agriculture and demanded a system of workers' control over factories based on the Yugoslav model. The three founders of the group awarded themselves the distinctly important sounding but faintly ridiculous roles of 'Chairman of the Department of Propaganda', 'Chairman of the Department of Provocation' and 'Chairman of the Department of Ideology'. Aside from the seeming delusions of grandeur, one's eye is immediately drawn to the fact that the trio considered these three tasks (propaganda, provocation and ideology) to be the most vital aspects of their work as a group: this was presumably a reflection of the extent to which the only substantial model that such groups had on which to base their ideas about 'the underground' came from propaganda about the pre-revolutionary Bolsheviks.

By the second half of the Khrushchev period, underground groups would increasingly speak of violence and revolution, but that was rarely the case in the mid to late 1950s. Maurice Hindus made this point best when, after his visit to Russia in 1957, he concluded that 'The intellectual underground into which the student or any inquiring youth moves produces only talk; protests, parodies, anecdotes, songs for the relief of his frustration; it hides no guns, manufactures no bombs.'[106] Of course, the authorities were unwilling to tolerate even that degree of political non-conformity. In fact, as Hindus travelled around the USSR, the response to the regime's domestic critics was already under way.

---

[105] See Voprosy istorii, 'Studencheskoe brozhenie'. The KGB surmised that 'from and to' was shorthand for 'from communism to capitalism'.
[106] M. Hindus, *House without a Roof*, p. 383.

CHAPTER 4

Turning back the tide: the clampdown on dissent

By November 1956 a meeting of the Central Committee Presidium saw the Party leadership taking an increasingly aggressive tone toward 'unhealthy elements' within Soviet society. The letters sent out to Party organisations earlier that year had begun to stem the tide of criticism within the CPSU and Komsomol, yet a considerable volume of dissent remained outside of these two bodies. Simply restoring discipline among communists was clearly not going to be enough to safeguard social stability in the longer term. The sense of confusion and the relative lenience of responses to criticism in the spring and summer of 1956 were soon to be replaced by a major clampdown that would firmly re-establish the regime's prerogative to punish dissent. As Elena Papovyan has noted: 'for people who are not normally interested in the subject, repression in the second half of the 1950s causes amazement'.[1] In fact, a total of 3,764 citizens were convicted of anti-Soviet activity between the end of 1956 and 1958: a figure comfortably exceeding that of any subsequent period during the entire post-Stalin era. This was to mark a key turning point in efforts to establish a more effective system of social control without recourse to terror.

On 10 November, *Pravda* published a speech that Khrushchev had delivered to a hall full of Komsomol members in which he explicitly linked the rebellious mood of Soviet students with the troubles in Hungary, a theme that was soon to become central to the policing of dissent.[2] With a major uprising in Berlin only three years previously, and disturbances in Poland preceding those in Hungary, the Eastern bloc was enduring its most tumultuous period prior to the late 1980s. Stalin's desired 'buffer zone'

---

[1] E. Papovyan, 'Primenenie stat'i 58-10 UK RSFSR v 1957–1958 gg. po materialam Verkhovnogo Suda SSSR i Prokuratury SSSR v GARF', in L. Eremina and E. Zhemkova eds., *Korni travy: sbornik statei molodykh istorikov*, Moskva: Zven'ya, 1996, p. 73.

[2] *Pravda*, 10 November 1956.

against the West was seemingly threatening to become a major source of instability.

With the Party leadership fully conscious of social and political ferment within the USSR, numerous sources have shown that they feared events in Hungary could spill over into neighbouring countries and ultimately into the Soviet Union, potentially unravelling the entire socialist bloc.[3] This judgement of the situation was perhaps a little far-fetched but not wholly unrealistic. When one considers the lack of popular legitimacy that the Eastern European regimes generally enjoyed, and the way that events in one country impacted on the next as the whole system began to collapse at the end of the 1980s, there is some justification for this assessment. As Amir Weiner has shown, the situation in Hungary had quickly begun to provoke considerable nationalist unrest in the USSR's western borderlands in particular.[4]

Events in Hungary ultimately left a distinct mark on the Khrushchev regime. It did not help Khrushchev's personal authority within the leadership that the Secret Speech had been a significant factor in rousing the hopes that had helped trigger the uprisings in both Poland and Hungary. Several of those who worked either within or around the political elite during the period subsequently left recollections suggesting that Khrushchev developed a kind of 'Hungary complex' after seeing the rapidity at which the situation had spun out of control in Budapest during autumn 1956.[5] Khrushchev's own memoirs offer only a brief hint at this 'complex' but do indicate a deep sense of strategic concern when he wrote that '... if NATO had penetrated through Hungary into the midst of the socialist bloc, things would turn hard for all of us'.[6] With the aftermath of the Secret Speech still so fresh in the memory, Communist Party functionaries around the country were also in a state of some considerable agitation and panic at this time.[7] Indeed, it would be surprising if they had not been at least a little concerned at the way events were unfolding in Hungary, since communists

---

[3] See, for example, M. Kramer, 'The Soviet Union and the 1956 Crises in Hungary and Poland: Reassessments and New Findings', *Journal of Contemporary History*, Vol. 33, No. 2 (April 1998), 192, and C. Gati, *Failed Illusions: Moscow, Washington, Budapest, and the 1956 Hungarian Revolt*, Stanford University Press, 2006.

[4] See A. Weiner, 'The Empires Pay a Visit: Gulag Returnees, East European Rebellions, and Soviet Frontier Politics', *The Journal of Modern History*, Vol. 78, No. 2 (June 2006), 333–76.

[5] See, for example, F. Burlatsky, *Khrushchev and the First Russian Spring: The Era of Khrushchev through the Eyes of his Adviser*, London: Weidenfeld & Nicolson, 1991.

[6] S. Khrushchev ed., *Memoirs of Nikita Khrushchev*, Vol. 3: *Statesman: 1953–1964*, University Park, PA: Pennsylvania State University Press, 2007, p. 650.

[7] E. Zubkova, *Obshchestvo i reformy 1945–1964*, Moskva: Izdatel'skii tsentr 'Rossiya molodaya', 1993, p. 153.

and members of the Hungarian security services were being physically attacked and even killed in the streets by protesters. One did not have to be a Stalinist to perceive that this was a distinctly dangerous moment for the established order of things inside the Soviet bloc.

Uncertain as to how best to proceed, Khrushchev despatched several members of the Central Committee Presidium to Budapest in order to assess the situation there. It was not without significance that the Party's chief ideologist, and perhaps its most unreformed Stalinist, Mikhail Suslov, had been one of the emissaries whom Khrushchev sent to Budapest during the rising, where he was apparently absolutely horrified by the chaos and anti-communist sentiment that he witnessed.[8] Presiding KGB chairman Ivan Serov was also sent to Hungary for a time during the rising and took a particularly hawkish line in pushing for military action.[9] Two of the most powerful members of the Soviet leadership, therefore, had direct experience of seeing a communist regime on the edge of collapse, and quite predictably pushed to redouble efforts against dissent inside the Soviet Union.

As subsequent developments showed, while there were differences of opinion within the Party leadership on any number of issues, including on whether to send Soviet troops into Hungary, by late 1956 there was undoubtedly a growing consensus among the Central Committee Presidium that dissent had to be reined in at home. After all, the Soviet Union had ultimately been able to maintain its Hungarian ally only by force of arms, and no power would be either willing or able to prop up Khrushchev's regime if a similar situation were to arise inside the USSR, a fact that the Party leadership would have been entirely aware of. Even though the communist system in the USSR had taken far deeper roots than its counterparts in the Eastern bloc, and the atmosphere at home was hardly revolutionary, there were still myriad grievances – such as those of Gulag returnees and of nationalists in the non-Russian republics – which existed close to the surface and gave the authorities little margin for error when it came to policing society at this point in time. Events following the XX Congress (both the discussions of the Secret Speech and responses to the Hungarian

---

[8] V. Sebestyen, *Twelve Days: Revolution 1956*, London: Weidenfeld & Nicolson, 2006, p. 121. Although not a major figure in the struggle against dissent during the Khrushchev years, it is also noteworthy that Yuri Andropov, the future KGB chairman who would go on to lead the fight against dissidents for a decade and a half, was the Soviet ambassador in Hungary at that time and apparently resurrected an ailing career through his deft handling of the uprising there. See V. Solovyov and E. Klepikova, *Andropov: A Secret Passage into the Kremlin*, London: Macmillan, 1983.

[9] Nikita Petrov has shown that the hawkish Serov had been one of the loudest voices demanding Soviet action in Hungary. Whilst in the country he had also led the arrest of a Hungarian negotiating party. N. Petrov, *Ivan Serov: pervyi predsedatel' KGB*, Moskva: Materik, 2005, p. 171.

rising) had already shown that the abandonment of widespread state violence had not yet yielded a system that could be guaranteed to maintain mass conformism. When combined with fears over events in Hungary potentially spreading to the USSR, the result was a distinct hardening in the authorities' responses toward dissent.

The form that this 'hardening' took was a major campaign of legal repression against dissenters. It was initiated by a secret letter sent out from the Central Committee to all Communist Party organisations on 19 December 1956, entitled 'On the Strengthening of the Political Work of Party Organisations among the Masses and the Suppression of Attacks by Anti-Soviet Enemy Elements'.[10] The KGB's own internal history textbook, written two decades subsequently, stated simply that 'the December letter began a merciless campaign against anti-Soviet elements'.[11] Boris Firsov has quite rightly argued that this was one of the key moments of later Soviet history.[12] Nikolai Obushenkov – a member of the Krasnopevtsev group discussed in the previous chapter – simply recalled how '. . . it was obvious that 19 December 1956 was the end of the Thaw. It meant that all hopes for renewal from above, henceforth and for a long time, were groundless, that the only possibility in the battle for renewal was illegal activity.'[13]

The immediate roots of the clampdown can be traced back to 10 November, when the Presidium requested that Nikolai Belyaev, Ekaterina Furtseva, Petr Pospelov, Petr Ivashutin and Roman Rudenko formulate another Party letter to help combat the rising tide of dissent.[14] On 21 November the commission reported back to the Presidium with its recommendations, but their draft letter was deemed unsatisfactory.[15] The records of a Central Committee Presidium session held on 6 December show the subject of dissent was again included on the agenda, with the aim of producing a draft letter to be sent out to Party organisations, KGB branches and regional procurators.[16] All of the top leadership were present

---

[10] RGANI, f. 89, op. 6, d. 2, ll. 1–15.

[11] V. Chebrikov et al., *Istoriya sovetskikh organov gosudarstvennoi bezopasnosti: uchebnik*, Moskva: Vysshaya krasnoznamenskaya shkola komiteta gosudarstvennoi bezopasnosti pri sovete ministerov SSSR, 1977, p. 527.

[12] B. Firsov, *Raznomyslie v SSSR 1940–1960 gody: istoriya, teoriya i praktika*, Sankt Peterburg: Izdatel'stvo Evropeiskogo universiteta v Sankt Peterburge, 2008, p. 261.

[13] Voprosy istorii, 'Vlast' i intelligentsiya: "delo" molodykh istorikov (1957–1958.)', *Voprosy istorii*, No. 004 (1994), 120.

[14] Leonid Brezhnev was also added to the commission at some point between 6 November and 21 November. Serov and Rudenko took the lead role in compiling the draft.

[15] N. Petrov, *Ivan Serov*, p. 170.

[16] GARF, f. 3, op. 12, d. 1006, in A. Fursenko et al. eds., *Prezidium TsK KPSS 1954–1964*, Tom 1: *Chernovye protokol'nye zapisi zasedanii stenogrammy*, Moskva: Rosspen, 2004.

at the session, including Khrushchev, Nikolai Bulganin, Lazar Kaganovich, Georgy Malenkov, Anastas Mikoyan, Vyacheslav Molotov, Kliment Voroshilov, Maksim Saburov, Mikhail Pervukhin and Georgy Zhukov.

The principal question on the agenda at the 6 December meeting was 'What should be done about anti-Soviets (*antisovetchiki*)?' The minutes of the session show that Malenkov proposed the strengthening of Party discipline; Molotov spoke of the need to improve propaganda and overcome shortages; Mikoyan emphasised that the views of the Party must be more clearly presented to the people; and Khrushchev proposed increased monitoring of potentially hostile elements, especially those who had recently been released from the camps, and particularly Trotskyites.[17] Clearly, there was consensus that the threat of rising unrest had to be dealt with. Indeed, even though the members of the Presidium were bitterly divided on a range of other matters – and several of those present would attempt to oust Khrushchev as First Secretary several months later – the session in question was surprisingly united.[18]

From his vacillating over the question of employing the army in response to events in Hungary, as well as his undoubted bravery in taking the lead on exposing Stalin's crimes at the XX Congress, we can be reasonably certain that Khrushchev was not by nature a leader inclined toward despotic repression. Nonetheless, as and when the question of domestic stability arose he consistently came down on the side of those who would brook no talk of compromise. In fact, of all the comments at the 6 December session, Khrushchev's were by far the most illiberal in tone and also the most disingenuous, since he had played a major role in bringing about the releases of those whom he now warned against. Similarly, while certain tropes of dissenting behaviour may have had a ring of Trotskyism about them, such as denunciations of growing bureaucratism, there was no explicit trend of support for Stalin's former nemesis.

The opinions expressed at the 6 December session were passed down to a Central Committee commission for editing before being transformed into a confidential Party letter. The drafting commission was headed by Leonid Brezhnev and included, among others, Georgy Malenkov, Averkii Aristov, Nikolai Belyaev, Ivan Serov and Roman Rudenko.[19] They met on 14 December to 'exchange opinions' on the results of the Presidium session

---

[17] GARF, f. 3, op. 12, d. 1006, ll. 1–54, in A. Fursenko et al. eds., *Prezidium TsK KPSS*, Tom I.

[18] See D. Watson, *Molotov: A Biography*, Basingstoke: Palgrave Macmillan, 2005, p. 259.

[19] RGANI, f. 89, op. 6, d. 1, ll. 1–15. At the time of the redrafting these men occupied positions of Central Committee secretary, deputy chairman of the Council of Ministers, two further Central Committee secretaries, chairman of the KGB and head of the Procuracy respectively.

and to compose the final letter that was to be sent out to all Party organisations.[20] By 19 December a new draft had been prepared and was sent back to the Presidium for final approval before being circulated to Party and state organisations all across the country. In terms of the authorities' changing methods of social control, this was an absolutely key period. The Party and Komsomol were steadily being brought back into line following the XX Congress, and now came the turn of society at large.

In its very earliest lines the Party letter asserted that the 'present harmful atmosphere' in the USSR was a product of events taking place elsewhere, particularly in Hungary, where the imperialist powers had increased their efforts to undermine the socialist camp. The ultimate goal of the West, according to the letter, was the forcible restoration of capitalism across Eastern Europe and the Soviet Union.[21] The letter went on to upbraid local Party organisations for allowing criticism to go without a decisive and timely response, and it again stated that bourgeois elements were attempting to 'hijack' the struggle with the Cult of Personality for their own ends. It then flagged up the challenge posed by 'so-called neo-Bolsheviks' and insisted that they must not be mistaken for political allies – a sure enough sign of the potential threat their accusations and demands posed for the official public sphere. The real crux of the document, however, could be found in the statement which simply declared: 'in the struggle against anti-Soviet elements we must be strong and unrelenting', demanding that all communists actively fight to defend the Soviet system against critics.[22]

It is not too hard to see why the KGB interpreted this as signalling a 'merciless' struggle against dissenters, even though such remarks were actually tempered somewhat in the letter. Only a few lines below the exhortation to be 'strong and unrelenting' toward anti-Soviet elements, a cautionary note was included, stating that 'we have to work on people who are being influenced by foreign propaganda. They should not be automatically considered enemy elements.'[23] This acceptance that critics were not necessarily enemies represented a major break with the doctrine of the recent past but it also sent out conflicting signals to those who were expected to do the policing at ground level. As it turned out, however, this particular recommendation went largely unheeded over the next eighteen months.

---

[20] RGANI, f. 3, op.14, d. 83, ll. 1–2, in A. Fursenko et al. eds., *Prezidium TsK KPSS*, Tom 1.
[21] RGANI, f. 89, op. 6, d. 2, ll. 1–5.   [22] RGANI, f. 89, op. 6, d. 2, l. 12.
[23] RGANI, f. 89, op. 6, d. 2, l. 12.

Although the Soviet authorities were at least partly correct to see outside
involvement in certain instances of unrest across the socialist camp (such as
Radio Free Europe's explicit encouragement of the Hungarian rising), they
consistently overstated the problem and, therefore, misjudged the nature of
most political criticism, seeing a treasonous influence that simply was not
there.[24] However, one can see where the assumption of a link between foreign
subversive activity and domestic dissent came from. The Eisenhower regime
in the US was speaking of pursuing a policy of 'rolling back' communism, and
helping to topple numerous regimes across Latin America in particular.
Rumours abounded inside the USSR that the CIA had allocated millions of
dollars to fund opposition groups throughout the Soviet Union.[25] No solid
evidence has yet appeared to corroborate this rumour but when one considers
the international climate of the time, it would be foolhardy to dismiss it
entirely: both in the West and the East, huge amounts of resources were being
invested in attempts to undermine the Cold-War enemy.

Once the new line on responding to critics had been set out in the
December letter, things began to move quickly. A telegram sent by the US
ambassador in Moscow, Charles 'Chip' Bohlen, to the Department of State
on 19 December indicated that a tightening of discipline had already begun,
even before the letter had chance to circulate. He wrote that: 'It is obvious
from the quantity of press treatment and from the geographically widespread discussion of shortcomings in ideological work that a campaign has
been inaugurated to eliminate manifestations of undesirable tendencies
among [the] population.'[26] The following month, a *Pravda* editorial
brought the key themes of the letter into the public domain, demanding
that individuals do more to defend the system against its critics and admitting that even communists were behaving incorrectly on occasion.[27] This
demand for ordinary citizens to be more active in helping the authorities
fight 'undesirable behaviour' was to become one of the hallmarks of policing
from the late 1950s onwards.

---

[24] In fact, the ethical questions that were raised by Radio Free Europe's role in the rising proved to be
far-reaching, since the CIA supervised the output of the station and had arguably provoked further
death and destruction in Hungary by urging the rebels on even though they had no intention of doing
anything concrete to help their cause. One of the most immediate results of this was that Radio Free
Europe's sister station which broadcast to the USSR changed its name from Radio Liberation to
Radio Liberty, thus striking a slightly less militant tone. See V. Petrov, 'Radio Liberation', *Russian
Review*, Vol. 17, No. 2 (April 1958), 106.

[25] See R. Pimenov, *Vospominaniya*, Moskva: Informatsionno-ekspertnaya gruppa 'Panorama', 1996,
p. 72.

[26] Telegram from Charles Bohlen to US Secretary of State, 19 December 1956. Budapest, HU OSA 299.

[27] *Pravda*, 29 January 1957.

Unsurprisingly, the relative cultural liberalisation that taken place earlier in 1956 was quickly halted and remained stalled for some time thereafter. The link between non-conformist cultural activity and burgeoning political dissent had been quite clear for all to see in Hungary. Khrushchev was even reported to have remarked years later that 'If ten or so Hungarian writers had been shot at the right moment, the revolution there would never have occurred.'[28] No Soviet authors were shot or even imprisoned, but they did find their wings clipped. Dudintsev's *Not by Bread Alone* was attacked in the December letter. Its author fell into long-term disfavour and Konstantin Simonov, the editor of *Novy mir*, was subsequently removed from his post.[29] At the end of December, the Department of Culture held a meeting in Moscow to familiarise prominent non-Party writers with the contents of the December letter, stating that it contained 'important directions for the work of writers and the press'.[30] Among the twenty-one authors present at the meeting were major names such as Il'ya Ehrenburg, Konstantin Chukovskii, Konstantin Fedin and Samuil Marshak. In short, the conservative turn in policy was to apply across the board.

Although the Central Committee Presidium had dictated the outlines for the ensuing clampdown on dissent, responsibility for its implementation was placed squarely with local officials. Correctly perceiving that they had not only been shown the green light to take measures against critics but also that there would be negative consequences for themselves if they did not do so, local police and courts began to act. The uncertainty of the spring was quite clearly over. As Boris Firsov described: '. . . the call was heard. All the links of the Party and state apparatus began to move and to respond, just like in the old days.'[31] Within only a few weeks, the number of individuals sentenced for dissent began to rocket.[32] In truth, the campaign that followed was nowhere near the scale of arbitrariness and severity of the 'old days': compared with the number of convictions for counter-revolutionary activity at almost any point under Stalin, the 1,964 political convictions

[28] V. Sebestyen, *Twelve Days*, p. 81.
[29] There is, however, some debate as to whether Simonov was sacked as a direct result of publishing *Not by Bread Alone*, not least because his removal saw the more liberal Aleksandr Tvardovsky reinstated as editor of *Novy mir*. See E. Rogovin-Frankel, *Novy Mir: A Case Study in the Politics of Literature, 1952–1958*, Cambridge University Press, 1981, p. 107.
[30] RGANI, f. 89, op. 17, d. 77, l. 22.   [31] B. Firsov, *Raznomyslie*, p. 261.
[32] Surviving records (which constitute around two-thirds of the original total for 1957) show only twelve convictions under article 58-10 in November 1956. This jumped to fifty-four during February 1957 and then to 134 by April and thereafter stayed around that monthly level for much of the next year. See V. Kozlov and S. Mironenko eds., *58-10 Nadzornye proizvodstva prokuratury SSSR po delam ob antisovetskoi agitatsii i propaganda: annotirovannyi katalog Mart 1953–1991*, Moskva: Mezhdunarodnyi Fond 'Demokratiya', 1999.

Table 4.1 *Annual sentences for anti-Soviet activity and
propaganda (article 58-10), 1956–64*

Year	Annual sentences	Proportion of all 58-10 sentences during the Khrushchev period
1956	384	6.7%
1957	1,964	34.3%
1958	1,416	24.7%
1959	750	13.1%
1960	162	2.8%
1961	207	3.6%
1962	323	5.6%
1963	341	6%
1964	181	3.2%
Total	5,728	100%

Source: Confidential communiqué from KGB chairman Viktor Chebrikov to CPSU General Secretary Mikhail Gorbachev in 1987, in *Istochnik*, No. 6 (1995), 153.

handed down in 1957 was a mere fraction. Nonetheless, judged by standards other than that of the Stalin era this was undeniably a period of extensive political repression and one that cannot easily be reconciled with the notion of 'thaw'.

Table 4.1 shows the number of Soviet citizens jailed for anti-Soviet activity across the entire Khrushchev period. The surge of convictions during 1957 and 1958 is particularly noticeable. As Fedor Burlatsky subsequently recalled in his *glasnost'*-era memoir, 'Later I learned that under Khrushchev many hundreds of people had suffered for so-called political crimes, that is, for voicing disagreement with his policies. Brezhnev developed this practice on a massive scale and with even greater deceit, but it must be acknowledged that it began under Khrushchev.'[33] The idea that there were no political prisoners in the Khrushchev years, at which Burlatsky hints, seems to have been reasonably widespread, both at the time and for years after.[34] The reality was very different. One would certainly not deny that policy against dissent became even more cynical during the Brezhnev era. However, the practice of jailing critics not only existed under Khrushchev but was actually much more

[33] F. Burlatsky, *Khrushchev and the First Russian Spring*, p. 97.
[34] See, for example, L. Alexeyeva and P. Goldberg, *The Thaw Generation: Coming of Age in the Post-Stalin Era*, Boston, MA: Little, Brown and Company, 1990, p. 139; A. Solzhenitsyn, *The Gulag Archipelago*, Vol. 3, London: Collins/Fontana, 1978, p. 476.

prevalent during his time as First Secretary – a fact that has not yet been fully assimilated into the literature either on Soviet dissent or on Khrushchev-era political affairs.

The statistics on sentences for anti-Soviet activity (Table 4.1) not only include those who were jailed for political dissent but also feature people convicted for nationalist and religious activity, since all came under the same article of the criminal code. However, case files from 1957 and 1958 show that the overwhelming majority of convictions during the period in question were for acts that can be considered 'political dissent'. In fact, the three different genres of dissenting behaviour were rarely targeted concurrently by the Soviet authorities, either under Khrushchev or Brezhnev. In managing heightened nationalist unrest in the western border regions around the same time, the authorities proved far less quick to resort to custodial sentencing and instead made much more of an effort to temper dissenting behaviour by other means, such as communal policing and co-opting returnees wherever possible. Amir Weiner was absolutely correct to view these borderlands as a kind of 'testing zone', where new processes of maintaining social order without recourse to widespread imprisonment were being tried out and modified before being applied across the USSR more widely.[35]

Unlike the better-known government campaigns of the era, such as those against parasitism and hooliganism (both being many times greater in terms of the number of people who were arrested, though also much less severe in terms of punishment handed down), increased legal repression against dissenters was conducted without any significant mobilisation of the public at large. Nonetheless, the authorities did not want the crackdown to go unnoticed. In this they were successful. Zinaida Schakovsky, for example, wrote of her visit to the USSR in 1957 that 'from reading Soviet newspapers you might get the impression that the only crimes Soviet citizens commit are crimes against the state . . .'[36] This crackdown and accompanying media coverage were intended not only to remove from wider society those engaging in protest and criticism but, perhaps more importantly, they were to send a signal to the population at large, reasserting both the bounds of permissible behaviour and the determination of the security organs to take on those who spoke out.

---

[35] It is also worth pointing out that many of the released nationalists whom Weiner discusses were far more hostile toward the Soviet regime than most of the 'politicals' who were rounded up during the on-going campaign. See A. Weiner, 'The Empires Pay a Visit'.

[36] Z. Schakovsky, *The Privilege Was Mine*, London: Jonathan Cape, 1959, p. 45. For purposes of context it is worth recalling that the regime generally chose to downplay the level of criminal activity around the country.

By providing only a rudimentary outline of what now constituted anti-Soviet behaviour in the new era of 'socialist legality', the drive against dissent saw a significant degree of unpredictability and arbitrariness return to the Soviet law-enforcement apparatus.[37] The provincial officials charged with conducting the clampdown were often poorly educated and insufficiently trained, as well as eager to appear vigilant after the problems that had followed the Secret Speech. This in itself was a cause of considerable inconsistency and one of the reasons why the December letter spawned so many jail sentences.[38] Local procurators and KGB branches frequently erred on what they saw as the side of caution and employed article 58-10 in a wide-ranging and at times wholly unsuitable fashion. As a subsequent review of convictions during the period noted, there were many cases where citizens were unjustly jailed for private conversations or for telling jokes, as well as instances of officials pursuing vendettas against individuals on the basis of personal animosities, and cases of entirely permissible letters of complaint about issues like poor housing conditions or financial difficulties leading to prosecution for anti-Soviet activity.[39]

The fact that the clampdown on dissent progressed throughout 1957 and beyond raises the point that this hard line toward critics was clearly not something that had been forced upon Khrushchev by Stalinists in the leadership: the most influential among them had been removed after unsuccessfully trying to oust him as First Secretary in June 1957, yet the crackdown continued unabated for another year afterward. Though it may not have been his default option, Khrushchev was quite prepared to backtrack a little on his promises of socialist legality as and when circumstances dictated. As Philip Boobbyer has pointed out, Khrushchev 'endorsed the Leninist moral position that there should be one system of ethics for a time of revolutionary transition, and another for after the enemy has been defeated'.[40] Reading 'time of transition' as 'period of heightened tension', there would be no compunction at expanding the bounds of what should be considered anti-Soviet during times of perceived or potential crisis.[41] Mistakes could always be rectified later, if need be. In fact, quite a few of

[37] As Brian LaPierre has shown, this was also the case with the Khrushchev-era campaign against petty hooliganism. See B. LaPierre, 'Making Hooliganism on a Mass Scale: The Campaign against Petty Hooliganism in the Soviet Union, 1953–64', *Cahiers du Monde russe*, Vol. 47, No. 1–2 (janvier–juin 2006), 349–75.
[38] E. Papovyan and A. Papovyan, 'Uchastie verkhovnogo suda SSSR v vyrabotke repressivnoi politiki, 1957–1958', in L. Eremina and E. Zhemkova eds., *Korni travy*, p. 86.
[39] GARF, f. 8131, op. 32, d. 5080, ll. 30–5.
[40] P. Boobbyer, *Conscience, Dissent and Reform in Soviet Russia*, London: Routledge, 2005, p. 62.
[41] This consistently proved to be the case, with raised tensions in Cold-War confrontations often going hand in hand with a more hard-line approach to dissenters.

those who were jailed during the clampdown would later have their sentences reclassified or else overturned, though this would have to wait until the rebellious atmosphere of late 1956 and 1957 had fully subsided.

Most notable was the sheer volume of those convicted as a result of apparently isolated, and often drunken, public outbursts: around 50% of all political sentences during the clampdown. A number of instances have already been cited when individuals found themselves arrested and jailed for anti-Soviet behaviour after drunkenly calling members of the militia 'fascists' or shouting slogans such as 'Long live Eisenhower'. Numerous underground groups, such as those of Pimenov and Krasnopevtsev, and anonymous letter-writers were also jailed at this time, yet the authorities largely declined to make a distinction between this kind of purposive and deliberate protest behaviour and spontaneous drunken outbursts. It seems that this failure to distinguish hooligan-type dissent from what we might call 'consciously political' protest activity was primarily about ensuring continued state domination of the public sphere.

As a subsequent review of convictions for dissenting behaviour noted, 'cases of anti-Soviet activity are important not just for individual reasons but for the atmosphere and conditions they create'.[42] Though they may not have reflected any real deep-seated opposition to the Soviet system, outbursts such as 'Long live Eisenhower' were nonetheless unacceptable for a regime that placed such value on its ability to control the flow of information and to dictate public discourse. At times of increased international tension, the authorities placed ever greater emphasis on liquidating challenges to their dominance of the public sphere. At other times, such statements might be classed as hooligan behaviour (which drew a markedly less severe response), but in the wake of the Hungarian rising they were seen as politically dangerous. This was not only a reflection of a deeply intolerant ideological outlook. Close control of the public sphere was absolutely vital to the wider goals of the Soviet project. Thus, encroachment upon that control was, to the eyes of the authorities at least, genuinely subversive.

The arrests continued. During the course of 1957, students began appearing in camps in growing numbers.[43] When Boris Vail' was sent to a labour camp in Siberia for his part in the Pimenov group, he came across fellow student-dissenters from Alma-Ata, Barnaul, Sverdlovsk and elsewhere.[44] As

[42] GARF, f. 8131, op. 32, d. 5080, l. 19.
[43] See K. Smith, 'A New Generation of Political Prisoners: "Anti-Soviet" Students, 1956–1957', *The Soviet and Post-Soviet Review*, Vol. 32, Nos. 2–3 (2005), 191–208.
[44] B. Vail', *Osobo opasnyi*, London: Overseas Publications Interchange, 1980, p. 235.

stated in the preceding chapter, often people such as these were not necessarily conscious opponents of the Soviet regime but frustrated communists who desired liberalisation and a more thorough-going revival of Party and Komsomol life. More often than not, imprisonment did not just fail to 'correct' these sentiments but actually caused that sense of frustration to harden. Repression, therefore, could often be counter-productive in the longer term. Tatyana Verblovskaya later wrote of her own arrest and sentencing as part of the group formed by Pimenov and Vail': 'to this day I never cease to wonder why they needed to turn a quiet, even somewhat shy, law-abiding young woman ... into an especially dangerous criminal, who had threatened the socialist system'.[45] In later years, the authorities would reach broadly the same view as Verblovskaya – and generally avoided use of custodial sentences for most first-time dissenters – though not before a great many others had found themselves in the same position as she did.

The number of expulsions from the Communist Party also rose again for the first time in many years. The total annual rate of expulsions rose only a little, from 35,058 in 1956 to 36,222 in 1957, but this anyway marked a reversal of several years of steep decline in the total number of expulsions.[46] Data on appeals against expulsion from the Party showed an increase in offences related to dissenting behaviour. Where there had been 306 appeals against expulsions for 'anti-Party discussions' in 1956 (of which ninety-one were subsequently upheld on appeal), there were 368 in 1957 (with 197 upheld). While 154 Party members appealed against expulsion for 'participation in anti-Party groups' in 1956, that figure rose to 229 in 1957 (of which sixty-five and 166 respectively were upheld).[47] Moscow *oblast'* and Moscow city CPSU organisations had eighty-seven and seventy-nine members expelled as unfit communists in 1957. In Sverdlovsk, Perm and Novosibirsk there were 115, 118 and 129 members expelled on the same grounds respectively. Chelyabinsk, Gorky, Kemerova, Krasnodar, Stavropol and Tula all ejected at least fifty members as 'undeserving of the title "communist"'.[48]

When broken down into categories such as geographical location and education level of offenders, convictions under article 58-10 reveal a number

---

[45] K. Smith, 'A New Generation of Political Prisoners', p. 207.

[46] E. Cohn, 'Disciplining the Party: The Expulsion and Censure of Communists in the Post-War Soviet Union, 1945–1961', Ph.D. Dissertation, University of Chicago, 2007, p. 58.

[47] E. Kulavig, *Dissent in the Years of Khrushchev: Nine Stories about Disobedient Russians*, Basingstoke: Palgrave Macmillan, 2002, p. 88–9. It is worth noting here that the proportion of expulsions subsequently upheld on appeal had also grown between 1956 and 1957.

[48] RGANI, f. 6, op. 6, d. 1100, ll. 1–10.

of interesting trends. In the first instance, records suggest that political dissent was an overwhelmingly urban phenomenon. While numerous socio-political factors, such as higher levels of education, closer proximity to political power and greater population density, indicate that urban dwellers are generally the more likely to engage in acts of political protest, it is also necessary to raise the point that these figures tell us about the number of people who were punished for dissent, rather than actual levels of dissenting activity around the country. With far fewer resources for policing located in the countryside, some forms of dissent (such as public outbursts in particular) in rural areas were less likely to draw official attention and be acted upon by the authorities. As such, one might well refer to rural dissent as a 'known unknown', for the historian and perhaps also for the Soviet authorities at the time.

Although statistics on the subject are incomplete, surviving records show that 476 of those convicted in 1957 were classified as having attained only 'lower'-level education – meaning anything from illiteracy up to several classes of elementary schooling – compared to almost 150 who were recorded as having undergone some form of higher education.[49] A large numerical majority of those jailed as 'anti-Soviets' at this point, therefore, had little or no formal education, a stark contrast with the overwhelmingly intelligentsia-based Brezhnev-era human-rights movements. To some extent this reflected the imprecise nature of the clampdown as much as it did the nature of dissenting activity. More importantly, data from the 1959 census shows that less than 2% of the entire Soviet population had actually undergone higher education at that point, indicating that although they were numerically less prevalent among victims of political repression, the most educated people were actually considerably over-represented as a proportion of those jailed for dissent at this point.[50] The traditional view of dissent as a primarily intelligentsia-based social phenomenon, therefore, requires some refining but is by no means entirely without validity.

Another noteworthy aspect of the drive against dissenters was the way that it was enacted across different parts of the USSR. Table 4.2 gives an indication of how matters played out in the individual union republics during 1957. The fact that the total number of sentences in 1957 provided by the Procurator's

---

[49] Unfortunately, the KGB proved less than meticulous at recording prisoners' education levels. Only around two-thirds of case files for individuals sentenced under article 58-10 give some basic data on educational achievement.

[50] See Tsentral'noe statisticheskoe upravlenie pri Sovete Ministrove SSSR, *Chislennost', sostav i razmeshchenie naseleniya SSSR: kratkie itogi vsesoyuznoi perepisi naseleniya 1959 goda*, Moskva: Gosstatizdat TsSU SSSR, 1961.

Table 4.2 *Sentences for anti-Soviet activity (article 58-10)*
by union republic in 1957

Union Republic	Total sentenced under article 58-10 in 1957	% of all 58-10 sentences in 1957	% of total Soviet population by union republic
Russia	957	53.3%	56.4%
Ukraine	443	24.7%	20.5%
Belarus	65	3.6%	3.8%
Moldova	27	1.5%	1.3%
Latvia	43	2.4%	1%
Lithuania	68	3.8%	1.3%
Estonia	39	2.2%	0.6%
Georgia	25	1.4%	2.1%
Armenia	11	0.6%	0.9%
Azerbaidzhan	10	0.5%	1.6%
Turkmenistan	22	1.2%	0.7%
Kyrgyzstan	11	0.6%	1.1%
Uzbekistan	27	1.5%	3.4%
Kazakhstan	44	2.4%	4.3%
Tadzhikistan	4	0.2%	1%
Total	1,796	99.9%	100%

Sources: 1958 Procurator review. GARF, f. 8131, op. 32, d. 5080, l. 5. Population statistics taken from the 1959 census (Tsentral'noe statisticheskoe upravlenie pri Sovete Ministrove SSSR, *Chislennost', sostav i razmeshchenie naseleniya SSSR*).

office (1,796) does not quite tally with KGB data on convictions cited earlier in the present chapter firstly reflects that Soviet statistics can be incomplete and contradictory at times. This discrepancy most likely stemmed from the fact that many legal records were apparently lost during the numerous administrative reshuffles of the Khrushchev era.[51] Since the KGB figures cited earlier in the present chapter were compiled three decades later, they most likely incorporated data that was unavailable or missing at the time of the original Procurator review in 1958 and, therefore, are probably the more accurate of the two. Nonetheless, the different totals provided by the Procuracy (1,796) and KGB (1,964) are sufficiently close that some considerable faith can be placed in the general patterns they show.

As we can see from Table 4.2, this was undoubtedly an all-Union campaign, with every republic seeing some political repression. Most strikingly, the volume of sentences in each union republic tended to be roughly

[51] V. Kozlov and S. Mironenko eds., *58-10 Nadzornye proizvodstva*, p. 6.

equivalent to that republic's proportion of the overall Soviet population.[52] In subsequent years, the Central Asian republics in particular would be marked by especially low numbers of arrests for dissenting behaviour, making the figures for 1957 all the more interesting. For example, more Kazakhs were sentenced under article 58-10 in 1957 than during the rest of the entire Khrushchev period combined. This was also true for Tadzhiks, Uzbeks, Turkmen and Kyrgyz. With such contrasting figures, one must conclude that these differences were caused by pronounced changes in government policy, rather than changes in dissenting behaviour.

No evidence has come to light to suggest that individual union republics were given quotas for arrests and sentences in 1957, and such a move would have been entirely at odds with the general path of post-Stalin legal reforms. It seems much more likely that regional KGB departments and prosecutors felt that they had better demonstrate their vigilance and promptly jailed at least some citizens for even the mildest criticism. As the far bigger drives against parasitism and petty hooliganism showed, a campaign mentality could be quick to take hold, and signals emanating from the centre had to be seen to be being acted upon. All kinds of offences could be made to fit the priorities of the time: what was considered anti-Soviet activity in 1957 might just as easily be considered hooliganism in subsequent years, for example. As such, the data again tell us at least as much about the authorities' policing of dissent as they do about the actual volume or nature of protest and criticism around the country. It is certainly true that one could be jailed for something in 1957–8 that would not have attracted serious punishment at an earlier or later date, but it also seems fair to suggest that one could be jailed for something in Tashkent or Alma-Ata that would not have resulted in the same outcome in Leningrad or Moscow, and vice versa.

It is also interesting to look specifically at the number of CPSU and Komsomol members jailed during the clampdown. The available records for 1957 – a total of 1,250 out of 1,964 cases – show that ninety-nine full CPSU members and 100 Komsomol members were jailed for acts that can be categorised as political dissent. When one looks at the kinds of behaviour that they engaged in, there was a strong trend for convicted Party and Komsomol members to have been involved in anonymous, rather than open activity. Most commonly among CPSU members this meant

---

[52] Interestingly, Theresa Smith and Thomas Oleszczuk have pointed to a similar trend in the use of punitive psychiatry across the post-Stalin era as a whole. See Chapter 8 of the present work and T. Smith and T. Oleszczuk, *No Asylum: State Psychiatric Repression in the Former USSR*, London: Macmillan, 1996, p. 82.

individual acts of protest such as writing anti-Soviet letters and leaflets. Among jailed Komsomol members there was a more pronounced trend toward collective activity, such as the formation of underground groups. This was perhaps a reflection of the respective impacts of living through the worst of Stalinist rule and of coming to maturity once those most dangerous years of the Soviet system had passed, though one should probably also make allowance for youthful exuberance as a factor which disposed the young generation toward underground group activity. Few CPSU or Komsomol members were jailed as a result of drunken outbursts or public clashes with the militia, a trend which reflected the fact that members of the two groups mostly still saw themselves as the vanguard of the Soviet system, standing apart from the 'rabble' that vented their anger in the streets and keen to retain the material and social status attached to the role of card-carrying communists.[53]

Party and Komsomol members also had some considerable success in evading custodial punishment for acts of dissent. Erik Kulavig has produced figures from the Party Control Commission showing that in 1957 a total of 166 CPSU members appealed against expulsion from the Party on the grounds of 'participation in anti-Party groups' and a further 197 appealed against expulsion for 'anti-Party discussions', figures that far exceeded the number of communists who were jailed that year.[54] This discrepancy was to some extent a result of the fact that Party organisations sometimes proved successful at protecting their members from punishment through the courts by a series of interminable delaying tactics, something that prompted legal officials to complain about there effectively being separate laws for communists and non-communists.[55] Eventually the Central Committee Presidium intervened to put a stop to this practice in December 1962, when it issued the resolution 'On Eliminating Mistakes and Deficiencies in the Practice of Sentencing Communists who have Committed Crimes', insisting that Party organisations cease trying to shelter their members from the law.

Because these people were Party and Komsomol members – and therefore communists in name at least – the authorities could be less quick to jump to the conclusion that they were genuine enemies of the Soviet regime, especially

[53] As numerous scholars have pointed out, CPSU membership had come to carry considerable social prestige and material benefits by the late socialist stage of Soviet history.

[54] Furthermore, these statistics represented only the number of expulsions that were subsequently upheld on appeal. If we were to include data on those who appealed successfully against their expulsion on these grounds the figures would be 229 and 368 respectively. Some of those who were expelled did not appeal at all. Those imprisoned were automatically expelled from the Party. E. Kulavig, *Dissent in the Years of Khrushchev*, p. 88.

[55] See E. Cohn, 'Disciplining the Party', pp. 105–7.

after Khrushchev's criticism of intra-Party repressions under Stalin and the regime's general turn toward re-education rather than punishment. A second reason for the reduced likelihood of dissenting communists facing jail terms was that these were citizens over whom the authorities already had a wide variety of sanctions available. For example, one could punish a CPSU member with Party disciplinary procedures (which included ten separate levels of Party reprimand) or expulsion, with all the negative consequences that these entailed, as well as a jail sentence if need be.[56] For a non-Party member who engaged in dissent at this time there were fewer responses available other than dismissal from one's job or imprisonment. However, this was an age when workers were in both short supply and high demand, and were therefore in a strong position when it came to finding employment. As such, simply having a dissenting worker fired from his or her job would not have been a major sanction, since alternative employment could often easily be found.[57] Subsequent years would see all citizens subjected to a more diverse and effective range of practices relating to dissenting behaviour, encompassing both prevention and punishment.

The processes involved in prosecuting acts of dissent on a legal basis provide a useful example of the way that different elements of the law-enforcement apparatus functioned in tandem, and sometimes in friction, with one another. More often than not, where acts of dissent involved some kind of open public manifestation, such as drunken outbursts, it was the militia that were first to respond, since they were the regime's most numerous and most visible representatives at ground level. If deemed 'political', a case would usually be handed over to the KGB, who had complete jurisdiction in investigating matters concerning political crimes.

The security organs' investigation techniques had changed significantly since the Stalin era. These were not quite the same sadistic thugs of the 1930s and 1940s, many of whom had been removed from their posts (though not punished) since Stalin's death and Beria's downfall. After his arrest in 1957 Revolt Pimenov recalled that his interrogators were almost unfailingly polite, and at times obsequiously so.[58] This, though, was an indication that the KGB was becoming more shrewd and skilled in its work rather than more lenient in its attitudes. Many of those who experienced KGB inter-rogations later recalled having felt that things were going well and they

---

[56] On the range of Party reprimands see E. Cohn, 'Disciplining the Party', p. 66.
[57] On the growing social power of the working class, see M. Lewin, *The Soviet Century*, London: Verso, 2005, p. 172.
[58] R. Pimenov, *Vospominaniya*, p. 103.

actually had the better of their interlocutor, but then realised they had been out-foxed by an apparently sympathetic interrogator and had consequently given away far more incriminating evidence than they had at first realised.[59] In fact, the security organs adapted surprisingly well to post-Stalin conditions, both in evading proper procedure as and when it hampered them and in learning how to get results without reliance upon classically Stalinist methods. As Boris Vail' later noted, the KGB was developing a real mastery of human psychology.[60] Violence and torture had ceased to be staples of investigations, though they had by no means disappeared entirely. Pressure could also be brought to bear through threats to arrest suspects' friends or to have a loved one fired from their job or expelled from university. Those arrested as members of a group were fed misleading details about each other's testimony. Other methods could be even less sophisticated. Lev Krasnopevtsev recalled that after his arrest in August 1957 he was subjected to interrogation sessions that lasted far longer than the law permitted – sometimes up to seventeen hours. One of his fellow group-mates, N.G. Obushenkov, remembered being handed interrogation protocols to sign at the end of each session in which the answers he had given to various questions had been seriously misrepresented in the official record.[61]

Arrests and searches had to be sanctioned by the procurator of a given *oblast'*, and new laws guaranteed defendants access to a defence lawyer – albeit usually one with somewhat questionable dedication to their client's case – and demanded that convictions be based on evidence (whereas earlier one's social origins alone had been a sufficient basis for repression). Nonetheless, countless cases testified to the highly subjective nature of such 'evidence', especially when the offence in question carried political overtones. Indicative of the improved legal procedures that emerged following Stalin's death was the creation of the 'Department for the Supervision of KGB Investigations' in 1955, within the Procuracy.[62] Its task was primarily to ensure that these new legal safeguards against judicial abuse were being adhered to by the security organs. This new department was endowed with the authority to challenge evidence provided by the security organs and to call for cases to be overturned where inconsistencies and abuses or lack of proof were found, though there is little evidence to suggest that it did so at this particular time. Subsequent years would show that divisions and

---

[59] See, for example, P. Grigorenko, *Memoirs*, New York: W.W. Norton, 1982, p. 285.
[60] B. Vail', *Osobo opasnyi*, pp. 187–96.   [61] *Voprosy istorii*, 'Vlast' i intelligentsiya', p. 114.
[62] The Procurator's office was not only responsible for prosecuting crimes but also for supervising the observance of legality more generally – two clearly conflicting roles. See H. Berman, *Soviet Criminal Law and Procedure*, Cambridge, MA: Harvard University Press, 1972.

Table 4.3 *Length of sentences under article 58-10 in
the period 1956–7*

Year	Up to 5 years	6–10 years	Over 10 years	Total
1956	95 (41.1%)	131 (56.7%)	5 (2.2%)	231 (100%)
1957	930 (52%)	829 (46.4%)	29 (1.6%)	1,788 (100%)

Source: *1958 Procurator review*. GARF, f. 8131, op. 32, d. 5080, l. 7

disputes between the security organs and the legal establishment certainly did exist, especially when the latter began, in the early 1960s, to reclassify and reverse sentences that had been passed during the campaign of 1957 and 1958. Whilst the drive against dissent was on-going, and the international situation looked unpredictable, the KGB had the whip hand.

Details on the length of prisoners' sentences are somewhat sketchy but nonetheless instructive. The twenty-five-year jail terms of the Stalin era had not yet been formally abolished but were very rarely applied to dissenters, though there were still plenty of Ukrainian and Baltic nationalists serving out long sentences such as these that had been handed down in the late 1940s and early 1950s.[63] Table 4.3 gives an indication of sentencing trends for article 58-10 during the first part of the campaign. Based on this evidence, we can see that the average length of sentence under article 58–10 at this time was about five years. In a way this typifies the progress of liberalisation during the era: political repression was still bad by most measures, but was nowhere near as bad as it had been under Stalin.

Perhaps most striking is the fact that so few dissenters were sentenced to periods of ten years or more. Even Revolt Pimenov and Lev Krasnopevtsev – ringleaders in two of the era's largest underground groups – were originally sentenced to six and ten years' corrective labour respectively, when both would have almost certainly been faced with a twenty-five-year sentence or the death penalty only half a decade earlier.[64] The slight decline in the length of sentences between 1956 and 1957 presents something of a conundrum, though it most likely reflected the continuation of a general decline

---

[63] The Fundamental Principles of Criminal Legislation in 1958 reduced the maximum tariff from twenty-five to fifteen years and restricted periods of exile to five years.

[64] Like those of several other members of the group, Pimenov's sentence was significantly increased (in his case, to ten years) after the Leningrad procurator's office appealed at the leniency of their sentences.

in the duration of jail sentences during the 1950s. Although Table 4.3 does not show this, no one was executed in punishment for acts of political dissent during the period in question – ultimate proof that the tariff for criticism had been considerably lowered since the Stalin era.[65]

The prisons and labour camps that remained by the middle of the 1950s had already changed considerably since March 1953. Following an immediate period of disarray at the announcement of Stalin's death, V.F. Abramkin and V.F. Chesnokova describe a generalised and significant softening of regime right across the Gulag.[66] The number of prisoners dropped at a startling rate. Where there had been 113,735 political prisoners on 1 January 1956, a year later the total stood at 18,187. From constituting over 20% of all inmates during much of the Stalin era, 'politicals' came to make up less than 2% under Khrushchev.[67] In a number of important ways, the camps had evolved too, as penal policy became a little less barbaric. Underpinning practically all of the changes that took place was the fact that increased emphasis was now being placed on re-education of prisoners, rather than punishment or economic exploitation. Numerous Western specialists were invited to see a selection of the new corrective-labour colonies and prisons: many of these pronounced themselves impressed at the humane and progressive practices employed.[68]

Prisoners convicted of counter-revolutionary crimes were spread across thirty-eight corrective-labour colonies by the mid 1950s, with notable concentrations of 'politicals' in the Vorkuta, Karaganda, Mordova and Perm camp complexes.[69] Although the relatively progressive turn in penal policy was not always consistently implemented, on the whole conditions had improved notably for inmates since Stalin's death. The culture of virtually unbridled violence against prisoners soon slackened, and guards were even

---

[65] For purposes of comparison, figures from the Pospelov report, on which the Secret Speech was based, indicated that 581,692 were shot for anti-Soviet activity during 1937–8. Seven death sentences were, however, handed down in the aftermath of the 1962 disturbances at Novocherkassk. It is also worth pointing out that Viktor Swoboda and Bohdan Nahaylo refer to the execution of several Ukrainian nationalists during the Khrushchev period. V. Swoboda and B. Nahaylo, *Soviet Disunion: A History of the Nationalities Problem in the USSR*, New York: The Free Press, 1990, p. 158.

[66] V. Abramkin and V. Chesnokova, *Tyurmennyi mir glazami politzaklyuchennykh*, Moskva: Sodeistvie, 1993, p. 6.

[67] J. Hardy, 'Khrushchev's Gulag: The Evolution of Punishment in the Post-Stalin Soviet Union, 1953– 1964', Ph.D. Dissertation, Princeton University, 2011, pp. 58, 70.

[68] Many visitors were nonetheless unconvinced that what they had seen was an entirely accurate reflection of the wider camp network. As Jeffrey Hardy points out, the colonies in question were not entirely typical of the penal system as a whole, but they were not simply for show either. See J. Hardy, 'Gulag Tourism: Khrushchev's "Show" Prisons in the Cold War Context', 1954–59', *Russian Review*, Vol. 70, No. 1 (January 2011), 49–78.

[69] GARF, f. 9401, op. 2, d. 492, l. 142.

instructed to show inmates a degree of respect. 'Criminal' prisoners were no longer free to dominate and abuse 'politicals' with impunity.[70] In prison in Leningrad awaiting trial, Vail' was held alone in a cell that had previously accommodated twenty men. He was fed three times per day and received 25 g (1 oz) of sugar and 750 g (20 oz) of bread each morning. Reshat Dzhemilev, who was jailed in 1958, recalled that he received hot food every day.[71] In the camps inmates were able to knock time off their sentence by carrying out labour tasks. Prisoners were able to participate in sports tournaments and were permitted conjugal visits lasting up to several days.[72] Incoming parcels were practically unrestricted in volume, as was outgoing mail (though censorship of prisoners' letters remained in place). Of course, one must not paint too rosy a picture of penal reform: this was still an environment into which few would wish to enter. Those defined as 'counter-revolutionary criminals' were expected to undertake higher work quotas than other inmates, they were 'supervised by the best qualified staff', and regularly had informers planted within their ranks. In places, political prisoners were still undertaking particularly strenuous corrective labour tasks, such as logging and mining for gold and for coal.[73] Furthermore, as Chapter 8 shows, the corrective-labour camps of the Khrushchev era were about to become considerably harsher.

The Soviet regime's struggle with domestic critics was, of course, to carry on virtually without pause up to the eventual collapse of the USSR, and later years featured two further important crackdowns on dissent – one in the early 1970s and another toward the end of that decade.[74] However, the clampdown that had been initiated in December 1956 lasted only until the summer of 1958, by which time over 3,000 individuals had been jailed for counter-revolutionary activity since the December letter had been circulated. By the middle of 1958, the immediate stimulus for the crack-down – the ferment that came to the surface after the impact of the Secret

---

[70] As V. Abramkin and V. Chesnokova point out, this was a result both of official attempts to rein in the power of criminal prisoners within the camps and of political prisoners themselves becoming more assertive in the post-war era. By the early 1960s, however, the power of the criminals was on the rise once again. V. Abramkin and V. Chesnokova, *Tyurmennyi mir glazami politzaklyuchennykh*, pp. 10–13.

[71] 'Interv'yu s Reshatom Dzhemilevym', in V. Ambramkin and V. Chesnokova, *Tyurmennyi mir glazami politzaklyuchennykh*, p. 89.

[72] J. Hardy, 'Gulag Tourism', 53.   [73] GARF, f. 9401, op. 2, d. 492, l. 144.

[74] The first of these two Brezhnev-era clampdowns began in 1972 and was primarily aimed at destroying the *samizdat* journal *The Chronicle of Current Events*. It proved to be a failure in the long term but did prevent *The Chronicle* from appearing for well over a year. The second campaign, in early 1977, was most notable for the fact that leading members of the Moscow Helsinki Group were arrested and subsequently jailed, including Yuri Orlov, Aleksandr Ginzburg and Anatoly Shcharansky.

Speech had combined with the heightened unrest prompted by events in Hungary – had all but evaporated and the rules of what could and could not be said had again been made clear to all. It took some months for the backlog of cases to thin out, but surviving records show a drop from seventy-seven convictions under article 58-10 in June 1958 to sixty-four convictions in October; fifty-two in December; forty-seven in February 1959; then thirty-two in June and fourteen in October.[75] After an eighteen-month show of force by the authorities the level of protest activity would have naturally declined somewhat, but such a precipitate drop in sentences was clearly prompted by the decision to bring the clampdown to a close.

Although the original causes of the campaign may have dissipated, a tangible catalyst had still been required for it to be decisively drawn to a close. It was the entreaties and advice of the legal establishment, in the form of the Procurator's office and the Supreme Court in particular, that played a leading role in winding down the wave of arrests and sentences as they sought to temper the arbitrary use of the law. The Supreme Court had already been expressing reservations about the legality of the drive against dissent for some months by the summer of 1958. Pressure had started to build for the campaign to be ended already in 1957 but, according to Aleksandr and Elena Papovyan, a combination of inertia within the political machinery and KGB resistance had prevented any softening of policy.[76] One document in which doubts were raised in respect of several specific cases of 'anti-Soviet activity' was a report entitled 'Information on the Results of Legal Practice in Cases of Counter-revolutionary Crimes'. Compiled in early 1958, and drawing upon numerous cases from late 1956 and early 1957, it essentially argued that too many of those who were being sentenced under article 58-10 should not have been branded 'anti-Soviet', but dealt with in some more appropriate manner. In May 1958 it was forwarded to the CPSU Central Committee. The timing of subsequent events indicates that this Supreme Court *spravka* was the basis for a major review of sentencing policy carried out during May and June of 1958.

The ensuing review began by presenting detailed figures on the numbers and social origins of those who had been sentenced during the campaign. It cited numerous individual cases of citizens arrested and jailed for anti-Soviet agitation and propaganda since Stalin's death, and particularly since the December letter. It still pointed to the unmasking of Stalin and the uprising

---

[75] See V. Kozlov and S. Mironenko eds., *58-10 Nadzornye proizvodstva*.
[76] E. Papovyan and A. Papovyan, 'Uchastie verkhovnogo suda SSSR', in L. Eremina and E. Zhemkova eds., *Korni travy*, p. 68.

in Hungary, combined with heightened imperialist subversion, as the main catalysts for raised levels of dissenting activity, and unambiguously stated that the increased number of convictions for dissenting activity showed that the KGB and Procuracy had been both vigilant and effective in following the instructions set out in December 1956.[77] After the traditional sugar-coated introduction, the review also painted a more complete picture. It stated that 'the [security] organs are essentially conducting the struggle well but are sometimes apprehending people who are not truly anti-Soviet'. It then insisted: '... complaints about individual shortages or personal problems are not anti-Soviet. This can include gossip about leaders, jokes of a political character, complaints about agriculture – all of which can be without counter-revolutionary meaning.'[78] It referred back to the largely overlooked statement in the December letter that had urged caution in sentencing as anti-Soviet those whose criticism did not display genuine political opposition but suggested some degree of mistakenness or naïvety. The closing lines of the review proved to be the most significant of all: 'mistakes are being made in cases of counter-revolutionary crimes. The courts require a clarification from the Plenum of the Supreme Court as regards what does and does not constitute anti-Soviet behaviour.'[79]

The Supreme Court resolution duly arrived on 13 June 1958. Its overall message can be summed up by the following line: 'for an act to be considered anti-Soviet it has to be consciously aimed at harming the Soviet state'. It recommended that those who drunkenly cursed the authorities or acted primarily out of material discontent should not *necessarily* (italics added) be charged under article 58-10. Courts and investigators should look at individuals' biographies, including their work and war record, their social status and age, in order to help distinguish between anti-Soviet activity and a 'faulty attitude toward certain events or policies'.[80] This was a crucial step in the creation of a more sophisticated and effective corpus of policy against dissent. It marked the point where the regime's 'fire-fighting' approach began to be replaced with a more proactive and sophisticated series of measures for policing dissent, which turned to custodial sentencing as a last resort rather than a default option.

---

[77] GARF, f. 8131, op. 32, d. 5080, l. 17.   [78] GARF, f. 8131, op. 32, d. 5080, l. 42.
[79] GARF, f. 8131, op. 32, d. 5080, l. 43.
[80] GARF, f. 8131, op. 32, d. 5080, l. 64. As Vatulescu has pointed out, biographical details always occupied an especially prominent place in Soviet investigation protocols, so much so that 'while the traditional police file can read like a detective story, the Soviet secret police file reads like a peculiar biography'. C. Vatulescu, 'Arresting Biographies: The Secret Police File in the Soviet Union and Romania', *Comparative Literature*, Vol. 56, No. 3 (Summer 2004), 245.

By the end of the 1950s the authorities duly began to distinguish between deliberate acts of dissent, such as those that tended to be carried out by members of the intelligentsia, and the spontaneous expressions of frustration that more commonly featured among workers, and subsequently tailored their response accordingly. Roughly speaking, the regime had come to accept that even when manifested in political language, material dissatisfaction was inherently less dangerous than political dissatisfaction, provided that it was kept at manageable levels. By distinguishing between the two, and by alleviating the former to some degree, the authorities were also able to prevent any significant fusion of worker and intelligentsia dissent of the kind that had rocked Hungary and would later do so in Czechoslovakia and Poland. While the impact that this differentiation had upon the development of nationalist and religious dissent seems to have been relatively minimal, it appears that it did contribute significantly to the small size and isolated nature of the later human-rights movement.

There was some considerable pragmatism in making this distinction between spontaneous worker dissent and more persistent and pre-planned criticism. Both were potentially dangerous in different ways, but the former was much more easily dealt with, since its roots were generally economic, rather than political. Furthermore, once the raised tensions of 1956 and 1957 had passed, there was no longer a need to treat hooligan-type political outbursts as quite such a serious danger. It is also true, however, that much of the pre-planned and more deeply politicised dissenting behaviour that took place around this time was still not 'consciously aimed at harming the Soviet state' or genuinely opposed to the communist regime – something that the authorities either did not see or chose to disregard.

This was neither the first nor last time that Soviet jurists were able to have a restraining effect on harsh Party policy.[81] That is not to suggest that one can consider the legal establishment to have been fundamentally 'liberal', however. Instead, one should view this as an attempt by an educated and skilled segment of society to become more 'professional' and a little less susceptible to the arbitrary dictates of the political authorities: this was a trend that was to surface most famously among some of the country's leading scientists. Even so, to suggest that the ending of the clampdown

---

[81] For example, Yoram Gorlizki has shown that justice officials also resisted Khrushchev's attempts to give Comrades' Courts the power to exile citizens for up to five years. Moshe Lewin also argued that the Supreme Court took the lead in pushing for further improvements to criminal justice during the 1970s. See Y. Gorlizki, 'Delegalization in Russia: Soviet Comrades' Courts in Retrospect', *American Journal of Comparative Law*, Vol. 46, No. 3 (Summer 1998), 403–25, and M. Lewin, *The Soviet Century*, p. 171.

showed the Soviet regime acquiescing to the rule of law would undoubtedly be a step too far. The reality of the situation in regard to dissenters was that methods more effective than imprisonment were being developed and deployed to deal with social ferment. Greater effort was put into creating a façade of 'socialist legality', though the authorities continued to be able to bend the law to their own will in order to tackle critics, as countless sham trials against dissenters over the years testified. If they perceived any threat to domestic stability, all other considerations – such as legal process and international public opinion – could still be brushed aside.[82] The legal establishment, it seems, was able to have a restraining influence on such a sensitive policy area only when the Party leadership allowed them to do so, and any such gains could always be reversed.

The clampdown had been intended not only to ensure that domestic tensions did not spiral out of control but also to send out a signal to the public: a general deterrent to dissuade citizens from speaking up. Arrests and sentences removed the danger posed by specific individuals and groups but a widespread show of strength from the security organs would have a useful effect on society as a whole in helping to restate the boundaries of acceptable and unacceptable comment – vital after the recent tumult and uncertainty. With popular perceptions of the KGB's effectiveness at tracking down dissenters a key factor in deterring unorthodox political behaviour, the campaign can be seen as a vital re-affirmation of the security organs' strength and their prerogative to tackle political non-conformity.[83]

This was the third and last of the key stages in bringing to a close most outward signs of dissension that had arisen during 1956. Firstly, Party and Komsomol activists and officials had been whipped into shape after struggling to respond effectively to remarks following the Secret Speech. Then, more rigorous ideological and behavioural discipline was re-established among ordinary CPSU and Komsomol members. Lastly, the univocality of the public sphere was protected, borders of permissible and impermissible were again elucidated, and the authorities' determination to clamp down on unacceptable political behaviour was more fully impressed upon the wider population. By about the middle of 1958, then, the genie was just about back in the bottle and the authorities now only had to keep it there.

---

[82] As Robert Sharlet pointed out, 'the Party continued to retain a meta-judicial or extra-constitutional status, reserving to itself an immense, unchecked residual power'. R. Sharlet, 'De-Stalinization and Soviet Constitutionalism', in S. Cohen, A. Rabinowitch and R. Sharlet eds., *The Soviet Union since Stalin*, Bloomington, IN: Indiana University Press, 1980, p. 100.

[83] See D. Bahry and B. Silver, 'Intimidation and the Symbolic Uses of Terror in the USSR', *American Political Science Review*, Vol. 81, No. 4 (December 1987), 1066–98.

From that point, a more stable and pliant post-Stalin social order began to emerge.

In regard to the way that dissent was policed in later years, it was the winding down of the 1957–8 campaign that left the most significant legacy. The insistence that acts of protest and criticism had to show genuine intent to undermine or weaken the Soviet regime for them to be regarded as 'anti-Soviet' became a keystone of responses to dissent, ensuring that no such widespread campaign would take place again. Of course, the authorities' perceptions of what constituted 'genuine intent to undermine the system' was rarely the same of that of the dissenters themselves, and often appeared entirely unconvincing to expert observers abroad, yet this was still an advance of some substance compared to the political repression of 1957 and early 1958.

At no other point in the entire post-Stalin era was a comparable number of citizens arrested and sentenced for dissenting activity. Although many times lower than the number of people jailed for political crimes in the Stalin years, the total of 1,964 convictions for anti-Soviet activity and propaganda in 1957 alone by far outstripped that of any subsequent year in Soviet history. It is worth noting that in the entire fourteen-year period of 1966 to 1980, when the Soviet dissident movement was most active and internationally prominent, the total number of political sentences is recorded as 1,829.[84] Of course, one must exercise caution in making sweeping comparisons between the two periods by reference only to the number of jailed dissenters. Later years saw a move away from the use of prison and camp sentences for all but the most serious offences. Other practices, such as the widespread use of 'prophylactic measures', are not represented in the above data. Again, this did not indicate a softening of attitudes toward criticism but instead showed that means other than labour camps and prisons were increasingly found to be effective tools for maintaining conformity among all but the most determined 'trouble-causers'.

---

[84] The figures on the Brezhnev period include sentences under article 70 (the principal successor to article 58-10) as well as article 190-1, which was introduced in 1967 as a means of strengthening existing legal provisions for dealing with dissent.

PART II

CHAPTER 5

The anti-Soviet underground

In many ways dissent in the first half of the 1960s was not fundamentally different to that of the late 1950s: people still produced political leaflets, formed underground groups and complained about poor living standards. As a social phenomenon in which most participants were almost entirely isolated from each other, dissent did not evolve quickly or evenly across years, regions or social groups. However, when one takes a wider view of the Khrushchev period as a whole, there were some important differences between the earlier and later parts of the era. Most notably, both underground activity and public acts of protest became considerably more volatile for a time in the early 1960s.

While the half-decade following Stalin's death had been a time of great political and social oscillation, for the country at large things had begun to settle down again by the end of the 1950s. Much of the idealism and enthusiasm that was released during the middle of the decade had subsided. There were further changes ahead, of course, but it was during the early 1960s that both dissenting behaviour and the authorities' responses to dissent began to develop forms that would remain broadly consistent until the 1980s. There were no political shocks comparable to the Secret Speech and no foreign activity as divisive as the Hungarian invasion. Even so, aspirations were rising faster and workers in particular were beginning to make greater demands of the system: demands that the regime increasingly had to accommodate. The problem of working-class dissent became particularly explosive for a time before the authorities managed to placate key workers' grievances and were largely able to reduce overt protest and criticism to a relatively small section of the intelligentsia by the middle of the 1960s.

Although there was still little in the way of enduring appetite for revolution or open rebellion, idealism and respect for the political authorities were declining markedly in certain quarters as the perceived gap between masses and elites widened. General acceptance of the Soviet system remained widespread and its fundamental political values still resonated, but ever since the mid 1950s mass compliance had been becoming more closely linked to the regime fulfilling basic functions such as providing employment and social benefits as well as ensuring the availability of goods. People were no longer quite so willing to sacrifice their own aspirations in the present for a goal far off in the future. It was entirely apparent to the authorities by the early 1960s that Soviet workers expected an acceptable standard of living and were, on occasion, prepared to fight in order to achieve it. Social infrastructure, consumer goods and working conditions all rose higher up the regime's list of priorities from this point and accordingly helped to keep popular dissent at a minimum for most of the next two and a half decades.

The kind of loyal and idealistic but misjudged criticism that had been a feature of the immediate post-Secret Speech period was almost entirely eradicated. The new post-Stalin boundaries of acceptable and unacceptable ideological discourse were firmly established by the end of the 1950s and would remain largely unchanged for much of the next three decades. Many dissenters and would-be dissenters had already been jailed, removed from the Party and Komsomol or otherwise intimidated into silence as it became entirely evident that there was still to be no legitimate outlet for even loyal political criticism available to the masses.[1] Most acquiesced to this new reality but some grew ever more alienated because of it.

While Maurice Hindus could justifiably assert that dissent in the second half of the 1950s 'hid no guns and manufactured no bombs', the same could not always be said of the early 1960s.[2] There was still relatively little in the way of outright anti-communist sentiment, and even less mention of preference for a capitalist political system, but one can clearly discern a growing sense of embitterment and alienation among many of those who spoke out. During the second half of the Khrushchev era this could translate into leaflets calling for the removal of the entire Party leadership, riots and demonstrations involving thousands of people, and underground groups that acquired weapons, called for revolution and plotted terrorist acts. Variations on Marxist-Leninist ideology continued to predominate among dissenters, though a growing number of them now argued that the whole regime had to be reconstructed rather than just fixed. Those who still

---

[1] Of course, there were still plenty of CPSU members and apparatchiks who desired reform and worked toward that goal from within the Party, though it would not be until Mikhail Gorbachev's accession to power in 1985 that they were able to pursue an openly reformist agenda.

[2] M. Hindus, *House without a Roof: Russia after Forty-Three Years of Revolution*, London: Victor Gollancz, 1962, p. 383.

sought to air dissenting opinions no longer laboured under the misapprehension that their remarks might be welcomed or even tolerated.

One symptom of this spreading disillusionment at the incumbent political leadership was the growing influence of the Yugoslav dissident Milovan Djilas's stinging critique against the state of the Soviet system: *The New Class* (1957).[3] Until his split with Tito in 1954, Djilas had been a high-ranking member of the Yugoslav regime and in this role had spent some considerable time among the Soviet leadership during the war years, seeing at first hand the ideological sclerosis and elite privilege that had taken hold there. After publishing a series of controversial articles, Djilas was expelled from the League of Communists of Yugoslavia and was then jailed in 1956, writing *The New Class* whilst imprisoned. It was immediately banned inside the USSR, though copies had begun to emerge by the end of the 1950s.[4] His fundamental argument was a compelling one: it stated that the Soviet Union was no longer a dictatorship of the proletariat on the path toward communism but had become a dictatorship of the bureaucracy, mired in self-interest. With criticism of bureaucrats and popular resentment at the privileges enjoyed by elites constituting regular staples of critical opinion in the USSR, there was a highly receptive audience for Djilas's work among those who wanted to build communism but felt deeply frustrated at the state of the communist project. In his preface to *The New Class*, Djilas tapped into a vein of sentiment that was becoming more widely held among dissenters at the time: '... even though I was disillusioned, I am not one of those whose disillusionment was sharp and extreme ... As I became increasingly estranged from the reality of contemporary Communism, I came closer to the idea of democratic socialism.'[5] In other words, the goals of the system were not in question, but the methods were. This was certainly a fair reflection of many dissenters' attitudes during the period, though some were already showing more far-ranging doubts and frustrations.

Concrete evidence on the number of underground groups that came into being during the era does not exist, nor could it, since at least some of them formed and disbanded without ever coming to the security organs' attention. There were, however, a few interesting snippets of information contained in communications between the KGB and Central Committee.

---

[3] M. Djilas, *The New Class: An Analysis of the Communist System*, London: Unwin, 1966.
[4] It was for attempting to reproduce a copy of *The New Class* that Vladimir Bukovsky was first jailed in 1963. GARF, f. 8131, op. 31, d. 97676, ll. 1–8.
[5] M. Djilas, *The New Class*, p. 14.

In 1961 the security organs reported that they had uncovered forty-seven different groups, with a total of 186 participants. In July 1962 they announced that sixty different anti-Soviet groups had been uncovered in the previous six months, including a total of over 200 participants.[6] These were hardly panic-inducing figures for the authorities, not least since groups remained almost entirely isolated from each other and showed little potential to connect with the masses, but they were troubling, nonetheless. Many of these groups showed signs of a deepening frustration and ideological drift away from the idealistic criticism of the mid to late 1950s. The Union of Freedom and Intellect, for example, distributed hundreds of leaflets around Moscow State University in February 1962 attacking the regime's 'ossified and dogmatic' Marxism and promising to revolutionise Soviet society.[7] Another of the group's leaflets branded the Soviet system 'totalitarian' and demanded a wide range of material and political improvements, ending simply by stating that 'we are fighting to overthrow the political hegemony of the CPSU Central Committee'.[8]

The most widespread manifestation of underground activity continued to involve composing, copying and distributing hostile leaflets. These began to appear in ever-greater numbers. A report from 25 July 1962 stated that in the first half of that year the security organs had discovered 7,705 different anti-Soviet leaflets and documents, distributed by some 2,522 authors – a figure twice as high as the same period in 1961. The main centres where they were found included Ukraine, Azerbaidzhan, Georgia, Latvia, Stavropol, Krasnodar, Rostov, Leningrad and Moscow.[9] According to the KGB, such leaflets were increasingly characterised by calls for active struggle against the Soviet authorities, malicious attacks on individual leaders, nationalist attitudes, lack of faith in the building of communism and slander against Soviet democracy. A growing number apparently also expressed hatred of the CPSU and made terrorist threats against communists, Komsomol members and Party activists.[10] This kind of content had existed in previous years but had been quite rare. While one must remain alive to the dangers of accepting at face value the language of the KGB on such matters, the available evidence certainly supports their overarching assertion that dissent was becoming increasingly vociferous.

This trend can be seen in many of the *listovki* of the early 1960s. A leaflet that was distributed in the Ukrainian cities of Donetsk, Zhitomir and

---

[6] RGANI, f. 5, op. 30, d. 454, l. 110.   [7] GARF, f. 8131, op. 31, d. 92669, l. 51.
[8] GARF, f. 8131, op. 31, d. 92669, l. 51.   [9] RGANI, f. 89, op. 51, d. 1, ll. 1–4.
[10] RGANI, f. 89, op. 51, d. 1, l. 1.

Rovensk and in Lugansk *oblast'* during May 1963 gives some indication of the themes and language that featured in the late Khrushchev period:

ALL-UNION DEMOCRATIC FRONT – REVOLUTIONARY
SOCIAL-DEMOCRATIC PARTY

> *The reaction is coming. Khrushchev is reviving Stalinism.*
> *His plan spells disaster.*
> *The people are rising for the struggle.*
> *We demand:*
> *1. 100 roubles minimum wage.*
> *2. 30-hour working week.*
> *3. Minimal bureaucracy and militarism.*
> *4. Democratic freedoms.*
> *5. Legalisation of the VDF and RSDP.*[11]
> *6. Amnesty for political prisoners.*
> *The state order in our country is a bureaucratic clique*
> *based on exploitation of the workers.*
> *Our aim is to replace this order with*
> *socialist democracy.*
> *Comrades!*
> *The struggle has begun.*
> *The strike movement is widening.*
> *The soldiers are refusing to fire on the people.*
> *All to the ranks of the revolution!*
> *We will win!*
> *Down with Khrushchev's reactionary clique!*
> *Long live socialist democracy!*
> *Long live the fourth Russian Revolution!*[12]

Over 800 copies of this particular leaflet, measuring 18 cm x 12 cm (7 in x 5 in), were scattered in the streets and sent by post to various private individuals and political figures in Ukraine. The subsequent KGB investigation confiscated a further 1,221 copies that had either already been distributed or were ready for distribution. The investigation soon revealed that the main culprit was one B.I. Bul'binskii, a thirty-year-old worker from Rovensk who had already been jailed once for the same offence in 1957 but had subsequently been released in 1961 and again began to produce and distribute political leaflets. Bul'binskii had prepared the leaflets alone but had been assisted in distributing them by three others, including a local student named N.M. Trofimovich, who had already scattered 1,200 leaflets in

---

[11] VDF refers to the All-Union Democratic Front (*Vsesoyuznyi demokraticheskii front*) and RSDP refers to the Revolutionary Social Democratic Party (*Revolyutsionnaya sotsial-demokraticheskaya partiya*).

[12] RGANI, f. 5, op. 30, d. 412, l. 67.

Odessa and Rovensk, and a former prisoner named S.A. Babich, who had posted or handed out over 1,000 copies around Zhitomir.[13]

One can see significant elements of Milovan Djilas's political philosophy in Bul'binskii's leaflet, especially where it read: 'the state order in our country is a bureaucratic clique based on the exploitation of workers'. Bul'binskii's language and political outlook were recognisably shaped by the Soviet system – as one would expect – but his stance was unmistakably belligerent. With Khrushchev's revelations about Stalin-era crimes still relatively fresh, since he had only recently revisited the subject at the XXII CPSU Congress in October 1961, the leaflet's warning that Khrushchev was 'reviving Stalinism' was a stark one. Even those who vehemently rejected Khrushchev's attacks on Stalin had no wish for a return to arbitrary terror. It may be that the claim about a widening strike movement referred to mass disturbances the previous summer – of which Novocherkassk was the most notable example – yet it could just as well be that this was simply bluster. Certainly, no widespread workers' struggle had begun and there is no literature to suggest troops had anywhere refused to fire on demonstrators, or had even had cause to do so since they opened fire at Novocherkassk.[14]

In some ways, therefore, the leaflet is most useful in that it tells us what kinds of rhetoric and political positions dissenters believed might win over the masses. Unlike many leaflets, this one explicitly combined both material and ideological themes. Interestingly, biographical details contained in the KGB file on Bul'binskii state that he was a worker in a cement factory but also that he had a higher education, which perhaps goes some way toward explaining this rather rare balancing of typically worker and intelligentsia concerns.[15] The fact that calls for a minimum wage and shorter working week come at the very beginning of the leaflet probably tell us it was primarily intended to appeal to workers. Similarly, its ideological content was simple and to the point, making it accessible to the widest possible audience. The sixth demand – amnesty for political prisoners – clearly shows the presence of the kinds of concerns that were later to play a major role in the subsequent dissident movement. It also tells us that Khrushchev's claims about there being no political prisoners left in the USSR were by no means universally accepted, not least because Bul'binskii had been in the Khrushchev-era camps himself.

---

[13] RGANI, f. 5, op. 30, d. 412, ll. 69–71.

[14] As the following chapter notes, MVD forces under attack from angry crowds at Aleksandrov in 1961 had actually requested permission to respond with arms but their request had been denied.

[15] RGANI, f. 5, op. 30, d. 412, l. 65. One would assume that his earlier spell of imprisonment was a factor behind Bul'binskii's lack of an occupation more fitting to his level of education.

That the leaflet concluded with a call for citizens to 'join the ranks of the revolution' was indicative of the sharpening tone of dissent in the early 1960s. It also demonstrated one of the fundamental differences between the political dissent of the Khrushchev era and the human-rights activity of the Brezhnev years. The former most frequently attempted to mobilise the masses and relied upon the threat of domestic unrest as its main lever for applying pressure on the authorities. The latter instead sought to appeal first to the Soviet leadership, before later shifting focus to winning popular support in the West, in order to marshal international diplomatic pressure that would then be brought to bear on the Soviet authorities. The major problem with the Khrushchev-era trend of dissenters appealing to the Soviet people was that the threat of civil unrest was for the most part a hollow one and was furthermore fraught with great danger for those involved, since the safeguarding of domestic stability remained an issue that would always prompt the most determined response from the Soviet authorities.[16]

One of the most interesting aspects of cases like Bul'binskii's was the sheer volume of *listovki* that were produced and distributed. In the 1950s a total of even twenty copies of any given tract could be quite rare, but one repeatedly finds KGB reports and interrogation protocols from the early 1960s in which leaflets and brochures were discovered in their hundreds or even thousands – all the more startling when one bears in mind the continuing scarcity of paper and disposable income inside the USSR. In February 1963, for example, Galina Zakharchenko and Viktor Khozyainov were arrested after distributing over 2,000 leaflets in Vinitsa and Zhitomir. In April of the same year, a batch of 500 leaflets was discovered in Tambov, and in September an underground group calling itself 'Oreol' distributed around 200 leaflets in Frunze.[17] Those who disseminated the *listovki* were also becoming more daring at times. The director of the Central Lenin Museum in Moscow reported that attendants had found *listovki* scattered in the exhibition halls there.[18] At a public lecture of the 'All-Union Society for the Dissemination of Political and Scientific Knowledge' in February 1962, leaflets were passed among the audience before being directed to the speakers on stage.[19]

---

[16] Of course, appealing to outsiders for help in dealing with the Soviet authorities could be equally, if not more, dangerous, especially in conditions of complete openness. Those whose names became known in the West, however, were offered at least a degree of protection by outside interest in their case.

[17] GARF, f. 8131, op. 32, d. 95164, ll. 1–4; RGANI, f. 5, op. 30, d. 429, l. 52; and GARF, f. 8131, op. 31, d. 96174, ll. 3–4.

[18] RGANI, f. 5, op. 30, d. 454, l. 125.   [19] RGANI, f. 5, op. 30, d. 378, l. 55.

Official ideological prescriptions were also being called into question in ever-sharper attacks. In April 1964 the 'Democratic Union of Socialists' sent out over 850 leaflets to destinations in Kiev, Kishinev, Odessa and Chelyabinsk which included statements such as 'the dictatorship of the Party means freedom for communists and unquestioning obedience for the vast majority of the people', 'the dictatorship of the Party is the reason for mistakes and exaggerations in its activity' and 'the idea of full communism is only a hypothesis'.[20] Before its six members were tracked down and arrested by the KGB the following month, the Democratic Union of Socialists also posted a huge batch of leaflets entitled *Pravda narodu* ('truth to the people' or 'truth to the nation') to various central newspapers, official organisations and selected private individuals.[21] Produced in small and extremely dense type, the leaflet ran to several pages of quite sophisticated ideological criticism of the contemporary political situation inside the USSR. Under the heading 'an appeal from the Democratic Union of Socialists to all workers of the Soviet Union', the leaflet insisted that the Soviet system did not constitute a dictatorship of the proletariat or an 'all-people's state' but was simply dictatorship by the Communist Party.[22]

One of the things that made the *Pravda narodu* leaflet so interesting was that copies turned up across an extremely wide geographical area. On 29 April the KGB reported that examples had been found in Leningrad, Khar'kov, Novosibirsk, Kazan and Kuibyshev, thus being spread over thousands of square kilometres. Days later, this list of destinations was expanded after further copies were discovered in Riga, Arkhangel' and parts of Lithuania. When combined with the group's previous despatch of leaflets to Kiev, Kishinev, Odessa and Chelyabinsk one can see that many of the USSR's biggest urban centres, across five separate union republics, had been targeted. The difficulty of acquiring the necessary resources (20 kg – 44 lb – of typescript were found in a house search once the culprits were uncovered) for such an undertaking, along with the inherent danger of disseminating them on such a scale, quite clearly showed that the authorities were not wholly unjustified in seeing those involved as subversives or would-be subversives. One did not need to be an inveterate Stalinist to presume that such behaviour reflected a degree of genuine enmity toward the political status quo.

---

[20] RGANI, f. 5, op. 30, d. 454, l. 72.   [21] RGANI, f. 5, op. 30, d. 454, l. 76.

[22] RGANI, f. 5, op. 30, d. 454, l. 72. The term 'all-people's state' was introduced in the 1961 Third Party Programme and replaced 'dictatorship of the proletariat' as the official description of the Soviet political order.

Quite how leaflets such as these were received by the people who came across them is a subject on which substantial evidence is naturally hard to find. However, having personally handed out around a dozen copies of his own group's leaflets at the gates of Moscow's Hammer and Sickle factory in early 1964, Petro Grigorenko provided some interesting anecdotal evidence of the experience: 'With my heart in my mouth I offered one to my first customer, who nodded and, without stopping, took it and hid it in his pocket. The second was successful, too, and the third. The fourth was a misfire. In response to my question he grimly shook his head and put his hands in his pockets.'[23] What we can say from even this small sample is that there was at least a degree of curiosity about such documents among the wider public. Whether or not people sympathised with the sentiments that they expressed is much less clear.

In many ways, the above scenario is a perfect example of what Lewis Siegelbaum described as a 'porous border' between public and private life.[24] These were leaflets about public matters, which were produced in private and then distributed in public places. They were most likely to then be read in private, often with the aim of prompting the reader to some form of public activity of their own. Most dissenting behaviour of the time either straddled public and private activity or else criss-crossed between the two in this way. As Siegelbaum also points out, private activities could compensate for avenues that were proscribed by the authorities yet still centred upon public life, one example being clandestine groups that met to discuss subjects such as 'the true history of the Russian Revolution'. During the earlier part of the Khrushchev era in particular, many of those who participated in such secretive activities were also intimately and even passionately engaged with the 'official' sphere of Soviet life – such as through membership of the Communist Party or Komsomol – though this was a trend in pronounced decline by the 1960s.

As someone who became an internationally celebrated dissident and in due course left behind a wealth of fascinating material about himself, Petro Grigorenko's group, the 'Alliance of Struggle for the Rebirth of Leninism', offers some further insights into the impulses behind dissenting activity such as this. While Grigorenko was in many respects one of the least

---

[23] As Grigorenko recounts, he handed the leaflets out dressed in his military uniform. Whether this had any impact on people's willingness to take the material he offered is unclear but certainly seems possible. P. Grigorenko, *Memoirs*, New York: W.W. Norton, 1982, p. 275.

[24] See L. Siegelbaum, 'Introduction: Mapping Private Spheres in the Soviet Context', in L. Siegelbaum ed., *Borders of Socialism: Private Spheres of Soviet Russia*, Basingstoke: Palgrave Macmillan, 2006, pp. 1–24.

'ordinary' of Soviet citizens – since he had previously been a general in the army and had met numerous members of the very top CPSU leadership, including Khrushchev – there was much about the group that fit into the wider trends of the time. Their leaflets centred on themes such as growing bureaucratism and low living standards; their membership was close-knit and based on already existing ties of family loyalty; and they were soon uncovered by the KGB without registering any notable impact upon society at large.

From Grigorenko's own account of how he came to be involved in underground activity, two particularly interesting themes stand out. Firstly, as for so many others, doubts and frustrations at the contemporary situation in the USSR had been brought to the surface by the Secret Speech and had led Grigorenko to seek answers in the works of Lenin. He managed to find succour only after some considerable effort, recalling later that 'I began to "sort out" Lenin unconsciously, selecting to retain that which suited my own views and totally bypassing some of his most important opinions.'[25] This was arguably the basis of neo-Bolshevism in a nutshell. Secondly, after being expelled from the Party for attacking the growing leadership cult around Nikita Khrushchev in 1961, Grigorenko decided that there was simply no use in presenting even loyal criticism to those in power, insisting to himself that 'there could be no dialogue with such monsters. They needed not to be persuaded but thrown out.'[26]

In his efforts to continue viewing himself as a 'Leninist' Grigorenko was going through a process experienced by many dissenters of the time, and presumably also by many others who never vented their doubts and frustrations so openly. Without rejecting the Soviet system or detaching himself from it, he was nonetheless struggling to reconcile his deep connection to Soviet ideals with the reality that surrounded him. This was clearly not someone who had remained aloof from the practices and goals of the Soviet project but had devoted his adult life to it and had enjoyed an exalted career in doing so. For such people, the tendency to turn against the authorities from a position of 'true Leninism' or 'neo-Bolshevism' was always much likelier than any kind of Damascene conversion to anti-communism. As Jochen Hellbeck's work on the diary of Stepan Podlubnyi has shown, any kind of internal doubts could be particularly hard to bear, especially without an alternative social and political framework in mind.[27] Thus, for many the

---

[25] P. Grigorenko, *Memoirs*, p. 267.   [26] P. Grigorenko, *Memoirs*, p. 270.
[27] See J. Hellbeck, *Revolution on my Mind: Writing a Diary under Stalin*, London: Harvard University Press, 2006.

first step was not to break with the ideological basis of the system at all, but to break with its present incarnation from what seemed a position of loyalty to the wider values and goals of October 1917. This, though, rarely proved to be a political endpoint. Over time, Grigorenko and others like him generally moved further away from the ideology they had once embraced.

The notion that there was simply no sense in pursuing a route of trying to 'fix' the system through open and loyal criticism was becoming widespread among dissenters by the end of the 1950s. Though there were some, such as Roy Medvedev and Lev Karpinsky, who continued to strive for change from within – and actually enjoyed a degree of success in doing so – the sense that genuine reform was possible, and could be furthered by the aid of conscientious citizens, had understandably dissipated since the XX Congress.[28] Leonid Borodin, who was himself originally an idealistic communist but later became a member of the avowedly anti-communist 'All-Russian Social Christian Union for the People's Liberation' (VSKhSON), recalled exactly this kind of attitude: 'my motive [for joining an underground group] was simple: a [political] party was not possible and nor were positive steps toward changing the state ...'[29] This is a problem which to some extent faces almost all regimes that do not allow for independent political activity. For the individuals and groups active in Khrushchev's USSR, however, the historical context of recent, mass repression and the perceived threat of its return (raised in the leaflet by B.I. Bul'binskii, for example) gave such acts an added sense of gravity and urgency.

Of all the underground organisations of the late Khrushchev era, the VSKhSON was certainly among the largest and most intriguing. Influenced by Milovan Djilas's critique of Soviet communism and by Nikolai Berdyaev's writings on spirituality and freedom, Igor Ogurtsov decided in mid 1963 to form a group with like-minded friends Evgeny Vagin and Mikhail Sado.[30] When it was finally uncovered by the KGB in late 1966, the group had twenty-eight full members and a further thirty candidate members, spread across several cities.[31] In its ethos at least, this was a

---

[28] As Nikolai Mitrokhin has shown, Russian nationalism was also emerging as a growing ideological force within the political apparatus, among liberals as well as conservatives. See N. Mitrokhin, *Russkaya partiya: dvizhenie russkikh natsionalistov v SSSR, 1953–1985*, Moskva: Novoe literaturnoe obozrenie, 2003.

[29] 'Beseda s Leonidom Borodinym', in V. Pimonov ed., *Govoryat 'osobo opasnye'*, Moskva: Detektiv-Press, 1999, p. 72.

[30] On the VSKhSON see in particular N. Mitrokhin, *Russkaya partiya*, pp. 221–35. See also J. Dunlop, *The New Russian Revolutionaries*, London: Nordland Publishing, 1976.

[31] Of course, the fact that the group even had formal 'candidate members' tells us that this was a well-developed organisation that clearly took itself seriously.

revolutionary organisation. New recruits were told that the group had thousands of members in clandestine cells dotted throughout the country. They were also expected to attract additional members, to donate 10% of their wages to a fighting fund, to obey an established system of party bylaws and to serve the group as both 'propagandist and soldier'. As with other underground organisations, there was more talking and thinking than actual action, though they preached revolution and were 'unambiguously prepared to resort to terror'.[32] They considered communism as a threat to Christianity and an anti-Russian phenomenon, insisting that 'the communist world is disintegrating. The people have found out from bitter experience that it brings poverty and depression, falsehood and moral degeneration.'[33] What they proffered instead was a Russian nationalism that occasionally spilled over into xenophobia and displayed more than a hint of anti-Semitism.

A survey of a few cases that arose in the first six months of 1963 highlights an emerging tendency toward political intransigence among underground groups, as witnessed in some of the positions adopted by the VSKhSON. In Sverdlovsk *oblast'* a factory technician, a stock keeper and a joiner (named Shefer, Sudakov and El'chin respectively) fashioned themselves as 'The Revolutionary Party' and in December 1962 produced a programme of action in which they pledged to establish contact with the embassies of capitalist states, to acquire weapons and to launch a wave of terror against the Soviet authorities. These were not simply adventure-seeking young boys playing at revolution, though: the eldest, Sudakov, was forty-five years old and had been jailed twice already. Typically of the early 1960s, none of the three was a member of either the Komsomol or Communist Party. The kind of activist idealism that had formerly prompted members of those two organisations to engage in dissenting activity was in clear decline. The group was uncovered and its participants arrested in January 1963 while attempting to attract new recruits from among the armed forces, according to the KGB. Their sentences, however, were surprisingly lenient: two years for El' chin and four years each for Shefer and Sudakov.[34]

On 13 March 1963, and then again on 31 August and 1 September, over 100 anti-Soviet leaflets were discovered in Tashkent that had been produced by a group calling itself the 'Secret Terrorist Union'.[35] The leaflets simply read: 'In the present conditions the existence of the Party is absurd. It does

[32] N. Mitrokhin, *Russkaya partiya*, p. 230.

[33] A. Yanov, *The Russian New Right: Right-Wing Ideologies in the Contemporary USSR*, Berkeley, CA: Institute of International Studies, 1978, p. 21.

[34] RGANI, f. 5, op. 30, d. 412, ll. 34–5.   [35] RGANI, f. 5, op. 30, d. 429, l. 88.

not oppose anyone and it does not fight for anyone.' This leaflet in particular offered an early insight into the ideological malaise that had already begun to take hold over many citizens in the Soviet Union.[36] While we cannot assume that moods among dissenters were a reliable reflection of the attitudes of 'ordinary' citizens, these kinds of sources do help strengthen the long-established but hard-to-quantify suspicion of declining ideological engagement from the 1960s onwards. At the top, the revolutionary ethos of earlier years was being supplanted by consolidation and conservatism, draining the system of its vitality but at the same time helping to provide stability. As the burst of political enthusiasm that had swept the system in 1956 showed, resurgent communist idealism had anyway been a particularly mixed blessing for the authorities, since the attitudes and expectations it could engender rarely fit perfectly with those of the Party leadership.

In May 1963 the Belarusian KGB arrested three participants of an underground group in Minsk, all of them students at the local polytechnic institute, who had managed to acquire several artillery shells and other explosives, which they had apparently found in the forest. The trio had drawn up detailed plans to blow up Minsk radio station number 3 – the city's jamming station – and had acquired almost 6 kg (13 lb) of typescript with which to produce leaflets.[37] On 27 May the group leader, Sergei Khanzhenkov, was apprehended by chance as he travelled into the centre of Minsk on a bus with a suitcase containing explosives. He was subsequently jailed for ten years. His co-conspirators, Viktor Khrapovitskii and Georgii Seregin, received sentences of ten years' and eight years' corrective labour respectively. Over forty years later, Khanzhenkov recalled how he had seen the radio jamming station as a symbol of Soviet power to be fought against in order to 'shake up' the peaceful and submissive life of the Belarusian SSR.[38] On reflection, he conceded it had been naïve to think that blowing up a radio station would have changed anything much in the country. Indeed, had their plan succeeded the likelihood would almost certainly have been public outrage and an intense crackdown on dissent.

---

[36] Some, such as Fürst, argue that this malaise had started to take hold among the masses in the years prior to Stalin's death. See J. Fürst, *Stalin's Last Generation: Soviet Post-War Youth and the Emergence of Mature Socialism*, Oxford University Press, 2010, p. 3.

[37] RGANI, f. 5, op. 30, d. 412, ll. 70–7. See also F. Feldbrugge, *Samizdat and Political Dissent in the Soviet Union*, Leiden: A.W. Sijthoff, 1975, p. 48.

[38] *Belgazeta*, 24 October 2005, pp. 26–7. Mikkonen shows that Soviet jamming of foreign broadcasts was widely unpopular, even amongst law-abiding citizens. See S. Mikkonen, 'Stealing the Monopoly of Knowledge? Soviet Reactions to Cold War Broadcasting', *Kritika*, Vol. 11, No. 4 (Fall 2010), 771–805.

This kind of naïvety about the mood of the masses was to be one of the hallmarks of the 1960s underground.

In Leningrad, Valery Ronkin's 'Kolokol' group, also known as the 'Union of Communards', came together at the city's Institute of Technology in the summer of 1964 and produced a Djilas-inspired manifesto entitled 'From Dictatorship of the Bureaucracy to Dictatorship of the Proletariat', which soon became well known in non-conformist circles. It insisted that the Soviet brand of socialism was entirely discredited and spoke of overthrowing the regime with a Hungarian-style popular revolution.[39] Nonetheless, the members of the Kolokol group were to a man dedicated socialists.[40] In the autumn of 1964 the group distributed more *listovki* in Leningrad, mostly among students and tourists. Their message was simple: conditions could only be improved by revolution, since the Soviet authorities understood only the use of force.[41]

Ronkin and several of his fellow group-mates were uncovered and jailed the following year. Wishing to demonstrate the seriousness of their offence, but using an ill-considered turn of phrase, the prosecutor at their November 1965 trial reportedly declared that 'they send people to jail for this even in the West'.[42] While one's eye may well be drawn to the prosecutor's tacit admission of Soviet political intolerance, his statement was not entirely inaccurate. There is no doubt that Sergei Khanzhenkov's Minsk group would have faced jail for their actions under any political system whatsoever, and many of the other groups outlined in the present work would have at least attracted the interest of domestic security forces. This in itself is a point worth raising, since we are used to the traditional paradigm of 'repressive regime' and 'persecuted dissidents'. Of course, the overwhelming majority of evidence supports this broad conception of the struggle between critics and authority inside the USSR. Even so, if one is to gain a better understanding of the dynamics of that conflict, it is important to acknowledge that matters were not always quite so straightforward.

One of the common denominators among those involved in underground activity, like Ronkin and Khanzhenkov, was that they saw themselves acting in what could be called 'the public interest' and consequently

---

[39] See V. Pimonov, *Govoryat 'osobo opasnye'*, p. 71 and V. Iofe, *Granitsy smysla: stat'i, vystupleniya, esse*, Sankt Peterburg: Nauchno-informatsionnyi tsentr 'Memorial', 2002, p. 120.

[40] See J. Fürst, 'Friends in Private, Friends in Public: The Phenomenon of the Kompaniia among Soviet Youth in the 1950s and 1960s', in L. Siegelbaum ed., *Borders of Socialism*, p. 233.

[41] V. Ronkin, *Na smenu dekabryam prikhodit yanvari ...*, Moskva: Obshchestvo 'Memorial', 2003, p. 150.

[42] L. Alexeyeva, *Soviet Dissent: Contemporary Movements for National, Religious and Human Rights*, Middletown, CT: Wesleyan University Press, 1987, p. 298.

assumed that 'the people' would ultimately rally to their side. Ideas of 'shaking up' or 'awakening' the masses were commonplace in the thinking of underground groups, who often liked to identify themselves as a would-be vanguard of 'the people' in their struggle with authority. As Alexei Yurchak asserts, however, such dissidents were often regarded by their contemporaries as 'fanatics' and 'obsessives' in much the same way that Party activists were.[43] In other words, they did not represent the views, ambitions and daily reality of 'the people'. Leaflets, manifestos and verbal tirades frequently reflected an assumption that 'the people' agreed with the opinions expressed by the complainant, though this assumption often proved illusory. The VSKhSON, for example, based its entire programme on the assumption that the country was ready to reject communism, something that Leonid Borodin later conceded was 'delusional'.[44] For some, the wish was perhaps father to the thought. The absence of any reliable information on public moods can only have exacerbated such a situation, since it allowed individuals and groups to presume a unity of popular opinion that did not exist in reality. By the middle of the 1960s, this was a mistake that groups made less and less frequently, as dissenters began to turn away from the evidently unrealistic aspiration of winning the open support of the Soviet masses against their political leaders.

Things were not always as they seemed at first glance, however. The reality was that some seemingly dangerous underground organisations existed only on paper. There were more than a few cases when dissenters drew up manifestos and leaflets in the name of groups that did not really exist. D. Kruritskii, for example – a Communist Party member of fifteen years' standing and a decorated war veteran – was arrested by the KGB in 1960 after pasting up leaflets around Moscow (which, in standard KGB rubric, included 'slander against the Party and state' as well as threats against Khrushchev) and sending over 230 anonymous letters to political leaders of the very highest rank. All this was done in the name of the 'Committee of Liberation', of which Kruritskii proved to be the only member.[45] Similarly, lone individuals could send anonymous letters threatening strikes and uprisings in the name of an entire factory or town. The main motive for this kind of behaviour most probably lay in the assumption that a collective complaint was more likely to be successful in gaining the authorities' attention, whereas the opinions and

---

[43] See A. Yurchak, *Everything Was Forever Until it Was No More: The Last Soviet Generation*, Oxford: Princeton University Press, 2006, p. 108.

[44] 'Beseda s Leonidom Borodinym', in V. Pimonov ed., *Govoryat 'osobo opasnye'*, p. 72.

[45] RGANI, f. 5, op. 30, d. 320, l. 156.

demands of a lone citizen could be easily dismissed in a system that did not prioritise the individual. Even so, as numerous scholars have shown, notions of collectivism were deeply embedded in Soviet society by this point, so expressing oneself in terms of 'we' rather than 'I' was not necessarily a purely tactical step. Leaflets that exaggerated the scale of underground activity (such as Bul'binskii's announcement that 'the strike movement has begun') probably also aimed to embolden others to action by showing those who suppressed their own doubts and frustrations that they were not alone. In practice, though, this kind of aim would hardly ever be achieved, since the attention of the security organs would be quickly aroused and strenuous efforts made to track down and remove all such leaflets before they came to the attention of the public.

The early 1960s also saw a number of KGB reports exposing mooted assassination plots aimed at the CPSU First Secretary in particular. In 1960, an underground group in Tbilisi prepared a bomb to be thrown at Khrushchev during an up-coming visit to the city, apparently as an act of retribution for the violent suppression of the riots there in 1956.[46] In December 1963, the Moscow student and CPSU member I.G. Lomov formed a group with a Lithuanian named Eidrigyavichyus and a Russian named Zubarev and plotted an attack on Khrushchev as he travelled between Moscow's Vnukovo airport and the Kremlin, though it remains unclear as to how advanced plans had become before the trio were arrested.[47] As Chapter 9 shows, an abortive assassination attempt in Moscow during 1961 was ironically to play a significant role in the evolution of the subsequent human-rights movement.

A handful of lower-level officials were physically injured and even killed during the period. In Kiev, for example, an unidentified individual managed to fire several rifle shots through a window at a Party meeting, hitting two people and killing one of them.[48] In February 1963 an intoxicated worker named V.T. Sharutin shot and killed one N.P. Sokolov, the chairman of a local electoral commission, with a hunting rifle.[49] A little over four months earlier, in Kalinin *oblast'*, a citizen had drunkenly called for communists and Komsomol members to be executed, before firing off twenty-five shots, wounding a local CPSU member and then burning her house

---

[46] V. Kozlov and S. Mironenko eds., *Kramola: inakomyslie v SSSR pri Khrushcheve i Brezhneve 1953–1982*, Moskva: 'Materik', 2005, p. 324.
[47] See V. Kozlov and S. Mironenko eds., *Kramola*, p. 324.   [48] RGANI, f. 5, op. 30, d. 231, l. 15.
[49] RGANI, f. 5, op. 30, d. 429, l. 22.

down.[50] With only scant details available, one cannot say for certain that these attacks were carried out either partly or wholly on political grounds, rather than out of simple personal animosity, yet the incident in Kalinin *oblast'* in particular seems to suggest a combination of both the personal and political.

Many of the above cases serve to highlight the extent to which underground activity was beginning to reflect an increasing degree of alienation from the existing regime. It is also true, however, that even though the dissenters may have been entirely earnest in their calls for demonstrations and resistance, most did not come anywhere near to putting their militant plans into action. In the case of Petro Grigorenko's underground group, 'The Alliance of Struggle for the Rebirth of Leninism', Andrei Grigorenko – himself a member of the organisation – conceded that although their leaflets spoke of uprisings and revolution there was never any real effort made to acquire weapons or to plot any kind of rising.[51] Even so, it would be too dismissive to suggest that such groups were essentially 'playing at revolution', especially since the dangers involved in even threatening an insurrection were so great. This kind of gap between words and deeds was not uncommon, though. Setting oneself huge political goals in an environment where there was such limited scope for unsanctioned political activity, and in which the KGB remained ever-vigilant, was always likely to end with total failure to live up to one's aims.

While 'Bolshevik methods' were still a useful template for underground group activity, neo-Bolshevik political thought was losing some of its former lustre as the years passed. The Soviet system had always put great effort into isolating the USSR from the harmful influences of the outside world, especially during the last few years of the Stalin era. The drive to shut out foreign cultural encroachment had never been comprehensive in its scope or completely successful, and new research is showing that cultural norms could be flouted quite widely even during the most stifling period of Stalinism.[52] Nonetheless, the ideological seal imposed around the country was almost airtight, leaving Soviet society overwhelmingly isolated from outside ideas and information. This 'information blockade' had been a great asset as the regime sought to build an entirely new society. It had never been able to stop all unsanctioned information from circulating, but it had kept

---

[50] RGANI, f. 5, op. 30, d. 378, l. 44.
[51] Interview with Andrei Grigorenko, New York, October 2006.
[52] See, for example, G. Tsipursky, 'Pleasure, Power and the Pursuit of Communism: Soviet Youth and State-Sponsored Popular Culture during the Early Cold War Period, 1945–1968', Ph.D. Dissertation, University of North Carolina at Chapel Hill, 2011.

society as a whole largely insulated against most of what the regime did not want its citizens to hear.[53] When this virtual monopoly on information began to weaken in the 1950s and 1960s, the system's failings, cruelties and lies were broadcast again and again for those who wished to hear them. This in itself would rarely provoke major acts of protest, but it could certainly facilitate listeners' declining engagement with key elements of official discourse. In fact, consciously disregarding government warnings on the 'dangers' of politically harmful phenomena such as foreign radio broadcasts, and tuning in anyway, of itself showed a degree of disengagement from official discourse.[54]

The first Radio Liberty broadcasts to the USSR began at almost exactly the same time that Stalin left the Soviet stage.[55] Official opening up to the outside world also began quickly, though rather more hesitantly, in the months and years after March 1953. An increased amount of Western literature was published; a handful of student and cultural exchanges were enacted; Soviet teams more frequently entered the international sporting arena and foreign tourism to the USSR was encouraged. These changes hardly revolutionised Soviet society all at once, but they were to bring the outside world a little closer: this had a lasting impact on dissenting behaviour, and one that continued to grow over time.

In the adversarial context of the Cold War, the capitalist powers were not averse to making ideological capital out of Soviet citizens' frustrations. Even so, the primary importance of the West in regard to Soviet dissent did not lie in overt attempts at encouraging subversion. It lay instead in the opening of new ideological and material horizons and in the further erosion of faith in the authorities' pronouncements and policies. As Vladimir Bukovsky recalled of the 1957 World Youth Festival and the 1959 American Exhibition in Moscow (which was attended by around 3,000,000 Soviet citizens over forty-two days), 'All this talk about "putrefying capitalism" became ridiculous. The importance of these events was comparable to the

---

[53] Zinaida Schakovsky, for example, recalled that the young people she met on her travels around the USSR in 1957 were 'superbly ignorant of the outside world'. Z. Schakovsky, *The Privilege Was Mine*, London: Jonathan Cape, 1959, p. 166. What almost all sources from the era point to, however, is a great curiosity about the West among youths in particular.

[54] Both Gleb Tsipursky and Juliane Fürst have raised an analogous point in regard to those who continued to dance proscribed Western dances during the early 1950s. See G. Tsipursky, 'Pleasure, Power, and the Pursuit of Communism', and J. Fürst, *Stalin's Last Generation*.

[55] Gene Sosin recalled that less than ten minutes into the first Radio Liberty broadcast the Soviet authorities located and began to jam the signal. G. Sosin, *Sparks of Liberty: An Insider's Memoirs of Radio Liberty*, University Park, PA: Pennsylvania State University Press, 1999, p. 13. Both the BBC and Voice of America had been broadcasting to the USSR for some years by this point, though their content was markedly less politicised than that of Radio Liberty.

exposure of Stalin.'[56] The latter part of Bukovsky's remark may have exaggerated the point somewhat, but the broader message it conveyed was undoubtedly realistic. Interaction with the outside world, especially the capitalist West, was problematic for social control on all kinds of levels. Although most people continued broadly to accept official pronouncements on subjects such as domestic and foreign events, those who no longer did so could be particularly vociferous in their rejection of state lies. An anonymous letter to Aleksandr Shelepin summed this up perfectly. The author wrote simply that: 'you say black is white ... stop writing and chattering about the happiness of the people. It is insulting that we know the opposite is true.'[57]

It is important to note, however, that citizens with a sense of interest in, and admiration for, aspects of life in the West did not necessarily reject the Soviet system either in whole or in part. There was no clean dichotomy of pro-West and anti-Soviet. Just as one could quite easily tolerate or enjoy certain aspects of life in the USSR whilst objecting to others, the same was true of attitudes to the West. It was entirely possible to consider oneself a good Soviet citizen whilst also enjoying American jazz or French cinema. Similarly, many of the most vociferous and classically subversive dissenters of the early Khrushchev period were unambiguous in their rejection of the capitalist system. Few doubted that its collectivism and global mission made the Soviet system morally superior to the apparent greed and individualism of the West. As Vladislav Zubok has pointed out, even the perennially persecuted *stilyagi* – who defined themselves by their love of Western fashions and music – often continued to support Stalin wholeheartedly in his last years.[58]

Most of those young people who were drawn toward the West did not focus primarily on its politics. The burgeoning interest in Western music and fashions that began to emerge soon after the war then flourished under Khrushchev and was to grow inexorably from a relatively minor, elitist trend to one that would dominate the youth culture of the later Soviet years, with the likes of the Beatles, Slade and Deep Purple gaining a huge fan-base inside the USSR. This was not without significance, even if it did not equate to outright rejection of the Soviet system. As Sergei Zhuk pointed out in his work on youth culture in post-Stalin Dnepropetrovsk: 'Rock and Roll was

---

[56] V. Bukovsky, *To Build a Castle: My Life as a Dissenter*, London: Andre Deutsch, 1978, p. 113.
[57] RGANI, f. 5, op. 30, d. 141, l. 2.
[58] V. Zubok, *Zhivago's Children: The Last Russian Intelligentsia*, Cambridge, MA: Harvard University Press, 2009, p. 44.

the battering ram the West drove into our collective psyche. Then every-thing else rushed in: art, fashion, books, and, sometimes, politics.'[59] Zhuk's use of the word 'sometimes' is worth noting. In the early 1960s this was still a situation in its infancy, though that did not stop the Soviet authorities from taking the kind of heavy-handed approach to cultural non-conformity that ultimately served to exacerbate the problems facing the regime by forcing those outside of the mainstream to satiate their cultural tastes through semi-legal and illegal means, thus setting in motion the margin-alisation of a growing swathe of the young population.

The enduring importance of material concerns in dissenters' complaints was demonstrated in numerous reports sent from the KGB to the Central Committee's General Department. On 30 December 1961 leaflets were pasted up on walls in the centre of Chita, asking: 'Loudmouth Khrushchev – where is your abundance?' and 'Comrades! How much longer will we live half-starving and destitute?'[60] An anonymous letter sent to the Central Committee presented the situation as follows: 'There are five million people who are living under communism – they are the government and the ministers. Ten million are living under socialism – these are the directors, generals, engineers and bureaucrats. The other one hundred and eighty-five million of us are waiting for socialism and we do not even know what it is.'[61] An anonymous letter left in a Kaliningrad ballot box lambasted 'communist millionaires', stating that 'They are stealing money, they are living in luxurious palaces and they see workers as beasts.'[62] Anger at such apparent breaches of social justice indicated a willingness to judge the performance of the system on its own terms, again suggesting an underpinning acceptance of the basic principles on which it stood. Perceived distinctions between 'us' and 'them' – with 'them' usually meaning bureaucrats and officials, rather than ordinary Party mem-bers – had long been a feature of Soviet life and was a wellspring of consid-erable resentment. This gap between leaders and masses was to continue growing as the privileges and self-aggrandisement of the Soviet elite, not just in politics but in culture, industry and much else besides, expanded further over the late Soviet period.

The issue of poor living standards among large elements of the popula-tion grew more pressing once it started to become evident from radio broadcasts and encounters with foreigners in the major cities just how

---

[59] S. Zhuk, *Rock and Roll in the Rocket City: The West, Identity, and Ideology in Soviet Dnepropetrovsk, 1960–1985*, Washington, DC: Woodrow Wilson Center Press, 2010, p. 9.
[60] RGANI, f. 5, op. 30, d. 378, l. 28.   [61] V. Kozlov and S. Mironenko eds., *Kramola*, p. 268.
[62] V. Kozlov and S. Mironenko eds., *Kramola*, p. 203.

superior material conditions were in other parts of the world. The fact that Khrushchev's incessant boasts about catching up and overtaking the West aroused such indignation among colleagues in the Central Committee Presidium suggests that they too were aware this was a source of tension within society, where envious glances were directed not only toward the West. With the growth of travel between the USSR and Eastern Europe, it became apparent that in places there, too, many people enjoyed a higher standard of living than those in the Soviet Union. A speaker at one Party meeting went so far as to claim that 'even in Africa they live better than we do': a useful demonstration of the hyperbole that questions of living standards could prompt.[63] This kind of overstatement was itself a response to the fact that the regime's consistently misleading discourse about improving material conditions set the bar for economic success impossibly high. Alexis de Tocqueville's dictum that 'material grievances become intolerable once it is made apparent that a better situation exists elsewhere' is particularly apt in regard to frustration at living standards as citizens learned more about the wider world. For years state propaganda had told of inhuman conditions endured by ordinary citizens in the West, a factor that had surely amelio-rated the many privations endured by the Soviet people in earlier years. By the later part of the Khrushchev era this kind of lie simply would not stick. With the post-Stalin Soviet regime increasingly basing its credibility on an ability to provide an acceptable standard of living for its citizens – as was the case across much of post-war Europe – tangible improvements were needed.[64]

Despite complaints about goods shortages and low wages, living standards were actually rising appreciably for most citizens during the Khrushchev era. The country's chronic housing shortage was being tackled with great fanfare and the availability and variety of consumer goods expanded along with widened access to higher education and improving healthcare.[65] Avenues for recreation and entertainment proliferated and were sometimes even shorn of their previously ubiquitous ideological messages.[66] Nonetheless, improving material conditions do not of themselves induce greater public contentment and conformity: quite the opposite in many cases. Broadening

[63] RGANI, f. 89, op. 6, d. 6, ll. 1–5.
[64] See S. Reid, 'Cold War in the Kitchen: Gender and the De-Stalinization of Consumer Taste in the Soviet Union under Khrushchev', *Slavic Review*, Vol. 60, No. 2 (Summer 2002), 211–52.
[65] On the Khrushchev-era housing programme, see in particular M. Smith, *Property of Communists: The Urban Housing Programme from Stalin to Khrushchev*, DeKalb, IL: Northern Illinois University Press, 2010.
[66] On this theme, see K. Roth-Ey, *Moscow Prime Time: How the Soviet Union Built the Media Empire that Lost the Cultural Cold War*, London: Cornell University Press, 2011.

horizons and improvements to everyday life served to arouse higher hopes for the future and fed desire for further advances – desires that Khrushchev's boasting about 'catching up and overtaking the US' hardly helped to contain.

In studies on dissent in the former East Germany, it has been argued that citizens there used the economically far superior West Germany as a yardstick to measure the successes and shortcomings of their own system, and this naturally went some way toward undermining the prestige of the GDR in the eyes of many of its people.[67] Although lacking in the racial and historical aspects of the German model, the analogy of Soviet citizens looking at the way that citizens of the world's only other superpower lived had a broadly similar effect.[68] While older citizens who had reached maturity by the 1930s tended to view their material situation in terms of improvement on the early Soviet and Tsarist past, by the 1950s younger people more often compared their own circumstances with those that existed in other countries, both socialist and non-socialist – further evidence that horizons were widening.[69] Such comparisons rarely reflected particularly well on the situation at home. As time went on it became harder to escape the conclusion that there were systemic economic problems that would not be overcome under existing conditions. With regime discourse on full communism tending to centre upon themes of material abundance, which plainly failed to be forthcoming, derision was never too far away.[70]

The increased emphasis on questions of material goods was indicative of the extent to which underground groups had increasingly become the preserve of workers, rather than members of the intelligentsia. One can attribute this tendency for workers to predominate in the underground group activity of the later Khrushchev years to a number of factors. As Chapters 2 and 4 showed, a concerted drive to silence political nonconformity within the student body and the Communist Party and Komsomol had already done much to stamp out signs of overt political criticism among many of those whom we might class as 'educated', yet that explains only one aspect of the change. Vladimir Shlapentokh pointed to a decline in the social prestige that the authorities allotted to the working

---

[67] J. Grix, *The Role of the Masses in the Collapse of the GDR*, Basingstoke: Macmillan, 2000, p. 10.

[68] Of course, this is not to suggest that Soviet, or East German, notions of Western living standards were always realistic, since they, too, were often a result of propaganda.

[69] See J. Millar, 'History, Method, and the Problem of Bias', in J. Millar, ed., *Politics, Work, and Daily Life in the USSR: A Survey of Former Soviet Citizens*, Cambridge University Press, 1987, p. 27.

[70] There were, of course, plenty of Soviet jokes regarding the regime's promises of material abundance. See in particular B. Lewis, *Hammer and Tickle*, London: Weidenfeld & Nicolson, 2008.

classes as a reason for growing worker discontent.[71] Elina Zavadskaya and Olga Edelman, on the other hand, point to the growing gap between material expectations and reality, combined with a lack of legitimate alternative outlets for frustration.[72] While the two approaches are not necessarily incompatible, it is the latter which feels the more convincing, particularly when we take into account the consumerist social contract of the time, along with popular resentment at elite privileges and the fact that ever since the crackdown that followed the Secret Speech it was entirely clear that there remained virtually no acceptable outlet for all manner of frustrations.

One of the most interesting dynamics regarding the growing predominance of workers among those who participated in underground groups was that of the relationship between education and dissent. Writing about the Stalin-era group 'the Communist Party of Youth', Juliane Fürst suggested that well-developed intellectual abilities were vital for those who engaged in this kind of underground activity, since these provided the necessary framework for individuals both to critique their existing environment and to visualise a better world.[73] Evidence from the initial part of Khrushchev's rule broadly supports this thesis, particularly when we draw a link between education levels and the kind of fundamentally ideological criticism witnessed during the second half of the 1950s. Data showing that the underground groups of the early 1960s tended to feature participants who were less well-educated appears somewhat problematic for Fürst's assertion, however. It is certainly true that education levels were rising generally during the post-Stalin era, yet this alone was not sufficiently pronounced as to account for what was a fairly sharp demographic change among dissenters.

In reality, the question was not necessarily one of being educated in the way that we typically conceive it today (roughly, based upon the level of schooling reached) but on the amount of information – whether scrupulously accurate or not – that was available to those willing and eager to receive it. Whether coming from inside the Soviet Union, in the form of leaflets and *samizdat* literature, or from the West, in the form of radio broadcasts, the field of non-official information becoming available to ordinary people in the USSR was growing markedly under Khrushchev.

---

[71] See V. Shlapentokh, *Soviet Intellectuals and Political Power: The Post-Stalin Era*, Princeton University Press, 1990.

[72] E. Zavadskaya and O. Edelman, 'Underground Groups and Organisations', in V. Kozlov, S. Fitzpatrick and S. Mironenko eds., *Sedition: Everyday Resistance in the Soviet Union under Khrushchev and Brezhnev*, New Haven, CT: Yale University Press, 2011, pp. 290–1.

[73] J. Fürst, 'Prisoners of the Soviet Self? Political Youth Opposition in Late Stalinism', *Europe–Asia Studies*, Vol. 54, No. 3 (May 2002), 358.

This ensured that far greater numbers of Soviet citizens had the ability to conceptualise new aspirations and to articulate political grievances. If, as a number of authors have suggested, the Stalin regime had enjoyed notable success in implementing a kind of Orwellian thought control in delimiting its citizens' political thought, this was an achievement that came under sustained and often sophisticated attack from the 1950s onwards.[74] The declining prevalence of idealistic Marxist political views among underground groups, therefore, was not only rooted in the fact that their participants now tended to be less well-educated than previously – and were thereby less versed in the classics of Marxism-Leninism and wider socialist theory – but also in the fact that the information on which their complaints were based was increasingly emanating from the avowedly anti-communist West, not just from the Soviet past (as in the case of neo-Bolshevism) or from the USSR's ideological close cousins, like Tito's Yugoslavia.

Social tensions over material shortages and hardships were naturally seized upon and exacerbated by a number of Western radio stations broadcasting to the USSR. Gene Sosin, an early Radio Liberty staff member, recalled that during the Cuban Missile Crisis his station regularly ran messages such as 'for every Soviet missile in Cuba, enough money, material and labour have been expended to provide shoes for 25,000 people'.[75] Already inflammatory in a country where basic necessities were lacking at times, broadcasting such material in late 1962 – after a summer of unrest sparked by the announcement of steep price rises – would surely have had some resonance among those who listened. This was the Cold-War propaganda battle at its most incisive: a battle in which the Soviet regime was consistently outfoxed by the US in particular.

The subject of Cuba raises another facet of dissenting behaviour in the Khrushchev period: that of criticism centred on Soviet aid to client states. While many idealistic communists continued to be enthused by the wider mission of Soviet involvement in the Third World, and by the romance of the Cuban revolution in particular, this was not the case for everyone. A leaflet distributed around Moscow in 1963, for example, insisted that 'The Soviet people tighten their belts every year, yet they suffer and stay silent, still clapping for Nikita when necessary. We work in order to feed "unlucky" Negroes and "poor" Germans yet the Soviet people have no bread.'[76] A 1963 CIA report pointed to anger in the Georgian port town of Sukhumi at the shipment of grain to Syria, when parts of the Soviet Union

---

[74] On the subject of 'Orwellian' mind control, see, for example, J. Fürst, 'Prisoners of the Soviet Self'.
[75] G. Sosin, *Sparks of Liberty*, p. 97.   [76] GARF, f. 8131, op. 33, d. 96712, l. 24.

received flour only a few times per year.[77] The Central Committee's General Department files also contain a number of anonymous letters in which the theme of foreign aid was raised, including one addressed to Aleksandr Shelepin from Komi ASSR which claimed Soviet standards of living were lower than in every capitalist country, stating 'prices are supposed to be coming down but you are skinning people' and 'it is no surprise that there has been trouble in Poland, Hungary and Germany, we have suffered even longer' before ending by insisting that 'the hunger here is because you and your colleagues are giving all of our products away'.[78]

It is important to point out that financial and material aid to client states was not a theme of dissent restricted solely to the Khrushchev era, and probably not to the USSR either for that matter. As mentioned in Chapter 1, calls for subscriptions to aid the Republican side during the Spanish Civil War had also met with a critical response in some quarters, even in the hellishly dangerous political environment of the late 1930s. Evidently, some of the Soviet people, and this seems to apply to workers most of all, had long resented giving away the fruits of their collective labour while there were major shortages to be addressed at home. It was they, of course, who faced many of these shortages and one can empathise with this sense of frustration at being overlooked as their political masters chased wider strategic goals – some of them bearing only the flimsiest relationship to the system's ideological mission – at their expense.[79]

Away from a few major Soviet cities, the chance to encounter the new influx of foreign students and tourists was rare, leaving radio broadcasts the main link to the outside world. These were usually hard to access because of jamming, especially in the big urban centres, though people were often prepared to go to considerable lengths in order to pick up broadcasts, such as learning how to customise receivers or heading out of town in order to pick up a signal beyond the range of the jamming stations. Western intrusion into Soviet airwaves increased dramatically throughout the period as the number of stations expanded along with the number of broadcasting hours, languages and signal strengths. A report sent to Khrushchev from the Ministry of Culture in May 1956 showed the extent to which this was a growing problem, pointing out that there were already 25,000,000 private shortwave radio sets in the USSR but by the end of the sixth five-year plan,

---

[77] 'Life and Attitudes in Soviet Georgia: Random Observations by Wife of Repatriated German Scientist'. Budapest, HU OSA 299.
[78] RGANI, f. 5, op. 30, d. 141, l. 2.
[79] Soviet support for Nasser's Egypt, for example, met with a degree of distaste since Nasser had until recently been repressing Egyptian communists.

in 1960, that figure was to rise to around 70,000,000.[80] As the year 1960 arrived, there were fifty to sixty foreign radio stations broadcasting to Soviet audiences, ensuring that the authorities could not even hope to block them all out.[81] Even allowing for variable factors such as signal strength and extensive jamming, it is evident that the potential audience for Western broadcasts was becoming truly massive.[82]

There is of course a question mark over how many people listened to such broadcasts and in what ways they were influenced by them. The evidence here is patchy. Sosin recalled that at the 1958 Brussels World Fair representatives of Radio Liberty managed to interview 300 Soviet tourists, with sixty-five of them reporting that they were regular listeners to the station.[83] These data, though, probably tell us relatively little about the true size of Radio Liberty's audience inside the USSR. People allowed to go on foreign trips to capitalist states like Belgium were usually those with unblemished political records and were probably less inclined to listen to foreign radio, or at least were less likely to admit doing so. Although various accounts suggest that 'virtually everyone' listened to Western broadcasts toward the end of the Soviet era, this was not the case under Khrushchev, for ideological and practical reasons, such as the fact that many people in rural areas still owned only the 'wired sets' which would not pick up foreign channels. The conditions these foreign stations operated in made it particularly hard for them to obtain reliable feedback from their audiences, and thus they could struggle to tailor their content effectively at times. Indeed, research carried out by Radio Liberty found that although those who opposed the regime thought the station's broadcasts too moderate in tone, others were offended by anything deemed sharply anti-communist.[84]

Even avid listeners to Western radio did not necessarily disregard official Soviet discourse. Many of them were interested first and foremost in hearing new music. Donald Raleigh's interviews with former Soviet citizens

[80] RGANI, f. 5, op. 30, d. 141, ll. 17–18. On the reasons for the Soviet regime's decision to mass-produce short-wave radios, which were by their nature better able than long-wave radios to pick up signals from outside the USSR, see K. Roth-Ey, *Moscow Prime Time*.
[81] As Simo Mikkonen shows, jamming was a complex and expensive operation which produced only mixed success. The proliferation of foreign signals ensured that the authorities had to concentrate their efforts only on jamming 'the most anti-Soviet' broadcasts. S. Mikkonen, 'Stealing the Monopoly of Knowledge'.
[82] Around this time there was also an initial concern among Soviet leaders that the rapidly emerging medium of television might be infiltrated by outside powers in the same way that radio had been. See K. Roth-Ey, 'Finding a Home for Television in the USSR, 1950–70', *Slavic Review*, Vol. 66, No. 2 (2007), 278–306.
[83] G. Sosin, *Sparks of Liberty*, p. 73.
[84] V. Petrov, 'Radio Liberation', *Russian Review*, Vol. 17, No. 2 (April 1958), 111.

who grew up in the provincial Russian city of Saratov during the post-Stalin era provide some useful insights on the impact of Western broadcasts.[85] We see, for example, that most of those whom Raleigh interviewed recalled accepting the Soviet regime's version of events, rather than that presented by the foreign radio stations they listened to, as late as the 1968 Prague Spring.[86] Evidently, people did not automatically accept that news coming from the West was 'the truth', but rightly recognised that the likes of Radio Liberty also had their own agenda. An excerpt from one of Raleigh's interviews, with Natalia Belovola, raises a further question over the impact of Western broadcasts on young people's behaviour when the interviewee said that: '. . . back then I didn't pay much attention to what was said, but was more interested in saying that I listened to Voice of America. Even more so because it was jammed and everything that's secretive and off-limits always elicits interest.'[87] As with Valery Ronkin's friends who had spoken of forming an underground group in the hope of meeting girls and finding Western music, for some young people this kind of behaviour was first and foremost about being fashionably rebellious.

It seems that many, perhaps most, who listened to foreign radio did not fundamentally change their political views as a direct result – or least they did not do so immediately. The most popular and most trusted stations were either those that played the most new Western music or else those that opted to forgo direct political attacks on the communist regime and instead attempted to provide relatively balanced information, such as the BBC and Voice of America. For those citizens already disenchanted at the Soviet system, however, the likes of Radio Liberty offered exactly what they wanted to hear: political hostility.

An important matter to note in regard to Radio Liberty in particular is that, roughly in line with the Soviet leadership's accusations, the station clearly was an integral part of US propaganda efforts against the communist regime. Set up, supervised and covertly funded by the CIA, the long-term goal of the station was not so dissimilar to that which the Soviet authorities loudly alleged: to undermine and discredit the communist system in the eyes of its citizens.[88] The name of its official parent company, Amcomlib –

---

[85] See, for example, interview with Arkadyi Darchenko, p. 133 or Gennadyi Ivanov, p. 257, in D. Raleigh ed., *Russia's Sputnik Generation: Soviet Baby Boomers Talk about Their Lives*, Bloomington, IN: Indiana University Press, 2006.

[86] D. Raleigh ed., *Russia's Sputnik Generation*, p. 20.

[87] Interview with Natalia Belovola in D. Raleigh ed., *Russia's Sputnik Generation*, p. 166.

[88] The fact that Radio Liberty was funded by the CIA was not fully exposed until 1971. The link between the two was officially severed soon after.

an acronym for 'American Committee for Liberation from Bolshevism' – clearly demonstrated that Radio Liberty had a distinctly political function. Furthermore, this was a truly major operation on the US government's part: by 1963 the station had thirty state-of-the-art transmitters spread across Germany, Spain and Taiwan and was broadcasting on twenty-six different frequencies in a multitude of Soviet languages.[89]

Even more ideologically hostile than Radio Liberty was the Frankfurt-am-Main-based 'People's Labour Union' or *Narodno trudovyi soyuz*, known as NTS.[90] Founded in Belgrade by White Émigrés fleeing Russia after the Bolshevik takeover in October 1917, NTS was bitterly anti-communist. It also had informal links to the CIA. Although largely neutralised and reduced to semi-mythical 'bogeyman' status by the 1970s, the organisation was still very real during the Khrushchev era and its efforts to stir unrest inside the Soviet Union were considerable.[91] In a July 1956 report to the Central Committee, KGB chairman Ivan Serov described the NTS strategy of sending unmanned hot-air balloons packed with anti-Soviet propaganda materials across Soviet and East European territory from bases in West Germany. Serov stated that in the preceding six months a total of 806 balloons had been found in Ukraine and Belarus, along with Russian regions including Moscow, Yaroslavl, Ivanov, Voronezh, Chelyabinsk, Omsk and Tyumen, containing over 106,000 leaflets, brochures and newspapers in total.[92] That NTS continued with this practice into the 1960s was evidenced by figures provided in the KGB's 1977 internal history textbook, which stated that over 5,000 such balloons were discovered on Soviet territory during 1961–2, containing a total of over 1,000,000 anti-Soviet leaflets.[93] In June 1960 the KGB also reported that NTS agents had been attempting to make contact with a party of Soviet tourists visiting West Germany, unsuccessfully trying to

[89] G. Sosin, *Sparks of Liberty*, p. 98.

[90] Less well-known anti-Soviet groups based overseas included the Union of Struggle for the Freedom of the Peoples of Russia (SBONR), the Union of Struggle for a Free Russia (SBSR) and the League for Struggle for People's Freedom.

[91] Numerous dissidents, including Aleksandr Ginzburg and Yuri Galanskov, were falsely accused of having links to NTS during the Brezhnev era. See J. Rubenstein, *Soviet Dissidents: Their Struggle for Human Rights*, Boston, MA: Beacon Press, 1980, p. 70. Yuri Orlov recalled that even in the late 1970s he had believed the group to be a fictional invention of the KGB. Yu. Orlov, *Dangerous Thoughts: Memoirs of a Russian Life*, New York: William Morrow and Company, 1991, p. 205.

[92] RGANI, f. 5, op. 30, d. 141, ll. 54–6.

[93] V. Chebrikov et al., *Istoriya sovetskikh organov gosudarstvennoi bezopasnosti: uchebnik*, Moskva: Vysshaya krasnoznamenskaya shkola komiteta gosudarstvennoi bezopasnosti pri sovete ministerov SSSR, 1977, p. 543.

persuade them to smuggle the organisation's leaflets into the USSR and to distribute them on their return.[94]

NTS had some sporadic successes in stirring up small-scale protest activity through its radio broadcasts. In Stavropol an assistant doctor named M.M. Ermizin posted dozens of anti-Soviet leaflets in the name of the NTS between 1962 and 1964. They were sent to the Central Committee Presidium and to newspapers including *Sovetskaya kul'tura*, *Stavropol'skaya pravda* and *Kazakhstanskaya zdravnitsa*, calling on others to produce and circulate anti-Soviet materials and to hold strikes and stage uprisings.[95] Another example could be seen in a case against I.I. Unger, I.I. Kuk and V.G. Neifel'd (all ethnic Germans) of Tomsk *oblast'* in which the trio had transcribed several NTS broadcasts. On 14 October 1962, an election day, they attached copies of these transcriptions to walls of factory buildings in the city and stuffed them into a ballot box. One of the leaflets discovered in a ballot box read as follows:

> *Voice of the People*
> *NTS calls on you to join the struggle*
> *against the Khrushchev dictatorship.*
> *Ask yourself a question:*
> *what exactly is 'Soviet power'?*
> *The radio and press say nothing about many events that are happening*
> *in our country.*
> *For example, the rising at Temirtau,*
> *the attempt on Khrushchev's life at the Soviet–Polish border*
> *and the strikes at the Kirov factory in Leningrad.*
> *Comrades!*
> *The time has come to struggle against the existing order.*
> *We have great faith in the strength of the people,*
> *Russia is waking up and we are hearing a new sound.*
> *It is the future!*
> *Of that there can be no doubt!*
> *NTS*[96]

The leaflet's complete lack of any reference to what NTS were proposing to replace Soviet power with was surely indicative of the fact that the organisation's ideological beliefs (essentially, activist anti-Marxism and rejection of collectivism) would have had limited resonance among the masses. Although there undoubtedly was a rising at Temirtau around this time, further research has so far failed to reveal evidence of the claimed strike in

---

[94] RGANI, f. 5, op. 30, d. 320, l. 12.   [95] GARF, f. 8131, op. 31, d. 97853, ll. 1–13.
[96] GARF, f. 8131, op. 31, d. 94153, ll. 1–9.

Leningrad.[97] It is wholly possible that the strike did happen and has not yet come to light, but it is perhaps more likely that it was entirely invented by NTS. After all, their aim was to provoke a public reaction, not to provide a reliable source of suppressed information. The point to be made here is that in such adversarial conditions one must regard information from practically all such sources with a degree of caution, not just those that were generated by the state.

In a 1972 *Russian Review* article, Sergei Levitsky claimed that NTS agitation inside the Soviet Union around this time was 'crowned with considerable success', while its publications came to 'enjoy great popularity among dissident Soviet citizens'.[98] However, there appears little in the way of hard evidence to support this claim and it is important to note that Levitsky was an émigré sympathiser of NTS. The number of Soviet citizens who responded positively to the incitements of NTS actually appears to have been very small. As far as one can judge these things, it seems that the general desire among most of the populace was generally not for revolution or for capitalism but more often for stability, a degree of liberalisation and a better standard of living. Even many active dissenters wished to have nothing to do with NTS. With much of the intelligentsia still broadly supportive of at least the principles on which the October Revolution was based, their interest in NTS was minimal. Workers, too, generally had little sympathy for their outright anti-communist messages, and Soviet patriotism still remained strong among Russians at least.

Among the most portentous facets of the increasing interaction between dissenters and the West in the early 1960s was the small but growing stream of communication flowing out of the USSR. With the exception of occasional personal encounters, up to the late 1950s communication between Soviet citizens and the West had been an overwhelmingly unidirectional affair – information was being beamed into the USSR but reliable news about events and attitudes inside Soviet territory was reaching the West far less often. By the early 1960s a few individuals were gradually beginning to open up small routes outwards. Later developed and expanded by the likes of Andrei Amalrik (an early expert at transmitting dissident literature to the West), this ability to communicate more effectively with the outside world would go on to become one of the cornerstones of the Brezhnev-era

[97] Similarly, Roy and Zhores Medvedev do mention an assassination attempt in Belarus (and also a second attempt in Stavropol), though it is far from clear whether this was the same event referred to in the above leaflet. See R. and Zh. Medvedev, *Khrushchev: The Years in Power*, New York: Columbia University Press, 1977, p. 21.
[98] See S. Levitsky, 'The Ideology of NTS', *Russian Review*, Vol. 31, No. 4 (October 1972), 398–405.

dissident movement and would eventually contribute to a major shift in the dynamics of dissenting activity in the USSR.

One of the first notable instances of this emerging route to the West could be seen in Yuri Galanskov's use of his personal connections among foreign journalists to transmit to the West information on riots that took place in Murom and Aleksandrov during 1961.[99] After hearing rumours of the disturbances, Viktor Khaustov, Eduard Kuznetsov and Vladimir Osipov immediately left Moscow to visit the two nearby towns in order to gather information on what had transpired there. They then wrote up the details in leaflet form and sent them abroad through Galanskov's contacts. In a sense, this was not unlike the kind of information-gathering that would later feature among the work of Brezhnev-era human-rights activists. In contrast to the sober and rigorously factual work of later dissidents, however, the trio produced a romanticised and politicised account of what were essentially hooligan riots rather than political demonstrations.

A growing number of Soviet citizens were arrested as a result of attempts to communicate with the West around this time. Veniamin Iofe documented numerous cases in Leningrad when citizens were jailed for translating and distributing articles from foreign newspapers, for possession of banned Western literature and for establishing too-close contacts with visiting tourists.[100] This spate of arrests reflected not only the growth of dissenters' contacts with the outside world but also increased sensitivity to 'harmful' Western influences on the part of the KGB and Central Committee Presidium, as the international strategic situation again turned increasingly frosty during the early 1960s.[101]

Nina Barbarchuk, a forty-three-year-old doctor from Minsk, was jailed in January 1961 after writing a series of anonymous letters to US President John F. Kennedy the previous month. A December 1960 letter from Barbarchuk included a warning to the President of her doubts about the Soviet leadership's desire for peace and outlined the poor living standards and frustrations of the Soviet people.[102] As an educated and mature individual it seems doubtful that Barbarchuk could have reasonably expected her letter ever to reach the US President – care of the American embassy in Moscow – without being intercepted. As such, Barbarchuk was most likely

---

[99] L. Polikovskaya, *'My predchuvstvie ... predtecha': ploshchad Mayakovskogo 1958–1965*, Moskva: Obshchestvo 'Memorial', 1997, p. 221. The riots in question are discussed in the following chapter.

[100] V. Iofe, *Granitsy smysla*, p. 181.

[101] Vladislav Zubok, for example, writes that the KGB were 'bombarding the Presidium with alarmist reports' about US plans to attack the USSR during 1960–2. V. Zubok, *Zhivago's Children*, p. 195.

[102] GARF, f. 8131, op. 31, d. 91673, ll. 23–5.

using the letter as a channel of communication between herself and the Soviet authorities, in order to make clear the nature of people's dissatisfaction with and cynicism towards officialdom without explicitly condemning the regime.[103] Most of all, it reflected the extent to which Barbarchuk considered it pointless to attempt to communicate directly with her own government, since Soviet political culture so rarely allowed for genuine input from the masses and provided minimal space for meaningful dialogue between ordinary citizens and authority on political matters.

The Western world, however, was not the only source of ideological antagonism for the Soviet authorities. One of the less widely raised themes of dissenting behaviour in the Khrushchev era is that of Chinese political agitation following the Sino-Soviet split – a new challenge to which Soviet leaders were very much alive as the two countries vied for leadership of the socialist world. The main catalyst for China's efforts to stir unrest in the USSR was the acrimonious personal rift between Khrushchev and Mao, a fact reflected in the extent to which the Soviet First Secretary himself was a particularly prominent target of Chinese criticism. As Sino-Soviet rivalry grew in intensity, the level of Chinese propaganda activity also increased. The Albanian regime, which had sided with Mao in the split, also colluded with the Chinese in this behaviour. In November 1960, for example, the KGB reported that 'information bulletins' and journals had been sent out to 356 addresses across the USSR from the Albanian embassy in Moscow.[104] A month later this figure had risen to 534 addresses.[105]

Chinese political agitation, like that of NTS, was not without some success, particularly in the southern and eastern provinces of the Soviet Union, where their radio signals were strongest. In August 1963 Komsomol members G.A. Svanidze, L.M. Kizilova and V.S. Miminoshvili were caught in Batumi pasting up leaflets that called for Khrushchev to be overthrown and declared 'Our leader is Mao-Tse Tung!'[106] In December of the same year, I.M. Panasetskii was sentenced for writing graffiti on walls in Chernigov *oblast'* with slogans including 'Long live the KPK' (Chinese Communist Party) and 'Long live Mao Tse-Tung'.[107] Leaflets supporting Maoist positions on a whole range of political questions were also discovered in Ukraine, Kazakhstan and Uzbekistan, in the Tatar and Bashkir ASSRs and in Novosibirsk and Omsk *oblasti*.[108] Some people, such as a former Party worker named Fedoseev and several underground groups,

[103] See V. Kozlov, and S. Mironenko eds., *Kramola*, p. 120.   [104] RGANI, f. 5, op. 30, d. 320, l. 167.
[105] RGANI, f. 5, op. 30, d. 320, l. 177.   [106] GARF, f. 8131, op. 31, d. 96151, ll. 1–3.
[107] GARF, f. 8131, op. 31, d. 95901, l. 1.   [108] RGANI, f. 5, op. 30, d. 454, l. 112.

including one named the 'Organisation of Idealistic Communists', reportedly attempted to establish contacts with representatives of the Chinese regime, offering to share with them 'hostile materials' and to agitate on their behalf inside the USSR, according to the KGB.[109] Like those dissenters who presented their challenge from a neo-Leninist position, the clearly communist political sensibilities of those involved did not make such views any less heretical in the eyes of the Soviet authorities. In the threat that it posed to the Party-state public sphere, Chinese communism was little less dangerous than American anti-communism.

On 4 May 1963, KGB chairman Vladimir Semichastnyi reported to the Central Committee that China was 'continuing to send propaganda into the Soviet Union' and in the previous month alone over 5,000 Chinese anti-Soviet brochures had been discovered and confiscated by the security organs.[110] This was followed on 20 May by a further communiqué that more explicitly linked the Chinese regime to the preparation of anti-Soviet leaflets. An informer named Chzhao Pin-Khyan reported to the KGB that the Chinese embassy in Moscow had been preparing anti-Soviet materials and was apparently forcing Chinese students studying in the USSR to distribute them. The report also claimed that regular meetings and seminars were being held inside the Chinese embassy in Moscow in which Soviet domestic and foreign policy were slandered, along with members of the CPSU leadership.[111] By January 1964, the Chinese were transmitting their 'schismatic views' in broadcasts amounting to eight hours per day.[112] A further report from the Ministry for the Protection of Public Order, dated 8 January 1964, stated that over 2,000 anti-Soviet leaflets had been discovered at the site of the recently vacated Albanian embassy.[113]

While tactics like these were especially provocative, they did not necessarily have a major impact at ground level. With many Soviet dissenters showing widespread revulsion at the poverty and violence of the Stalin era, the appeal of Mao's China as an alternative model of communist development was always likely to be relatively limited. The attractiveness of the US clearly had a much wider resonance among elements of the Soviet population, yet even there the situation tended to be more ambiguous than

---

[109] RGANI, f. 5, op. 30, d. 435, ll. 3–6. Unfortunately, the report did not give any details on exactly what these 'hostile materials' consisted of.
[110] RGANI, f. 5, op. 30, d. 424, l. 67.   [111] RGANI, f. 5, op. 30, d. 424, l. 82.
[112] RGANI, f. 5, op. 30, d. 435, ll. 1–2.
[113] RGANI, f. 5, op. 30, d. 454, l. 8. The Ministry for the Protection of Public Order (MOOP) was established in Russia after the Soviet MVD was abolished in 1962 and its powers passed to republican ministries of internal affairs. During the Brezhnev period the organisation reverted to its former shape and name.

the authorities in Moscow assumed, since it only occasionally touched upon matters ideological. The role played by the outside world in dissenting behaviour during the Khrushchev period can essentially be divided into two categories. The first was overtly subversive: activity promoted by the likes of NTS or the Chinese, aimed at directly provoking resistance to authority. While this may have occasionally yielded some immediate results in the form of leaflets and manifestos, its impact was limited and relatively easy for the Soviet authorities to 'nip in the bud'. The second was a much more gradual and less visible process that nonetheless had a significant impact on dissenting behaviour in the longer term, and probably also on many people's private views. By making available to Soviet citizens all manner of new information, opinion and debate, political and material horizons gradually began to widen, faith in the pronouncements of the authorities accordingly declined over time and vocabularies and frameworks for the articulation of political dissatisfaction, which had been largely absent in earlier years, began to emerge.

CHAPTER 6

Taking to the streets

The later part of the Khrushchev era did not just see the embitterment of small and isolated underground groups. It also threw up a series of major public disorders across the USSR, culminating in what Rudolf Pikhoya described as 'an explosion of popular discontent at Khrushchev's policies' during the summer of 1962.[1] In a 1991 article entitled 'Uprisings the Country Did Not Know About!' the newspaper *Novoe vremya* listed fourteen different Soviet cities that had experienced significant public disturbances between 1960 and 1962: Novocherkassk, Aleksandrov, Murom, Nizhnyi Tagil, Odessa, Dneprodzerzhinsk, Lubna, Kuibyshev, Kemerova, Krivoi Rog, Grozny, Donetsk, Temirtau and Yaroslavl.[2] The geographical spread and volatility of these disorders – some of which even included mob attacks on police stations and Communist Party buildings – meant that this last major spell of open working-class protest for more than two decades could not be ignored by those in the Kremlin.

Mass disorders in the USSR were by no means restricted to the early 1960s. In fact, the post-war years saw all manner of gang fights, work refusals and clashes between police and angry mobs. Starting in the late Stalin era and reaching a climax at Novocherkassk in the summer of 1962, disturbances ranging in size from a few dozen to many thousands of people had already taken place at labour-camp complexes including Kolyma (1949), Norilsk (1953), Vorkuta (1953) and Kengir (1954) and among free citizens in Tbilisi (1956), Grozny (1958) and Temirtau (1959). Each of these risings was important in its own right, but those of the early 1960s were to play a crucial role in shaping the Soviet system of the post-Stalin era.

While these disturbances may have been largely unknown at the time of the *Novoe vremya* article's publication in 1991, the intervening years have

---

[1] R. Pikhoya, *Sovetskii soyuz: istoriya vlasti, 1945–1991*, Moskva: Rossisskaya akademiya gos. sluzhby pri Prezidente Rossiisskoi Federatsii, 1998, p. 387.
[2] *Novoe vremya*, 22 April 1991.

seen emerge a fairly detailed picture of events, with Vladimir Kozlov's *Mass Uprisings in the USSR* (2002) and Samuel Baron's *Bloody Saturday in the Soviet Union* (2001) likely to prove benchmarks on the subject for many years to come.[3] With this in mind, there is no need here to attempt a blow-by-blow account of events that have been more than amply outlined elsewhere. Nonetheless, it is important to tie in these disorders with what we know of dissenting behaviour and policy against dissent during the era in question. In doing this we can better contextualise these disturbances, the way in which they were dealt with by the authorities and what they said about the wider socio-political situation of the early 1960s.

A brief outline of some of the major disorders of the period is clearly a useful place to start. In the present context it is worth revisiting the disturbances that took place in Tbilisi during March 1956 and ended with hundreds of arrests and dozens of deaths. Popular anger and hurt national pride had begun to spread in the Georgian capital once the Secret Speech's revelations about Stalin became known, and on 7 March a crowd of approximately 70,000 gathered at a Stalin monument in the centre of the city. The next day and the day after, angry crowds again massed in Tbilisi as the atmosphere turned increasingly volatile.[4] Finally, late at night on 9 March protesters attempted to seize control of the Georgian capital's communications infrastructure and attacked the city police department. When soldiers tried to disperse the crowds they encountered widespread and violent resistance, prompting a series of set-piece confrontations to break out around the city. Tanks were brought in and soldiers fired on protestors, turning the demonstration into a disaster that rankled for many years to come in the Georgian SSR.[5]

A number of clashes also erupted between returning members of the deported nationalities, whom Khrushchev had pardoned and released from exile, and those who had since settled in their places.[6] The situation reached

[3] V. Kozlov, *Mass Uprisings in the USSR: Protest and Rebellion in the Post-Stalin Years*, London: M.E. Sharpe, 2002 and S. Baron, *Bloody Saturday in the Soviet Union: Novocherkassk, 1962*, Stanford University Press, 2001.

[4] Some of the best primary accounts of these events can be found in L. Lur'e and I. Malyarova, *1956 god: Seredina veka*, Sankt Peterburg: Neva, 2007.

[5] Indeed, Georgia's first post-Soviet President, Zviad Gamsakhurdia, was jailed in April 1957 for his part in an underground nationalist group that had pasted up leaflets in Tbilisi calling on fellow Georgians to 'remember the bloody night of the ninth of March'. GARF, f. 8131, op. 31, d. 77022, ll. 1–5.

[6] Not all of the deported nationalities were allowed to return to their homelands. The Crimean Tatars, for example, were denied the right to return en masse to the Crimea until the Gorbachev era. The Meskhi were also prevented from returning to their native lands in southern Georgia. See L. Alexeyeva, *Soviet Dissent: Contemporary Movements for National, Religious and Human Rights*, Middletown, CT: Wesleyan University Press, 1987.

a peak in Grozny – though troubles were also registered in nearby Dagestan, Ingushetia and Kalmykiya around the same time – where simmering conflict between returning Chechens and Russian settlers resulted in the murder of a young Russian sailor in August 1958. This in turn provoked mass riots and pogroms against Chechens that ended with police coming under attack as they tried to keep the peace between the two groups.

Mass disturbances then broke out in Kazakhstan during the Virgin Lands campaign of the late 1950s but were again largely prompted by ethnic tensions between incomers from the cities and members of the indigenous population, rather than any overt animosity toward the political authorities. As with events in Chechnya, the troubles there were most often manifested in gang fights in which the militia's main role was to intervene between the warring factions, though this could still result in the police coming under attack from angry crowds. In terms of politicised complaint, the most significant disorders of the Virgin Lands campaign took place at Temirtau, in Kazakhstan, from 1 to 3 August 1959 and 'paralysed normal life in the city for three days', according to a subsequent official report.[7] Although squalid and unsuitable living conditions, along with shortages of basic necessities, subsequently left a bitter taste in the mouth for many of those who had volunteered to go out to Kazakhstan and elsewhere, most of the young 'Virgin Landers' had embarked with a great sense of idealism and adventure for the task of helping to open up new parts of the country for cultivation.[8] As reactions to the Secret Speech had shown, mobilising such idealism carried its own dangers and could easily lead to frustration and doubt. The saxophonist Alexei Kozlov would later recall of his own experiences in Kazakhstan: 'It was in the Virgin Lands that I found my animosity toward Soviet propaganda ... Even the most immature and unengaged young people left the Virgin Lands with the feeling of some kind of absurdity.'[9] As the Soviet system matured and later ossified, this kind of mass mobilisation of idealistic energy was increasingly shunned. This was not only a reflection of the leadership's declining utopianism, and the consistent failure of such drives to produce results, but also of the fact

---

[7] RGANI, f. 3, op. 12, d. 576, ll. 30–48, in A. Fursenko et al. eds., *Prezidium TsK KPSS 1954–1964*, Tom 3: *Postanovleniya 1959–1964*, Moskva: Rosspen, 2008.

[8] On the Virgin Lands scheme see M. Pohl, 'The Planet of 100 Languages: Ethnic Relations and Soviet Identity in the Virgin Lands', in N. Breyfogle, A. Schrader and W. Sunderland eds., *Peopling the Russian Periphery: Borderland Colonisation in Eurasian History*, London: Routledge, 2007, and M. Pohl, 'Women and Girls in the Virgin Lands', in M. Ilič, L. Attwood and S. Reid eds., *Women in the Khrushchev Era*, Basingstoke: Palgrave Macmillan, 2004, pp. 52–74.

[9] See V. Zubok, *Zhivago's Children: The Last Russian Intelligentsia*, Cambridge. MA: Harvard University Press, 2009, p. 128.

that activist idealism could be hard to control and direct, quickly turning instead into a source of trouble for the authorities, just as it had in 1956.

From late spring 1959, several thousand young volunteers had been suffering particularly testing conditions at Temirtau, such as shortages of food and water for drinking and for washing, and had seen their complaints consistently rebuffed or ignored by the authorities there. Around midnight on Saturday 1 August over 500 youths, predominantly from Belarus and Ukraine, began to protest, looting shops and stores. When the police duly made arrests, crowds responded with vehemence, erecting barricades in the street, attacking a police station and throwing rocks at members of the militia. Protesters wrote political graffiti on walls and shouted slogans in demand of a shorter working day, higher wages and the right to go on strike.[10] As frequently happened in such disorders, the rioters quickly gained the upper hand over startled authorities and for a short time managed to force concessions from panicked local officials – in this case the release of two arrested protesters – before the state could muster the resources to reassert its authority.

Violence also broke out just over 100 km (60 miles) from Moscow, in Murom (Vladimir *oblast'*), in June 1961 after a local worker named Kostikov died in police custody. A rumour spread that he had been killed by the militia and tension began to mount in the town.[11] Three days later, Kostikov's funeral procession descended into a mass riot after mourners attacked a local militia station en route. When the *oblispolkom* chairman attempted to placate the swelling crowd he was drowned out by catcalls and abuse, eventually giving up in his attempts to assert some authority over the angry mob.[12] A subsequent report on events in Murom stated that protesters there went on to do significant damage to militia and KGB buildings, breaking windows, doors and furniture, severing telephone connections and stealing documents and firearms, before the authorities could reassert control.[13] Partly inspired by events in Murom, another major disturbance was registered in nearby Aleksandrov the following month, after a fracas that had begun when a policeman attempted to arrest a pair of drunken soldiers again degenerated into a riot. The resulting disorders were short-lived and localised but involved extensive alcohol-fuelled hooliganism and anti-police sentiment. According to the secretary of Aleksandrov *gorkom* there were

---

[10] RGANI, f. 3, op. 12, d. 576, ll. 30–48.

[11] Kozlov reports that the man in question had died of a brain haemorrhage incurred during the drunken accident for which he had originally been arrested. V. Kozlov, *Mass Uprisings*, p. 194.

[12] RGASPI, f. 17, op. 91, d. 1498, in A. Fursenko et al. eds., *Prezidium TsK KPSS*, Tom 3.

[13] GARF, f. 8131, op. 31, d. 91127, ll. 1–5.

calls to 'strangle communists' and to 'throttle the Soviet regime'. Crowds threw bottles of burning petrol into a militia station and an attempt to storm the city jail was beaten back thanks only to the 'true Party-mindedness' of workers at the prison.[14]

The climax of these mass disorders came in the summer of 1962, soon after the announcement of a series of sharp price rises on a host of staple goods, including meat and butter, which naturally aroused widespread consternation after years of decreasing prices. This was obviously a prob-lematic development at a time when the Soviet regime was staking an increasing degree of its domestic and international credibility on raising levels of consumption.[15] KGB monitoring reports from that summer give an idea of the volume of discontent, referring to instances of angry crowds and anti-Soviet leaflets with calls for strikes and demonstrations appearing in numerous major cities. In Riga citizens gathered round a Lenin statue, shouting political slogans. In Kiev leaflets were found across the city calling for people to hold a protest meeting against the rises. Among students at Moscow's Mendeleev Chemical Technical Institute there were calls to organise a strike. In Perm *oblast'* leaflets spoke of people having to make soup out of sawdust and eating coal.[16] The volume of *listovki* being discovered more than doubled on the previous year, and there was a 'considerable' increase in the number of letters containing terrorist threats against communists and members of the government, something that the KGB explicitly linked to the price rises.[17] A communiqué dated 3 June 1962 referred to workers in Gorky attempting to organise a strike, unspecified 'problems' with stevedores in Odessa and a series of terrorist threats against the government emanating from Kirov *oblast'*.[18] While the authorities could realistically view underground groups as troublesome fringe elements, and previous disorders like those at Murom and Aleksandrov as the work of drunken hooligans, the wave of discontent that swelled in 1962 was not so easily dismissed.

In Novocherkassk the impact of the country-wide price rises was exacer-bated by a decision to raise work quotas at the town's main factory, the Novocherkassk Electric Locomotive Works (NEVZ). This effectively meant that workers had to do more work to earn the wages they had previously received, or else accept less money for doing the same amount

[14] RGASPI, f. 17, op. 91, d. 1498, l. 7 in A. Fursenko et al. eds., *Prezidium TsK KPSS*, Tom 3.
[15] On this theme see S. Reid, 'Cold War in the Kitchen: Gender and the De-Stalinization of Consumer Taste in the Soviet Union under Khrushchev', *Slavic Review*, Vol. 60, No. 2 (Summer 2002), 211–52.
[16] RGANI, f. 89, op. 6, d. 12, ll. 1–4 and RGANI, f. 89, op. 6, d. 14, ll. 1–3.
[17] RGANI, f. 89, op. 51, d. 1, ll. 1–4.   [18] RGANI, f. 89, op. 6, d. 14, l. 3.

of work. Thanks to the new price rises, even the wages that they did earn were now worth less in real terms. Once added to existing food shortages in the city, and the factory management's brusque rejection of workers' complaints, tensions quickly escalated. At around 8 am on 1 June, NEVZ workers decided to withdraw their labour and gathered outside the plant before seizing control of the factory building itself, ransacking the interior of the administration block and cutting the nearby train line from Saratov to Rostov. The next day, striking workers, with women and children along-side, proceeded to march the 10 km (6 miles) from the outlying factory district toward the centre of town. Sympathisers from other factories joined along the way but the procession remained peaceful, eventually coming to an end at a public square in the centre of Novocherkassk. Panicked by news of the protest, the leadership in Moscow had already despatched several high-ranking Party figures, including Anastas Mikoyan and Frol Kozlov, to take control of the situation there and drafted in thousands of troops to police the swelling crowd.

As the crowd headed toward the town, a decision had been taken for the recently arrived deputation to be evacuated from the Communist Party building in the centre of Novocherkassk. When it became evident to the masses on Lenin Square that they would not be met by the high-ranking delegation flown in from the capital, the mood began to turn increasingly hostile. Frustration boiled over as more aggressive elements in the crowd forced their way into the town's Communist Party building and promptly began to vandalise and loot its interior. Soon afterwards, a group of protest-ers attempted forcibly to release prisoners from the police station, though there were in fact none being held there at the time. It was then that armed forces began to fire indiscriminately into the crowd that had gathered outside the town's *gorkom* building. Dozens of people were killed and many more were wounded as the authorities seized back control of the situation.

The widespread anger of summer 1962 came as final confirmation for the leadership in Moscow that material conditions were becoming ever more important to mass conformity. While more overtly ideological issues, such as the expulsion of the anti-Party group[19] or the invasion of Hungary, might provoke passionate opposition in some quarters, it was matters that touched on wages and the provision of goods that had the potential to cause the greatest damage to social passivity among the masses, largely because their effects would be so much more tangible and potentially ruinous to the

---

[19] See Chapter 1.

average citizen. The economic cost to the regime of widespread worker discontent may well have been largely invisible – most commonly taking forms such as absenteeism and general labour indiscipline – but this was in itself serious, since the price rises that sparked the 1962 unrest had come as part of a 'belt-tightening' exercise prompted by the stuttering economy. It was not by chance that price rises like those of 1962 were not repeated by Khrushchev or his successors, though such rises were badly needed at times. Even as the Soviet economy teetered on the brink of collapse in the late 1980s, Mikhail Gorbachev was loath even to consider urgently needed increases in the price of goods lest they again provoke uproar. Once improved living standards had become an entrenched facet of the Soviet social contract, they would have to be maintained at least.

What made a number of these disturbances so notable was the level of violence involved, with protesters attacking the tools and symbols of authority with frightening vehemence at times. Exceptional though they were in the bigger picture of things, such behaviours betrayed a deepening problem for the authorities. As previous chapters have already shown, this kind of working-class volatility was not entirely without precedent. It had been witnessed in word, if not always in deed, a great many times before the end of the 1950s, most notably in the form of individual public outbursts and confrontations with members of the militia. The anti-police sentiment that characterised the two major disorders in Vladimir *oblast'*, for example, had clear forebears in the countless outbursts on the streets, on buses and in train stations for which so many citizens had been jailed in 1957 and 1958. At this time in particular, it took only a few such individuals, combined with insensitive or indecisive policing, before a conflagration between authorities and citizens might escalate. To a considerable extent, therefore, mass disorders such as those at Murom and Aleksandrov can be viewed as an intensification or an extension of protest behaviours that already existed, rather than a wholly novel phenomenon.

As the preceding chapter showed, there was also a marked intensification of dissenting behaviour and intransigent rhetoric among underground groups during the early 1960s. Indeed, this 'hardening' of dissent was also present among elements of the liberal intelligentsia, though there it translated not as a more aggressive stance toward authority but as bolder ideological criticisms and a more tenacious refusal to be cowed into silence. There were several factors that lay behind this general 'hardening' of dissent – including the continued weakening of the regime's monopoly on information and the private reassessments of the system that had begun with the Secret Speech – but perhaps the most important was the fact that the authorities' own position had already hardened sufficiently for it to be abundantly clear that there was to be no meaningful dialogue with those who showed even a degree of political discontent.

Once the authorities had restated the bounds of acceptable comment and behaviour, and then began to enforce them, those still determined to air their grievances were well aware that peaceful and loyal protest would not work: they neither protected the protester from punishment nor resulted in problems being remedied. When protest did flare up it would be more serious because of this, either in the form of explosive disorders, subversive underground activity or the organised and enduring criticism by the subsequent dissident movement. Under Stalin, this process was largely short-circuited by the application of mass terror. The Brezhnev years saw rising living standards and more sophisticated methods of social control having the desired effect on almost all but those few who threw in their lot with the dissident movement. In Khrushchev's time, terror had already been abandoned but improving material conditions and new policing practices were only beginning to take hold.

Bearing in mind the combustible nature of some of these mass protests, one of the striking aspects of the public disturbances of the Khrushchev era was the relative restraint shown by the authorities, who could quite conceivably have resorted to violence earlier and much more often than they ultimately did.[20] At Temirtau, for example, an MVD official caught up in the mob attack on a militia station twice requested that he and his militiamen be allowed to respond to the crowds with armed force, yet the *obkom* first secretary refused to sanction such a move, doubtless preventing many deaths.[21] While the use of devastating force was still very much a live option, it was by no means the authorities' default position. Justified as their frustrations may have been, it was consistently protesters rather than government forces who were the first to resort to violence. While the deaths at Tbilisi and Novocherkassk were unquestionably a tragedy that showed the worst possible side of the Soviet regime, it is still worth remembering that by the time events there degenerated into a bloodbath, the protesters – albeit a minority of them – had already gone to extremes, attacking and ransacking official buildings. With this in mind, it is also worthwhile to

---

[20] Whether this reflected greater humanitarian concern on the part of the authorities or was primarily about trying to prevent further unrest is a subject open to debate. Both probably played a part to some extent.

[21] RGANI, f. 3, op. 12, d. 576, l. 33. As Kozlov notes, members of the militia did 'open fire' on the crowds but only with blanks. Accordingly, protesters did not disperse for long before returning with a vengeance. V. Kozlov, *Mass Uprisings*, p. 36.

point out that neither the Soviet Union nor the communist world had a monopoly on gratuitously violent policing of public protest either at that time or since.

For a whole host of reasons it would have been simply impossible to arrest all those involved in such disorders. As was the case with the underground groups of the time, the authorities focused their energies on jailing the supposed ringleaders. At Novocherkassk this meant a little over 100 individuals were tried on charges of anti-Soviet activity for their part in the rising there, with seven of the 'worst offenders' facing the death sentence (itself a demonstration of how badly the affair had shaken the authorities, since the death sentence was so rarely employed against dissenters after Stalin's death). Because the vast majority of those who had participated in riots around the country remained at liberty, and many others throughout the USSR were clearly also deeply disgruntled, the government had little choice but to address at least some of the frustrations that had created the conditions for unrest. This could be seen at a micro-level in the way that the recently announced price rises were subsequently suspended in Novocherkassk and additional food supplies were quickly despatched to the town. In itself, this was a useful reflection of the emerging post-Stalin system. The Party leadership remained more than willing to clamp down hard on those few who stuck their head above the parapet, but they were also increasingly wary of provoking confrontation with the masses, preferring instead to assuage their most serious material frustrations.

Aleksandr Solzhenitsyn's claim that Novocherkassk represented a key turning point for the Soviet regime was broadly correct, though he misdiagnosed the substance of that change. His argument – that the massacre there sounded the death knell for the last remaining idealistic believers in communism, and thereafter left the regime with the support only of cynical careerists – does not stand up well to scrutiny.[22] The claim founders on several issues, but perhaps the most important lies in its implicit assumption that knowledge about the brutal suppression of the disturbance at Novocherkassk was widespread, something which remains unsupported by evidence. From the very start of the protests there, the army, police and KGB went to great effort to prevent news of the events from spreading, and in this they seem to have been reasonably successful.[23]

---

[22] See A. Solzhenitsyn, *The Oak and the Calf: A Literary Memoir*, London: Collins and Harvill Press, 1980.

[23] For example, Samuel Baron recalled that even during *glasnost'* the Soviet authorities went to considerable effort to prevent details of the tragedy from entering the public domain. S. Baron, *Bloody Saturday*, pp. xi–xii.

Phone lines were cut, mail was suspended and roads in and out of the town were blocked. Although rumours inevitably began to emerge, and were soon repeated by foreign radio stations, concrete details were thin on the ground outside of the affected area. Very few *listovki* explicitly referred to events in Novocherkassk, for example. It may well have been true that those who did find out about what had transpired there reacted as Solzhenitsyn suggested, but there is little to show that such knowledge was particularly common at the time. More accurately, we can point to the popular responses to the 1962 price rises in particular as representing a turning point for the Soviet system in the sense that they presented the authorities with conclusive proof of the link between living standards and social passivity. While the consumerist Soviet social contract had already begun to emerge in the 1950s, it was the early 1960s which saw it take on a more final form.

Vladimir Kozlov's interpretation of these public disturbances as a vital communication channel between masses and political elites, in which 'both the bosses and the populace adapted to the new historical reality' as they thrashed out the rules of the game for the post-Stalin era, is especially convincing.[24] Most of all they made plain that the suffering and intense hardships of previous years would not be tolerated again. The disorders and wider rumblings of discontent during the summer of 1962 were a perfect example of this type of communication. As events in the early 1960s showed, some of the standard channels of information on popular moods, such as Party and Komsomol reports, were proving far from perfect, giving the leadership in Moscow at best a highly selective reading of tensions and frustrations among ordinary citizens.

A prime example of this could be seen in a report from Penza *obkom* on 1 June 1962, informing the CPSU Central Committee of local Party members' reactions to the imminent price rises that were to provoke such unrest elsewhere that summer. The missive listed nothing but support and even praise for the planned price hike.[25] Out of over 400 communists present at the meeting, apparently none disapproved. It cited comments such as those of the metal worker D.P. Lepilin who stated that 'These are difficult times and we are ready to get through them. I approve these measures' and the *kolkhoznitsa* G. Zaburdaeva who even expressed gratitude for the price rises as a 'major new help in quickly raising the level of Soviet agriculture and

[24] V. Kozlov, *Mass Uprisings*, p. 5.
[25] Party members in Penza were given advance notice of the rises at a meeting on 30 May. The rises were announced to ordinary, non-Party, citizens on the radio and in newspapers the next day. See O. Khlevnyuk et al. eds., *Regional'naya politika N.S. Khrushcheva. TsK KPSS i mestnye partiinye komitety 1953–1964*, Moskva: Rosspen, 2009.

creating an abundance of food products'.[26] While they may well have reflected accurately what was said openly at the meeting, they were clearly nothing like a useful indicator of the popular mood. Reports like this did not constitute 'good information' but rather told those in Moscow what they wanted to hear. Such communications did not help the Party leadership make sound judgements about how policies might play out at ground level. If taken at their word, they were liable to do more harm than good. Sometimes it was only when mass disturbances actually broke out, and problems in any given locality could no longer be 'varnished' by officials, that the centre got its 'good information'. By that time such information was useful only for future planning, though this was anyway an important process as the regime continually sought to improve upon measures aimed at better handling and prevention of such disturbances.

Sometimes Moscow did learn of tensions around the country before they reached dangerous levels, though not always through local officials. Just before the events in Murom and Aleksandrov, workers at a combine-harvester plant in Tula had gone out on strike for four days in a row during May 1961 in protest at the imposition of new work norms that had effectively reduced wages at the plant by around one-third. The workers withdrew their labour yet the management of the factory and its Party cell chose to turn a blind eye, neither dealing with the problem nor reporting it to their superiors. When the striking workers sent a telegram to the Central Committee requesting that they send a commission to investigate the situation there, an envoy was duly sent from the local *obkom*. The strikers' grievances were then addressed and they were persuaded to return to work.[27] However, a whole host of officials at the factory and in the local Party organisation were punished for covering up the strike and for failing to resolve the matter properly, several of them receiving strict Party reprimands, others facing the sack and some suffering expulsion from the CPSU, while the *gorkom* organisation itself was also censured.

A similar situation played out at a timber plant in Petrozavodsk several months later, in September 1961, when staff refused to work in protest at recent changes to labour norms and wages. When Moscow sent officials to investigate, they again found in favour of the workers, branding the changes

---

[26] The report concluded by listing some of the questions that were asked at the meeting. Some touched on slightly more sensitive areas, such as whether there would be a reconsideration of recent restrictions on private plots, but even these were overwhelmingly innocuous in the way they were phrased. GAPO (State Archive of Penza *oblast'*), f. P-148, op. 1, d. 4126, ll. 73–7, in O. Khlevnyuk et al. eds., *Regional'naya politika*.

[27] RGASPI, f. 556, op. 21, d. 351, in O. Khlevnyuk et al. eds., *Regional'naya politika*.

to norms 'unsatisfactory' and pointing out that workers stood to lose 150–70 roubles per month.[28] The director of the plant was sacked, along with several local Party officials, and work was resumed.[29] Situations like these might not have become explosive in themselves, but this was broadly the way in which the trouble at Novocherkassk would first develop. While events there ultimately proved to be a one-off, they had clearly not come entirely out of the blue. After trouble had flared up for real in the summer of 1962, the KGB would take an ever more active role in monitoring affairs in workplaces up and down the country.

As it turned out, the early 1960s saw the last major outbreaks of mass disorders for some years. Some commentators argue that the decline in acts of protest such as these was actually a negative sign for the long-term health of the regime, on the basis that it showed workers were becoming disconnected from communist beliefs, though this is a little problematic. It is firstly important to note that these mass protests did not grow fewer entirely of their own accord but also because the authorities devoted time and resources to preventing them. Among the most significant contributors to this shrinking of worker dissent was the fact that the authorities in Moscow actually took heed of some of what they learned through this implicit communication channel created by public disorders. Most notably, that meant not undertaking policies which ran such a high risk of provoking a hostile response from the public. When social tensions centred primarily upon economic matters, rather than ideological ones, the price of defusing those tensions was generally considered worth paying, or else turning a blind eye to, in the case of the swelling black market.

Of course, the motivations and aims of large crowds are naturally diverse and can be subject to radical change in a short space of time, but how far mass worker protests had actually been driven by communist idealism in the first place is somewhat open to question. Deeply held political values could be an important catalyst in some acts of protest, but this was not always the case. While protesters at Novocherkassk and Temirtau clearly demonstrated some element of identification with the purported values of the Soviet system, the same can hardly be said of the riots that took place in Murom and Aleksandrov. Even so, according to KGB reports from Novocherkassk (which essentially evaluated the NEVZ workers' main grievances as being

---

[28] Crude statistics on average wages for manual workers during the period in question show that a drop of 150–70 roubles would equate to a monthly shortfall of around 25–30%. See M. Matthews, *Class and Society in Soviet Russia*, London: Allen Lane, 1972, pp. 72–107.

[29] RGASPI, f. 556, op. 21, d. 351, in O. Khlevnyuk et al. eds., *Regional'naya politika.*

justified), the primary frustrations on show were not ideological ones but were overwhelmingly economic, with protesters demanding 'meat, milk and butter', and showing anger at the insensitivity of factory bosses and Party officials.[30] There was little perception of ideological betrayal any more sophisticated than the sentiment that workers' living standards should not be declining under a regime that purported to rule in their name. Indeed, the wider discontent of 1962 was clearly not the same as the wave of dissent that had swelled in the wake of the Secret Speech – when idealistic communists had imagined that their criticism would contribute to healing the political damage done by Stalin – but was essentially about protecting oneself and one's family from privation: as universal a theme as one could hope to find.

The sense of political loyalty to the Soviet system that protesters showed was primarily centred upon the broad ideals and principles of the revolution (sometimes crudely understood and almost always idealised), rather than its contemporary incarnation under the stewardship of Nikita Khrushchev. This differentiation between the credibility of the existing leadership and of the wider basis of the Soviet system could also be seen in the fact that Lenin was so rarely a target of criticism and many still revered him almost unquestioningly. As Samuel Baron wrote of events that took place when demonstrators forced their way into the NEVZ factory director's office at Novocherkassk: 'they did not tear down the portraits of Lenin; it was Khrushchev they reviled'.[31]

While for the intelligentsia much of Khrushchev's legitimacy as leader was rooted in the progress of deStalinization, for workers it tended be based on promises of improved consumption. Both of these foundations proved vulnerable at different points in the early 1960s. In subsequent years, the Brezhnev regime bolstered the credibility acquired from improved consumption levels with increasing emphasis on Soviet victory in the Second World War as the system's main legitimating achievement. By pinning a good deal of the regime's credibility on past achievements rather than on those of the present or future, Brezhnev had made an astute move, since the past could not let him down. Additionally, by exaggerating his personal contribution to the Great Patriotic War, he more effectively wove his own leadership into the legitimacy of the system than did Khrushchev, whose emphasis on 'return to Leninism' left him without the same kind of personal 'anchor' in Soviet legitimacy. After all, his own political career had taken shape entirely under Stalin and he had even defeated and

---

[30] RGANI, f. 89, op. 6, d. 16, ll. 1–9.   [31] S. Baron, *Bloody Saturday*, p. 37.

disgraced most of the last members of the Party leadership who did have direct ties to the revolutionary era that he so eulogised, such as Stalin, Molotov, Voroshilov and Kaganovich.[32]

Time and again, the Communist Party leadership in Moscow picked out two groups of people to blame for such public disorders: 'criminal elements' and local officials. Both, it seems, were deserving of at least some blame. Assessing the role of 'criminal elements' or 'marginals' in these disturbances is a challenging task for the historian. They certainly featured prominently when the authorities subsequently apportioned culpability for disorders and have been a central component of the subsequent historiography.[33] However, bearing in mind the extent to which official reports on dissent showed a tendency to reflect what the authorities in Moscow wanted to hear, one is inclined to show a degree of caution here. There were certainly plenty of these marginals at liberty within society at the time – not least because of the amnesties that drained the Gulag after Stalin's death – and there was an especially high concentration of such people in towns on the edge of Moscow's 101-km (60-mile) ring (inside which certain categories of former prisoner were forbidden to live), including Murom and Aleksandrov. They were not, however, the sole wellspring of explosive discontent.

While there seems no doubt that marginals were at the heart of the two hooligan disturbances in Vladimir *oblast'*, the picture of events in summer 1962 was rather more ambiguous. At Novocherkassk, KGB reports spoke of 'hooligan elements' who joined the peaceful workers' procession as it approached the town from the factory district, yet the authorities had gone to great lengths to prevent this, stationing troops, police and Party activists inside the town before the demonstration reached there, including the deployment of police to prevent students in the city's dormitories from coming out in support of the marchers. More importantly in the present context, they also sought to track down and remove over 1,500 known 'criminal elements' from Novocherkassk before the crowd had reached the town centre.[34] The biographical materials on protesters who were subsequently jailed for anti-Soviet activity certainly do show that a few of them fit

---

[32] The irony was that Khrushchev's own involvement in the Second World War was considerably more extensive than that of Leonid Brezhnev, having been present as a political commissar at both the fall and recapture of Kiev and the iconic battles at Stalingrad and Kursk.

[33] On 'marginals' in the Khrushchev era, see E. Zubkova and T. Zhukova eds., *Na 'krayu' sovetskogo obshchestva: sotsial'nye marginally kak ob"ekt gosudarstvennoi politiki, 1945–1960-e gg.*, Moskva: Rosspen, 2010.

[34] RGANI, f. 89, op. 6, d. 16, ll. 4–7.

the bill as 'marginals'. Nonetheless, the biographies of the majority of those who were jailed after the riot pointed to a much more 'decent' social status, showing respectable jobs and a lack of previous convictions.[35] There is no doubt that it suited all concerned (including those who would continue to live and work in Novocherkassk afterward) for the protest there to be presented as a peaceful and loyal demonstration that had been hijacked by a small band of malignant trouble-makers, but social ferment was by no means restricted to hooligan elements that summer. A July 1962 KGB report announced that 1,039 authors of anti-Soviet leaflets had recently been uncovered and stated that 364 of the authors were workers, 192 were white-collar workers, 210 students, sixty *kolkhozniks*, 105 pensioners and 108 people without defined employment: the latter is the category where one would usually find such 'marginals'.[36] Of course, producing leaflets and participating in mass disorders were by no means the same thing, and each could attract rather different social constituencies. Nonetheless, there can be little doubt that the frustration which facilitated the unrest of summer 1962 had percolated throughout much of society.

As Novocherkassk had demonstrated most clearly, incompetent and insensitive behaviour by officials was clearly a source of public ire and a concern for the Party leadership in Moscow. After the 1961 riots in Aleksandrov and Murom, the Central Committee turned its anger on the local authorities' 'unsatisfactory leadership in the struggle against criminality' and on their failure to take 'decisive measures' to prevent the disorders there.[37] An inquest into the two riots took place on 9 August 1961 at a plenum of Vladimir *obkom*, where the events were labelled a 'shameful episode' for the two cities' Party organisations and the local leadership was branded 'unreliable', with several of its members described as 'political ignoramuses'.[38] One local official's concession to the angry crowd at Aleksandrov, in which he admitted that the work of the local *druzhinniki* (volunteer police force) had been poor and required attention, was branded 'worse than cowardice'.[39] Heads duly rolled, as the first secretary of Vladimir *obkom* was dismissed from his position, along with a secretary of Murom *gorkom* (who was even expelled from the Communist Party) and the first secretary of Aleksandrov *gorkom*.

[35] See GARF, f. 8131, op. 31, d. 98328; d. 98327; d. 95432, in V. Kozlov and S. Mironenko eds., *58-10 Nadzornye proizvodstva prokuratury SSSR po delam ob antisovetskoi agitatsii i propaganda: annotirovannyi katalog Mart 1953–1991*, Moskva: Mezhdunarodnyi Fond 'Demokratiya', 1999.
[36] RGANI, f. 89, op. 51, d. 1, l. 4.   [37] See O. Khlevnyuk et al. eds., *Regional'naya politika*, p. 442.
[38] RGASPI, f. 17, op. 91, d. 1498, in O. Khlevnyuk et al. eds., *Regional'naya politika*.
[39] RGASPI, f. 17, op. 91, d. 1498, l. 4, in O. Khlevnyuk et al. eds., *Regional'naya politika*.

All manner of problems were highlighted at the inquest. Local Party organisations were accused of failing in their political work among the masses and of not understanding popular moods in the area. It was pointed out that the *oblast'* had witnessed a marked rise in the overall number of crimes being committed, and also in the number of crimes going unpunished, over the previous year but that little had been done to remedy this deteriorating situation. Attempts to bring the disturbances in Murom to a close were criticised for being disorganised, indecisive and too conciliatory toward protesters. The secretary of Aleksandrov *gorkom* justifiably pointed to the fact that the area faced a fairly unique problem in the number of transient criminal elements it attracted, stating 'we know the working class here well. We do not know the former prisoners who have been arriving here.' He insisted that Party activists and volunteer policemen had been in the thick of the action the whole time in Aleksandrov and had continually tried to reason with the protesters but the crowd had simply been too big, too angry and too drunk for their efforts to succeed.[40]

Taken together, these claims and counter-claims present most of the key failures and weaknesses – both systemic and individual – that usually characterised the way events panned out. Naturally, though, the inquest barely touched upon deeper problems of generalised resentment toward officialdom and the indefinite social alienation of huge numbers of marginals. Such matters remained out of bounds for open and frank discussion among even *oblast'*-level officials. These kinds of blockages in the flow of information – where certain important subjects were deemed too sensitive or too impolitic to be raised and debated – were to be a lingering obstruction to the chance of a solution to the problems that the system faced at any given time.

A little over a month after the protest at Novocherkassk, on 19 July 1962, a communiqué was sent from the Communist Party's Administrative Organs Department to the General Department which effectively constituted a review of the authorities' existing practices for dealing with public disturbances.[41] To give some idea of the report's significance it is worthwhile pointing out that its contributors included Aleksandr Shelepin, Vladimir Semichastnyi, Matvei Zakharov, Roman Rudenko, Vadim Tikunov and Petr Ivashutin. Respectively, these men were the former KGB chairman, presiding KGB chairman, deputy KGB chairman, the

---

[40] RGASPI, f. 17, op. 91, d. 1498, l. 5, O. Khlevnyuk et al. eds., *Regional'naya politika*.
[41] RGANI, f. 89, op. 6, d. 20, ll. 1–16.

head of the Procurator's office, the head of the MVD and the head of military intelligence.

Unsurprisingly, the overarching conclusions of the report were clear: more men, resources and attention should be devoted to combating dissent. It stated that the KGB was penetrating deeper into workers' organisations and had improved its 'prophylactic work', but conceded that there was still much to be done. Sticking to the traditional formula, it connected the recent growth in anti-Soviet activity with an increase in imperialist intelligence work and stated that there were only a few 'anti-social elements' who, under the influence of foreign propaganda, were 'continuing to try to use temporary hardships for their own ends'. On the negative side, links between the KGB and militia were described as 'weak' and it was acknowledged that the security organs were not 'mobilisationally prepared' for major disorders such as Novocherkassk, and that they had struggled to influence events there once the disturbance was under way.[42]

The review then insisted that decisive measures had to be taken in order to strengthen the work of the KGB against anti-Soviet elements. Surveillance of 'suspicious types' and released prisoners needed to be stepped up, the recruitment of informers and KGB operatives had to be expanded and specific training undertaken for future scenarios of mass disturbances in built-up areas. In order to combat weaknesses in the deployment and utilisation of undercover operatives, the review called for an increase in the availability of technological services for observation purposes as well as improvements in the training and political education of agents.[43] This last point touched upon a pattern that was already well under way by the 1960s: education and training levels within both the security organs and the militia were rising substantially from the second half of the 1950s, especially in comparison to the Stalin era. Indeed, according to a number of well-respected observers, one of the defining characteristics of the KGB was that it continually grew more effective with each passing year.[44]

It was clearly too dangerous to rely solely on local officials to detect, report and head off swelling unrest. As well as stepping up the monitoring activities of the KGB and moving to alleviate the main sources of material

---

[42] RGANI, f. 89, op. 6, d. 20, ll. 1–6.
[43] RGANI, f. 89, op. 6, d. 20, ll. 6–9. As Yoram Gorlizki also points out, soon after the disorders at Novocherkassk the militia were given truncheons, teargas and handcuffs. Y. Gorlizki, 'Policing Post-Stalin Society: The Militsiia and Public Order under Khrushchev', *Cahiers du Monde russe*, Vol. 44, Nos. 2–3 (avril–septembre 2003), 479.
[44] See, for example, V. Shlapentokh, *A Normal Totalitarian Society: How the Soviet Union Functioned and How it Collapsed*, New York: Oxford University Press, 2001, p. 92.

discontent, Moscow became quicker to act when flashpoints threatened to arise. With bread queues forming even in Ukraine in the autumn of 1963, Khrushchev opted to import over ten million tonnes of grain from abroad, rather than risk famine that might cost untold lives and would surely threaten further disorders. This was a humiliating step, both for the regime as a whole and for Khrushchev personally, since agriculture had long been hailed as his personal field of expertise, but it clearly demonstrated how determined the leadership was to avoid a re-run of the strife of the previous summer. Nonetheless, agricultural failures were regularly integral to personal attacks on the First Secretary. *Listovki* that were scattered on a bus in Odessa *oblast'* by a twenty-two-year-old construction worker and Komsomol member named Pavel Otchenashenko simply read: 'Increased prices and lowered wages. Agriculture is collapsing. This is Khrushchev's work!'[45] Vladimir Bukovsky recalled spending summers labouring on a collective farm in his youth and being woken daily by the sound of peasant women outside cursing and singing vulgar songs about Khrushchev while they worked.[46] His largely unsuccessful meddling in agricultural matters and the imposition of fresh restrictions on private plots were almost guaranteed to leave Khrushchev lacking in popularity among the peasantry in particular, despite a number of major improvements that his rule had brought for them.

The lessons of 1962 had quite clearly shown the leadership that any onset of food shortages would likely prompt dangerous levels of unrest. In previous times bad harvests had meant widespread hunger and even starvation on a massive scale – a cycle that Khrushchev broke, yet for which he was nonetheless pilloried. Evidently, the immediate wound that was inflicted on people's sense of pride in the achievements of the Soviet system (which remained strong in Russia at least) had the greatest impact on contemporary evaluations, but those looking back on events with a little more distance and objectivity would struggle to argue that Khrushchev had done the wrong thing, especially on a humanitarian level.[47] As such, anger at the decision to buy grain abroad was a useful reflection of the occasionally paradoxical nature of dissent. To assume that people who protested always did so with their own, or their country's, best interests (particularly their long-term

---

[45] GARF, f. 8131, op. 31, d. 96255, ll. 1–7.

[46] Interview with Vladimir Bukovsky, Cambridge, March 2007.

[47] Even so, the Medvedevs – far more sober and informed analysts of the situation than most of those who criticised Khrushchev – suggest that his ouster in October 1964 practically 'saved' Soviet science and agriculture. R. and Zh. Medvedev, *Khrushchev: The Years in Power*, New York: Columbia University Press, 1977, p. 135.

interests) in mind is to impose a logic that did not always exist at the time. Bearing in mind how big a volte-face this was for a regime whose leader endlessly boasted of its present and future achievements, it is hardly surprising that people did not always view the matter in its wider context.

Like other Soviet leaders, Khrushchev was the subject of mocking nicknames, caricatures and jokes, but the amount of derision and vitriol aimed at him tells an important story that has not always emerged in the existing literature, dominated as it has traditionally been by Western commentators and members of the Soviet intelligentsia whose perceptions of Khrushchev and the 'thaw' period have often been the more positive. Workers and peasants, on the other hand, could be quick to round on Khrushchev's perceived failings and failures. To a considerable extent, he played the role of a 'lightning rod' for anger at all kinds of issues, and particularly at the gap seemingly opening up between ordinary citizens and privileged elites. Khrushchev's frequent and occasionally lengthy trips abroad and the holding of opulent state banquets for visiting dignitaries aroused considerable anger among elements of the population, especially the working class.[48] Letters complained of Party leaders and officials fencing themselves off from the masses or else living the high life at the expense of the people. In Kuibyshev, a Party member named Brigachev Politov insisted that the only people who lived well in the USSR were precisely those who contributed least: namely bureaucrats and officials.[49] An anonymous letter sent to *Sovetskaya molodezh* from Latvia attacked the growing disparity in living standards, asserting that many people could afford to eat meat only three times per year, before branding factory directors and public officials 'crooks and embezzlers'.[50] Bulganin was accused of doing nothing but attending banquets.[51] Khrushchev's own rather sizeable waistline did not go unremarked either. For a system that proclaimed egalitarianism as one of its fundamental principles, this perception of entrenched social injustice was always likely to be an area of contention, especially after Khrushchev's predecessor had been so widely (and in many ways quite falsely) portrayed as having led such a Spartan lifestyle.

Many people initially viewed favourably the contrast between Khrushchev's ebullient and informal manner compared with that of his predecessor, yet a degree of anti-Khrushchev sentiment already existed

[48] See V. Kozlov and S. Mironenko, *Kramola: inakomyslie v SSSR pri Khrushcheve i Brezhneve 1953–1982*, Moskva: 'Materik', 2005.
[49] GARF, f. 89, op. 6, d. 5, ll. 1–3.   [50] Budapest, HU OSA 300-80-1, Box 44.
[51] See K. Aimermakher et al. eds., *Doklad N.S. Khrushcheva o kul'te lichnosti Stalina na XX s"ezde KPSS: dokumenty*, Moskva: Rosspen, 2002, p. 605.

virtually from the start of his time in office. Of course, those who had spoken up in defence of Stalin, and later also in defence of members of the anti-Party group, had been quick to round on Khrushchev, often accusing him of seeking to raise his own position by blackening the names of his rivals. As Chapters 1 and 3 showed, a cruder, hooligan-type opposition to Khrushchev could also be seen in numerous case files of individuals convicted of anti-Soviet agitation and propaganda at the time. One such example was N.P. Ipatov, a twenty-four-year-old docker from Kirovskaya *oblast'* who was jailed after drunkenly declaring at a railway station cafeteria in February 1957 that 'Khrushchev and Bulganin drink the people's blood.'[52] Another case that proceeded through the courts a month previously had seen a CPSU member and factory director from Azerbaidzhan named M.K. Yusubov convicted after sending anonymous letters to *Pravda* in which he accused Khrushchev and Bulganin of having disgraced Stalin and of 'leading the country toward disaster'.[53] In fact, terms like 'disaster' and 'disgrace' were to be a staple of many dissenters' personal attacks on Khrushchev throughout the era, though these disasters and disgraces were often only vaguely formulated.

As the above examples show, much of the criticism aimed at Khrushchev was usually only crudely articulated, constituting a kind of hyperbolic catch-all assault on the character and achievements of the First Secretary, with little sign of any genuinely constructive or considered criticism. Notable by their absence in the attacks on Khrushchev, just as they were largely missing from the mass disorders of the era, were substantive ideological critiques. Accusations of 'betraying the working class' or of 'leading the country to disaster' most often centred upon issues such as price rises or shortages of goods, rather than any kind of controversial interpretation of Marx or Lenin. With the consumerist social contract of the post-Stalin years increasingly well established by the early 1960s, this conflation of living standards and ideological propriety was perhaps inevitable. It can only have been exacerbated by the fact that discourse on the future attainment of full communism centred so heavily upon a projected material abundance that was not to be on the horizon any time soon.

Some of the main themes of this burgeoning anti-Khrushchev dissent could be seen in a series of leaflets distributed by Yuri Grimm and Abdulbai Khasyanov in November 1963. The pair produced 500 copies of three

[52] GARF, f. 8131, op. 31, d. 81365, in V. Kozlov and S. Mironenko eds., *58-10 Nadzornye proizvodstva*.
[53] GARF, f. 8131, op. 31, d. 80118, ll. 1–5, in V. Kozlov and S. Mironenko eds., *58-10 Nadzornye proizvodstva*.

different leaflets and scattered them in the area around Moscow's Kiev train station as well as across the Kuibyshev and Pervomaiskii districts of the capital. The first leaflet said simply, 'You are nothing to Nikita, just as you were nothing to Stalin.'[54] The second included comments such as 'Are you a patriot for your homeland? If yes, then you cannot calmly accept the disaster that our leaders are taking us to' and 'for almost half a century of this regime we have strained with titanic labour and yet we still live worse than other peoples'.[55] The final leaflet is reproduced in its entirety below:

> *Comrades!*
> *In the name of a happy life for the Soviet people,*
> *in the name of a bright future for our children,*
> *in the name of saving our country from the disgrace*
> *that the windbag Khrushchev has brought us to,*
> *demand that the Supreme Soviet quickly removes him*
> *from all of his positions, together with all his toadies*
> *and names them enemies of the people.*
> *Wake up comrades!*
> *Don't wait for a change, make it happen!*[56]

The resulting KGB file on Yuri Grimm reported that he 'had a long-standing and unhealthy interest in the broadcasts of Voice of America and the BBC as well as capitalist films and literature which caused him to relate negatively to Soviet activity'. What makes this remark so interesting is the fact that the leaflet's language and political framework were unambiguously Soviet, from the opening salutation through to the (naïve) faith in the Supreme Soviet's ability to remove Khrushchev from office at the bidding of the masses. In fact, there is no discernible sign of any overt Western input into either the tone or content of the leaflet in question. However, this may well be explained by the fact that the relationship between content and audience was always a crucial one in terms of dissent. An attempt to connect with a domestic Soviet audience would need to employ language and ideas that were both familiar ('enemy of the people') and important ('a bright future for our children') to the reader. Their tendency not to do this was to be one of the reasons why the subsequent Brezhnev-era dissident movement largely failed to capture the imagination of ordinary Soviet citizens. This is not at all to say that Sakharov et al. were oblivious to the everyday frustrations of the man and woman in the street, however: for the most part they were not seeking to appeal to Soviet citizens but to governments

---

[54] GARF, f. 8131, op. 33, d. 96712, l. 22.   [55] GARF, f. 8131, op. 33, d. 96712, l. 23.
[56] GARF, f. 8131, op. 33, d. 96712, l. 24.

and peoples in the West, and thus relied on discourse and ideas more appropriate to those bodies.

Another of the themes that saw the First Secretary provoke consternation among elements of the population was that of a burgeoning 'Khrushchev cult': this was something that could only ever be regarded as rank hypocrisy in light of his own denunciation of the Stalin cult. One of the leaflets circulated by Yuri Grimm and Abdulbai Khasyanov in 1963, for example, alluded to this 'Khrushchev cult' when it mockingly posed the question: 'Isn't it time for Khrushchev to claim his pension before he converts to a god?'[57] While official celebration of Khrushchev never approached the scale of that enjoyed by Stalin, accusations of cult-building were not wholly unfounded. For example, despite the government's 1957 ban on naming places after living political leaders, 1961 saw the Ukrainian port of Novogeorgievsk renamed in Khrushchev's honour.[58] Celebrations of his seventieth birthday in April 1964 were particularly fawning. The First Secretary was awarded the title 'Hero of the Soviet Union' (again) while the state media overflowed with fulsome praise of his achievements from home and abroad. By this time, though, even most of his colleagues in the Central Committee Presidium had already had enough of Khrushchev and would soon move against him.[59]

As a number of commentators have pointed out, many Soviet citizens still favoured Stalin over Khrushchev. Yuri Glazov, for example, wrote that ordinary workers had liked Stalin and saw him as a strict father but 'felt nothing but contempt' for Khrushchev.[60] Even though Glazov rather over-states the point, and some dissenters' pro-Stalin rhetoric was primarily a means of insulting officialdom once he had been denounced, there is little doubt that many workers in particular still held the late *vozhd* and his achievements – most notably the victory over Nazi Germany – in far greater regard than they did the incumbent First Secretary. While the prospect of liberalisation was the major theme that brought many members of the intelligentsia to Khrushchev's side, this was not as important in shaping attitudes to the First Secretary among workers and peasants. Of course, workers and peasants hardly opposed the ending of mass terror, but issues such as democratisation and free speech were on the whole not among their most pressing concerns. Conversely, themes that caused consternation

[57] GARF, f. 8131, op. 33, d. 96712, l. 19.
[58] G. F. R. Bursa, 'Political Changes of Names of Soviet Towns', *Slavonic and East European Review*, Vol. 63, No. 2 (April 1985), 181.
[59] See W. Taubman, *Khrushchev: The Man and His Era*, London: The Free Press, 2003, pp. 614–15.
[60] Yu. Glazov, *The Russian Mind since Stalin's Death*, Boston, MA: D. Reidel, 1985, p. 30.

among the intelligentsia, such as the occasional hounding of liberal writers and artists, probably did little or no harm to Khrushchev's standing with other parts of the population. Indeed, we can reasonably assume that there was some popular approval for these attacks on 'pampered' intellectuals.[61]

With members of the intelligentsia rightly viewing Khrushchev as the best, or perhaps only, force for reform among the political elite, there was ample reason for them to take a more positive view of him, especially in the early part of his rule when he and the intelligentsia implicitly allied against more overtly conservative elements within the Party leadership. Although no intellectual himself, Khrushchev quickly won the allegiance of many among the intelligentsia through his criticism of Stalin and his encouragement of cultural liberalisation. Nonetheless, as the clampdown on many of those who had spoken out against Stalinism after the Secret Speech showed, along with occasionally vitriolic attacks on errant writers, the First Secretary remained determined that the tail would not wag the dog. His vision of the right course of action for the USSR was what mattered, and that was only sometimes in accord with the desires of liberal intellectuals, whose visions of liberalisation often went much further than he was willing to be pushed. While Khrushchev's relationship with the liberal intelligentsia had always been at least a little fractious in the second half of the 1950s, the political outlook was becoming much less promising during the early 1960s. Prospects for continued liberalisation were receding whilst outbursts of crude anti-intellectualism on the part of the First Secretary were becoming louder and more frequent.

For many, it was only with the benefit of hindsight that Khrushchev's standing began to improve significantly. Looking back two and a half decades after his ouster, Ludmilla Alexeyeva felt that 'in his uneven and boorish way, Khrushchev was one of the greatest leaders Russia ever had'. However, Alexeyeva also conceded that this degree of admiration had not developed until some time after he had been deposed.[62] That time lag between Khrushchev's removal from power and approval of his achievements should not be overlooked, since it allowed Alexeyeva to evaluate Khrushchev in the light of his successor, under whom things had grown more difficult for the liberal intelligentsia. When the Soviet regime took an

---

[61] As Boris Kagarlitsky has pointed out, there was a conscious effort on the part of the regime to sow division between the working class and the intelligentsia by painting a picture of the latter as 'whingers' and 'cry-babies'. B. Kagarlitsky, *The Thinking Reed: Intellectuals and the Soviet State from 1917 to the Present*, London: Verso, 1989, p. 110.

[62] L. Alexeyeva and P. Goldberg, *The Thaw Generation: Coming of Age in the Post-Stalin Era*, Boston, MA: Little, Brown and Company, 1990, p. 105.

unmistakably conservative turn following the arrest of Andrei Sinyavsky and Yuli Daniel in 1966 and, more notably, after the Prague Spring in 1968, one of the main beneficiaries was Khrushchev's reputation as an earlier force for liberalisation. Masha Gessen summed this up perfectly when she wrote that: 'from the vantage point of October 1964 ... the thaw seemed like a long sequence of missed opportunities and squelched reforms. From the vantage point of 1968 and later, the thaw was a magical era that ended as quickly as it had begun.'[63] Although not made explicit in Gessen's argument, we can add that this subsequent reappraisal of the 'thaw' took place most clearly among the liberal intelligentsia, since it was they who had generally had the best of the Khrushchev era, if fleetingly, and would have the worst of the Brezhnev era. They would also be the ones whose status and connections consistently enabled them to shape popular perceptions of both periods, especially in the West.

In addition to his inconsistent liberalisation and intermittent hectoring of the intelligentsia, some simply judged Khrushchev's behaviour on the world stage an embarrassment. For a society becoming increasingly well-educated and more sophisticated – and especially for the growing ranks of professionals who were by now far better educated than their political leaders – Khrushchev could certainly look a buffoon at times, and one who reflected poorly on the Soviet system. William Taubman's account of an incident that took place during a 1964 state visit to Egypt is instructive: 'He ate and drank like a peasant, downing six large sweet cakes at one sitting even after his daughter Rada had begged him to stop, guzzling brandy and pouring his soup into a saucer and then drinking it without a spoon.'[64] Alexeyeva recalled Khrushchev's 'kitchen debate' with Richard Nixon – when the pair had a particularly heated exchange in a mocked-up kitchen at the 1959 American Exhibition in Moscow – as an event that caused a deep sense of shame in herself and her friends.[65] His alleged 'shoe-banging' episode at the UN and rumours of frequent drunkenness and unrefined manners all went some way to undermining Khrushchev as a dignified and statesmanlike leader of a superpower. Some of these charges were ultimately rather unfair, and he certainly seems to have left a favourable impression on many of those who actually met him in person, though one would undoubtedly struggle to think of a major world leader quite so colourful as Nikita Khrushchev.

---

[63] M. Gessen, cited in S. Bittner, *The Many Lives of Khrushchev's Thaw: Experience and Memory in Moscow's Arbat*, London: Cornell University Press, 2008, p. 15.

[64] W. Taubman, *Khrushchev*, p. 611.   [65] L. Alexeyeva and P. Goldberg, *The Thaw Generation*, p. 105.

For others, the question was not simply one of embarrassment, but fear for the consequences of the First Secretary's antics. Eduard Kuznetsov recalled how he had felt certain that Khrushchev's reckless diplomacy would provoke a Third World War even before the Cuban Missile Crisis brought such an event perilously close to reality.[66] There were a whole host of factors one could point to in justification of this sentiment, such as the increasingly bitter and personalised Sino-Soviet split, Khrushchev's continuing brinkmanship over the unsettled Berlin question and his bellicose and occasionally bullying behaviour toward other world leaders.[67] In short, during a period of remarkable international tension there was no lack of grounds for believing that the rather volatile and often less-than-diplomatic Soviet leader might provoke disaster at some point.

By the time of his ouster, Khrushchev had alienated numerous important sectors of Soviet society, from Party members who either opposed deStalinization or else were frustrated at the slow pace of it, to bureaucrats affected by unpopular administrative reorganisations, soldiers who lost jobs thanks to military cuts, scientists dismayed by the continued support for Stalin's charlatan biologist Trofim Lysenko, and many others besides. While it is impossible to make definitive claims about the state of popular opinion on the matter, since reliable data on the subject does not exist, what we can say with certainty is that signs of discontent at Khrushchev personally seem to have been fairly widespread by the later stages of the era. This was also reflected in the complete absence of protest at his enforced retirement after the 'palace coup' of October 1964. Even more damningly, an August 1965 report from KGB chairman Vladimir Semichastnyi to the CPSU Central Committee stated that since Khrushchev's removal from power, not only had the number of anti-Soviet leaflets in circulation dropped by around 50% compared to the same period of the previous year, but a large proportion of those that had been found in recent months actually expressed satisfaction at his fall from grace.[68]

If anything, Khrushchev's occasionally unpredictable policy shifts and his combustible personality threatened to become an impediment to the achievement of lasting stability. That he could arouse hostility among large elements of the population was certainly known to his colleagues in the political elite. Reports frequently came in from the KGB and MVD that

---

[66] Interview with Eduard Kuznetsov in L. Polikovskaya, '*My predchuvstvie ... predtecha': ploshchad Mayakovskogo 1958–1965*, Moskva: Obshchestvo 'Memorial', 1997, p. 223.

[67] One of the best examples to cite in this respect is Khrushchev's casual boast to British Prime Minister Anthony Eden that Soviet missiles could 'easily' reach Britain. See W. Taubman, *Khrushchev*, p. 357.

[68] RGANI, f. 89, op. 6, d. 28, l. 2.

touched upon this unpopularity, describing instances of dissent around the country that featured 'abuse of specific individuals among the leadership' or mentioned 'attacks on a leading Party and state figure': these practically always meant Khrushchev. As such, an awareness of popular antipathy toward him must have helped reassure those who would begin plotting their coup in summer 1964 that it could be pulled off without too much risk of a major domestic backlash, if successful.

CHAPTER 7

Less repression, more policing

While the development of policy against dissent during the early Khrushchev period had been broadly characterised by a sense of trial and error, the first half of the 1960s saw the Soviet regime developing a more consistent and sophisticated approach. Neither the uncertainty of the immediate post-Secret Speech period nor the increased repression that had followed December 1956 were to be repeated. Instead, the authorities began to deploy a multifaceted body of measures in which greater efforts were made to induce compliant behaviour among the population at large and to isolate dissenters, whilst continuing to employ harsh punitive responses against those remaining critics who were deemed to be 'genuinely anti-Soviet'.

In many ways this period marked the final emergence of a new kind of post-Stalin, post-terror dictatorship: one that the Party leadership had been fumbling its way toward during the half-decade since Stalin's death. While the second half of the 1950s can be seen as a time when the regime broke forever with the most brutal aspects of Stalinism, it was during the early 1960s that new methods of managing the masses began to crystallise and the contours of a new type of social control took on a more concrete form. Living standards rose. Minor political transgressions were treated with greater lenience while more serious offences could be met with even harsher coercion.[1] The authorities also took an increasing interest in studying and shaping the minutiae of citizens' everyday lives. Popular opinion was more effectively monitored and shaped. Volunteer groups and informants came to play a significant role in policing as the distinction between 'state' and 'society' became more blurred.

As Oleg Kharkhordin has pointed out in regard to the policing of post-Stalin society, the system consolidated the move away from the chaotic and

[1] See F. Feldbrugge, 'Soviet Criminal Law. The Last Six Years', *The Journal of Criminal Law, Criminology and Police Science*, Vol. 54, No. 3 (September 1963), 263.

punitive terror of the Stalin years and toward a 'relentless and rational system of preventative surveillance'.[2] The authorities were becoming much more sure-footed in dealing with dissent. In addition to providing a higher standard of living, this meant less outright repression but more intimate policing of citizens' everyday lives. Pressure to conform did not come solely 'from above' but was also increasingly embedded in the very fabric of everyday life. Citizens were increasingly expected to take an active interest in each other's personal lives and ideological affairs for the wider good of the collective. As Elena Zubkova succinctly pointed out: 'private life was considered a public matter'.[3]

Combining a variety of positive inducements for citizens to refrain from non-conformist behaviour with the threat of tough sanctions against 'troublemakers', Brian Silver labelled the new system 'welfare-state authoritarianism', and with some justification.[4] The state provided a growing range of social benefits but expected public conformity in return. In practice, this meant that large-scale discontent based on material factors was generally placated wherever possible, but political grievances – such as those of intelligentsia dissenters – were still liable to provoke a particularly stern response. The regime's ideological claims to legitimacy, such as its revolutionary heritage and the scientific infallibility of Marxism-Leninism, were still foregrounded in official discourse, and socialist values continued to resonate among much of the population, but in practice they were increasingly bolstered and even supplanted by 'covert' claims to legitimacy that were based on more practical and tangible issues, such as providing full employment, improving living standards and advancing technological progress.[5]

Whereas practically all of the Party's 'big guns' had been involved in shaping the clampdown that began in December 1956, members of the top leadership were less involved in dictating the terms of the struggle against dissent by the early 1960s. In fact, the KGB's own history textbook later

---

[2] O. Kharkhordin, *The Collective and the Individual in Russia: A Study of Practices*, Berkeley, CA: University of California Press, 1999, p. 299. Even so, Kharkhordin's assertion that 'the remaining spaces in the grid of mutual surveillance were successfully eliminated' feels somewhat overstated. As ever, the extent of the authorities' control was considerably greater in theory than in practice.

[3] E. Zubkova, *Obshchestvo i reformy, 1945–1964*, Moskva: Izdatel'skii tsentr 'Rossiya molodaya', 1993, p. 121.

[4] See B. Silver, 'Political Beliefs of the Soviet Citizen: Sources of Support for Regime Norms', in J. Millar ed., *Politics, Work, and Daily Life in the USSR: A Survey of Former Soviet Citizens*, Cambridge University Press, 1987, p. 102.

[5] On this broad theme see J. Pakulski, 'Legitimacy and Mass Compliance: Reflections on Max Weber and Soviet-Type Societies', *British Journal of Political Science*, Vol. 16, No. 1 (January 1986), 53.

claimed it was they, rather than the Central Committee Presidium, who took the more active role in drawing up measures to deal with dissent from the end of the 1950s onwards.[6] In other words, control passed from the politicians to the professionals. While local Party organisations and officials had often failed to satisfy the leadership in Moscow with their handling of protest and criticism, there were few such problems with the policing work of the security organs. Of course, the Presidium was still kept abreast of developments around the country and could play a much more hands-on role during times of heightened unrest, such as the summer of 1962. While the very top leadership was provided with occasional summaries of dissenting behaviour, the General Department of the Central Committee continued to receive regular updates on even quite banal instances of protest and criticism around the country from the KGB, and less frequently from the MVD and Procurator's office. Even when it did not present any kind of tangible threat to social stability, monitoring dissenting activity remained high on the regime's list of domestic priorities.

Aside from the disturbance at Novocherkassk, there were only a few instances where members of the CPSU leadership were actively and openly involved in responding to political non-conformity. Most often, this meant dealing with high-profile critics or those who were in some sense a part of the establishment elite.[7] Nowhere was this more visible than in the cultural sphere, as typified by Khrushchev's occasional splenetic harangues aimed at writers and artists. On an institutional level, the Ideological Commission was an important new facet of the Central Committee's battle to keep tabs on the cultural intelligentsia.[8] Typically of the time, its role was to exert a controlling influence rather than to punish or repress. Leonid Il'ichev – the notoriously dogmatic head of the Central Committee's Department of Agitation and Propaganda – insisted in June 1963 that the aim was 'not to subject writers to criticism, but to help them understand their ideological mistakes'.[9] In reality, this was essentially another layer of control intended to keep in check potentially wayward elements among the creative

[6] V. Chebrikov et al., *Istoriya sovetskikh organov gosudarstvennoi bezopasnosti: uchebnik*, Moskva: Vysshaya krasnoznamenskaya shkola komiteta gosudarstvennoi bezopasnosti pri sovete ministrov SSSR, 1977, p. 581.

[7] As the following chapters show, examples of this included the writer Valery Tarsis, the nuclear physicist Andrei Sakharov and General Petro Grigorenko.

[8] The Ideological Commission was not entirely new as an institution, though its responsibilities and prerogatives had undergone significant change since its original incarnation in January 1958. See V. Afiani, 'Ideologicheskie komissii TsK KPSS (1958–1964 gg.) v mekhanizme upravleniya kulturoi', in E. Afanas'eva and V. Afiani eds., *Ideologicheskii komissii TsK KPSS, 1958–1964: dokumenty*, Moskva: Rosspen, 1998, pp. 23–8.

[9] K. Aimermakher, 'Partiinoe upravlenie kul'turoi i formy ee samoorganizatsii (1953–1964/67)', in E. Afanas'eva and V. Afiani eds., *Ideologicheskii komissii*, pp. 5–22.

intelligentsia through shaming, self-criticism and intimidation. The fact that the Commission was headed by two of the dominant Party leaders of the era (Suslov and Il'ichev) gives some idea of its political weight as an organ intended to bully non-conformist intellectuals back into line. For the most part, it achieved this task.

Maintaining outward conformity among the masses was by no means solely based upon intimidation and thunderous rhetoric, however. One of the issues that has not always been addressed in studies on dissenting activity in the USSR is the role of positive inducements in ensuring either social passivity or active engagement with the regime. Indeed, the theme of conformity is one of the key areas that must be explored in greater depth as scholars' focus on the post-Stalin era continues to grow. As Gleb Tsipursky has shown, the Khrushchev era saw a major expansion in the recreational opportunities made available to Soviet youth in particular, as a notably softer line was adopted on how best to instil the necessary values and goals into the next generation of builders of communism. Millions of young people poured great energy and enthusiasm into participating in officially sponsored activities such as photography clubs, musical ensembles and night-schools.[10] Even for those growing disenchanted at political life inside the USSR, there were still myriad interstices at which one voluntarily interacted with the system on its own terms. Furthermore, the regime controlled a great array of benefits and favours that it could hand out to those who were at least outwardly loyal. From granting members of the intelligentsia privileged access to coveted consumer goods, foreign travel and various honorary titles, through to keeping the price of foodstuffs artificially low and providing free healthcare and education for the masses, the authorities deployed a variety of positive measures aimed at engendering both active support and widespread conformism. For the intelligentsia in particular, these were often benefits which could easily be taken away again. As such, the majority were usually content to conform to political expectations – which had anyway become much less exacting since Stalin's death – in order to protect the privileges and security that had only recently been won.

To some extent, this placating of material frustrations was also a feature of efforts aimed at tackling citizens' interest in the West. As Lev Karpinsky noted during his time as head of the Komsomol's Department of Propaganda, bourgeois influence upon Soviet youths was intimately linked

---

[10] G. Tsipursky, '*Pleasure, Power and the Pursuit of Communism: Soviet Youth and State-Sponsored Popular Culture during the Early Cold War Period, 1945–1968*', Ph.D. Dissertation, University of North Carolina at Chapel Hill, 2011.

to the fulfilment of emerging cultural tastes.[11] Listening to foreign radio stations, for example, did not just bring one into contact with the latest Western music, but potentially also Western political content. In fact, this was exactly how a number of foreign stations deliberately worked: attracting listeners with the latest music and then adding ideological material.[12] One way around this was to make a more convincing attempt at satisfying popular cultural desires within the framework of the Soviet system.[13] For example, the authorities showed a willingness to respond to young people's frustrations over the style and quality of their apparel by producing more modern and fashionable clothing. A limited amount of approved Western music was also allowed once it became abundantly clear that young people would otherwise find it for themselves.[14] Similarly, while the regime sought to block foreign radio broadcasts they also looked to make Soviet radio shows more appealing to the general public, often by reducing their overt ideological content, particularly during those time slots when foreign stations such as Radio Liberty were broadcasting to the USSR.[15] As Kristin Roth-Ey shows, the subsequent rise of 'mass culture', in the form of increasingly entertainment-centred (as opposed to ideologically based) cultural output, was to be one of the hallmarks of the post-Stalin years and would go hand in hand with a declining focus on the Soviet grand narrative of constructing communism.[16]

Of course, widespread social passivity was never rooted solely in the regime's ability to provide a reasonable standard of living for its citizens, nor upon universal affinity to the stated values of the communist project. Even without reliance upon terror, coercion and control remained central planks of the post-Stalin system. Perceptions of the KGB were often absolutely vital to the process of weighing up the costs and benefits of pre-planned protest behaviours in particular. In short, if the bulk of society believed that the KGB was effective at tracking down 'enemies', it provided a valuable general deterrent against dissenting behaviour. After a difficult period following

---

[11] G. Tsipursky, 'Pleasure, Power, and the Pursuit of Communism', p. 348.
[12] See S. Mikkonen, 'Stealing the Monopoly of Knowledge?: Soviet Reactions to Cold War Broadcasting', *Kritika*, Vol. 11, No. 4 (Fall 2010), 771–805.
[13] Here one is reminded of Gleb Tsipursky's argument that improved levels of consumption did not just relate to foodstuffs and consumer goods, but also to cultural desires.
[14] See S. Zhuk, *Rock and Roll in the Rocket City: The West, Identity, and Ideology in Soviet Dnepropetrovsk, 1960–1985*, Washington, DC: Woodrow Wilson Center Press, 2010.
[15] RGANI, f. 11, op. 1, d. 340, in V. Afiani et al. eds., *Kul'tura i vlast' ot Stalina do Gorbacheva: apparat TsK KPSS i kul'tura, 1958–1964*, Moskva: Rosspen, 2005.
[16] K. Roth-Ey, *Moscow Prime Time: How the Soviet Union Built the Media Empire that Lost the Cultural Cold War*, London: Cornell University Press, 2011.

Stalin's death and the Secret Speech, when the security organs' standing had taken a heavy blow, there began a drive to 're-brand' the KGB as a slick and highly efficient organisation serving the interests of the masses. In a move that succinctly characterised the on-going changes, the forty-year-old, university-educated Komsomol first secretary Aleksandr Shelepin replaced the strongman and career *Chekist* Ivan Serov as KGB chairman in December 1958.[17] Soon, many of the remaining Stalin-era officers were being dismissed in favour of younger and better-educated replacements.

The available evidence suggests that this remodelling of the security organs had the desired effect. Out of almost 3,000 interviews with Soviet émigrés in the 1980s, Donna Bahry and Brian Silver found that the majority rated the KGB as more competent than the Politburo and almost 80% regarded it as 'difficult or very difficult' to tell who might be an informer. Crucially, around half felt that it was either 'easy or very easy' to avoid getting into trouble with the KGB.[18] This perceived combination of efficiency, omnipresence and predictability proved a powerful cocktail that went a long way towards keeping dissenting activity at a minimum without recourse to mass violence. Rather than simply lashing out at critics, the authorities had clearly put some thought into creating effective and durable methods of social control. Deterrence was to be based not just upon harsh punishment but also upon the threat of social alienation and perceptions of a high likelihood of being caught and punished by the increasingly effective security organs.[19] In ensuring that repressive activity became more predictable, the authorities not only made it easy for ordinary citizens to conserve any gains that had been achieved by staying on the right side of the law, but also created an impression of apparent legitimacy around the rump of political repression that continued to take place.

Alongside this revamping of the security organs came a blurring of the line between state and society, as ordinary citizens were increasingly expected to play a greater role in supervising their fellow countrymen and women. Officially sponsored volunteer initiatives saw millions of citizens

[17] See J. Elkner, 'The Changing Face of Repression under Khrushchev', in M. Ilič and J. Smith eds., *Soviet State and Society under Nikita Khrushchev*, London: Routledge, 2009, pp. 140–61.

[18] The data in question were produced by the Soviet Interview Project, conducted in the United States during the early 1980s. See D. Bahry and B. Silver, 'Intimidation and the Symbolic Uses of Terror in the USSR', *American Political Science Review*, Vol. 81, No. 4 (December 1987), 1066–98. For discussion of the strengths and weaknesses of the data produced by the project see J. Millar ed., *Politics, Work, and Daily Life in the USSR.*

[19] On Gulag officials' acceptance that lengthy jail sentences did not serve as an effective deterrent, see J. Hardy, '*Khrushchev's Gulag: The Evolution of Punishment in the Post-Stalin Soviet Union, 1953–1964*', Ph.D. Dissertation, Princeton University, 2011, p. 80.

policing the streets in People's Patrols, participating in the rehabilitation of released prisoners and sitting in judgement of their peers in Comrades' Courts. While such measures at least in part showcased the intermittent idealism of the era, others were more distinctly insidious. KGB agents and informers penetrated deeper into practically all social strata, workplaces and housing blocks.[20] Technological advances were also taking place that made it easier for the security organs to listen in on and observe the population at large.[21] All this formed the basis of the 'relentless and rational' system of social control that Kharkhordin diagnosed.

There was a growing reliance upon details provided by informants and so-called 'trusted people' (*doverennye litsa*) throughout society.[22] These were not quite the same as the 'denouncers' of the Stalin years, though: they were ordinary citizens co-opted by the KGB, or less often by the militia, to inform from time to time on the activities of those in whom the authorities had taken an interest. The security organs quickly proved skilful at nurturing a web of such informers. As Louise Shelley pointed out: 'They offered powerful inducements to comply and severe punishments for disobedience[;] few citizens of the USSR were capable of resisting the power of the police.'[23] Doubtless, many required no such pressure. From some, cooperation with the organs was demanded. Postal workers were to alert the authorities if they suspected packages of containing anti-Soviet materials.[24] Residents of ground-floor flats in apartment blocks were expected to keep the organs informed about any suspicious conversations they overheard on the lobby telephone, and a promise of cooperation with the KGB was often a precondition for jobs as security guards and building superintendents.[25] Failure to report a criminal act that one knew to be imminent now became a crime in itself. Even when millions of citizens began moving out of communal apartments and into private flats, privacy remained rather limited, since shoddy

[20] RGANI, f. 89, op. 6, d. 20, ll. 1–9.   [21] V. Chebrikov et al., *Istoriya sovetskikh organov*, p. 510.

[22] Actual numbers of 'trusted people' are all but impossible to find. One of the few estimates available has been made by Evgeniya Albats, who suggests that *perestroika*-era documents show somewhere between 30% and 60% of the population co-operated with the security organs in some way. The gap between the two figures (which would constitute close to 70,000,000 people at this point) and the vagueness of the term 'co-operate' induce a degree of caution in the reader. See Ye. Albats, *KGB: State Within a State*, London: I.B. Tauris, 1995.

[23] L. Shelley, *Policing Soviet Society: The Evolution of State Control*, London: Routledge, 1996, p. 6.

[24] This was actually one of the ways in which the KGB managed to track down the Union of Freedom and Intellect in February 1962. See V. Kozlov and S. Mironenko eds., *Kramola*, p. 360.

[25] L. Shelley, *Policing Soviet Society*, p. 120.

construction methods and materials often meant that neighbours could still hear practically every word that was said in the home.[26]

By drawing members of the public into the work of the state through involvement in activities like volunteer policing, the authorities firstly hoped to bind participants more tightly to the regime, thereby ensuring that official views on critics and other undesirables permeated wider society.[27] Accordingly, one of the key aims of policy against dissent was that the erring individual should 'feel the shame of society': they should be pushed back into line not just by government actions but by social pressure, too.[28] Just as importantly, by harnessing the power of the ordinary citizenry more effectively, the scope for what could be seen and heard by the authorities grew to an entirely new level. In itself, this had significant deterrent value, since many volunteers went about without uniforms and were therefore indistinct from the wider mass of society.

As time passed, a growing proportion of the regime's efforts to forestall dissenting behaviour inside the USSR were focused overseas. In addition to maintaining a grip on criticism and protest at home, more and more resources were put into tackling the efforts of hostile groups beyond the borders of the Soviet Union. The *Narodno trudovyi soyuz* (NTS)[29] in particular exercised the minds of the security organs. Undercover KGB agents soon penetrated its structures at practically every level. From then on, when NTS dispatched agents to the USSR (which it did on a semi-regular basis) they were almost immediately apprehended at the border.[30] The organs' internal history textbook boasted of uncovering and liquidating 'many military and political plans aimed at the Soviet Union and other socialist powers' as well as 'arresting many foreign intelligence agents masquerading as tourists'.[31]

Soviet diplomats were deployed to persuade foreign governments to prevent subversive organisations like NTS from operating on their territory and to force hostile radio stations to tone down their anti-communist rhetoric.[32]

---

[26] On this theme see S. Harris, '"I Know All the Secrets of My Neighbours": The Quest for Privacy in the Era of the Separate Apartment', in L. Siegelbaum ed., *Borders of Socialism: Private Spheres of Soviet Russia*, Basingstoke: Palgrave Macmillan, 2006, pp. 179–81.

[27] See G. Breslauer, 'Khrushchev Reconsidered', in S. Cohen, A. Rabinowitch and R. Sharlet eds., *The Soviet Union since Stalin*, Bloomington, IN: Indiana University Press, 1980, pp. 50–70.

[28] See V. Abramkin and V. Chesnokova, *Tyurmennyi mir glazami politzaklyuchennykh*, Moskva: Sodeistvie, 1993, p. 12.

[29] See Chapter 5.   [30] Interview with Vladimir Bukovsky, Cambridge, March 2007.

[31] V. Chebrikov et al., *Istoriya sovetskikh organov*, p. 566.

[32] By falsely denying that Radio Liberty was attached to the US government, the Americans were able to claim they had no influence over its output and thus could do nothing on this matter.

Threats and intimidation were also used against those radio stations that broadcast to Soviet audiences from the West. Gene Sosin recalled that Soviet agents were regularly 'planted' at Radio Liberty by the KGB and would gather whatever information they could before returning to the USSR to denounce the station. Émigrés working at the station's Munich offices regularly received silent telephone calls, anonymous threats and letters from relatives in the Soviet Union begging them to stop slandering their motherland and return home.

Most seriously, there were also murders. Two Radio Liberty staff members were killed in Munich – almost certainly by the KGB, according to Sosin.[33] A number of NTS officials were also abducted or killed in Western Europe during the 1950s. Aleksandr Trushnovich, the NTS leader in West Berlin, was killed by the KGB in April 1954 and an assassin was engaged to murder NTS President Vladimir Poremsky in late 1955. In October 1957 the Ukrainian nationalist leader Lev Rebet was stalked and then killed with a poison spray in Munich.[34] Stepan Bandera was also killed by the same KGB assassin in Munich during October 1959.[35] Others faced slightly less instantaneous retribution. In a January 1963 report to the CPSU Central Committee the KGB announced it had 'managed to find and bring back to the USSR' two former citizens who had fled the country and had subsequently been speaking out against the Soviet regime from Frankfurt-am-Main (where they were alleged to have been working for the US intelligence service), further demonstrating both the risk that émigré critics ran and the reach of the Soviet security organs.[36] What became of the two men in question remains unknown.

Inside the Soviet Union, the resources available for the policing of dissent were practically limitless – again showing that even though the authorities were not actually panicked by the level of protest activity around the country, they took the threat very seriously indeed. The case file of Mikhail Ermizin, an assistant doctor from Stavropol who had posted over forty political leaflets between 1962 and 1964, gave a useful demonstration of

[33] G. Sosin, *Sparks of Liberty: An Insider's Memoir of Radio Liberty*, University Park, PA: Pennsylvania State University Press, 1999, p. xiv.

[34] C. Andrew and V. Mitrokhin, *The Sword and the Shield: The Mitrokhin Archive and the Secret History of the KGB*, New York: Basic Books, 1999, pp. 361–2.

[35] The assassin in question was Bohdan Stashynsky. On the theme of government-sponsored assassinations of 'enemies' overseas at this time, see also N. Petrov, *Ivan Serov: pervyi predsedatel' KGB*, Moskva: Materik, 2005, pp. 152–6.

[36] RGANI, f. 5, op. 30, d. 412, l. 56. The report presents no evidence to indicate that the individuals in questions were actively working for the US intelligence service, though there was an American base in Frankfurt-am-Main.

this. The investigation protocol reported that Ermizin had been traced by 'graphic expertise' and 'forensic methods' (probably meaning handwriting or typeface analysis and fingerprinting); yet one of the most notable details in the file was that it listed no fewer than twenty separate KGB specialists who had been working on the investigation and a further two 'scientific experts' who had also been involved in tracking down the perpetrator of what was ultimately a fairly low-level act of protest.[37] Accordingly, investigations into the larger underground groups could be huge in scope. Boris Vail', for example, recalled that after having been subject to clandestine surveillance prior to his arrest in 1957, around 120 acquaintances and family members were interrogated in connection with the KGB investigation into his underground activities.[38] As Chapter 9 shows, the operation to track down and punish the writers Abram Tertz and Nikolai Arzhak was a particularly huge and complex undertaking that rumbled on for several years before coming to a conclusion when the pair were convicted of anti-Soviet activity in early 1966.

Details on another of the most interesting practicalities of policing dissent can be gleaned from a report sent by secretary of the Kazakh Communist Party, Putintsev, to the CPSU Central Committee on 24 May 1960. Describing the discovery of over 450 NTS leaflets in Aktyubinsk *oblast'*, Putintsev reported that the Party *obkom* had immediately mobilised 200 people to track down and remove the leaflets from public places, including local soldiers, Komsomol members, Party workers and KGB staff.[39] That the Kazakh authorities saw fit to devote so many people to this operation was indicative of the extent to which these leaflets were seen to constitute a threat to the regime's univocal public sphere and one that had to be quickly neutralised. The need to utilise civilians, like Party and Komsomol members, for this task also demonstrated that taking such documents out of circulation could be a rather ad hoc exercise in peripheral regions. In major cities there would most likely have been no such mobilisation of non-police manpower, since the authorities did not want ordinary Party members or soldiers to come into contact with these kinds of materials. Indeed, even internal KGB reports were not allowed to cite the full content of dissenters' remarks, in order to shield against the danger that they represented.

Unlike the KGB, the militia was not systematically involved in the policing of dissent during the Khrushchev years – a practice that was later

---

[37] GARF, f. 8131, op. 31, d. 97853, ll. 10–14.
[38] B. Vail', *Osobo opasnyi*, London: Overseas Publications Interchange, 1980, p. 196.
[39] RGANI, f. 5, op. 30, d. 320, ll. 9–10.

to be reversed under Brezhnev – though more often than not it was they who first responded to public protests and outbursts by virtue of their being the main government force on the ground. They were also obliged to assist the security organs as and when requested to do so, something that could involve acts such as temporarily detaining citizens on trumped-up charges, creating diversions that allowed the KGB to carry out unsanctioned apartment searches, and conducting provocations against individuals whom the KGB had taken an interest in, such as starting fights in the streets or making false accusations of wrongdoing. Another of their more important responsibilities was to register typewriters, printing presses and photographic equipment: this played an important role in tracing the authors of anonymous letters, anti-Soviet leaflets and *samizdat* documents.

In fact, the militia was at rather a low ebb during the Khrushchev years. As we have already seen, there was considerable anti-police sentiment bubbling close to the surface within society, and popular regard for the MVD was not high. Yoram Gorlizki, for example, notes that during a 1958 riot in Grozny, members of the militia took off their uniforms in order to evade assault by angry rioters.[40] Like the KGB, the reputation of the MVD was damaged by the Secret Speech. Khrushchev and his colleagues initially did little to reverse the declining resources, prestige and morale of the militia, preferring instead to mobilise the populace in order to bolster policing. The mass disturbances of the early 1960s, however, helped engineer a rethink on the subject. The situation then began to change, as new laws designated the death penalty for violent attacks on members of the militia, police were to be armed with handcuffs, teargas and truncheons, and a new 'militia day' was instituted in an attempt to restore some pride and professional stature to an organisation that was one of the key public faces of the Soviet system.[41]

As official reports and anecdotal evidence testified, the relationship between the KGB and militia at times proved a weak link in the state's efforts to combat dissent and could also be somewhat fractious at ground level.[42] The volunteer police force, the *druzhinniki*, were an even weaker link in the law-enforcement apparatus, not least because many of them were not truly volunteers at all, and consequently showed little enthusiasm for

---

[40] Y. Gorlizki, 'Policing Post-Stalin Society: The Militsiia and Public Order under Khrushchev', *Cahiers du Monde russe*, Vol. 44, Nos. 2–3 (avril–septembre 2003), 473.
[41] See Y. Gorlizki, 'Policing Post-Stalin Society'.
[42] See, for example, RGANI, f. 89, op. 6, d. 20, ll. 3–9. See also V. Bukovskii, *I vozvrashchaetsya veter . . .*, Moskva: Zakharov, 2007.

policing.[43] The inquest into the hooligan disorders at Murom, for example, complained that volunteer police there had done little more than report problems they saw to the militia, rather than actually dealing with any difficulties themselves.[44] How far this was an attempt by the militia to pass some of the blame for the events that unfolded in Murom is unclear, though one can easily picture the lack of zeal displayed by an amateur force of cajoled citizens when confronted by a rampaging crowd. In short, there were limits to the effectiveness of the new model of 'less repression but more policing'.[45]

As the previous chapter showed, it had not escaped the attention of the leadership that local officials tended to prove unable to handle challenging or potentially volatile situations with sufficient sensitivity and decisiveness. By the early 1960s, there was an increasing oversight of procedures and centralisation of decision-making on the subject of dissent. This was a trend that continued throughout the Brezhnev era, especially in regard to the most high-profile dissidents, such as Andrei Sakharov and Aleksandr Solzhenitsyn. While the period immediately following the Secret Speech and the December letter saw numerous instances when regional offices botched or mishandled investigations, by the turn of the decade more stringent control of affairs was being imposed by the centre.

The case file of Andrei Danilovich Mosin, who was arrested in Kursk in October 1962 after sending two anonymous letters to the editor of *Izvestiya*, testified to this pattern of growing central interest in the conduct of regional affairs. The local procurator at Kursk first contacted the USSR Procuracy in Moscow on 26 October to inform them that an arrest had been sanctioned, and then contacted Moscow again on 16 November to advise that the investigation was complete and the case was about to proceed to court. On 7 January 1963 – almost two months later – the Moscow office demanded Kursk bring them up to date on the trial's outcome, which it did four days later, stating that on 28 November Mosin had been sentenced to seven years' corrective labour. On 23 January Moscow then requested to be informed of the content of Mosin's letters and set a deadline of 1 February. When no response was forthcoming, on 2 February another

---

[43] Levies of recruits were set for individual workplaces, which then had to persuade – or more often, force – workers to 'volunteer' in order to meet that factory's obligations to the state.

[44] RGASPI, f. 17, op. 91, d. 1498, in A. Fursenko et al. eds., *Prezidium TsK KPSS 1954–1964*, Tom 3: *Postanovleniya 1959–1964*, Moskva: Rosspen, 2008.

[45] Indeed, their rather limited success as instruments of law enforcement was undoubtedly a factor in the move away from such volunteer initiatives as the 1960s progressed.

letter was sent from the capital demanding that the Kursk office speed up its work and provide the requested information – which it eventually did eleven days later.[46] The message was clear, Moscow was taking an active interest in matters all across the country and weak links in the policing of dissent were being eradicated, even where cases might appear largely inconsequential.

New tactics for tackling critics were being rolled out across the USSR as a whole. Following the wave of criticism and questioning that had occurred at meetings and discussions in the wake of the Secret Speech, plans were drawn up to deal with such remarks more effectively in the future. Public political interchange would become ever more carefully managed, as ideological questions were increasingly stripped of ambiguity and vitality and more effective firewalls were erected to 'nip in the bud' any dissonant voices that did arise. A demonstration of this last point was provided by events at Moscow's Lenin District Party conference on 7 September 1961, when Petro Grigorenko took to the rostrum to make an impromptu address. In the speech he criticised the continuing lack of internal Party democracy and the air of servility and careerism within the CPSU, before attacking the leader cult that was developing around Nikita Khrushchev. After a motion to deprive Grigorenko of the floor in mid-speech was voted down by delegates in the hall, his remarks were immediately followed by an unscheduled intermission, during which the heads of delegations were assembled in a closed room and ordered personally to instruct their members to condemn Grigorenko's comments.[47]

When proceedings at the conference resumed, a motion was straight away put forward that Grigorenko be deprived of his delegate's credentials on the grounds of 'political immaturity'. Despite the motion receiving the backing of less than one-third of the delegates, it received no opposition and was passed accordingly. The key to success lay in the clear and timely reassertion of 'right' and 'wrong' and in making plain the responsibility of individuals to defend the system from its critics. There was clearly some sympathy for Grigorenko in the hall, since support for the motion was far from overwhelming, but the fact that nobody was willing to vote in his defence was telling of the extent to which discipline had been thoroughly restored within the Party, especially in comparison with the period following the XX Party Congress. Needless to say, Grigorenko's Party membership, like his military career, was soon a thing of the past.

---

[46] GARF, f. 8131, op. 31, d. 924020, ll. 1–11.
[47] P. Grigorenko, *Memoirs*, New York: W.W. Norton, 1982, p. 250.

Grigorenko later wrote of how he was subsequently informed that this tactic was specifically worked out in preparation for the XXII Party Congress, when Khrushchev was to renew his criticism of Stalin.[48] The available evidence clearly suggests this assertion was not without foundation. On the very same day as Grigorenko's remarks in Moscow, Valentin Ovechkin also delivered a similarly contentious speech at a Party conference in Kursk and was dealt with in exactly the same manner.[49] At about the same time in the late summer of 1961, a pensioner identified by Edward Cohn only as 'Comrade P' had also attacked the emerging cult around Nikita Khrushchev and criticised the draft of the new Party Programme at a CPSU conference in Kalinin *oblast'*. The outcome was again similar: Comrade P was quickly criticised and condemned for making 'harmful, politically incorrect, demagogic and slanderous statements ... aimed at undermining the Central Committee of the CPSU and its leadership'. After making another controversial speech the following day, he was expelled from the Party.[50]

Having been shaken by the period of confusion and disunity within the Party ranks that had arisen after Khrushchev's original exposure of Stalin, it would indeed have been remiss of the leadership not to have put some kind of preventative plans into place before returning to the issue with redoubled energy in October 1961. As events panned out, there was to be no re-run of the confusion and confrontation of spring 1956. Few communists again misjudged the borders of permissible and impermissible. There were far fewer expulsions from the Party in the wake of the XXII Congress than there had been during the mid to late 1950s. Data on appeals against expulsion for 'participation in anti-Party groups' give evidence of this trend, dropping from 154 in 1956 to only sixteen in 1961. Figures from the Party Control Commission show that 306 Communist Party members were ejected on the basis of 'anti-Party discussions' during 1956: the analogous total for 1961 was only sixty-three.[51] In fact, when the figures for 1961 are broken down on a month-by-month basis there is no real evidence of any notable rise in expulsions for 'anti-Party discussions' following the XXII Congress: a quite remarkable fact

---

[48] P. Grigorenko, *Memoirs*, p. 250.

[49] L. Alexeyeva, *Soviet Dissent: Contemporary Movements for National, Religious and Human Rights*, Middletown, CT: Wesleyan University Press, 1987, p. 271.

[50] E. Cohn, '*Disciplining the Party: The Expulsion and Censure of Communists in the Post-War Soviet Union, 1945–1961*', Ph.D. Dissertation, University of Chicago, 2007, p. 204.

[51] E. Kulavig, *Dissent in the Years of Khrushchev: Nine Stories about Disobedient Russians*, Basingstoke: Palgrave Macmillan, 2002, p. 88. The figures cited here are for the number of expulsions prior to appeal. Symptomatic of the declining ideological vigilance within the CPSU, the proportion of successful appeals against expulsion also grew considerably over the course of the era.

when we take into consideration the vehemence with which Khrushchev returned to the 'Stalin question' at the Congress.[52]

The authorities had learned the lessons of the XX Congress and subsequently managed discourse on the Stalin issue much better the second time around. Not least of all, they published the latest round of attacks on Stalin in the press, so as to prevent the ambiguity and emergence of independent public opinion that had arisen 1956. It was also no coincidence that Khrushchev's attack on Stalin in 1961 did not again come with the vaguely defined promise of a 'return to Leninism'. Of course, Lenin and Leninism would always remain at the very heart of Soviet political discourse, but 1956 had already shown that even this was a tool which had to be wielded with some considerable caution lest it arouse passions that might again prove hard to square with existing conditions in the country. The seeming pattern of decline in communist activism and idealism across much of the post-Stalin era (or even across the post-war era more widely), therefore, was not entirely inconvenient for the political authorities: it may have drained the system of its vitality but it also helped contribute to political passivity.

By the turn of the decade, Khrushchev had already announced that prophylactic measures (*profilaktika*) were to become the main feature of what he called the state's 'educational work'.[53] The exact origins of this new policy have yet to be documented, though some commentators suggest that the Central Committee decreed its introduction as a way of bringing down the number of citizens convicted of anti-Soviet activity.[54] Bearing in mind that Khrushchev's January 1959 announcement on the introduction of prophylactic measures came only a few months after the Supreme Court had told the Party leadership that too many people were being inappropriately jailed for anti-Soviet activity, this appears an eminently sensible hypothesis. Interestingly, Nikita Petrov notes that former KGB chairman Ivan Serov – who was dismissed from his post at the end of 1958 – had been a major obstacle to plans for prophylaxis to be rolled out some time earlier

---

[52] A monthly breakdown of expulsions from the CPSU for anti-Party discussions in 1961 is as follows: January – 4; February – 5; March – 3; April – 2; May – 2; June – 3; July – 5; August – 5; September – 1; October – 2; November – 4; December – 2. RGANI, f. 6, op. 6, d. 1183, l. 64.

[53] The English term 'education' does not quite cover the whole meaning of the Russian *vospitanie*, which also indicates notions of 'upbringing' and 'cultivating'. The announcement was made at the XXI CPSU Congress in January 1959. See E. Papovyan and A. Papovyan, 'Uchastie Verkhovnogo Suda SSSR v vyrabotke repressivnoi politiki, 1957–1958', in L. Eremina and E. Zhemkova, eds., *Korni travy: sbornik statei molodykh istorikov*, Moskva: Zven'ya, 1996, pp. 54–73.

[54] J. Elkner, 'The Changing Face of Repression', in M. Ilič and J. Smith eds., *Soviet State and Society under Nikita Khrushchev*, p. 154.

than it eventually was.[55] While more recent scholarship has largely moved beyond traditional assumptions of internecine struggle between clearly demarcated 'liberals' and 'conservatives' within the CPSU leadership, details like this do tell us that noticeably harder or softer lines were put forward by individuals and institutions on any given issue.

As Julie Elkner pointed out, the semantic imagery of dissent as some kind of unhealthy phenomenon or infection from which society had to be protected is immediately apparent, but the actual meaning of the term 'prophylactic measures' was less clear.[56] Vasily Mitrokhin's lexicon of KGB terminology defines *profilaktika* in the following way: 'Activity carried out by Soviet state bodies and social organisations aimed at the prevention of crimes against the state, politically harmful misdemeanours and other acts which affect the interests of the state security of the USSR'.[57] The fact that Mitrokhin's description was still rather vague indicated the imprecise and flexible nature of the new policy – which naturally gave the security organs considerable latitude in how and when it was used.

There were two basic forms of prophylaxis: a first aimed at minimising protest and criticism throughout society as a whole, using methods such as mass political agitation (open prophylaxis), and a second which brought the KGB face to face with specific individuals who were perceived to be insufficiently compliant or in some way unreliable (individual prophylaxis). Both centred upon a shifting balance of persuasion and intimidation. When combined, they provided an effective inter-locking mechanism of social control that played a major, though largely unseen, role in maintaining passivity throughout the vast majority of Soviet society for many years to come.

One of the key facets of attempts to forestall dissenting behaviour throughout Soviet society as a whole lay in the studying and shaping of public moods. The former made the regime better able to predict and head off potential flashpoints and the latter provided a more enduring foundation for stifling and isolating critics in the longer term. This was hardly a fundamentally new field of activity, since the Soviet authorities had always taken a deep interest in monitoring and shaping the popular mood, but it was being put on a more rigorous scientific footing by the start of the

---

[55] Petrov also points to the lingering impact of the Hungarian rising as a factor which had prevented an earlier move toward prophylaxis. N. Petrov, *Ivan Serov*, p. 169. Jeffrey Hardy notes that Serov had also been a staunch opponent of liberalisation within the Gulag. J. Hardy, 'Khrushchev's Gulag', p. 245.

[56] See J. Elkner, 'The Changing Face of Repression', in M. Ilič and J. Smith eds., *Soviet State and Society under Nikita Khrushchev*.

[57] V. Mitrokhin, *KGB Lexicon: The Soviet Intelligence Officer's Handbook*, London: Frank Cass, 2002, p. 329.

1960s.[58] Sociological study of public opinion through mass questionnaires and surveys – on top of more traditional Soviet information-gathering activities, such as reading intercepted mail – began in earnest when the Institute of Public Opinion was established at *Komsomolskaya pravda* in 1960.[59] The fact that a newspaper aimed at young people had been chosen as the home for this new institute was no coincidence. Firstly, the print media was reinvigorating its status as a key tool for shaping the socialist present and future.[60] Secondly, the authorities continued to be most concerned by the apparent disengagement of the younger generation from the Soviet project.

As Thomas Wolfe points out, by the early 1960s the Soviet media had come to display an increasing degree of negativity, focusing on what socialist man should not be and should not do.[61] Dissent was increasingly tied to naïvety and immorality. Among the media's main targets during the later part of the era were young people who dared to voice positive views of the West, a fact not unrelated to the escalating Cold-War tensions of the time. Often branded 'demagogues', they were portrayed as ungrateful and disloyal, but rarely as outright ideologically hostile. This could be seen in a September 1963 article in the newspaper *Kazakhstanskaya pravda*, entitled 'From an Alien Voice'. In the article, two miners from Leninogorsk were lambasted for 'lavishing praise upon life in America at every opportune moment' and 'being unashamed to slander their homeland'.[62] A similar case was played out in the Georgian newspaper *Zarya vostoka* two months later. The piece, entitled 'A Bark behind the Gate', lambasted citizens who listened to foreign radio stations and spread anti-Soviet literature 'with a foreign voice'. The author's conclusion was succinct and emotive: 'we have no right to be indifferent'.[63] This last line was especially telling: as we have already seen, the Soviet people, and communists in particular, were increasingly expected to take an active role in combating critics, rather than simply leaving such work to the state.

Media excoriation was not restricted to those who praised the West, however. In March 1964 *Izvestiya* published a letter, purporting to be from a

---

[58] See, for example, P. Holquist, '"Information is the Alpha and Omega of Our Work": Bolshevik Surveillance in its Pan-European Context', *The Journal of Modern History*, Vol. 69, No. 3 (September 1997), 415–50.

[59] See B. Firsov, *Raznomyslie v SSSR 1940–1960 gody: istoriya, teoriya i praktika*, Sankt Peterburg: Izdatel' stvo Evropeiskogo Universiteta v Sankt Peterburge, 2008, and B. Grushin, *Chetyre zhizni Rossii v zerkale oprosov obshchestvennogo meniya: epokha Khrushcheva*, Moskva: Progress-Traditsiya, 2001. Both Firsov and Grushin worked at the Institute of Public Opinion from the time of its inception.

[60] On this theme see in particular T. Wolfe, *Governing Soviet Journalism: The Press and the Socialist Person after Stalin*, Bloomington, IN: Indiana University Press, 2005.

[61] T. Wolfe, *Governing Soviet Journalism*. [62] *Kazakhstanskaya pravda*, 27 September 1963.

[63] *Zarya vostoka*, 13 November 1963.

Magadan miner named Nikolai Kuritsyn, entitled 'This Must Be Fought!' After apparently overhearing two youths mocking that year's poor harvest while he was waiting in line at the bank, Kuritsyn wrote to *Izvestiya* describing such people as 'toadstools' and insisting that the Soviet way of life must be defended. On the question of how to respond to such individuals, Kuritsyn was unequivocal: '. . . we cannot act like our woodcutter acted, passing himself off as a gardener for thirty years. However, we must fight them, disgrace them, shame them, un-mask them in front of honest people.'[64] The disavowal of Stalin ('the woodcutter') and his methods was central to the letter's message: we are not reverting to the 'bad old days' but criticism of the system will not be tolerated. While the notion of 'un-masking' had a distinct Stalin-era ring to it, the juxtaposition of 'shame' and 'disgrace' with 'honest people' again demonstrated the manner in which dissenting behaviour (even as mild in form as that which Kuritsyn claimed to have overheard) was to be presented to the masses.

In fact, subsequent research by Radio Liberty stated that Kuritsyn was not a miner at all, as the letter in *Izvestiya* had claimed, but a professional journalist.[65] If we assume that this allegation was accurate – and that is distinctly possible, though not absolutely certain – it again serves to flag up the point that the media remained an integral tool in the authorities' efforts to mobilise popular opinion and shape public attitudes to dissent. The fact that this theme was raised in *Izvestiya*, which was sold right across the USSR and had a circulation of many millions, guaranteed a huge audience. As such, Kuritsyn's rallying call was heard far and wide. Numerous letters in support of his remarks were carried in *Izvestiya* later that month, attacking 'rumour-spreaders' and those who told anti-Soviet anecdotes. They included comments such as 'It becomes offensive to the point of pain when you hear base, rotten anecdotes from the mouths of some young people' and '. . . just some difficulty, some troubles in our huge economy and they are already buzzing like nasty autumnal flies'.[66] Again, these letters raised images of 'dirtiness' and 'naïvety', rather than outright treachery.

Probably the best example of using the media to whip up ill-feeling against critics could be seen in a February 1964 edition of *Trud*, where it was said of the 'anonymous calumniator' G.R. Levitin (who had apparently written a series of anonymous letters to *Trud*, though their content was never elucidated): '. . . he poured dirt on Soviet reality and blackened the state which

[64] *Izvestiya*, 1 March 1964.
[65] Radio Liberty Monitoring report, 6 March 1964, Budapest, HU OSA 300-80-01, Box 44.
[66] Research Notes on Soviet Affairs, 13 March 1964, Budapest, HU OSA 300-80-1, Box 44.

gave him an education, a well-built home and guaranteed him a pension'. It then accused Levitin of attempting to extort and threaten several of his own friends before concluding that 'he is not only abominable but he is also dangerous. Here is an evil which we must not tolerate.'[67] One can immediately see that Levitin was being attacked not on ideological grounds, but as a person of dubious morality.[68] The consumerist discourse ('well-built home', 'pension') and the emphasis on his apparent ungratefulness for all that the Soviet state had bestowed upon him quite clearly demonstrated what Jeffrey Brooks termed 'the ideology of the gift', whereby material benefits like these were depicted as a symbol of generosity, and one that should be repaid with 'correct' behaviour.[69] In fact, post-Stalin discourse on material improvements such as these usually tended to present them not in terms of state benevolence, but of fulfilling a duty to meet citizens' legitimate desires and aspirations.[70] Once dissenting behaviour became a part of the equation, however, a more traditional discourse could always be asserted to help ensure there was no risk of 'contagion' from criticism. Still, it is also important not to overlook the point that under Stalin, and even at earlier points in the Khrushchev era, behaviours like those of the miners in Leninogorsk, the youths in Magadan and G.R. Levitin could easily have led to a lengthy spell in a corrective-labour camp rather than scathing press coverage.

Over the course of the following year, similar articles, editorials and letters cropped up in newspapers with a degree of regularity. A Radio Liberty analysis of developments in the Soviet media showed that in February and March 1964 alone, *Izvestiya*, *Trud* and *Komsomolskaya pravda* all ran articles or editorials on issues including anonymous letters, anti-Soviet jokes, anti-Soviet rumours and public discussion of 'thorny problems'.[71] These were all newspapers with huge circulation figures, particularly *Izvestiya*, which carried four separate stories relating to various forms of political non-conformity during the two-month period in question. However, these were a few well-placed articles, rather than dozens. A high-profile campaign was not always the ideal option for dealing with dissenters, since it would implicitly communicate that frustration and discontent were more widespread than the

---

[67] *Trud*, 25 February 1964.
[68] This was to become a fairly common feature of attacks on dissidents throughout the Brezhnev era. In later years Elena Bonner in particular would be subject to all manner of slurs and scurrilous rumours in the Soviet press.
[69] See J. Brooks, *Thank You Comrade Stalin: Soviet Public Culture from Revolution to Cold War*, Princeton University Press, 1999.
[70] See G. Tsipursky, 'Pleasure, Power and the Pursuit of Communism', p. 225.
[71] Radio Liberty Analysis of Current Developments in the Soviet Union, Budapest, HU OSA 300-80-1, Box 632.

authorities were willing to admit and might also run the risk of criticisms resonating with the wider population.

Articles attacking dissenters and other non-conformists were also about reconfirming boundaries and norms: they transmitted the simple message of what was and was not acceptable, especially in public. That these attempts to silence critics were conveyed through newspaper articles, editorials and letters purporting to be from respectable members of the public represented a clear attempt to engineer public opinion via the voice of a kind of 'moral majority', rather than reliance solely on proclamations by political leaders. Perhaps the most notable aspect of these newspaper attacks on critics was the change of discourse on dissent. Up to the late 1950s attacks on dissenters had often been somewhat ideologically shrill, such as *Pravda*'s April 1956 accusation that Yuri Orlov and his colleagues had 'sung with the voices of Mensheviks and Socialist Revolutionaries'. By the turn of the decade, however, the media had begun to take a slightly more subtle approach to tackling the subject. Instead of the earlier ideological outrage, newspapers now employed language intended to invoke shame and hostility toward dissenters on patriotic, moral or material grounds. The usual ideological rhetoric was seemingly becoming less capable of arousing a sufficiently passionate response throughout society, but traditional moral values were still likely to strike a chord for most people.

In fact, the theme of morality was an increasingly important one in regime discourse of the early 1960s.[72] Edward Cohn, for example, has noted that the media was increasingly used to stigmatise alcoholics and bad parents around this time.[73] Media coverage on released prisoners and marginals had also begun to strike a much more condemnatory tone. When the Third Party Programme was unveiled at the XXII CPSU Congress in 1961 it included a novel addition in the form of the twelve-point 'Moral Code of the Builder of Communism'. As well as overtly ideological tenets such as 'devotion to the cause of communism', 'intolerance toward the enemies of communism' and 'collectivism and solidarity with working people of all countries', there featured a number of more 'universal morals', such as 'mutual respect within the family', 'sense of public duty' and 'honesty and modesty', that would not have been out of place in almost any political system. These values were not entirely new to Soviet discourse on morality; what had changed was the greater importance ascribed to

---

[72] As Chapter 9 shows, questions of morality were also becoming more prevalent among intelligentsia dissenters during the 1960s.
[73] E. Cohn, 'Disciplining the Party', p. 514.

them, as witnessed by their inclusion in the official Communist Party programme.[74] However, this new emphasis on morality was not so much about creating a new 'communist man' as it was about creating an obedient man to live within the mature socialist system. As Philip Boobbyer has rightly argued, the Code '... interpreted morality in functional terms, as something reinforcing the power of the state'[75]. This was broadly true of the wider efforts at reshaping society during the post-Stalin era. There is plenty of evidence that the regime was still trying to change the way that people conducted their everyday lives, but this now tended to focus on refining citizens' outward behaviours rather than their inner thoughts.[76]

The theme of appealing to citizens' patriotism and suspicion of foreigners could also be seen at work in the propaganda that attacked foreign broadcasts being beamed into the USSR. Media salvoes against the Munich-based Radio Liberty, for example, saw its Soviet émigré staff branded 'fascist riff-raff' and 'Vlasovites'.[77] In regard to Chinese political agitation, equally bellicose imagery could be employed, with *Izvestiya* claiming at one stage that Mao's regime was comparable to those of Hitler, Napoleon and Genghis Khan.[78] The intention to stir up some kind of patriotic fervour was entirely evident. The extent to which these names (particularly the more distant Napoleon and Genghis Khan) resonated among the USSR's non-Russian population, however, must have been rather limited. It certainly seems unlikely that the Mongol conquest of ancient *Rus'* or the battle of Borodino would have roused a great deal of pro-Soviet passion in Riga, Vilnius or Tallinn. Evidently the authorities in Moscow were primarily interested in shoring up the regime's Russian heartland.[79]

---

[74] D. Field, 'Irreconcilable Differences: Divorce and Conceptions of Private Life in the Khrushchev Era', *Russian Review*, Vol. 57, No. 4 (October 1998), 601.

[75] P. Boobbyer, *Conscience, Dissent and Reform in Soviet Russia*, London: Routledge, 2005, p. 64.

[76] Here it is worth drawing the connection with the fact that the penal system's earlier emphasis on 're-educating' or 're-forging' prisoners, rather than simply punishing them, was also waning by the early 1960s. See also S. Reid, 'Cold War in the Kitchen: Gender and the De-Stalinization of Consumer Taste in the Soviet Union under Khrushchev', *Slavic Review*, Vol. 60, No. 2 (Summer 2002), 211–52, and B. LaPierre, 'Making Hooliganism on a Mass Scale: The Campaign against Petty Hooliganism in the Soviet Union, 1953–64', *Cahiers du Monde russe*, Vol. 47, No. 1–2 (janvier–juin 2006), 349–75.

[77] G. Sosin, *Sparks of Liberty*, p. 71. 'Vlasovites' were Soviet WW2 collaborators who fought under General Andrei Vlasov for the Nazis.

[78] *Izvestiya*, 22 August 1963.

[79] Even so, by ratchetting up the use of Russian nationalist narrative in this way the authorities were presumably both reflecting and fuelling the emergence of a growing Russian national sentiment that would itself begin to pose a challenge to the communist regime's ideological hegemony in the 1970s and 1980s. See, for example. G. Hosking, *Rulers and Victims: The Russians in the Soviet Union*, Cambridge, MA: The Belknap Press of Harvard University Press, 2006, and N. Mitrokhin, *Russkaya partiya: dvizhenie russkikh natsionalistov v SSSR, 1953–1985*, Moskva: Novoe literaturnoe obozrenie, 2003.

It is hard to say with any real certainty just how successful the authorities were at shaping popular opinion against dissent and 'enemies' with methods like these. Numerous personal accounts certainly tell us that Soviet citizens had long since become skilled at 'reading between the lines' when it came to stories carried in the official media.[80] Still, anecdotal evidence seems to suggest that the new approach may well have had a significant impact on public attitudes. Ludmilla Alexeyeva, for example, recalled of her own experience as a human-rights activist during the Brezhnev era that 'a Soviet dissident quickly became a pariah even among those who privately shared his views' and 'isolated from society, we lived in what amounted to a ghetto'.[81] Plenty of people did not just 'go along' with the authorities' attacks on dissenters and other offenders, but actively embraced them.[82]

This was not simply about fear. Alexei Yurchak, for example, has argued that many Soviet citizens – particularly young people – of the 1960s, 70s and 80s did not feel any attachment to the Soviet dissidents who were so widely celebrated in the West at the time.[83] Individuals such as Andrei Sakharov would shift to the very centre of the political stage as the Soviet collapse loomed, but that did not indicate they had enjoyed mass support, whether silent or otherwise, in earlier years. When compared with the popular approval, or at least continued personal friendship, with which critics had often been met by their peers in the wake of the Secret Speech, this change in atmosphere was notable.

When all these society-wide measures failed to prevent non-conformist behaviour, more precise measures would be taken in the form of 'individual prophylaxis', the central feature of which was the 'prophylactic chat' (*profilakticheskaya beseda*). What this usually involved was for individuals who were considered to be ideologically wayward or potentially troublesome, but not implacably hostile, to be summoned to their local KGB offices. During the course of the ensuing 'chat' with the KGB, the individual in question was usually cajoled or bullied into admitting, and then renouncing, any kind of non-conformist activity that they or their acquaintances were involved in.[84]

---

[80] See, for example, V. Bukovsky, *To Build a Castle: My Life as a Dissenter*, London: Andre Deutsch, 1978.

[81] L. Alexeyeva and P. Goldberg, *The Thaw Generation: Coming of Age in the Post-Stalin Era*, Boston, MA: Little, Brown and Company, 1990, p. 244.

[82] See, for example, Alexeyeva's account of a public discussion on the Sinyavsky and Daniel case in 1967. L. Alexeyeva and P. Goldberg, *The Thaw Generation*, pp. 151–4.

[83] A. Yurchak, *Everything Was Forever Until it Was No More: The Last Soviet Generation*, Oxford: Princeton University Press, 2006, p. 106.

[84] Ludmilla Alexeyeva provided an account of one such prophylactic chat in *The Thaw Generation*, pp. 154–7.

It was made clear that they were being watched by the security organs and that a resumption of 'undesirable behaviour' would have serious consequences, such as the loss of one's job, the denial of a university place to one's children or the failure to be allocated a new apartment, all of which would be major blows in an increasingly materialistic social order. Of course, the threat of imprisonment also hung in the air. Again, the implicit emphasis on dealing with behaviours, rather than the attitudes that underpinned them, was clear.

The criteria for what kinds of cases were dealt with by the use of these prophylactic chats were broadly predictable but never entirely consistent. Those who were judged politically misguided in their behaviour – often this referred to youths, people with otherwise clean records and individuals who had played only a minor role in any given act of protest – were generally 'subjected to prophylactic measures'. These were people who could most easily be 'nudged back into line' and intimidated into silence with minimal effort, for whom harsher measures such as custodial sentencing would have been unnecessary and perhaps even counter-productive. Nonetheless, there remained a deliberate element of unpredictability in the use of prophylaxis. One could not bank entirely on avoiding jail. This was intended to induce a certain sense of caution, to keep people off balance and to prevent individuals from being able to 'go right up to the line without crossing it'. It was also true that the authorities themselves did not have absolutely fixed criteria on which cases were to be met with prophylaxis, but instead operated on a case-by-case basis, taking into account the wider domestic and international situation and individuals' personal biographies before deciding whether a 'chat' with the KGB would prevent further dissenting behaviour.[85]

An example of this could be seen in the case against Yuri Grimm and Abdulbai Khasyanov, the authors of a series of anti-Soviet leaflets discussed in Chapter 6. Perceived to be the ringleaders of their group, Grimm and Khasyanov were respectively sentenced to six years' and four years' corrective labour. However, the investigation into their dissenting activity named a further nine accomplices who had helped the pair to distribute their leaflets around Moscow but faced prophylaxis rather than jail.[86] Another case that was uncovered, in Voronezh *oblast'* during July 1963, even saw a self-styled fascist group – that had managed to acquire various explosives, a rifle and a machine gun – spared jail after they were uncovered by the

[85] On the use of personal biographies in Stalin-era repression, see in particular C. Vatulescu, 'Arresting Biographies: The Secret Police File in the Soviet Union and Romania', *Comparative Literature*, Vol. 56, No. 3 (Summer 2004), 243–61.

[86] GARF, f. 8131, op. 33, d. 96712, ll. 1–33.

KGB.[87] The four members of the 'National Socialist Party' – all of whom were still in their teens – and their parents were subjected to a series of prophylactic chats instead of imprisonment. This case was clearly at the extreme end of the scale, and it was surely the fact that they were so young which saved the quartet from jail, but it is nonetheless instructive of how widely prophylaxis could be applied. The four could easily have been jailed in far less authoritarian regimes than Khrushchev's USSR. Cases such as these leave one with a sense that as and when (or if) detailed KGB records pertaining to the use of these individual prophylactic sessions become available, historians may well see that the volume and intensity of dissenting behaviour across the USSR was considerably greater during the post-Stalin era than has been supposed up to the present time.

Exactly how many of these 'prophylactic chats' were undertaken by the KGB is hard to say, since only a limited amount of data has been made available.[88] Nonetheless, there are sufficient scraps of evidence to show that this had become by far the most widely deployed form of response to breaches of political norms by the early 1960s. A KGB report to the Central Committee from 25 July 1962, for example, stated that in the first half of that year 105 people had been jailed for preparation and distribution of anti-Soviet documents, while a further 568 had been subjected to prophylactic measures for the same offence.[89] An analogous report sent a little under two years later informed that out of 385 authors of anti-Soviet documents uncovered in the first five months of 1964, thirty-nine had been jailed while 225 had faced prophylactic measures.[90] The above figures, therefore, suggest a ratio of prophylaxis to imprisonment of approximately 5:1, representing a pretty dramatic sea-change in policy.

Evidently, the authorities had come to accept that imprisonment was not always the most appropriate or effective means of response to the majority of dissenters, especially since corrective-labour camps and prisons were by this time becoming 'schools of revolution', in the words of Vladimir Kozlov.[91] As such, they often opted to clamp down hard on ringleaders

---

[87] RGANI, f. 5, op. 30, d. 412, ll. 50–1. There was no suggestion in the KGB report that the group had planned to use this weaponry for any kind of concrete activity. The guns and explosives were presumably left over from the fighting around Voronezh during the war.
[88] The majority of the relevant information is held in the archives of the KGB and in the Presidential Archive of the Russian Federation. Both are closed to researchers.
[89] RGANI, f. 89, op. 51, d. 1, ll. 1–4.
[90] RGANI, f. 5, op. 30, d. 454, l. 110. The remaining 121 cases were still in process at the time the report was written.
[91] V. Kozlov and S. Mironenko eds., *Kramola: inakomyslie v SSSR pri Khrushcheve i Brezhneve 1953–1982*, Moskva: Materik, 2005, p. 54.

and allowed others to remain at liberty, though still under suspicion, thus ensuring that repressive policy did not permanently marginalise an overly large group of people whom the state had branded 'anti-Soviet'.[92] By presenting such individuals as 'mistaken' or 'naïve' they were not truly 'enemies', but had somehow been 'tricked' and could be put back on the right path with the help of the security organs, a picture that suited all concerned. There were a multitude of benefits for the authorities in adopting this new course of action. Where Stalin's massive and arbitrary terror had done untold damage to the morale of society and the economic development of the regime, prophylaxis came at limited financial, demographic and political cost. Just as significantly, it avoided provoking the kind of large-scale antagonism of society and international opprobrium that mass imprisonment would have incurred and which the post-Stalin leadership were becoming increasingly keen to avoid. Like most other measures aimed at reinforcing control over society after the abandonment of terror, they did not reflect any greater acceptance of heterodox opinions and tastes. One would therefore struggle to justify applying the term 'liberalisation', though they undoubtedly did mean that only a fairly small minority of critics now faced the harshest reprisals.

Most importantly, these individual prophylactic sessions seem to have been highly effective at stifling dissent. Once their value had been proven, the Brezhnev years would see the ratio of prophylaxis to imprisonment rise as high as 100:1.[93] In a classified account of the period, the KGB stated simply that 'the majority of those subjected to prophylactic measures did not offend again'.[94] Had prophylaxis not been effective in keeping dissent at manageable levels around the country the authorities would more than likely have reverted to far more aggressive means of maintaining domestic stability – as continued to be the case with the hard core of dissenters who refused to bow to either intimidation or inducement.

[92] Elena Zubkova has written about marginalised elements of Soviet society during the period, arguing that the regime generally also took a less uncompromising line against people like thieves, prostitutes and 'parasites' for the reasons outlined above. See E. Zubkova, 'Na "krayu" sovetskogo obshchestva. Marginal'nye gruppy naseleniya i gosudarstvennaya politika.1940–1960e gody', *Rossiiskaya istoriya*, No. 5 (2009), 101–18.

[93] Rudolf Pikhoya has cited figures from the Presidential Archive which show that for the period of 1967 to 1970 there were 58,291 cases where prophylactic measures were applied; between 1971 and 1974 the figure rose further to 63,108. When one compares these figures to the number of sentences under political articles of the criminal codes, the ratio between imprisonment and prophylaxis rises to approximately 1:100. R. Pikhoya, *Sovetskii soyuz: istoriya vlasti, 1945–1991*, Moskva: Rossisskaya akademiya gos. sluzhby pri Prezidente Rossiiskoi Federatsii 1998, p. 597.

[94] V. Chebrikov et al., *Istoriya sovetskikh organov*, p. 564.

CHAPTER 8

The application of force

As the preceding chapter showed, by the end of the 1950s the Soviet regime's approach to policing dissent had become less overtly repressive, even if it had not become significantly more tolerant. Nonetheless, the application of particularly harsh punishment for political non-conformity had by no means ceased entirely. If social pressure and peer-policing would not force dissenters back into line, more traditional responses could still be deployed. As F.J.M. Feldbrugge pointed out in a 1963 article on legal developments in the USSR: 'The social straggler is invited to rejoin the ranks immediately, and if he cannot or will not do so, he is annihilated.'[1] The tone of Feldbrugge's assessment may have been a touch hyperbolic, but its message was not misleading.

Even though the authorities were showing an increasing tendency to refrain from employing custodial sentences against critics, the number of people jailed for dissent during the early 1960s was far from insignificant. Over 1,200 individuals were sentenced for anti-Soviet activity between the turn of the decade and Khrushchev's ouster almost five years later.[2] When contrasted with contemporary regimes in Western Europe and the US, it becomes clear that post-Stalin liberalisation remained something of a relative concept. Nonetheless, perhaps the most important point of comparison can be seen in the fact that in the year 1960 there were 162 convictions for anti-Soviet activity, where a decade earlier the number of convictions under the same article was 53,179, and had been almost 130,000 two years prior to that.

In addition to the measures aimed at preventing non-conformist behaviour that were discussed in the previous chapter, there were two principal ways of punishing dissenters and neutralising the danger that they posed to the Soviet social order. The first, and more widely employed, was through

[1] F. Feldbrugge, 'Soviet Criminal Law: The Last Six Years', *The Journal of Criminal Law, Criminology, and Police Science*, Vol. 54, No. 3 (September 1963), 263.
[2] *Istochnik*, No. 6, 1995, p. 153.

recourse to corrective-labour camps and prisons, such as those at Mordova, Perm and Vladimir. The second involved confining critics to psychiatric units in Leningrad, Dnepropetrovsk, Kazan and elsewhere. For Western observers of the 1960s, 70s and 80s both of these practices were to become synonymous with the Brezhnev regime's efforts to crush the dissident movement, but by that time they had already been a key component of the Soviet struggle against protest and criticism for many years.

By the turn of the decade, however, legal reforms had begun to codify the progress of deStalinization, providing at least a semblance of proper judicial procedure. One of the most notable legal changes in regard to the policing of dissent came when a new Law on State Crimes was published in the all-Union Fundamental Principles of Criminal Legislation at the end of December 1958, along with a new Code of Criminal Procedure governing the authorities' ways and means of investigating and prosecuting dissent.[3] The legal principles laid out in the Law on State Crimes were subsequently included in the new criminal codes that were enacted across all fifteen union republics during 1960 and 1961.[4] These legal reforms were intended to prevent a return to the arbitrary abuses that had characterised the Stalin era, though they still left plenty of scope for the repression of dissenters.

A symbolically significant point of the new legal principles as they related to dissenters was that they abolished the legal classification of 'counter-revolutionary crimes', and thus also the notorious article 58, under which vast numbers of Soviet citizens had been jailed since the 1930s. The principal motivations for the move were apparently to reduce the arbitrariness that the vague legal concept of 'counter-revolutionary' had entailed and to emphasise the regime's break with the mass illegalities of the Stalin era.[5] Instead of 'counter-revolutionary crimes' the new criminal codes featured the classification of 'crimes against the state' and 'especially dangerous crimes against the state'.[6] In the place of article 58-10 came articles 70 and

---

[3] See K. Grzybowski, 'The Extraterritorial Effect of Soviet Criminal Law after the Reform of 1958', *American Journal of Comparative Law*, Vol. 8, No. 4 (Autumn 1959), 515–18, and V. Gsovski, 'Reform of Criminal Law in the Soviet Union', *Social Problems, Symposium on Social Problems in the Soviet Union*, Vol. 7, No. 4 (Spring 1960), 315–28.

[4] The 'Law on State Crimes' came as part of a package of reforms concerned with the general principles of criminal law and criminal procedure at an all-Union level and included the 'Basic Principles on Criminal Legislation', the 'Basic Law on Criminal Procedure in the USSR' and the 'Law on Military Crimes'.

[5] See P. Taylor, 'Treason, Espionage and Other Soviet State Crimes', *Russian Review*, Vol. 23, No. 3 (July 1964), 247–58.

[6] The difference between 'ordinary' crimes against the state and 'especially dangerous' crimes against the state was defined by the presence of 'anti-Soviet intent'. Thus, for example, fraud would generally be

72: the former dealt with 'anti-Soviet agitation and propaganda' and the latter with 'participation in anti-Soviet organisations'. In reality, the difference between the old and new articles was minimal.[7] Crimes under article 58-10 had been defined in the RSFSR criminal code as 'propaganda and agitation, containing calls for the overthrow, undermining or weakening of the Soviet regime or the committing of individual counter-revolutionary crimes, as well as distributing, preparing or possessing literature for that aim'. Article 70, on the other hand, dealt with 'agitation or propaganda carried out for the purpose of subverting or weakening the Soviet regime or of committing particular, especially dangerous crimes against the state, or the circulation for the same purpose of slanderous fabrications which defame the Soviet state and social system . . .'[8] This hardly represented an expansion of the boundaries of permissible political behaviour.

Most importantly, the Soviet concept of justice still continued to be centred upon the ideals and aims of the CPSU. Although the regime had begun to make a more convincing pretence at operating within its own laws, legal process could always be bent to the authorities' will when necessary, since the law-enforcement apparatus and judiciary remained very much under the sway of the Communist Party, and the Party leadership consistently refused to be constricted by the law. In this light, Louise Shelley provided a convincing assessment of the post-Stalin legal system when she wrote that: 'commitment to the rule of law, intrinsic to democratic policing, was conspicuously absent from the Khrushchev reforms'.[9] The Code of Criminal Procedure demanded that concrete evidence be produced in order to secure a conviction and guaranteed the accused access to a lawyer, showing that some of the worst practices of the Stalin era were receding into the past. The fact that dissenters on trial were, without fail, found guilty, and the state-appointed lawyers in question rarely made a convincing attempt at defending their clients, gives an indication as to how limited that progress really was.

One of the general trends that was witnessed across numerous articles of the new criminal codes, including those dealing with crimes against the state, was a lowering of the maximum tariff prescribed. In the case of

regarded as an 'ordinary' crime against the state, but if it could be shown that the fraud intended to harm the regime in some way it would then be tried as an 'especially dangerous' crime against the state. See H. Berman, *Soviet Criminal Law and Procedure*, Cambridge, MA: Harvard University Press, 1972.

[7] H. Berman, *Soviet Criminal Law*, p. 81.

[8] H. Berman, *Soviet Criminal Law*, p. 153. It is also worth pointing out that Vladimir Kozlov's anthology on article 58-10 in the post-Stalin era includes those jailed under articles 70 and 72 after the changes of December 1958. V. Kozlov and S. Mironenko eds., *58-10 Nadzornye proizvodstva prokuratury SSSR po delam ob antisovetskoi agitatsii i propaganda: annotirovannyi katalog Mart 1953–1991*, Moskva: Mezhdunarodnyi Fond 'Demokratiya', 1999.

[9] L. Shelley, *Policing Soviet Society: The Evolution of State Control*, London: Routledge, 1996, p. 45.

anti-Soviet agitation and propaganda, this meant a reduction from a maximum sentence of twenty-five years' corrective labour down to seven years,
with the possibility of a supplementary period of internal exile ranging from
two to five years. Nonetheless, with this apparent softening of penal policy
in mind it is instructive to refer back to the 1958 Procurator statistics cited in
Table 4.3, which show that even prior to the new code's promulgation, the
average sentence under article 58-10 had been approximately five years in
length.[10] As such, this shortening of the maximum tariff for dissent can be
seen as a codification of existing post-Stalin practice, rather than a liberalising measure in its own right. Typically of the authorities' new approach,
recidivists who were convicted of political crimes more than once faced an
increased tariff of three to ten years' imprisonment, again with the same
period of additional exile tacked on at the end.

In the application of the new laws, the authorities largely hewed closely to
the recommendations made by the Supreme Court in June 1958 in regard to
what constituted 'anti-Soviet' acts. In the first instance, this meant distinguishing 'genuine enemies' from those who had simply 'made political
errors'. Interestingly, though, there was a growing divergence in the use of
legal sanctions among the different union republics. Most intriguing was
the fact that, when taken together, the citizens of the USSR's five Central
Asian republics (Kazakhstan, Kyrgyzstan, Tadzhikistan, Turkmenistan and
Uzbekistan) made up almost 11% of the overall Soviet population yet
accounted for a combined total of less than 1% of all sentences for political
crimes in 1960–4.[11] Back in 1957, 136 political sentences had been handed
down in the Central Asian republics. Between 1960 and 1964, these five
republics combined witnessed only seven sentences for anti-Soviet activity –
a considerably lower number than even small individual republics such as
Belarus (seventeen political sentences), Georgia (eleven sentences) and
Armenia (eight sentences) in the same period. Nowhere else in the USSR
was the drop in convictions quite so precipitate, suggesting above all else
that this trend reflected developments in the internal affairs of the Central
Asian republics.[12] Already, the Brezhnev-era system of local elites running
these republics as personal fiefdoms was beginning to take hold by the end

[10] GARF, f. 8131, op. 32, d. 5080, l. 7.
[11] Population data on this subject are taken from the 1959 census. See Tsentral'noe statisticheskoe
upravlenie pri Sovete Ministrove SSSR, *Chislennost', sostav i razmeshchenie naseleniya SSSR: kratkie
itogi vsesoyuznoi perepisi naseleniya 1959 goda*, Moskva: Gosstatizdat TsSU SSSR, 1961, pp. 3–8. Data on
the nationality of those sentenced for anti-Soviet activity has been taken from the files of the USSR
Procurator. See V. Kozlov and S. Mironenko eds., *58-10 Nadzornye proizvodstva*.
[12] In this respect it is also worth noting that the USSR's large Muslim population was almost entirely
absent from figures on religious repression – unlike practically all of the USSR's other major religions.

of the 1950s and there was thus a growing desire to avoid arousing Moscow's interest in local affairs across much of the region – something that political arrests and trials would have been sure to do.[13]

While not nearly so precipitate as in Central Asia, the number of people being jailed for crimes against the state dropped markedly right across the USSR. The year after the crackdown on dissent ended in 1958 had still seen 750 citizens jailed for anti-Soviet activity, though the total would never again exceed 350 people sentenced in a single year. Owing to the disturbances and tensions of that summer, the second half of 1962 witnessed something of a surge in convictions, though when we consider the many thousands of people involved in public disorders around that time, it is immediately apparent that only a fraction of them were jailed. Even so, it proved possible quickly and effectively to smother those frustrations that had prompted the disturbances. As the previous chapter showed, the authorities were becoming increasingly sure-footed and proactive in terms of managing society without reliance upon widespread repression, a reflection of the fact that the uncertainty of the early post-Stalin years was fading away as new measures to combat dissent showed their worth.

Things were changing inside the camps, too. While the immediate period following Stalin's death was described by Aleksandr Solzhenitsyn as 'the mildest three years in the history of the [Gulag] archipelago', and the mid to late 1950s had seen increased emphasis on 're-educating' prisoners rather than just punishing them, conditions subsequently deteriorated to the point where the same author could write that the main difference between the camps of Khrushchev and those of Stalin lay in their size and demographic composition, rather than in the extent of their brutality.[14] While Solzhenitsyn overstated the case somewhat, one need only read Anatoly Marchenko's memoir of his time in the Mordova camp network during the early 1960s to see that conditions within the penal system had grown significantly harder since the early Khrushchev era.[15]

---

[13] For example, in the Uzbek SSR Sharof Rashidov remained in office from 1959 until 1983. In the Kyrgyz SSR Turdukan Usubaliev was first secretary from 1961 to 1985 and in the Tadzhik SSR Dzhabar Rasulov was head of the Communist Party between 1961 and 1982.

[14] A. Solzhenitsyn, *The Gulag Archipelago*, Vol. 3, London: Collins/Fontana, 1978, pp. 427 and 493. The difference in composition that Solzhenitsyn referred to was that the majority of political prisoners during the Khrushchev years tended to be from Ukraine or the Baltic states rather than from Russia. As Jeffrey Hardy asserts, a comparison of the primary literature on Stalin-era camps and those of the later Khrushchev years shows that the differences were still pronounced. J. Hardy, 'Gulag Tourism: Khrushchev's "Show" Prisons in the Cold War Context, 1954–59', *Russian Review*, Vol. 70, No. 1 (January 2011), 76.

[15] A. Marchenko, *My Testimony*, Harmondsworth: Penguin Books, 1969.

Numerous scholars have posited explanations for this hardening attitude toward penal policy.[16] In the most detailed study yet on the Khrushchev-era Gulag, Jeffrey Hardy paints a particularly compelling picture of institutional and public pressure being brought to bear for a tightening-up of conditions in the camp network.[17] With the camp population overwhelmingly made up of hardened criminal prisoners by the 1960s, attempts to maintain discipline and to re-educate generally met with mixed success at best. Having initially been somewhat optimistic in the middle of the 1950s, regime discourse on prisoners and former prisoners began to harden considerably as criminality steadfastly remained a serious problem across much of Soviet society. Accordingly, members of the public grew more anxious and displayed increasing frustration and opposition to attempts at treating prisoners more humanely, especially once a fresh crime wave struck the USSR at the end of the 1950s. Officials within the MVD and the Procuracy, journalists, members of the CPSU leadership and academic experts on penology fought over the merits of the mid-1950s Gulag reforms for a number of months before the more hard-line attitudes achieved a decisive ascendancy by the beginning of 1960. The Central Committee gave a damning indictment of failure in the reformed Gulag – citing prisoners' abuse of privileges, conditions that were likened to health spas and an apparent lack of success in re-educating inmates – and ordered two review committees to recommend a new course of action in the camps. Both committees pushed for the 'excessive liberality' of the previous reforms to be reined in.[18]

First-hand accounts by those incarcerated in the Soviet penal system at this time consistently portray a distinct turn for the worse from 1961 onwards.[19] The focus on re-educating prisoners never disappeared entirely but emphasis increasingly turned instead toward retribution. On 3 April 1961 the Council of Ministers issued the decree 'On Measures for Improving the Activity of Corrective Labour Colonies of the Ministries of Internal

---

[16] See, for example, M. Dobson, *Khrushchev's Cold Summer: Gulag Returnees, Crime and the Fate of Reform after Stalin*, Ithaca, NY: Cornell University Press, 2009 and V. Abramkin and V. Chesnokova, *Tyurmennyi mir glazami politzaklyuchennykh*, Moskva: Sodeistvie, 1993.

[17] J. Hardy, 'Khrushchev's Gulag: The Evolution of Punishment in the Post-Stalin Soviet Union, 1953–1964', Ph.D. Dissertation, Princeton University, 2011. Hardy's recent work on the Khrushchev-era Gulag has done a great deal to help build a more sophisticated picture of the institution after Stalin's death.

[18] J. Hardy, 'Khrushchev's Gulag', pp. 250–3.

[19] See, for example, A. Marchenko, *My Testimony*, p. 209; V. Abramkin and V. Chesnokova, *Tyurmennyi mir glazami politzaklyuchennykh*; and Voprosy istorii, 'Vlast' i intelligentsiya: "delo" molodykh istorikov (1957–58.)', *Voprosy istorii*, No. 004 (1994), 114.

Affairs of the Union Republics'.[20] The new guidelines provided for 1.75 square metres (20 square feet) of living space per inmate and decreed an eight-hour working day of heavy physical labour, though sources suggest that in practice work was often prolonged well beyond ten hours per day.[21] Prisoners' daily lives were again more strictly regimented and their rations were decreased by around 20%.[22] They could then be reduced further as punishment for failure to cooperate with the camp authorities, making the threat of starvation a powerful tool. An increased number of prisoners were forced to undertake labour tasks, such as logging and mining. Another noticeable result of the hardening punitive system was the scrapping of the early-release programme for those who consistently met their production targets. As with the authorities' emerging practices amongst wider society by the early 1960s, responsibility was increasingly put on prisoners to police each other, through acting as informers and establishing 'voluntary organisations' to co-opt more and more inmates to assist with camp administration.[23]

Four new grades of confinement were defined for prisoners: in ascending order of severity these were 'normal', 'intensified', 'strict' and 'special'. As Rasma Karklins noted: 'the more severe the camp regime, the worse the conditions and the harder the work'.[24] Political prisoners immediately began their sentences on the 'strict' regime and were liable to be 'upgraded' to 'special' at the slightest infraction of the rules. Vladimir Men'shikov, for example, a former member of the underground group centred around Lev Krasnopevtsev at Moscow State University, recalled his own status changing from 'normal' to 'intensified' and then to 'strict' all within a few months.[25] Visitation rights were also curtailed. Prisoners on 'strict' regime were now granted a public visit once every four months and a conjugal visit once a year. They were permitted to send two letters per month, were no longer allowed to receive food parcels and could spend only 5 roubles each month in the camp shop. Those on 'special' regime were granted a public visit only twice a year, were allowed no conjugal visits, could send only one outbound letter per month and could spend only 3 roubles in the camp shop. They

[20] Because the all-Union MVD had been broken up by Khrushchev in 1960, each of the fifteen republics had to enact its own legislation, though they were all much the same in tone and content.
[21] R. Karklins, 'The Organisation of Power in Soviet Labour Camps', *Soviet Studies*, Vol. 41, No. 2 (April 1989), 276–97.
[22] Hardy cites a decline from 3,000 to 2,413 calories per day for prisoners on standard rations. J. Hardy, 'Khrushchev's Gulag', p. 255.
[23] See O. Kharkhordin, *The Collective and the Individual in Russia: A Study of Practices*, Berkeley, CA: University of California Press, 1999, p. 306.
[24] R. Karklins, 'The Organisation of Power', 277.   [25] *Voprosy istorii*, 'Vlast' i intelligentsiya', 114.

were also to be located in more remote regions and assigned to heavy physical labour.[26]

There was no full reversion to the Stalinist Gulag archipelago, however. Firstly, the size of the Gulag was of a far smaller scale, both in terms of inmates and number of facilities. Even though orders for guards and officials to deal with prisoners respectfully were now dropped, the intensive brutality of the preceding era never returned entirely, and in fact some of the harshest of the new regulations were toned down again by the middle of the decade. It is also important to note that with political prisoners constituting less than 2% of the total Gulag population by the early 1960s, this whole process did not of itself reflect hardening attitudes toward dissent alone. Nonetheless, as the previous and present chapters show, around this time the regime was refining its methods of social control and punitive activity right across the board: these changes to the camp system were not only rooted inside the camps but in the final emergence of a settled and recognisably post-Stalin, post-terror Soviet system. For those deemed to be 'misguided' in their criticism, responses to dissent may have become less overtly repressive, but the 'genuinely anti-Soviet' minority, like criminals deemed 'unreformable', were being met with a renewed sense of purpose.

The total labour-camp population had been in numerical decline ever since Stalin's death but began to climb again in 1961. Looking at this issue in the context of the era as a whole, Miriam Dobson has rightly pointed out that 'If the release of prisoners and the massive down-sizing of the Gulag are to be considered important elements of Khrushchev's reform package, then it is significant that earlier trends were being reversed in 1961, the year he was understood to be at the peak of his political career.'[27] Though there were always other powerful figures within the Presidium who were able to impose themselves on the policy-making process – Mikhail Suslov being perhaps the most notable – this was indeed a time when Khrushchev's power within the Central Committee Presidium reached its apex and he was most able to throw his weight around within the political elite. Indeed, Nuriddin Mukhitdinov recalled this as a time when Khrushchev was almost entirely unable (or unwilling) to tolerate opinions that conflicted with his own.[28]

Signals implying that liberalisation was progressing, however, were still being emitted, especially when Khrushchev returned to his earlier criticism of Stalin. While the attacks on Stalin at the XXII CPSU Congress were

---

[26] J. Hardy, 'Khrushchev's Gulag'.   [27] M. Dobson, *Khrushchev's Cold Summer*, p. 185.

[28] N. Mukhitdinov, '12 let s Khrushchevym: vospominaniya byvshego chlena Prezidium TsK', *Argumenty i fakty*, No. 44 (1989), 5.

more numerous and much sharper in tone than those of 1956, this was to a considerable extent a case of Khrushchev 'playing the Stalin card' for personal political ends – most notably by weakening rivals within the political elite and delivering the *coup de grâce* to the failed plotters of the anti-Party group. As such, anti-Stalin pronouncements heard at the Congress did not consistently translate into a widespread renewal or deepening of liberalisation. Indeed, one could argue that Khrushchev's occasional attacks on Stalin and the enactment of concrete steps toward political liberalisation were always far less intimately linked than has often been assumed. While many dissenters explicitly linked their own anti-Stalinism with desires for genuine liberalising reform, the First Secretary was rather more ambiguous. On the nationalities question, for example, the XXII Congress actually marked the start of new curbs on cultural expression in the non-Russian republics. It also saw Khrushchev taking an increasingly belligerent line toward 'marginals'. In regard to dissent, the authorities were in fact already taking a tougher stance by this point, though many of their public pronouncements gave little suggestion that this was the case.

The chairman of the Party Control Commission, Nikolai Shvernik, declared at the Congress that no Party members had been expelled on political grounds that year. Records from his own department, however, clearly show thirty-six members expelled for 'anti-Party conversations' and a further eight members expelled for 'participation in anti-Party groupings' in 1961.[29] More notably, KGB data cited in Chapter 4 show that over 200 people were jailed for anti-Soviet activity that year (a rise on the previous year) and over 300 suffered the same fate the following year. In other words, the big set-piece moments of deStalinization, such as Congress speeches and literary works, did not necessarily reflect a fundamental change in practices regarding non-conformity at ground level. While the speeches made at the XXII Congress may well have enjoyed great resonance among Soviet citizens, and were clearly the subject of wide-ranging public interest, the extent to which they signalled a new wave of political liberalisation should not be overstated.

The process of reviewing and re-evaluating convictions under article 58-10 and its successors also provides a useful commentary on attitudes to dissenters during the period in question. The case of Yakov Rizoi, already raised in Chapter 3, was an instructive one. After he had been arrested for preparing and sending out a series of political leaflets, the KGB investigation noted the fact that Rizoi had been a dedicated CPSU member for twenty

---

[29] RGANI, f. 6, op. 6, d. 1183, ll. 1–64.

years, had acquitted himself well in the airforce during the Great Patriotic War and was twice decorated but had lost his job because of the military cutbacks decreed in April 1958. In spite of his previously exemplary personal record, on 21 December 1962 Rizoi was sentenced to seven years' corrective labour followed by three years of internal exile, the maximum sentence possible.[30] He immediately appealed against the judgement of the Odessa court and subsequently had his case reviewed by a higher authority: the Ukrainian Supreme Court. The review acknowledged that he was guilty of producing and distributing the documents in question but argued that the original case had not properly established whether Rizoi had actually intended to undermine the Soviet regime by his actions. It then cited a remark that the defendant had made at his trial: 'I have never been an enemy of Soviet power. After we were demobilised it was a blow to the heart. Where I saw any kind of shortages I incorrectly understood this to be the fault of improper policies by our leaders.'[31] With such an immaculate biography and a humble acceptance of mistakenness, which explicitly pointed to economic distress rather than political disenchantment as having lain at the heart of the problem, the appeal was a compelling one. It was decided that there were no grounds for considering Rizoi an 'especially dangerous state criminal', and on 17 January 1963, less than a month after he had originally been convicted, the sentence handed down by the Odessa *oblast'* court was revoked by the Ukrainian Supreme Court and Rizoi was freed.

While there is no overt basis to cast doubt upon the sincerity of Rizoi's disavowal of his dissenting activity, his stance did fit with the most frequently successful tactic for averting punitive action around this time. Those who attempted to protest their innocence or doggedly insisted that they had not meant any real harm by their actions implicitly called the authorities' judgement into question.[32] As Edward Cohn has showed, Party members facing disciplinary measures were consistently more likely to escape with a limited degree of censure if they declared their loyalty to the Party, confessed to their misdeeds and recanted. As the 1958 Supreme Court review of sentences under article 58-10 had emphasised, a strong personal biography (like that of Rizoi) could also give clues as to the presence or absence of 'genuine anti-Soviet intent'. Nonetheless, the most important thing for the accused was to back down from whatever political position it

---

[30] GARF, f. 8131, op. 31, d. 94020, ll. 1–4.   [31] GARF, f. 8131, op. 31, d. 94020, l. 6.
[32] See E. Cohn, 'Disciplining the Party: The Expulsion and Censure of Communists in the Post-War Soviet Union, 1945–1961', Ph.D. Dissertation, University of Chicago, 2007, p. 92.

was that had aroused disfavour. Once this had been done, and the demand for self-criticism fulfilled, it often became possible to return to the status quo ante. While all that Rizoi said in contrition may well have been entirely heartfelt, the fact that his conviction was overturned represented a sure sign of the regime's declining ideological vigilance.[33]

The Rizoi case also demonstrated the extent to which there remained an 'infantilisation' of lower-level offices and officials, who were granted minimal scope for flexibility or initiative in their work. Essentially, apparatchiks operating at lower and middling levels of power – in this case the Odessa *oblast'* court – were the least likely to respond to acts of dissent with any notable clemency. The people who occupied these positions effectively 'erred on the side of caution' since it was still far safer in career terms for them to respond to dissent with too much, rather than too little, vigour. After the personal danger that had faced such people during the Stalin years, and the dramatic political oscillation of the mid to late 1950s, few were willing to take any reasonably bold step until directed to do so from above. If the impulse for any lenience in evaluating these kinds of affairs did not come from the top, then it did not come at all, something that would become increasingly clear after October 1964.

Looking at the theme of release and rehabilitation from a slightly wider perspective, there are two striking trends that one notices. The first is how few victims of Khrushchev-era repression were subsequently rehabilitated under Gorbachev – when the wounds of the Soviet past were most fully brought to light – and the second is how many victims of Khrushchev-era repression, like Yakov Rizoi, were either rehabilitated, reclassified or had their sentences reduced while Khrushchev himself was still in power.[34] The lack of rehabilitations in the late 1980s for political prisoners from the Khrushchev period was partly a result of the way in which the public and political mind was most closely focused upon uncovering the horrors of the Stalin era during *glasnost'*, a time when regime pronouncements viewed Khrushchev in a broadly positive light.[35] It probably also indicated that, owing to the improvements in the post-Stalin legal system, few convictions from the Khrushchev era were deemed as having been 'unsafe'. In the sense that political repression was no longer entirely arbitrary, this was just about correct: cases were rarely entirely baseless. In the sense that victims of

---

[33] On this theme see E. Cohn, 'Disciplining the Party'.

[34] See A. Yakovlev et al. eds., *Reabilitatsiya: kak eto bylo. Fevral' 1956 – nachalo 80-x godov*, Moskva: Mezhdunarodnyi fond 'Demokratiya', 2003.

[35] See, for example, D. Nordlander, 'Khrushchev's Image in the Light of Glasnost and Perestroika', *Russian Review*, Vol. 52, No. 2 (April 1993), 248–64.

Khrushchev-era political repression had undertaken acts that were deserving of imprisonment, and had rightly been branded anti-Soviet, the answer was a much more subjective one, especially whilst the communist regime remained in power.

For the most part, those released and rehabilitated under Khrushchev were people who had been jailed during the clampdown of 1957–8, a clear acknowledgement that errors had been made at that time. Even so, judgements as to which cases were or were not deemed worthy of re-examination could be telling of the extent to which attitudes toward critics had shifted. Criminal prisoners were still viewed as 'socially closer' to the regime than were politicals. Those who were released early tended to have been jailed for hooligan-type dissent, rather than more consciously political forms of protest. For example, the worker N.A. Derzhavin of Osh *oblast'* in Kyrgyzstan had been sentenced in May 1957 after publicly cursing the regime and declaring his support for the Hungarian rising, yet he appealed and was then released as early as June 1958.[36] Others who could point to better work and war records received neither rehabilitation nor a reduction in their sentence. F.F. Shul'ts was a case in point: he was a pensioner and Communist Party member since 1919 who had been jailed two months prior to Derzhavin for sending critical letters to *Pravda*, but was not released until June 1964, by which time he had already served seven years in camps.[37] Evidently, the process of reconsidering convictions did not reflect any softening of attitudes toward 'genuinely' anti-Soviet protest.

In fact, it seems that the best chance of release and rehabilitation could lie in the status and connections of the appellant. Isaak Barenblat was a perfect example of this. He had been jailed under article 58-10 in September 1957 but was released on the direct order of Mikhail Suslov in early 1958. As it transpired, Barenblat's son worked at the Arzamas-16 secret nuclear installation alongside the rising star of Soviet physics, Andrei Sakharov. Barenblat junior convinced Sakharov to intervene on his father's behalf, which he did in a personal audience with Suslov in January 1958, quickly winning Barenblat senior's freedom.[38] Revolt Pimenov, too, eventually gained some useful backers after being jailed for underground activity. In March 1962 an

[36] GARF, f. 8131, op. 31, d. 78317, ll. 1–9. [37] GARF, f. 8131, op. 31, d. 74356, ll. 1–6.
[38] J. Bergman, *Meeting the Demands of Reason: The Life and Thought of Andrei Sakharov*, Ithaca, NY: Cornell University Press, 2009, p. 90. Bergman's account sees the elder Barenblat jailed for telling jokes about Khrushchev, for criticising certain aspects of the Secret Speech and for having unlawfully obtained 300,000 roubles. The official case file states that Barenblat's conviction was based on condemning Soviet support for the Arab states in their on-going conflict with Israel, for criticising Nasser (a Soviet ally) and for claiming that Marshall Zhukov was really in charge of the USSR. GARF, f. 8131, op. 31, d. 78291, ll. 1–5.

appeal from Pimenov's mother was forwarded to the Soviet Chief Procurator Roman Rudenko by Mstislav Keldysh, who at that time was both the head of the Soviet Academy of Sciences and a deputy of the Supreme Soviet. The appeal simply requested that Pimenov at least be allowed to do scientific work whilst imprisoned. References testifying to the value of Pimenov's mathematical work were provided by Academician P.P. Smirnov and by Corresponding Member of the Academy of Sciences A.D. Aleksandrov. Presumably as a result of Keldysh's exalted position, the details of the case were sent all the way up to the Central Committee Presidium. The situation was then reviewed on the order of the Procuracy and a July 1963 addition to the case file simply stated that 'Pimenov is now engaged with scientific work.'[39]

Without important backers and essential skills, others were less success-ful. Lev Krasnopevtsev's wife, Lyubov, wrote directly to Khrushchev in July 1960 asking for lenience and insisting that her husband had admitted his guilt and had simply been young and naïve in forming an underground group back in 1957. Her appeal was ignored. Appeals from the mothers of Pimenov's group-mates Mikhail Semenenko and Leonid Rendel' that same year similarly failed to register any impact.[40] After he was jailed in August 1963, Vladimir Bukovsky's mother also wrote an appeal to the Central Committee on her son's behalf but seemingly without success.[41] There are two important themes to raise here. Firstly, we can see that at least some important people with good careers were willing to involve themselves in helping virtual strangers convicted of anti-Soviet activity, something that clearly told of the more relaxed atmosphere of the time. Secondly, though, we can also see that people without powerful connections and special skills were not always able to gain access to the same kind of 'socialist legality' as those closer to the top of the social pyramid – just as ordinary citizens did not experience the same degree of liberalisation enjoyed by Soviet elites in politics, culture and elsewhere.

As Elena and Aleksandr Papovyan noted of the legal establishment's initial attempts to curtail the 1957–8 crackdown on dissent, the repressive apparatus did not take lightly any encroachment upon its prerogative to deal with critics.[42] There seems to have been considerable resistance from the security organs in regard to re-evaluating cases against convicted dissenters,

[39] GARF, f. 8131, op. 31, d. 73957, ll. 1–105.   [40] GARF, f. 8131, op. 31, d. 79866, ll. 80–98.
[41] GARF, f. 8131, op. 31, d. 97676, l. 8.
[42] E. Papovyan and A. Papovyan, 'Uchastie verkhovnogo suda SSSR', in L. Eremina and E. Zhemkova eds., *Korni travy: sbornik statei molodykh istorikov*, Moskva: Zven'ya, 1996, p. 68.

such as those caught up in the campaign of 1957–8. This could be seen in a letter written by the head of the Ukrainian KGB, V. Nikitchenko, in November 1960 to KGB chairman Aleksandr Shelepin in Moscow, complaining that a lack of unity between the courts, Procurator's office and security organs meant that dissenters who had been painstakingly tracked down by the KGB were being freed by the courts or else having their sentences downgraded on appeal.[43] Clearly, the KGB had little interest in seeing that 'justice' was done. It should also be borne in mind, however, that the security organs were already struggling to fulfil their duty to keep tabs on the huge numbers of Stalin-era 'counter-revolutionaries' who had been released.[44] As such, the KGB's motives for resisting the reclassification and release of those who had only recently been jailed were at least partly also of a practical nature. Even so, when Shelepin forwarded Nikitchenko's letter to the Supreme Court and demanded greater unity from all parties involved in combating dissent, he was rebuffed. The Court defended its right to re-evaluate cases that it considered to have been incorrectly conducted, though it rarely did so in practice after a short spell around the turn of the decade. Nonetheless, the united front that Soviet officials and institutions were able to show to the outside world was at times achieved only after some considerable differences of opinion and conflicting interests had been ironed out behind the scenes.

Bearing in mind the fundamental absence of the rule of law in regard to the policing of dissent, it is also worth reflecting on the question of how frequently the authorities opted to circumvent the process of arrest and sentencing under the overtly political articles of the criminal code in favour of alternative charges, such as hooliganism or parasitism, thus avoiding potentially awkward political trials and helping keep to a minimum the number of those branded 'anti-Soviet'. Although one cannot say how often this happened, we know that it did happen on occasion. The prosecution of the poet Joseph Brodsky on parasitism charges in 1964, for example, is widely acknowledged to have been politically motivated, as demonstrated by the fact that the apparently 'anti-Soviet' content of his poetry and diaries were a major focus of the prosecution's attention throughout his trial.[45]

---

[43] V. Kozlov and S. Mironenko eds., *Kramola: inakomyslie v SSSR pri Khrushcheve i Brezhneve 1953–1982*, Moskva: Materik, 2005, p. 45.

[44] On this theme see A. Weiner, 'The Empires Pay a Visit: Gulag Returnees, East European Rebellions, and Soviet Frontier Politics', *The Journal of Modern History*, Vol. 78, No. 2 (June 2006), 333–76.

[45] GARF, f. 8131, op. 31, d. 99616. See also R. Burford Jr, 'Getting the Bugs Out of Socialist Legality: The Case of Joseph Brodsky', *The American Journal of Comparative Law*, Vol. 22, No. 3 (Summer 1974), 464–508.

When Aleksandr Ginzburg was arrested in July 1960 it was, officially at least, not on account of his activity as the compiler of the underground *samizdat* anthology *Syntaksis*. The charges were instead based upon the fact that Ginzburg had sat an exam on behalf of a friend. However, only eight days prior to the Procurator's office sanctioning his arrest (and three days prior to the fraudulent exam in question) Ginzburg had been the subject of a report from KGB chairman Shelepin to the CPSU Central Committee in which it was alleged that he regularly engaged in anti-Soviet conversations, produced oppositional documents and slandered the Soviet order and its leaders. The report concluded by recommending that Ginzburg be imprisoned.[46] Eight days later, he was. According to his case file, a subsequent search of Ginzburg's apartment turned up several abstract artworks, copies of Milovan Djilas's *The New Class* and Aleksandr Esenin-Volpin's *A Leaf of Spring*, as well as what it described as 'an anti-Soviet document entitled *Skalpel'* – another poetry almanac he was compiling at the time.[47] These were all viewed as sufficiently important evidence to warrant extensive mention in the investigation protocol, despite their being entirely unrelated to the official charge in question.[48]

The sheer number of people detained in the campaign against parasitism during the early 1960s made it particularly easy for dissenters to be swept up with all manner of other 'undesirables'. The campaign mentality that had previously reared its head in 1957–8 now saw the decidedly amorphous criteria of 'parasitism' applied ever more widely as police and courts strained to meet the Party leadership's current domestic priority. Between May 1961 and May 1962 almost a quarter of a million Soviet citizens were detained under the new anti-parasite legislation, including over 65,000 for the potentially catch-all offence of 'miscellaneous anti-social crimes'. It is impossible to say how many of these detentions came as a result of dissenting activity, though we can be certain that at least some did.

As Elena Zubkova has pointed out: 'even during the "thaw" the regime made little distinction between criminals, parasites and dissenters. They were all treated as parasites.'[49] It may be that the threat of arrest for parasitism was more widely used against dissenters than the actual application of

[46] RGANI, f. op. 30, d. 320, l.14–16.
[47] Ginzburg fought his corner and refused to acknowledge that *Skalpel'* was in any way anti-Soviet. GARF, f. 8131, op. 31, d. 89189a, l. 7.
[48] GARF, f. 8131, op. 31, d. 89189a, in V. Afiani et al. eds., *Kul'tura i vlast' ot Stalina do Gorbacheva: apparat TsK KPSS i kul'tura, 1958–1964*, Moskva: Rosspen, 2005.
[49] E. Zubkova, 'Na "krayu" sovetskogo obshchestva. Marginal'nye gruppy naseleniya i gosudarstvennaya politika.1940–1960e gody', *Rossiiskaya istoriya*, No. 5 (2009), 115.

the measure, for the threat certainly was used relatively often. The admittedly limited primary accounts available on this theme, such as Andrei Amalrik's memoir of his own experiences as a convicted 'parasite' in *Involuntary Journey to Siberia*, suggest that the anti-parasite campaign did not ensnare whole hordes of political non-conformists but mostly pulled in drunks, petty thieves and thugs. As Amalrik's case and that of Joseph Brodsky had demonstrated, though, the authorities ultimately had no qualms about using the campaign to remove all manner of 'difficult' individuals.[50]

Aside from camps and prisons, the other significant strand of punitive policy employed against dissenters in the Khrushchev period was psychiatric internment. During the Brezhnev years, the state's confinement of dissidents to psychiatric hospitals grew more frequent, becoming a subject that caught the world's attention and provoked widespread revulsion as major publicity campaigns were undertaken in the West to free imprisoned dissidents like Leonid Plyushch and Anatoly Koryagin.[51] There was no such outside interest in punitive psychiatry during the Khrushchev era, however, since hardly anyone knew that the practice even existed at the time. It was not until Vladimir Bukovsky managed to smuggle a series of case files on interned dissenters out of the USSR in 1971 that the political use of psychiatry fully came to the attention of Western doctors, governments and societies. By that time, it had already been a fixture of the authorities' measures aimed at combating dissent for well over a decade. Though there is little in the way of hard data on the number of people interned, since records would hardly be kept confirming fake diagnoses, the likelihood seems to be that the number of victims ran quite probably at least into the hundreds over the duration of the period.

One can find cases of political offenders being held in psychiatric units during the Stalin years, too, but the evidence strongly suggests that there was no real systematic use of psychiatry as a deliberate tool of political repression at that time. Aleksandr Esenin-Volpin, for example, was confined to Leningrad's Prison Psychiatric Hospital for a year as early as 1949 but later told a 1972 US Senate hearing that he believed this to have been an act of kindness on the part of the diagnosing doctors, who had hoped to save him from a potentially much more dangerous spell in the Gulag.[52] Naum

---

[50] See A. Amalrik, *An Involuntary Journey to Siberia*, Newton Abbot: Readers Union, 1971.
[51] On the Western campaigns against punitive psychiatry see R. van Voren, *On Dissidents and Madness: From the Soviet Union of Leonid Brezhnev to the 'Soviet Union' of Vladimir Putin*, Amsterdam: Rodopi, 2009.
[52] Interview with Aleksandr Esenin-Volpin, Revere, MA, November 2006. See also US Congress, Senate, Committee on the Judiciary, *Abuse of Psychiatry for Political Repression in the Soviet Union:*

Korzhavin, who was arrested in 1948 for writing supposedly 'anti-Soviet poetry' and temporarily detained at Moscow's Serbsky Institute for Forensic Psychiatry, also recalled that staff there had tried to declare him 'not responsible' for his actions and thus spare him a potentially very long and possibly fatal confinement in the camps.[53] Indeed, under Stalin the leadership in Moscow actually felt the need to make it harder for psychiatrists to declare those who had been convicted of criminal offences 'not responsible', in the belief – seemingly accurate – that some doctors were trying to protect patients in this way.[54]

By the mid 1950s, with labour camps far less brutal than before and custodial sentences shorter, and with executions for political crimes effectively abandoned, the use of psychiatry within the penal system had begun to take on a very different meaning. Dissenters were no longer 'saved' by a diagnosis of ill health. Psychiatric confinement became just about the very harshest form of political repression and could completely wreck the lives of its victims. Those few who still assumed that a diagnosis of mental ill health might be preferable to a stretch in the camps were soon disabused of that view.[55]

Even before the legal clampdown on dissent had begun at the end of 1956, there were already instances of critics being silenced by punitive psychiatry. When the forty-year-old engineer Petr Lysak wrote to a Party agitator asking 'why is it that in such an allegedly free country as the USSR, foreign radio broadcasts are being jammed?', the authorities responded with a spell of hospitalisation that was to last for more than two decades. When accused of slandering the Soviet regime with his comments, Lysak had responded testily by insisting that such an accusation only constituted a slander against himself.[56] He was duly convicted of anti-Soviet activity in July 1957 and was thereafter transferred to a psychiatric unit. Once in

Hearings before the Subcommittee to Investigate the Administration of the Internal Security Act and Other Internal Security Laws, 92nd Congress, 2nd Session, Washington, DC: US Government Printing Office, 1972, p. 2.

[53] In Korzhavin's case the doctors trying to protect him were unsuccessful. A second commission was summoned to examine the patient and declared him 'responsible'. After eight months in the Lubyanka he spent the next seven years in exile before being released in the amnesties that followed Stalin's death.

[54] Ian Spencer also points out that the kinds of psychotropic drugs that were used on some dissenters during the Khrushchev and Brezhnev eras were hardly ever used under Stalin. I. Spencer, 'An Investigation of the Relationship of Soviet Psychiatry and the State', Ph.D. Dissertation, University of Glasgow, 1997, p. 162.

[55] Joseph Brodsky, for example, was apparently one of those who mistakenly assumed that being held in a psychiatric ward would be preferable to exile. See R. Burford Jr, 'Getting the Bugs Out of Socialist Legality'.

[56] See US Congress, Senate, Committee on the Judiciary, *Abuse of Psychiatry for Political Repression*, p. 9.

Leningrad Special Psychiatric Hospital (SPH), Lysak refused to recant and was forcibly medicated before being transferred to Sychyovka Psychiatric Prison Colony (in Smolensk *oblast'*) in 1965, where he was to remain until the 1980s.[57] Clearly, his fate was in no way preferable to the jail terms that were being handed down for acts of dissent at the time. However, early cases like this were not necessarily a reflection of wider state policy at the time, but instead seem to have been conducted on local initiative. In regard to this specific case at least, it may even be that the atmosphere created by the Secret Speech – in which condemnation of earlier intra-Party abuses soon rubbed up against demands for lower-level officials to rein in critical remarks stemming from Khrushchev's revelations – had inadvertently contributed to the use of this 'back-door' form of repression.

That members of the Party elite quite soon became cognisant of the political use of psychiatry is undoubted.[58] In large part this was thanks to the efforts of Dr Sergei Pisarev. A psychiatrist by profession and a Communist Party member, Pisarev himself had been forcibly hospitalised in early 1953 after writing to protest that the Doctors' Plot (see Chapter 1) was a fabrication. Upon his release in 1955, Pisarev undertook to expose the use of punitive psychiatry and bring an end to the practice. Eventually his efforts at tackling the problem achieved a degree of success in 1956 when a commission was established under the Central Committee official A.I. Kuznetsov to investigate Pisarev's accusation that Moscow's Serbsky Institute was being used to diagnose and imprison healthy people on political grounds. The commission was made up of numerous eminent professors of psychiatry and directors of psychiatric institutions. In essence, Pisarev's allegations were found to have been accurate. The commission concluded that the process of diagnosing patients needed to be radically revised and recommended that prison-psychiatric hospitals should be transferred from the jurisdiction of the MVD to that of the Ministry of Health.[59] As Harvey Fireside records, however, leading members of the commission soon began to lose their Party posts, while the likes of Daniil Lunts – who

---

[57] See US Congress, Senate, Committee on the Judiciary, *Abuse of Psychiatry for Political Repression*.

[58] There were personal connections between the Serbsky Institute and the top members of the CPSU: Georgi Morozov, the head of the Serbsky Institute, was married to a close relative of Boris Ponomarev, a long-standing associate of Mikhail Suslov and at one stage a candidate member of the Central Committee Presidium.

[59] C. Mee, *The Internment of Soviet Dissenters in Mental Hospitals*, Cambridge: John Arliss, 1971, p. 3. Mee notes that these findings did not reach the Central Committee Presidium. The subject does not appear on any official agenda, though it is entirely possible that (owing to the sensitivity of the subject-matter) the findings of the commission were communicated informally to some or all of the top leadership.

would become one of the Brezhnev era's most notorious 'psychiatrist executioners' – found their careers in the ascendancy.[60]

Sources differ as to the ultimate outcome of the investigation. Fireside stated that the main changes which took place were cosmetic ones (such as changing the names of institutions from Prison Psychiatric Hospitals to Special Psychiatric Hospitals), while Ludmilla Alexeyeva asserted that hundreds who had been misdiagnosed were released and numerous 'bad' psychiatrists were demoted.[61] Although Alexeyeva's many years of ground-level involvement in the struggle against punitive psychiatry make her a particularly credible voice on the subject, it is Fireside's account that feels the more convincing. What we now know of subsequent events in the field – not the least of which is the fact that the use of punitive psychiatry was considerably expanded in subsequent years and Special Psychiatric Hospitals remained under the control of the MVD, rather than the Ministry of Health – tends to corroborate Fireside's rather more pessimistic take on the matter.

One of the most compelling pieces of evidence suggesting that those at the very highest level of power had given the nod to the practice of hospital-ising dissenters came in May 1959, when *Pravda* published a recent speech by Khrushchev. In his speech the First Secretary declared that '. . . to those who start calling for opposition to communism . . . we can say that now, too, there are people who fight against communism . . . but clearly the mental state of such people is not normal'.[62] Whether this had been intended as an off-the-cuff quip by the First Secretary, who was certainly prone to extemporising and bombast, or whether it was a genuine signal to those charged with policing dissent, remains unclear. In a political system where the utterances of the Party leader carried so much authority – and where such remarks could quite easily have been kept out of the press if desired – Khrushchev's words were clearly of some significance.

Even more incriminating was the writer Valery Tarsis's claim that his own six-month internment at Moscow's Kashchenko Psychiatric Hospital came at the direct order of Khrushchev. According to Tarsis, the First Secretary had been shown an unflattering portrait of himself in Tarsis's

---

[60] H. Fireside, *Soviet Psychoprisons*, London: W.W. Norton, 1979, p. 38. The term 'psychiatrist executioner' was coined by the 1972 US Senate committee investigation into the Soviet use of punitive psychiatry.

[61] H. Fireside, *Soviet Psychoprisons*, p. 38, and L. Alexeyeva, *Soviet Dissent: Contemporary Movements for National, Religious and Human Rights*, Middletown, CT: Wesleyan University Press, 1987, p. 311.

[62] *Pravda*, 24 May 1959. See S. Bloch and P. Reddaway, *Russia's Political Hospitals*, London: First Futura Publications, 1978.

1962 novel *The Bluebottle*, which had been smuggled out of the USSR and published in the United Kingdom. Khrushchev had apparently then flown into a rage and demanded that the author be locked away at once.[63] The story certainly feels plausible: William Taubman, for example, has shown that Khrushchev could be particularly sensitive to personal criticism, and the occasional volatility of the First Secretary is beyond question.[64] Still, bearing in mind the seriousness of the matter, it is important to present this as an allegation rather than a fact. It is, however, worthwhile here to raise the point that a number of other dissenters who were hospitalised during the period had also been detained after criticism aimed specifically at Khrushchev. Yuri Grimm – the co-author of a series of anti-Khrushchev leaflets discussed in Chapter 6 – was transferred to Leningrad Special Psychiatric Hospital soon after his arrest, where he made the acquaintance of Petro Grigorenko, whose own break with the regime had come when he publicly criticised the burgeoning 'Khrushchev cult' in September 1961. Both men were released a few months after Khrushchev was ousted in October 1964.

Based on Theresa Smith and Thomas Oleszczuk's study of 410 dissenters who were subjected to psychiatric detention between 1960 and 1981, it is possible to draw some tentative outlines of trends in psychiatric confinement across the post-Stalin era as a whole. Those committed to psychiatric institutes on the back of court cases for anti-Soviet activity were held for substantially longer spells than were other patients. We can see that the vast majority of those interned were men (92.7%), the average first internment came at almost thirty-five years of age, and the average duration of internment was almost 5.5 years. Victims were overwhelmingly from urban areas but were spread among the major Soviet nationalities roughly in accordance with their proportion of the overall Soviet population, with the exception that Jews and citizens of the Baltic states were considerably over-represented while citizens from the Central Asian republics were markedly under-represented.[65] As has already been shown in previous chapters, much the

---

[63] Tarsis informed Bukovsky, who was to put the story into print, that his information on the matter came from senior KGB officers disgruntled at their being ordered to detain him. As a reasonably prominent writer it is highly unlikely that Tarsis could have been hospitalised without the express permission of very senior figures within the regime. Interview with Vladimir Bukovsky, Cambridge, March 2007. See also V. Bukovsky, *To Build a Castle: My Life as a Dissenter*, London: Andre Deutsch, 1978.
[64] See W. Taubman, *Khrushchev: The Man and His Era*, London: The Free Press, 2003.
[65] T. Smith and T. Oleszczuk, *No Asylum: State Psychiatric Repression in the Former USSR*, London: Macmillan, 1996, pp. 82–93.

same situation already prevailed in regard to custodial terms handed down by Soviet courts.

The conditions in which victims of psychiatric repression were held could be especially harrowing. After being sent for psychiatric evaluation at the Serbsky Institute in 1964, for example, Joseph Brodsky recalled that on his first evening there the patient in the next bed slit his wrists and died.[66] Interned dissenters were liable to find that their cell-mates were genuinely insane, and sometimes violently so. Petro Grigorenko shared a cell with a man who had murdered his six-year-old daughter, while Vladimir Bukovsky was detained alongside a man who had killed his entire family and cut off his own ears.[67] By no means all patients were subjected to forced medication, but many were and those who have since borne witness to this portray a scenario of immense cruelty and suffering.[68] Pavel Borovik, an accountant from Kaliningrad who was declared mentally ill at the Serbsky Institute in 1964, wrote upon his eventual release that 'From the drugs I have completely lost my appetite, my limbs tremble, every bone aches, and I can't walk.'[69] Rations at Leningrad SPH consisted of 'thin oatmeal, watery cabbage soup that was mostly water and no cabbage; bread and fish once a week'. Combined with inadequate heating, flimsy uniforms and damp conditions, many prisoners' health deteriorated badly there. After a fifteen-month spell in Leningrad SPH that he described simply as 'hell', Bukovsky emerged with rheumatism and a heart murmur while still in his twenties.[70] Others were to emerge almost completely ruined in both body and mind.

Those detained would be held either in what were known as Ordinary Psychiatric Hospitals (OPHs) or, if they were particularly unfortunate, in Special Psychiatric Hospitals (SPHs). In SPHs in particular, inmates were isolated from the outside world and entirely at the mercy of their supervisors. The orderlies, usually criminal prisoners themselves, were notoriously abusive toward their charges and had plenty of scope for brutality under the guise of restraining aggressive patients. Bukovsky in particular paints a compelling picture of virtually unbridled violence, with inmates being beaten senseless and threatened with a variety of pharmacological

[66] S. Volkov, *Conversations with Joseph Brodsky*, New York: The Free Press, 1998, p. 68.
[67] Z. Grigorenko, 'Open Letter', March 1970. See US Congress, Senate, Committee on the Judiciary, *Abuse of Psychiatry for Political Repression*, p. 51.
[68] See, for example, V. Bukovsky, *To Build a Castle*, pp. 209–10, and L. Plyushch, *History's Carnival: A Dissident's Autobiography*, London: Harvill Press, 1979.
[69] Leeds Russian Archive, Terlecka Collection, International Association on the Political Use of Psychiatry, 'Political Abuse of Psychiatry: A List of Victims', 1985, p. 11.
[70] US Congress, Senate, Committee on the Judiciary, *Abuse of Psychiatry for Political Repression*, p. 34.

tortures.[71] With conditions in the Gulag now more closely regulated, SPHs served as a repository of lawless abuse that remained virtually unaffected by post-Stalin reform.

The most common mechanism for confining dissenters to psychiatric wards was through criminal confinement. In 1977 the Working Group on the Internment of Dissenters in Mental Hospitals (a Western research group composed of psychiatrists, human-rights experts and Soviet-affairs specialists) described the process thus: 'typically the dissenter is arrested and charged with some kind of anti-Soviet activity. During the investigation he undergoes a psychiatric examination by a forensic commission which declares him insane and non-responsible. The subsequent trial becomes a formality: the court accepts the commission's judgement, the proceedings are brief, and the defendant, almost invariably barred from attending his trial (because of his illness), is deprived of the chance to defend himself.'[72] This Kafkaesque scenario was not uncommon. The tactic of debarring defendants from their own trial was another firewall erected to prevent dissonant voices from reaching even the most limited of audiences.

One man who was dragged into the labyrinth of punitive psychiatry in this way was Yuri Belov, a Russian tourist in Moscow. Belov had been staying at the hotel *Zarya* over 14 and 15 February 1962. Whilst in residence, he wrote several anti-Soviet slogans on the door of the men's toilet and a number of other public places around the capital. He also visited the Kremlin on a sightseeing trip and again left political graffiti on a toilet door.[73] A KGB investigation was immediately initiated and Belov was tracked down a couple of days later. Before the matter had a chance to proceed to court, an entry in his case file on 12 April 1962 stated that 'in the course of this investigation doubts have arisen regarding Belov's psychiatric state ... the case will be suspended until further medical assessment'. He was then sent to the Serbsky Institute to be assessed. The resulting evaluation asserted that he was 'unfit to be held responsible and constitutes a social danger', indicating that Belov was to be interned in a psychiatric unit.[74] While it is not possible to assert that Belov was definitely in a state of perfect mental health, the link between his dissenting activity and psychiatric confinement is entirely apparent.

---

[71] See V. Bukovsky, *To Build a Castle*, pp. 160–6.

[72] Working Group on the Internment of Dissenters in Mental Hospitals, *The Political Abuse of Psychiatry in the Soviet Union*, London: Working Group on the Internment of Dissenters in Mental Hospitals, 1977, p. 2. On the Group itself, see S. Bloch and P. Reddaway, *Russia's Political Hospitals*.

[73] GARF, f. 8131, op. 31, d. 92580, ll. 1–3.   [74] GARF, f. 8131, op. 31, d. 92580, l. 4.

A similar series of events took place with Vasilii Lopatin, who was arrested in January 1964 after scattering anti-Soviet leaflets around the streets of Tomsk on the night of 3 to 4 November 1963. A search of his home apparently revealed a pistol and further leaflets that Lopatin had prepared for distribution, in which he allegedly 'praised terrorist groups struggling against the Soviet regime'. An entry into his case file on 6 February 1964 stated that investigators had raised doubts about Lopatin's psychological state and he was to be sent for assessment. A further note on 30 March then said that he had been submitted for forced medical treat-ment, before a final addition to the file on 14 April simply stated that Lopatin had been directed to a 'closed psychiatric hospital', meaning one of the dreaded Special Psychiatric Hospitals.[75] What became of Lopatin thereafter remains unclear, since his case did not feature on any of the five major registers of hospitalised dissenters.[76]

Lopatin's absence from these lists serves to indicate that in spite of strenuous and admirable efforts by human-rights activists in the USSR and campaigners in the West, there are still numerous cases of psychiatric abuse that have gone unrecorded, particularly from the Khrushchev era, when less attention was being paid to the matter. In fact, three further cases can now be added. Firstly, in March 1960 a pensioner from Dnepropetrovsk *oblast'* named Petr Vasil'evich Evstaf'ev was arrested in Moscow after making threats against Party leaders when he was refused entry to the Kremlin.[77] On 2 April it was reported that Evstaf'ev was being held in Moscow Hospital No. 7 and was about to be transferred to the Serbsky Institute. A subsequent entry stated that he had been transferred to a Special Psychiatric Hospital. The second case also centred on events in the very heart of the Soviet capital. On 14 July 1960, Kasym Minibaev, who had flown to Moscow from Frunze in Kyrgyzstan, vaulted over barriers inside the Lenin and Stalin mausoleum and proceeded to attack the casket in which Lenin's body lay, kicking and breaking the glass that encased the bier before he was overpowered by security guards. Like so many others before and after him, Minibaev was despatched to the Serbsky Institute, found to have 'schizophrenia-like symptoms', and hospitalised.[78] The third case is

---

[75] GARF, f. 8131, op. 31, d. 96455, ll. 1–7.

[76] The five major registers of interned dissidents have been produced by Bloch and Reddaway, Koppers, Mercer, Podrabinek, and Smith and Oleszczuk. For a comparison of the five see T. Smith and T. Oleszczuk, *No Asylum*, pp. 205–37.

[77] Evstaf'ev's case file also revealed that he had written several critical letters to the newspaper *Dnepropetrovskaya pravda* and a search of his Dnepropetrovsk apartment turned up a further seven 'anti-Soviet documents'. GARF, f. 8131, op. 31, d. 88488, ll. 1–23.

[78] GARF, f. 8131, op. 31, d. 89189, ll. 1–16.

that of Yu.P. Pintans, an Australian citizen of Latvian origin who returned
to the Soviet Union in 1960 and took a job at Riga zoo, but quickly grew
disillusioned at life in the USSR. He began to write hostile letters, refused to
undertake military service or to vote in elections and eventually tried to
return to Australia. He was denied an exit visa because the Soviet authorities
insisted that his Latvian roots made him a Soviet citizen.[79] After repeated
complaints and refusals to 'toe the line', Pintans was convicted of anti-
Soviet activity in July 1962 and sent to Leningrad SPH.[80]

The process of evaluating prisoners' mental health often belied the true
grounds for internment. After he was caught attempting to smuggle the
unpublished manuscript of his book *The Unsung Song* out to the West via a
visiting French tourist in 1961, Mikhail Naritsa was arrested and subsequently declared 'not responsible for his actions' in March 1962. The
psychiatric evaluation committee, he wrote, '... was composed of about
twenty physicians seated along the walls of the room. My manuscripts were
there. One copy between all of them. As I entered they were distributing the
pages amongst themselves. Several pages for each one.' Upon enquiring
whether any of those present had actually read his work in full, Naritsa was
told only that 'it has been assessed by an expert'. The outcome was entirely
predictable: he was declared insane and confined to an asylum, where he
remained for the next three years. The amateurish nature of the session is
immediately obvious, not least since its consequences were so serious.

The fact that a total of twenty doctors had been involved in this rather
farcical process against Naritsa was also particularly striking, and presumably reflected the fact that the authorities were especially eager to make the
diagnosis appear a legitimate one, lest the case arouse significant interest
because of Naritsa's standing as a writer.[81] There is a wider point to be made
here, though, in that the use of punitive psychiatry offered the authorities a
'back-door route' for dealing with troublesome individuals: a way to conduct political repression without having to do so on a formal basis. The use
of medical diagnoses provided a certain sheen of legitimacy, since they were
provided by doctors, rather than the penal apparatus. Indeed, in theory at
least, the outward image that hospitalisation presented was one of healing
and helping. With the attacks on Stalinist brutality and the renewed
emphasis on 'socialist legality', this was an important way to short-circuit

[79] GARF, f. 8131, op. 31, d. 92010, ll. 1–5.
[80] See US Congress, Senate, Committee on the Judiciary, *Abuse of Psychiatry for Political Repression*, Appendix II, p. 33.
[81] In fact, the Naritsa case did arouse a degree of interest in the West, though nothing on the scale of later campaigns in the 1970s and 80s.

practically all of the changes that had taken place since Stalin's death, enabling the authorities to deal with 'enemies' quickly and virtually as they pleased without being seen to be turning to the 'old methods' of the Stalin years.

Not all psychiatric evaluations resulted in hospitalisation, however. In December 1956 Efim Yakovlevich Shatov, a Jewish pensioner from Odessa, was arrested after sending critical leaflets to a number of regional and national officials (including chairman of the Supreme Court Kliment Voroshilov). When charged, Shatov acknowledged only partial guilt of anti-Soviet activity, on the basis that he had produced the leaflets in question but had not intended to harm the Soviet state. He was then referred to the Serbsky Institute 'on account of his failing memory and a serious nerve problem'. There, he was found sufficiently healthy to be responsible for his actions but was not permitted to attend his own trial owing to his condition. A note in his case file from 14 February stated only that Shatov was to be confined to hospital at the Butyrka Prison, where he could be monitored.[82] On 10 June 1957 the case against him was abandoned.

The machinery of psychiatric repression did not always function smoothly. The case of Viktor Rafalsky was an extreme but telling example of the lack of diagnostic uniformity. A school headmaster from western Ukraine, Rafalsky was first arrested in 1954 for involvement in an underground Marxist group. Between 1954 and 1959 he went through six separate psychiatric examinations: three found him mentally 'responsible' (and thus liable to be sent to a corrective-labour camp) and the other three found him 'not responsible' (meaning confinement in a psychiatric ward). The three 'responsible' verdicts came from assessments in Leningrad, and the 'not-responsible' verdicts were produced by the Serbsky Institute. This was indicative of a wider rift between the Moscow and Leningrad schools of psychiatry at the time, in which (despite the city playing host to one of the most notorious SPHs) the former capital's doctors resisted submitting to the more politically motivated diagnoses being made in the Soviet capital. As often proved to be the case, it was the hardliners in Moscow who were to win the wider battle for control of Soviet psychiatry.

Rafalsky's tale was to be a particularly eventful one. He first emerged from psychiatric confinement in March 1956 only to be rearrested and returned to Leningrad SPH six months later. He was again interned for two years in 1959 when leaflets he had written several years earlier came to the attention of the KGB. Rafalsky was once again detained in 1968, this

---

[82] GARF, f. 8131, op. 31, d. 76978, ll. 1–7.

time at Dnepropetrovsk SPH, where in 1971 doctors eventually diagnosed him as mentally sound and requested his release, which was rejected by the courts. He was to have another brief period of freedom before being hospitalised yet again, when he was subjected to large doses of sulfazine before eventually being released and declared sane.[83] As Rafalsky's case showed, once a diagnosis of long-term illness had been made, it became easy for the authorities to hospitalise an individual over and over again without the need for any credible evidence of wrongdoing: this was one of the main advantages of punitive psychiatry from the authorities' point of view and one of the main dangers facing those detained.

In other cases, hospitalised dissenters were not charged with any kind of recognised crime before they were apprehended. Civil confinement was essentially the equivalent of 'sectioning' that exists in practically all countries (and is not entirely without controversy anywhere) for emergency hospitalisation of the mentally unwell. This entailed forcibly removing an individual from wider society on the basis that their behaviour constituted a danger either to themselves or to those around them.[84] Despite the system being already open to abuse – since the regime demanded 'political loyalty' from its psychiatrists and held huge influence over them through powers such as the conferment of promotion and the allocation of housing and other privileges – in 1961 new guidelines for civil confinement were issued, entitled 'Directives on the Immediate Hospitalisation of Mentally Ill Persons Who Are a Social Danger'. The directives contained sufficiently vague medical provisions as to allow practically untrammelled scope for the immediate and forcible incarceration of anyone.[85] This piece of legislation undoubtedly facilitated many instances whereby healthy individuals were confined in asylums over the next three decades. Importantly, it was consistent with the general hardening of policy against dissent during the early 1960s and thus can be viewed as part of an evolving framework of responses to the system's most troublesome critics.

Petro Grigorenko, who was to become one of the most famous victims of psychiatric repression, was first hospitalised by civil confinement in 1964, not long after his underground group, the Alliance of Struggle for the

---

[83] Leeds Russian Archive, Terlecka Collection, International Association on the Political Use of Psychiatry, 'Political Abuse of Psychiatry: A List of Victims', 1985, p. 27. See also T. Smith and T. Oleszczuk, *No Asylum*, p. 15.

[84] The most famous instance in which this process was employed was in the confinement of Zhores Medvedev at Kaluga OPH in June 1970. See R. Medvedev and Zh. Medvedev, *A Question of Madness*, New York: Alfred Knopf, 1971.

[85] S. Bloch and P. Reddaway, *Russia's Political Hospitals*, p. 152.

Rebirth of Leninism, was discovered by the KGB. The medical notes from Grigorenko's internment make explicit the link between his political views and the subsequent diagnosis of mental illness.[86] In the doctors' assessment of Grigorenko it stated that 'It was established that he had reformist ideas, in particular for the reorganisation of the state apparatus, linked with an overestimation of his own personality, messianic ideas, and paranoid interpretation of particular neutral facts.'[87] The remark about reformist ideas for the reorganisation of the state apparatus was a sure sign that Grigorenko's diagnosis was a deeply politicised one. His apparent 'paranoid interpretation of neutral facts' and 'overestimation of his own personality' were the kinds of flexible, catch-all symptoms that could be diagnosed in almost anyone and were just about impossible to disprove. Indeed, fighting against such a tendentious diagnosis would only be cited as conclusive evidence of its rightness.

Accordingly, one of the key facets of punitive psychiatry was to intimidate. In a number of cases where individuals refused to testify against a friend or family member, the spectre of forced hospitalisation quickly loomed. In 1959 Aleksandr Esenin-Volpin's third spell of psychiatric incarceration (his second under Khrushchev) came after he had refused to denounce a friend accused of treason, as a result of which he was to spend a year in Leningrad SPH. Prior to his being sent for psychiatric evaluation after an arrest in 1960, Aleksandr Ginzburg's case file also noted that he had refused to offer testimony when questioned on his friend Natalya Gorbanevskaya's *samizdat* activities.[88] When Mikhail Naritsa's wife had refused to acknowledge that her husband was sick, doctors began to suggest that maybe she too was ill and attempted to secure a warrant for her arrest.[89] Since the Soviet authorities consistently strived to keep the practice of hospitalising dissenters from being exposed publicly, we can safely assume that it was not overtly intended to have a deterrent effect on society at large. As the above cases show, it was clearly used to intimidate or deter those already connected to dissenting activity in some way. How successful it was at fulfilling this aim is not entirely clear – it certainly failed to produce the

---

[86] Grigorenko's supposed condition was diagnosed as 'paranoid development of the personality combined with the first signs of arterio-sclerosis of the brain'. Along with 'sluggish schizophrenia', 'paranoid development of the personality' was one of the most common politically based diagnoses used against dissenters.

[87] 'Forensic Diagnosis of P.G. Grigorenko', 18 August 1969, in US Congress, Senate, Committee on the Judiciary, Abuse of Psychiatry for Political Repression, p. 59.

[88] GARF f. 8131, op. 31, d. 89189a, l. 2.

[89] Having helped her husband to type up the offending book, *The Unsung Song*, Naritsa's wife was in real danger of facing punitive action herself.

desired result in the cases of Esenin-Volpin, Ginzburg and Naritsa – though most victims did indeed recant their dissenting behaviour once interned. With the potential damage that psychiatric imprisonment could do to an individual's health, and the possibility for indefinite hospitalisation, this could be the only viable route to survival.[90] While such measures may, at best, have changed the surface-level behaviours of those who were punished, it was highly unlikely that any of them were genuinely reconciled with the authorities' point of view. By the 1960s, however, that was entirely sufficient: the point was either to remove dissenters from society or to impose silence upon them.

There were plenty of benefits for the authorities in hospitalising dissenters. Firstly, a psychiatric diagnosis stigmatised the patient and implicitly rejected the validity of criticism by presenting dissenters' remarks as the product of a diseased mind and even as a symptom of abnormality. Secondly, a diagnosis of ill health meant that potentially embarrassing political trials could be entirely circumvented, or at least conducted with the accused *in absentia* and thus unable to fight the accusations against them. Thirdly, and most menacingly, by providing the accused with a diagnosis rather than a defined jail term, it was possible for critics to be detained indefinitely, until they were judged to have 'recovered', for which we can read 'recanted'. Many of the most famous cases of psychiatric abuse lasted for several months or a few years at most, but there were plenty who endured truly marathon stretches of incarceration. Indeed, the data compiled by Theresa Smith and Thomas Oleszczuk show that the late 1950s saw dissenters confined for the longest spells of the entire post-Stalin era, a trend most likely related to the fact that few in the outside world knew of the practice at that time, meaning there was no pressure on the regime to undo politically motivated diagnoses.[91]

The possibility of indefinite detention was not simply theoretical. After fleeing the country and gaining asylum in the UK in 1956, Mikhail Ivankov-Nikolov was lured back to the USSR, with the explicit promise that he would not be punished for his illegal emigration. On his return, he was arrested and subsequently declared mentally ill. With spells in Kazan, Chernyakhovsk and Dnepropetrovsk SPHs, Ivankov-Nikolov was thereafter to remain in a psychiatric unit until the 1980s.[92] In another case, Vasily

---

[90] See V. Bukovsky and S. Gluzman, 'A Manual on Psychiatry for Dissenters', 1974, in H. Fireside, *Soviet Psychoprisons*, Appendix I, pp. 92–117.
[91] T. Smith and T. Oleszczuk, *No Asylum*, p. 104.
[92] Leeds Russian Archive, Terlecka Collection, International Association on the Political Use of Psychiatry, *Information Bulletin No. 2*, October 1981, p. 3.

Shipilov had the importance of recanting his religious beliefs made perfectly clear to him at Sychyovka SPH, where a psychiatrist warned him that 'until the day you renounce your faith, you'll remain here forever – unless you're killed first'. The psychiatrist was just about true to his word: having been detained in 1960 Shipilov was still hospitalised over a quarter of a century later.[93]

Numerous interpretations have been put forward as to how and why psychiatric confinement came to be a feature of government responses to political critics in the Soviet Union. The three most prevalent explanations argue, firstly, that there was a long-standing predisposition toward the practice within Russia's political culture; secondly that the very nature of the Soviet psychiatric system made it particularly susceptible to such abuses; and, thirdly, that the Soviet regime simply used psychiatry as a deliberate and rational tool of state policy.[94] Peter Reddaway and Sidney Bloch – the pre-eminent Western scholars on the subject since the Brezhnev years – pointed to a use of political psychiatry in Russia that predated even the Bolshevik seizure of power, suggesting its use in the post-Stalin era was essentially an expansion of existing practice, rather than a fundamentally new development.[95] This long history of political psychiatry was certainly true, though the remarkable expansion of its application during the post-Stalin era points to something more than just a continuation of earlier practices. Indeed, it may even be more useful to draw a tentative link between the growth of psychiatric internment and the post-Stalin reforms which placed new limits on the authorities' use of more traditional repressive activity.

While contemporaneous Western arguments that psychiatric abuse was essentially a direct product of 'cruel' Soviet ideology testified to a deeply politicised, Cold-War perspective on the matter, Harvey Fireside and Ian Spencer took a less overtly ideological approach, suggesting that fundamental weaknesses and inefficiencies in the structure of Soviet medicine, like the systemic problems that existed in Soviet industry, agriculture and much else besides, lay at the root of psychiatric detention of critics.[96] The fact that professional training and medical resources were often limited, while social

[93] Leeds Russian Archive, Terlecka Collection, International Association on the Political Use of Psychiatry, 'Political Abuse of Psychiatry: A List of Victims', 1985, p. 31.
[94] For a fuller exploration of these arguments see T. Smith and T. Oleszczuk, *No Asylum*, pp. 65–74.
[95] Most famously, Petr Chaadaev was declared insane and effectively subjected to house arrest for a year under Nicholas I in 1836 after his 'Philosophical Letter', criticising what he perceived as Russia's cultural backwardness, was published in the journal *Teleskop*, subsequently triggering the 'Slavophiles and Westerners' debate of the nineteenth century.
[96] See, for example, I. Spencer, 'An Investigation of the Relationship of Soviet Psychiatry'.

conventions prescribed a very narrow definition of 'normal' behaviour, meant that the possibility of being adjudged mentally unwell could be higher in the Soviet Union than other places. Furthermore, Soviet psychiatrists swore under oath to serve not the wellbeing of their individual patients but 'the interests of society'.[97] To this can also be added the earlier point that Soviet psychiatrists were to a far greater degree in thrall to the political authorities than were their colleagues in the West. Nonetheless, there were many – maybe most – Soviet psychiatrists who refused to participate in the practice and even some who sought to expose it.[98] While they may be mostly circumstantial, ties linking members of the political elite to the use of punitive psychiatry suggest one ought to look beyond the medical world for an explanation.

Both of the above approaches make a real contribution to our understanding of how psychiatry came to be a part of the authorities' arsenal of measures to combat dissent. Most importantly, though, we can see that punitive psychiatry simply became a rationally employed, and often effective, policy to isolate, intimidate and punish dissenters. As Theresa Smith has showed, the level of psychiatric internments rose and fell roughly in accordance with the level of dissenting activity around the country; the threat of forced medication was used to blackmail patients' relatives into cooperating with various demands; and Special Psychiatric Hospitals were headed by MVD officers until the late 1980s.[99] Much as the Soviet authorities tried to claim otherwise, and in fact continued to do so right up until the fall of the regime, the evidence to show that the use of psychiatry became a calculated arm of policy against dissent is overwhelming. Like prophylaxis, its application continued to grow under the succeeding Brezhnev regime. This was a particularly dubious legacy for Khrushchev and for an era that is often still remembered as a time of thaw.

In fact, developments in punitive psychiatry tended to fit neatly with the broader evolution of penal policy. Most notably, we can see that Khrushchev's 1959 remarks linking acts of protest with mental illness fitted into a wider pattern of hardening state responses to dissent around the end of that decade. It came less than a year after the Supreme Court had called a halt to the excessive use of article 58-10 and only a couple of months after Khrushchev had announced at the XXI CPSU Congress that prophylactic

---

[97] S. Bloch and P. Reddaway, *Russia's Political Hospitals*, p. 43.
[98] The most well-known Soviet psychiatrists who protested against the abuse of psychiatry were Dr Semyon Gluzman and Dr Aleksandr Podrabinek.
[99] See T. Smith and T. Oleszczuk, *No Asylum*, pp. 72–92.

measures were to become the bedrock of policing. Similarly, the new guidelines which made it easier for the authorities to have dissenters sectioned also coincided with the worsening of conditions for 'politicals' in corrective-labour camps and prison as well as with the first upturn for many years in the total number of prisoners in the USSR.

Taken together, the changes coming into force across the Soviet punitive apparatus in the early 1960s were an integral part of the Khrushchev regime's evolving responses to critics. After the abandonment of mass terror with Stalin's death, and the somewhat uncertain handling of dissent during the mid to late 1950s, the second half of the Khrushchev era saw the beginning of the appearance of a more effective set of measures for dealing with dissent. This was basically founded on the principle of less outright repression but closer policing of the masses. The overt repression that did remain was intended to appear more legitimate, with open trials, lawyers and professional medical diagnoses, as the regime strove to distinguish the post-Stalin policing of dissent from Stalinist arbitrariness. When it came to dealing with those deemed 'genuinely anti-Soviet', however, the resulting court verdicts and diagnoses were in little doubt. This system was to last virtually up to the fall of the Soviet regime and went a long way toward stifling the expression of political discontent among the vast majority of Soviet citizens.

CHAPTER 9

A precursor to the Soviet human-rights movement

In addition to witnessing a dramatic escalation and subsequent decline in worker protest, the later part of the Khrushchev era also proved to be a vital stage in the evolution of dissent among that section of the intelligentsia which remained defiant. From around the end of the 1950s, Ludmilla Alexeyeva's depiction of the Khrushchev years as a kind of 'incubation period' for the subsequent Soviet human-rights movement becomes much more convincing. There was still no real 'movement' to speak of, but it was during the early 1960s that many important networks were first forged and new themes of dissenting activity emerged. The names of some of those already becoming involved in various forms of dissent at this stage constitute a veritable 'who's who' of the Brezhnev-era human-rights movement, such as Aleksandr Esenin-Volpin, Vladimir Bukovsky, Yuri Galanskov and Aleksandr Ginzburg, to cite just a few.

Once the volatile outbursts of worker protest in the early 1960s had subsided, the dissent that remained was largely dominated by the intelligentsia and generally eschewed the more overtly subversive and vociferous forms of activity. Even so, they, too, less and less often spoke in terms of 'fixing' the system. As the decade progressed many dissenters increasingly focused specifically on questions of conscience and the observance of legality – on their own part and on that of the authorities. After the disappointed hopes of the mid to late 1950s, for much of the dissenting intelligentsia the early 1960s were a period of searching for new philosophies and forms of expression. This was, according to Veniamin Iofe, a process that had been largely completed by the middle of the decade.[1] Although assuming a clear form and coming to prominence only with the emergence of the human-rights movement after Khrushchev's ouster, the move toward more open and legalistic activity was deeply rooted in the late 1950s and early 1960s.

[1] V. Iofe, *Granitsy smysla: stat'i, vystupleniya, esse*, Sankt Peterburg: Nauchno-informatsionnyi tsentr 'Memorial', 2002, p. 119.

As previous chapters have shown, the authorities had also been learning lessons and refining their methods of dealing with critics. These Khrushchev-era experiences would go a long way towards defining the contours of the confrontation between dissenters and authority over the next couple of decades.

One of the first significant events of the new decade was the passing of Boris Pasternak, whose most famous creation, Yuri Zhivago, had personified many of those humanist values that intelligentsia dissent was moving toward. Having never truly recovered from the distress caused by the attacks that followed his 1958 Nobel Prize win, Pasternak succumbed to lung cancer at the end of May 1960 and was buried at the writers' colony of Peredelkino, 25 km (15 miles) southwest of Moscow. With the author still in semi-disgrace by the time of his death, the authorities were eager to prevent his funeral from turning into a rallying point for discontented admirers.[2] Nonetheless, officials from the Department of Culture who were in attendance at the funeral reported that around 500 people arrived at Peredelkino to mark Pasternak's passing, including 150 to 200 members of the intelligentsia, foreign correspondents, students and writers, among whom was Konstantin Paustovsky – who had so vehemently denounced 'Drozdovs' back in 1956 – while numerous other leading cultural figures had sent wreaths.[3] Although one of the youths present loudly admonished the authorities' refusal to publish *Dr Zhivago* and declared that no other Soviet writer came close to the artistic heights scaled by Pasternak, the attendant officials from the Department of Culture reported that 'attempts to use the funeral to stir unhealthy moods were unsuccessful', though they did urge the strengthening of 'educational work' among creative youths and students.

That the authorities viewed Pasternak's funeral as a potential flashpoint could be seen in the fact that the above report was forwarded to Frol Kozlov, Otto Kuusinen and Nuriddin Mukhitdinov, all members of the top leadership.[4] While it may not have produced an immediate and visceral response from those in attendance, many have since seen the funeral as a moment heavy with significance. Most recently, Vladislav Zubok's history of the late-Soviet intelligentsia described the death and subsequent burial of

[2] V. Zubok, *Zhivago's Children: The Last Russian Intelligentsia*, Cambridge, MA: Harvard University Press, 2009, p. 19.
[3] RGANI, f. 5, op. 36, d. 119, l. 63–4, in V. Afiani and Tomilina, N. eds., 'A za mnoyu shum pogoni ...': *Boris Pasternak i vlast': dokumenty, 1956–1972*, Moskva: Rosspen, 2001.
[4] RGANI, f. 5, op. 36, d. 119, l. 64, in V. Afiani and N. Tomilina, eds., 'A za mnoyu shum pogoni ...' At the time in question, all three men were members of the Central Committee Secretariat.

Pasternak as a 'moment at which another spiritual and civic community emerged in the popular mind' and 'the first sizeable demonstration of civic solidarity in Soviet Russia', marking a re-emergence of the traditional values and ideals of the pre-revolutionary Russian intelligentsia.[5]

While there is a natural tendency to ascribe a kind of epoch-making status to notable events such as Pasternak's funeral, the response it generated was actually broadly of its time. The Soviet student body, for example, had already witnessed more than a few demonstrations of civic solidarity by this point, including protests in defence of fellow students who had been expelled from institutes and demonstrations against the Soviet invasion of Hungary. Responses to literary works such as Dudintsev's *Not by Bread Alone* in 1956 had also shown that questions of conscience and morality bubbled close to the surface. The biggest change would lie in the fact that earlier such demonstrations of solidarity had been quickly beaten back by the authorities. As the preceding chapters have shown, dissenters' positions were hardening by the 1960s. Though smaller in scale than the political dissent that had blossomed during 1956 in particular, that which arose among the liberal intelligentsia of the early 1960s was to prove far more enduring.

More divisive is the question of how far the intelligentsia dissent of the period genuinely represented a turn toward the values and moral codes of the pre-revolutionary Russian intelligentsia. While the likes of Vladislav Zubok and Jay Bergman have asserted this to be the case, others such as Serguei Oushakine and Thomas C. Wolfe see the dissenting intelligentsia of the post-Stalin era as a more distinctly Soviet phenomenon.[6] The superficial links to the old intelligentsia were clear enough, such as Valery Ronkin's Kolokol group naming itself after Aleksandr Herzen's nineteenth-century underground newspaper, or the tendency for non-conformist literary gatherings to style themselves as 'salons' and for dissenters to write approvingly of the Decembrists or to liken their own suffering to that of Petr Chaadaev.[7] Nonetheless, the language and ideals of dissenting intellectuals at this point could still be startlingly close to those propounded (if not always practised) by the government of the day and their aims were often recognisably Soviet in that they primarily demanded the system abide by its own rules and

[5] V. Zubok, *Zhivago's Children*, pp. 19–20.
[6] See S. Oushakine, 'The Terrifying Mimicry of Samizdat', *Public Culture*, Vol. 13, No. 2 (Spring 2001), 191–214 and T. Wolfe, 'Comment [On Komaromi and Nathans]', *Slavic Review*, Vol. 66, No. 4 (Winter 2007), 646–66.
[7] See J. Bergman, 'Soviet Dissidents on the Russian Intelligentsia, 1956–1985: The Search for a Usable Past', *Russian Review*, Vol. 51, No. 1 (January 1992), 16–35.

promises.[8] Indeed, many of them were still either CPSU or Komsomol members at this point. A wealth of anecdotal evidence does seem to suggest that there was some kind of 'rebirth of conscience' that began during the Khrushchev era.[9] Certainly the theme of morality began to appear more frequently in dissident thinking.[10] As Philip Boobbyer points out, though, this was a sense of conscience that did not just hark back to pre-revolutionary days, but was also heavily influenced by both global and Soviet thinking on questions of morality.[11] Most dissenters were hardly opponents of communism – even many of those who eventually fled the USSR still approved of fundamental planks of the Soviet system, such as universal healthcare, free education and state control of heavy industry – but they wanted it to be fairer and to work more effectively in practice. That these hopes faded over time is hardly doubted, though they were not quite dead yet.[12]

While Boris Pasternak's own family background and upbringing were unmistakably of the old intelligentsia milieu, the majority of the post-Stalin intelligentsia bore a more than considerable imprint of Soviet social-ism: to expect otherwise would be artificially to detach them from the very environment that nurtured and enveloped them. There is little doubt that many of them showed a certain nostalgia for the ethos of the pre-revolutionary intelligentsia yet, as Thomas C. Wolfe asserts, they still 'represented one of the many possible permutations of *Soviet* personhood'.[13] Indeed, we might even view dissenters' images of the old intelligentsia as another 'imagined past' like the notions of 'true Leninism' that had pre-dominated in the mid to late 1950s. Accordingly, even conscious attempts at emulating the old intelligentsia did not necessarily mean a genuine rebirth of their ideals and values. What we can say with certainty is that at least some members of the late Soviet intelligentsia, such as Andrei Sakharov and

---

[8] See, for example, S. Oushakine, 'The Terrifying Mimicry of Samizdat'.

[9] See, for example, 'Beseda s Vladimirom Timovym', in which Vladimir Timov speaks of abandoning a promising career with the KGB on moral grounds after monitoring religious believers. V. Pimonov, *Govoryat 'osobo opasnye'*, Moskva: Detektiv-Press, 1999, pp. 208–18. See also P. Boobbyer, *Conscience, Dissent and Reform in Soviet Russia*, London: Routledge, 2005.

[10] We see, for example, in V. Bukovsky and S. Gluzman's 'A Manual on Psychiatry for Dissenters' (in H. Fireside, *Soviet Psychoprisons*, London: W.W. Norton, 1979, Appendix I, pp. 92–117) that the authors assert the importance of 'the ability to act immorally towards persons and organisations which profess the morality of savages' and describe the Soviet human-rights movement as 'a purely moral opposition'. P. Boobbyer, 'Vladimir Bukovskii and Soviet Communism', *Slavonic and East European Review*, Vol. 87, No. 3, July 2009, 481.

[11] P. Boobbyer, *Conscience, Dissent and Reform*, p. 3.

[12] On this, see in particular P. Vail' and A. Genis, *60-e: mir sovetskogo cheloveka*, Ann Arbor, MI: Ardis Publishers, 1989.

[13] T. Wolfe, 'Comment', 665.

Andrei Amalrik, were interested in and came to seek inspiration from their pre-revolutionary forebears, like Aleksandr Herzen, Aleksandr Radishchev and the Decembrists.[14] This was not true for all of them, however. Aleksandr Solzhenitsyn, for example, came to display a deeply moralistic opposition to the Soviet system, though he explicitly rejected the values of the old intelligentsia, whom he blamed for the revolution that had brought the Bolsheviks to power in the first place.[15]

As earlier chapters have shown, this was a time when people were becoming better able to conceive of alternative political practices, values and goals to those which existed in the USSR, something that had not always been evident during earlier years. The intelligentsia were very much at the forefront of this trend. As faith in the system's capacity for genuine reform further dissipated among those who had previously considered themselves fundamentally loyal but not unquestioning citizens, and as the flow of unsanctioned information entering the Soviet Union grew, horizons began to widen, prompting an increasing ideological and cultural heterodoxy. In fact, one of the things that would later make the Soviet dissident movement so remarkable was the veritable rainbow of ideological positions its members adopted inside a one-party state, a stark contrast to the ideological homogeneity of political criticism in the mid 1950s. Nationalism, too, was very much on the rise in the non-Russian republics and in Russia itself, especially among the intelligentsia. Many others – young people in particular, according to Juliane Fürst – had been completely turned off by politics and simply sought to evade ideological activity wherever they could.[16] Undramatic though it may have been, this was in itself deeply problematic for the long-term wellbeing of the Soviet system.

Among the key landmarks in the evolution of intelligentsia dissent, which helped make public some of these emerging cracks in the Soviet monolith, were two series of public poetry readings, held at Mayakovsky Square in central Moscow. The initial meeting that started events there took place in July 1958, following the unveiling of a statue of the popular futurist poet Vladimir Mayakovsky. After officially approved speakers had given recitals, enthusiastic members of the crowd took it upon themselves to continue the evening with impromptu readings of their own. Having enjoyed the evening, many of the participants arranged to meet again at

---

[14] See J. Bergman, 'Soviet Dissidents on the Russian Intelligentsia'.
[15] See A. Solzhenitsyn ed., *From under the Rubble*, London: Harper Collins, 1975.
[16] See J. Fürst, *Stalin's Last Generation: Soviet Post-War Youth and the Emergence of Mature Socialism*, Oxford University Press, 2010.

the Square a week later, and soon the open-air poetry sessions were taking place regularly. Although they were not oppositional in tone, the meetings were characterised by a somewhat rebellious, free-wheeling atmosphere and a celebration of the 'spirit of the XX Congress'. In other words, they represented something akin to the post-XX Congress mood of 'anti-Stalinist but not anti-communist'. Initially the authorities looked quite benignly on these gatherings but became increasingly uneasy about them as time passed, using volunteer police to intimidate and apprehend participants as they approached the Square. Neither their relative spontaneity nor their utilisation of public space for the expression of unorthodox cultural tastes (in the very heart of the Soviet capital, no less) sat comfortably with regime's desire to maintain tight control of the Soviet public sphere. By the spring of 1960 the first series of meetings had been successfully brought to a close.

On the initiative of Vladimir Bukovsky and Vladimir Osipov, the poetry readings were revived in September 1960 and again drew crowds of up to a few hundred people to the centre of the capital on Saturday and Sunday evenings, often running from 9 or 10 pm through to 2 or 3 am.[17] While many who attended the readings did so primarily as poetry lovers rather than dissenters, there was undoubtedly an ideological undercurrent to events. Indeed, Bukovsky later recalled that his motivation for resurrecting the gatherings had been to draw together like-minded critics of the regime.[18] Even more subversively, Osipov had apparently conceived of the meetings as a Soviet equivalent to the Petöfi Circle, the Young Communist literary group that had played such an important role in triggering the uprising in Hungary only a few years earlier.[19] While Osipov's aims went unfulfilled, Bukovsky's did not. These poetry readings would go on to play a crucial role in bringing together various non-conformist elements from across Moscow and in attracting occasional sympathisers from as far away as Leningrad, Kiev and Saratov. With plainclothes KGB agents and Komsomol informers dotted throughout the audience, speakers avoided making overtly political statements and stuck to reading poetry, but often this, too, displayed deeply troubling sentiments of discontent. Yuri Galanskov's 'Manifesto of Man' – a regular staple of the

---

[17] TsKhDMO (former Komsomol archive), f. 1, op. 32, ed. khr. 1026, ll. 39–40, in L. Polikovskaya, *'My predchuvstvie … predtecha': ploshchad Mayakovskogo 1958–1965*, Moskva: Obshchestvo 'Memorial', 1997.
[18] Interview with Vladimir Bukovsky, Cambridge, March 2007.
[19] Interview with Apollon Shukht (fellow attendee at poetry readings) in L. Polikovskaya, *'My predchuvstvie … predtecha'*, p. 66.

meetings – declared 'I'll go to the square, and in the city's ear, I'll force a cry of despair, then take out a pistol, and press it to my temple . . .'[20]

Even without calling for outright resistance, these meetings represented a potentially serious problem for the authorities. They showed an embryonic public sphere that was becoming a little more independent of the behavioural and ideological expectations set out by the authorities. The meetings began to allow those who participated to see themselves as standing apart from the mainstream of society: a sentiment which later proliferated among young people in particular and implied a 'critical distance from the regime's ortho-doxy'.[21] In other words, events such as these enabled participants to feel something more than merely cogs in the giant Soviet machine, facilitating a shift whereby dissent became intertwined with questions of identity rather than just ideology.[22] This was a limited and unspectacular process but, if repeated widely enough, one that posed a real threat to ideological homogeneity. Of course, Soviet society had never truly been monolithic, but showing as much in the very centre of Moscow was a move of real significance.

Events surrounding the poetry readings were not restricted to the public gatherings in the centre of Moscow. Participants also congregated at friends' apartments and held 'salons' consisting of anywhere between ten and thirty people. Conversations there would turn far more open and critical than anything that was said during the sessions at the Square. There was talk of loss of faith in socialism, of the need for greater democratisation and of the desirability of establishing some form of loyal opposition to the existing regime.[23] That these 'open' and 'closed' facets of the Mayakovsky Square meetings differed notably in tone clearly demonstrated some degree of separation between public and private spheres, yet the fact that even in private they spoke of 'loyal' opposition tells us that the two were by no means diametrically opposed to one another.

---

[20] Yu. Galanskov, 'Chelovecheskii manifest', in M. Barbakadze and E. Shvarts eds., *Antologiya samizdata: nepodtsenzurnaya literatura v SSSR 1950–1980*, Tom 1: *Do 1966 goda*, Moskva: Mezhdunarodnyi institut gumanitarno-politicheskikh issledovanii, 2005, pp. 108–10. A Komsomol report of 28 October 1961 branded this particular poem as consisting of 'slander and hatred toward the Communist Party and Soviet system' and 'openly calling for rebellion', a particularly hysterical reading of Galanskov's work. TsKhDMO, f. 1, op. 3, ed. khr. 1062, in L. Polikovskaya, *'My predchuvstvie . . . predtecha'*.

[21] See G. Rittersporn, J. Behrends and M. Rolfe, 'Exploring Public Spheres in Regimes of the Soviet Type: A Possible Approach', in G. Rittersporn, J. Behrends and M. Rolfe eds., *Public Spheres in Soviet-Type Societies: Between the Great Show of the Party-State and Religious Counter-Cultures*, Frankfurt-am-Main: Peter Lang, 2003, p. 33.

[22] See B. Tromly, 'Re-Imagining the Soviet Intelligentsia: Student Politics and University Life, 1948–1964', Ph.D. Dissertation, Harvard University, 2007.

[23] Interview with Vitalii Skuratovskii, in L. Polikovskaya, *'My predchuvstvie . . . predtecha'*, p. 114.

A brief look at the policing of the readings at Mayakovsky Square provides a useful snapshot of efforts to stifle dissent at the time. The fact that those who gathered at the Square were not immediately arrested, and were never arrested in the vast majority of cases, tells us something about the extent to which the regime's approach had changed since even the early Khrushchev period. Nonetheless, the security organs and the Komsomol kept a very close eye on events. Komsomol detachments patrolled the meetings (though the security organs accused them of doing nothing useful), KGB agents furtively photographed participants, carried out heavy-handed searches for banned literature, apprehended would-be readers at nearby metro stations, tried to provoke fights at the Square and summoned individual attendees for prophylactic 'chats'. Moscow's Komsomol Central Committee ordered lists to be drawn up containing the names of all those who either read at Mayakovsky Square or attended the sessions. These individuals were then to be targeted for public censure at Komsomol meetings and criticised by name in a selection of major newspapers and journals.[24] More than a few also found themselves expelled both from university and the Komsomol. Rather than simply shutting down the poetry readings by force, the Moscow city Komsomol first offered to set up a discussion club to replace the open-air gatherings. Of course, this was not simply a kind gesture. In the first instance, they wanted to put an end to the 'public' aspect of the meetings so as to protect official dominance of the public sphere. Once under the stewardship of the Komsomol, it would also have been possible for the authorities to monitor participants' political positions more effectively, stifling any unwelcome ideological currents.[25] Doubtless aware of all this, the Mayakovsky Square attendees rejected the Komsomol's offer.

When initial measures failed to keep people from attending the readings, the next step was always liable to be more forceful. Vladimir Bukovsky, for example, wrote of an occasion when he was accosted on his way home one evening, bundled into a passing car and driven to an unknown location where he was beaten for several hours before being warned that he would be killed if he went to the Square again.[26] The assailants were, according to Bukovsky, members of the 'Komsomol Operative Detachments': volunteer

[24] TsKhDMO, f. 1, op. 3, ed. khr. 1062, in L. Polikovskaya, *'My predchuvstvie . . . predtecha'.*

[25] See G. Tsipursky, 'Pleasure, Power and the Pursuit of Communism: Soviet Youth and State-Sponsored Popular Culture during the Early Cold War Period, 1945–1968', Ph.D. Dissertation, University of North Carolina at Chapel Hill, 2011, p. 253.

[26] V. Bukovsky, *To Build a Castle: My Life as a Dissenter*, London: Andre Deutsch, 1978, p. 126.

youth groups that were formed to assist the work of state organs.[27] Groups such as these were another element of the on-going attempt to involve society in the work of the Party-state, blurring the traditional state–society dichotomy. They not only helped to embed the authorities' viewpoint on dissenters, and increased the number of 'boots on the ground' in terms of policing, but they were also a useful way of carrying out the dirty work (such as the beating of Bukovsky) that the KGB and police were no longer quite so free to do themselves. As Oleg Kharkhordin has shown, volunteer groups drunk on their own sense of power could be even harsher than the official law-enforcement agencies.[28] With this point in mind, one is drawn to Joseph Brodsky's withering assessment of such state-sponsored initiatives as 'a cheap way to make fascists out of the population'.[29] They also showed that although ideological energy may have been dimming on the whole, plenty of Soviet citizens were still entirely prepared to participate in helping suppress alternative currents of behaviour.

The policing of the poetry readings was a fairly useful reflection of the way that most dissent was handled by the authorities throughout much of the post-Stalin era. There was generally a semblance of legality on the surface of events but all manner of machinations, provocations and abuse took place out of sight. Acts such as beatings were probably not explicitly sanctioned at the highest level – and almost certainly would not have been committed to paper by anyone involved – but neither would events like the assault suffered by Bukovsky have happened entirely spontaneously. There would certainly have been an institutional acceptance of such practices within the KGB. In short, improvements to the legal system were never intended to benefit dissenters and non-conformists, and there was no real institutional commitment to observing legality on the part of the security organs.[30]

Nevertheless, running concurrently with the tightening-up of punitive policy that was largely taking place away from the public gaze, the onset of the 1960s also witnessed a renewed attempt at revitalising the ideological appeal of the Soviet system. In fact, there seemed to be plenty of grounds for optimism in the communist future at the start of the 1960s. The USSR had

---

[27] Louise Shelley also wrote that the Komsomol Operative Detachments were often involved in conducting heavy-handed searches for *samizdat* literature among students. L. Shelley, *Policing Soviet Society: The Evolution of State Control*, London: Routledge, 1996, p. 113.

[28] See O. Kharkhordin, *The Collective and the Individual in Russia: A Study of Practices*, Berkeley, CA: University of California Press, 1999, p. 286.

[29] S. Volkov, *Conversations with Joseph Brodsky*, New York: The Free Press, 1998, p. 59.

[30] R. Sharlet, 'De-Stalinization and Soviet Constitutionalism', in S. Cohen, A. Rabinowitch and R. Sharlet eds., *The Soviet Union since Stalin*, Bloomington, IN: Indiana University Press, 1980, p. 104.

just put the first man in space, it was the reigning champion in European football, it had topped the medals table at the 1960 Rome Olympics, and boasted many of the world's leading names in science and culture. New clients and allies were emerging all the time in Latin America, Africa and Asia. For many people both inside and outside of the USSR, the Soviet Union seemed to be winning the Cold War as the world entered the 1960s.

One of the most notable attempts to reinvigorate the Soviet system in the 1960s was the Third Party Programme, which was adopted at the XXII CPSU Congress in October 1961 and represented an attempt to 'reunify society in the wake of deStalinization and to revive the Soviet project'.[31] Asserting that socialism had now been built in the USSR and the Party's next goal was to move on toward the final construction of communism, the Programme returned to the concept of the withering away of the state. It promised greater intra-Party democracy and improving living standards for all, and declared the end of class struggle under the dictatorship of the proletariat, reclassifying the USSR under the distinctly inclusive title of an 'all-people's state'. Seemingly offering something for everyone, the new Programme was deeply idealistic and progressive, but equally unrealistic.

Although it again faded quite quickly, there was once more a renewed sense of optimism among those who hoped for reform within the existing system. It was at this time, for example, that Elena Bonner – who would later become one of the regime's most trenchant critics – decided to join the Party out of a desire to help 'correct' its problems.[32] Some of the hopes for reform that had been expressed in the spring of 1956 resurfaced, though they usually tended to be expressed neither so publicly nor so optimistically the second time around.[33] When one of the participants in the Mayakovsky Square readings – which were being forcefully curtailed even as the XXII Congress took place just a few hundred metres away – wrote to the Central Committee protesting at the way attendees were being hounded by the KGB and Komsomol, the discourse of the XXII Congress was immediately foregrounded. The Mayakovsky Square participant wrote that 'it has become entirely clear that the questions being discussed at Mayakovsky Square correspond with those which were raised by delegates at the XXII

---

[31] A. Titov, 'The 1961 Party Programme and the fate of Khrushchev's Reforms', in M. Ilič and J. Smith eds., *Soviet State and Society under Nikita Khrushchev*, London: Routledge, 2009, p. 8. The previous two Party Programmes had been produced in 1903 and 1919.

[32] Bonner left the Party in 1972, though Jay Bergman notes that she had 'left in all but name' by 1968. J. Bergman, *Meeting the Demands of Reason: The Life and Thought of Andrei Sakharov*, Ithaca, NY: Cornell University Press, 2009, p. 186.

[33] See also B. Tromly, 'Re-Imagining the Soviet Intelligentsia'.

Congress and were included in the Party's resolutions. It is exactly among the participants of these readings that the decisions of the XXII CPSU Congress find understanding and support.'[34] This was to some extent a tactical feint but, on certain themes and in certain quarters, the political positions of dissenters could still be quite close to official pronouncements. While its aftermath may not have been as uproarious as that of the XX Congress – in large part because the authorities had made sure they were better prepared to deal with critics this time – the XXII Congress did at least seem to promise a return to deStalinization, though that promise was to go largely unfulfilled.

There was little or nothing that most Soviet citizens could stridently oppose in the content of the Third Party Programme, and it remained the regime's principal ideological statement until the collapse of the Soviet system, but it also reflected the onset of a deeper problem. As Petr Vail' and Aleksandr Genis argued in their influential study on the 1960s USSR, nobody really believed in the literal meaning of the Programme, but instead saw in it whatever they wanted to.[35] This was a far less dangerous way to reanimate society than the promise of a 'return to Leninism'. However, the result was that people were increasingly able to support and display loyalty to what they saw as the fundamentals of the system without actually implementing its specific pre-scriptions in their everyday lives, a process that Alexei Yurchak termed 'reproducing the system and participating in its continuous internal displace-ment'.[36] Within the framework of the present study there is little that can be said in regard to Yurchak's assertion that this displacement helped facilitate the way that Soviet communism eventually collapsed, though the evidence pre-sented throughout much of this book does support his pinpointing of the early 1960s as a time in which key changes that had allowed this displacement to emerge were taking place within the Soviet system.

Just as the themes of dissent were evolving amongst the intelligentsia around this time, so were the forms that it took. Participation in under-ground groups and attempts to stir up the masses were to a large extent becoming a thing of the past.[37] This was partly because they had

---

[34] 'VTsK KPSS po povodu publishniikh chtenii i discussii na ploshchadi Mayakovskogo', in L. Polikovskaya ed., *'My predchuvstvie . . . predtecha'*.

[35] P. Vail' and A. Genis, *60-e: mir sovetskogo cheloveka*, p. 5.

[36] A. Yurchak, *Everything was Forever Until it Was No More: The Last Soviet Generation*, Oxford: Princeton University Press, 2006, p. 283.

[37] As Elina Zavadskaya and Olga Edelman point out, the number of groups uncovered by the KGB actually grew around the end of the 1960s. See E. Zavadskaya and O. Edelman, 'Underground Groups and Organisations', in V. Kozlov, S. Fitzpatrick and S. Mironenko eds., *Sedition: Everyday Resistance in the Soviet Union under Khrushchev and Brezhnev*, New Haven, CT: Yale University Press,

consistently proved both dangerous and ineffective but also because there was a growing belief that such behaviour could only ever lead to a different kind of tyranny. As Petro Grigorenko famously wrote years later: 'in the underground one can meet only rats'.[38] In place of the often isolated and ephemeral nature of underground activity, more flexible, enduring and dynamic forms of protest emerged. One of the most important conduits facilitating this shift was *samizdat* literature.

Groups of friends coming together and reading proscribed or unknown writers was not an entirely new phenomenon, having existed even during the Stalin years. By the late 1950s, though, this kind of behaviour had started to grow beyond intimate groups, taking in ever-larger circles of like-minded individuals and incorporating a widening array of proscribed works. Prose by Evgeny Zamyatin, Ivan Bunin and Mikhail Bulgakov was joined by the poetry of Osip Mandelshtam, Nikolai Gumilev and Marina Tsvetayeva. Home-made translations of banned works by Western authors such as Arthur Koestler, George Orwell and Ernest Hemingway also began to surface inside the USSR.[39] Bearing in mind the extent to which the first two of these three Western authors had already done so much to influence foreign perceptions of the Soviet system, and had fundamentally shaped discourse on totalitarianism in the West, this was a development that bore clear political overtones for readers inside the USSR.[40]

One of the most important social environments for literature such as this were the *kompaniya* that emerged in the years following Stalin's death: these were informal and often overlapping groups of anything up to about fifty friends meeting – usually in private – to talk politics and share stories, jokes, drinks, music and much else besides. Again, they tended not to be politically hostile in tone – since many participants retained a desire to make the Soviet system work – though they can broadly be described as culturally and ideologically non-conformist, and they more than once spawned overtly oppositional sub-groups from within their midst. As Juliane Fürst points out, they represented both an attempt to withdraw into the private sphere of friends and family and an attempt to create

2011, p. 285. By that stage, however, a growing number of those groups were primarily nationalist or religious in nature. There were still some political groups coming to light, primarily among disgruntled workers in the provinces.

[38] P. Grigorenko, *V podpol'e mozhno vstretit' tol'ko krys*, New York: Letinets, 1981.
[39] See A. Daniel, 'Istoki i smysl sovetskogo samizdata', in M. Barbakadze and E. Shvarts eds., *Antologiya samizdata*, pp. 17–33.
[40] On the influence of Koestler's *Darkness at Noon* and Orwell's *1984* in shaping the totalitarian school of Sovietology see A. Krylova, 'The Tenacious Liberal Subject in Soviet Studies', *Kritika: Explorations in Russian and Eurasian History*, Vol. 1, No. 1 (Winter 2000), 119–46.

something resembling an independent public sphere.[41] They were, how-ever, to be a quite short-lived phenomenon, dying out by the mid 1960s.[42] While one could not truly speak of anything resembling civil society in the USSR until well into the 1980s, the Khrushchev years did at least witness some initial attempts at creating such an environment among members of the intelligentsia.

From out of this milieu a handful of self-published literary journals also began to appear around the end of the 1950s. Widely regarded as the principal pioneer of *samizdat*, Aleksandr Ginzburg compiled three volumes of his literary anthology *Syntaxis* (*Sintaksis*) and distributed around 300 copies of each among friends in Moscow and Leningrad between 1959 and 1960.[43] Although its primary importance lay in the role it played in marking the emergence of the *samizdat* genre, the journal was not without real cultural significance: among the notable authors whose work featured in *Syntaxis* were Joseph Brodsky, later to win the Nobel Prize for Literature, and Bulat Okudzhava, who would go on to become the most famous of the Soviet 'guitar-poets' and whose statue now stands in the Arbat district of central Moscow. Having already compiled and distributed three issues of *Syntaxis*, Ginzburg was in the process of completing a fourth when, on 14 July 1960, the Moscow *oblast'* Procurator's office sanctioned his arrest.

The scope and number of unofficial materials like these soon grew quickly. In Lithuania and Ukraine, too, *samizdat* journals began to appear around the end of the 1950s, soon spreading to other republics and lan-guages of the USSR. In Armenia, nationalists would begin to publish their own underground newspaper. By the 1960s Soviet Baptists were distribut-ing their *Fraternal Pamphlet*, encouraging support for the Initiative Group of Baptists. In Kiev, the Club of Creative Youth became a hotbed of intellectual ferment and Taras Shevchenko a rallying point for the defence of Ukrainian culture.[44] Starting in the October that Khrushchev was ousted, Roy Medvedev's monthly *Political Diary* was to circulate widely among intellectuals and members of the political establishment for a

[41] See J. Fürst, 'Friends in Private, Friends in Public: The Phenomenon of the *Kompaniia* among Soviet Youth in the 1950s and 1960s', in L. Siegelbaum ed., *Borders of Socialism: Private Spheres of Soviet Russia*, Basingstoke: Palgrave Macmillan, 2006, pp. 229–49.

[42] A. Alexeyeva and P. Goldberg, *The Thaw Generation: Coming of Age in the Post-Stalin Era*, Boston, MA: Little, Brown and Company, 1990, p. 83.

[43] Since these 300 copies would most likely have been reproduced potentially many times by those who acquired them, it impossible to say how many copies circulated altogether.

[44] See B. Tromly, 'An Unlikely National Revival: Soviet Higher Learning and the Ukrainian "Sixties", 1953–65', *Russian Review*, Vol. 68, No. 4 (October 2009), 607–22.

number of years.[45] Following Ginzburg's arrest in 1960, Mayakovsky Square attendees Vitalii Skuratovskii and Anatolii Yakobson produced their own *samizdat* poetry journal named *Cocktail* (*Kokteil'*), while Yuri Galanskov compiled the almanac *Phoenix* (*Feniks*) and Vladimir Osipov created *Boomerang* (*Bumerang*). Soon after, Mikhail Kaplan put together and circulated two volumes of *Sirens* (*Sirena*) in the first half of 1962 – both of which were dominated by the poems of people who had read out their work at the Square.[46] This cycle of dissent followed by repression, which then generated its own secondary protests, was the mark of an increasing refusal to be cowed among the dissenting intelligentsia.

While such overt acts of dissent still remained limited, there were plenty of signs of a wider cultural non-conformity and political heterodoxy growing within society. Much as later years would see a thriving black market in Western music emerging in Soviet towns and cities, so the early 1960s witnessed the appearance of seemingly extensive trading in banned literature. A 1963 KGB report detailing a series of surprise checks on marketplace bookstalls in the capital outlined findings including pornography, political works by Trotsky and copies of *Dr Zhivago*.[47] Some of these early Soviet entrepreneurs were making good money out of such literature. In June 1964 *Vechernyaya Moskva* called one such trader 'Valya the Millionaire', branding him 'an inveterate speculator and parasite'.[48] The same article then complained that instead of fighting against it, respectable citizens, such as scholars and artists, were embracing this trade in illegal literature. Pirate radio, which the authorities referred to as 'radio hooliganism', was also on the increase by the end of the 1950s. Although pirate stations were most often dedicated to playing Western music, rather than raising political issues, legislation soon appeared banning it throughout the USSR's fifteen republics.[49] By this point the constantly proliferating challenges to cultural and political orthodoxy, even though they did not present a direct or immediate threat to the authority of the regime, were truly

---

[45] See S. Cohen ed., *An End to Silence: Uncensored Opinion in the Soviet Union, from Roy Medvedev's Magazine 'Political Diary'*, New York: W.W. Norton, 1982.

[46] See M. Barbakadze and E. Shvarts, eds., *Antologiya samizdata*. Other notable *samizdat* journals from the Khrushchev era included *Vremena goda*, *Fonarb*, *Masterskaya* and *Bom!* See E. Afanas'eva and V. Afiani eds., *Ideologicheskie komissii TsK KPSS 1958–1964: dokumenty*, Moskva: Rosspen, 1998.

[47] RGANI, f. 5, op. 55, d. 21, ll. 264–5, in V. Afiani et al. eds., *Kul'tura i vlast' ot Stalina do Gorbacheva: apparat TsK KPSS i kul'tura, 1958–1964*, Moskva: Rosspen, 2005.

[48] Budapest, HU OSA 300-80-1, Box 44.

[49] See S. Zhuk, *Rock and Roll in the Rocket City: The West, Identity, and Ideology in Soviet Dnepropetrovsk, 1960–1985*, Washington, DC: Woodrow Wilson Center Press, 2010, p. 32. See also P. Taylor, 'Underground Broadcasting in the Soviet Union', *Russian Review*, Vol. 31, No. 2 (April 1972), 173–4.

alarming as they were entirely incompatible with the regime's desire for tight control of public life.

From the early 1960s, *samizdat* began to undergo qualitative and quantitative shifts that would see the volume of uncensored literature in circulation growing exponentially and tackling ever more politically sensitive themes. By the middle of the decade it was '. . . no longer about texts that had been rejected by the censor, but about texts that were never intended for the censor'.[50] *Samizdat* authors were therefore moving further beyond the boundaries of acceptable comment. Like Western radio broadcasts, the genre represented another breach in the regime's information blockade that had long been so important in helping to keep society compliant.[51]

Unlike Western radio, *samizdat* was a distinctly polyphonic medium whose content was dictated not just by foreign information and agendas but by Soviet citizens themselves: it raised the political, intellectual and moral issues that were most important to them. It created a new forum for the spread of information, debate and discussion, helping to expand further the philosophical horizons of its audience and creating what Vyacheslav Igrunov termed 'an infrastructure of independent thought' of the kind that had been just about stamped out by Stalinism.[52] Nonetheless, this point can rather easily be overstated. *Samizdat* literature could also be distinctly Soviet in content and outlook. As Serguei Oushakine points out, this was still a forum that relied heavily upon the themes, discursive framework and rhetorical devices employed by the authorities.[53] Like those who wrote it, *samizdat* was not wholly detached from the stimuli provided by the Soviet system but was recognisably a part of it. Indeed, this was true of alternative public spheres more widely: stepping outside of the direct control of the authorities did not at all add up to being free of the influence of the Soviet system.[54]

Importantly, *samizdat* also contributed to the establishment of rudimentary networks of dissenters as works were passed from hand to hand. All those involved in the production, reproduction, reading and dissemination

[50] A. Daniel, 'Istoki i smysl sovetskogo samizdata', in M. Barbakadze and E. Shvarts eds., *Antologiya samizdata*, pp. 19–20.
[51] Outside of the biggest cities, though, *samizdat* could be particularly hard to come by. See, for example, D. Raleigh ed., *Russia's Sputnik Generation: Soviet Baby Boomers Talk about their Lives*, Bloomington, IN: Indiana University Press, 2006.
[52] V. Igrunov, 'Vvedenie', in M. Barbakadz and E. Shvarts eds., *Antologiya samizdata*, p. 10.
[53] S. Oushakine, 'The Terrifying Mimicry of Samizdat'.
[54] See, for example, G. Rittersporn, M. Rolfe and J. Behrends, 'Thoughts on the Public Sphere in Soviet-Type Systems', in G. Rittersporn, J. Behrends and M. Rolf, eds., *Public Spheres in Soviet-Type Societies*, p.40.

of illicit material shared a conscious disobedience of official political dictates. These emerging networks also provide further evidence of a private
sphere that was 'in dynamic interactive tension with the public sphere',
rather than one that had been entirely eviscerated or else hermetically sealed
off from public life.[55] Like the *listovki* discussed in previous chapters, these
were documents that tended to centre upon the policies and behaviour of
the authorities and were produced (and reproduced) in private among the
public. Where *samizdat* literature represented an advance on the already
declining practice of distributing *listovki* was in the secondary reproduction
and further diffusion of the works in question.[56] Leaflets would be distributed in a town or city and then within a matter of hours disappeared forever
from the public domain. Provided they aroused people's interest, *samizdat*
works could be continually retyped and circulated to an ever-wider audience, both inside the USSR and abroad, allowing the ideas they expressed to
accumulate, evolve and grow.

The growth of *samizdat* literature and the forging of personal bonds
between critics of the regime were not the only ways that events at
Mayakovsky Square had a tangible influence upon the future human-rights
movement. The ending of the poetry readings in October 1961 proved the
catalyst for a further shift in the evolution of Soviet dissent. The reason
the meetings had finally been brought to a decisive halt by the authorities
was the arrest of two of the main organisers: Vladimir Osipov and Eduard
Kuznetsov. Both had been involved in an abortive plot to assassinate
Khrushchev, though by the time of their arrest friends had actually persuaded
the pair to call off the attempt.[57] Nonetheless, the KGB got wind of the plan,
arrested those involved and initiated a decisive crackdown at the Square.

The most significant outcome of the affair with Osipov and Kuznetsov
was a growing rejection of underground activity and an increasing adher-
ence to the legalistic and non-violent forms of protest that were already
being espoused by Aleksandr Esenin-Volpin.[58] The obvious futility of the

[55] L. Siegelbaum, 'Introduction: Mapping Private Spheres in the Soviet Context', in L. Siegelbaum ed.,
Borders of Socialism, p. 3. These views on private spheres in the USSR are best represented by
O. Kharkhordin, *The Collective and the Individual in Russia*, and V. Shlapentokh, *A Normal
Totalitarian Society: How the Soviet Union Functioned and How it Collapsed*, New York: Oxford
University Press, 2001.

[56] On the theme of what did and did not constitute *samizdat* literature, see A. Daniel, 'Istoki i smysl
sovetskogo samizdata', in M. Barbakadze and E. Shvarts eds., *Antologiya samizdata*.

[57] The plot had been drawn up by an acquaintance named Anatoly Ivanov. The actual assassin was to be
a man named Vitaly Rementsov. Both were arrested and subsequently confined in psychiatric
institutes.

[58] Interview with Aleksandr Esenin-Volpin, Revere, MA, November 2006.

assassination plot was of itself important, but events at the trial left a more lasting mark. Like the public statements of Soviet leaders, the Soviet constitution promised all manner of rights and freedoms that were not granted in practice. Most of society had come to acquiesce in this reality and showed little interest in laws that seemingly existed only on paper. The answer, Esenin-Volpin argued, was to take the regime at its word: to behave within the law and to demand that the state did the same. It was an argument that few of Esenin-Volpin's circle had taken seriously at first, though this began to change in 1962.

Although Osipov and Kuznetsov's spring 1962 trial was officially declared 'open', like most other proceedings against dissenters it was in reality very much closed. Nonetheless, Esenin-Volpin had studied the Soviet constitution, had learned his rights under the law and demanded access to the trial. Bukovsky summed up his successful entry to the court in the following way: 'Little did we realise that this absurd incident, with the comical Alik Volpin brandishing his criminal code like a magic wand to melt the doors of the court, was the beginning of our civil-rights movement and the movement for human rights in the USSR.'[59] Of course, there were also plenty of other factors at play in the emergence of the human-rights movement, but this undoubtedly was a pivotal moment that demonstrated the changing dynamics of dissenting behaviour. What Esenin-Volpin had done was to hasten a change in the rules of engagement between dissenters and authority. At the same time, however, this emerging emphasis on the laws and rights that were set out in the constitution ensured that the discourse of dissidents and authorities remained joined at the hip, which was to prove both a strength and a weakness for the subsequent dissident cause. As Serguei Oushakine points out, it gave dissidents a framework to represent themselves as political subjects but also meant that they struggled to offer a coherent and compelling alternative view on the Soviet system, whether they hoped to or not.[60]

Interestingly, the security organs' perception of this change in the nature of dissent was very different to that of Esenin-Volpin and friends. Vasily Mitrokhin's cache of KGB files, spirited out of the Russia shortly after the Soviet collapse, provide a telling insight in this regard. They indicate that the dissent of the early Khrushchev years was retrospectively viewed by the

---

[59] V. Bukovsky, *To Build a Castle*, p. 131. Esenin-Volpin also attempted to file a libel case against an *Ogonek* journalist named Shatunovskii after he had written in the journal that Volpin was a 'villain'. See B. Nathans, 'The Dictatorship of Reason: Aleksandr Vol'pin and the Idea of Rights Under "Developed Socialism"', *Slavic Review*, Vol. 66, No. 4 (Winter 2007), 632.
[60] S. Oushakine, 'The Terrifying Mimicry of Samizdat'.

organs as fundamentally loyal, but that of the 1960s onwards was seen as distinctly subversive.[61] To our eyes this presents a rather startling paradox: dissenters who emphasised the observance of the law and peaceful protest were viewed as more subversive than those who had formed underground groups and called for the country's political leaders to be beaten or even killed. In the first instance, this tells us that Andrei Amalrik was probably right to argue that the Soviet authorities found it much harder to deal with open and legalistic protest than they did with earlier, more volatile, forms of dissent.[62] Much as criminal prisoners in the camps were seen as 'socially closer' to the regime than were politicals, so the hooligan dissenters were socially closer than intelligentsia liberals.

Evidently, we are also looking at a slightly different conception of 'subversion' to that with which we are familiar today. One of the key issues here was the authorities' determination to preserve their hegemony over popular discourse. The isolated and unknown dissenters of the early Khrushchev years in particular were never likely to have a major impact in this regard outside of a few brief periods of heightened domestic and international tensions. In later years dissidents did at least have the means available to them (primarily through *samizdat* and foreign-radio broadcasts) to make a genuine impact on popular consciousness. Most important in shaping the KGB's assessment, however, was dissenters' increased interaction with Western media and Western political figures from the 1960s onwards. On both an ideological and a practical level, there was little that could be more subversive in the eyes of the Soviet authorities than this link to 'the main enemy'. Indeed, many ordinary Soviet citizens found this new focus on the West more than a little unpalatable.[63]

While Esenin-Volpin's own experiences of arrest, interrogation and imprisonment, as well as his contrarian personality and his mathematician's emphasis on logic over emotion, were a vital catalyst for this emerging change of direction in dissenting behaviour, it was also rooted in the events

[61] See V. Mitrokhin, 'Non-conformism. Evolution of the 'democratic movement' as a politically harmful process since the mid 1950s', Folder 9, Woodrow Wilson Center, Washington, DC, Cold War International History Project Virtual Archive, Mitrokhin Archive.

[62] See F. Barghoorn, 'Regime–Dissenter Relations after Khrushchev: Some Observations', in S. Gross Solomon ed., *Pluralism in the Soviet Union: Essays in Honour of H. Gordon Skilling*, London: Macmillan, 1983, p. 135.

[63] Ludmilla Alexeyeva, for example, recalled of her initial response to Andrei Sinyavsky and Yuli Daniel smuggling satirical literary works out to the West that 'It was one thing to tell the truth at home. It was something else to tell it to outsiders, many of whom were genuine enemies of our country.' L. Alexeyeva, *The Thaw Generation*, p. 113.

of the preceding decade.[64] The new law codes and codes of criminal procedure that had been introduced since the late 1950s, for example, were to become fundamental tools of the human-rights movement. The re-establishment of 'socialist legality' and the ending of arbitrary rule had been central themes of discussion during the era. Some, such as Khrushchev and Chief Procurator Roman Rudenko, had gone to considerable lengths to emphasise that the authorities were serious about legal propriety; this was not entirely window-dressing. Again, we can see the extent to which dissident thought and official discourse could be intimately connected. In November 1962 they would briefly become closer than they had been at any time since the Secret Speech.

Khrushchev's renewed attack on Stalin at the XXII CPSU Congress, and *Novy mir* editor Aleksandr Tvardovsky's call for writers to submit more challenging works to his journal, had found a willing audience in the Ryazan schoolteacher Aleksandr Solzhenitsyn. With the encouragement and assistance of his friend and former camp-mate Lev Kopelev, Solzhenitsyn took his story named simply *Shch-854* out of its hiding-place and submitted it to *Novy mir*.[65] With a little careful manoeuvring and some vital inside help, his manuscript landed on the editor's desk on 7 December 1961.[66] Upon reading it, Tvardovsky immediately threw his entire weight behind Solzhenitsyn's story. He managed to evade the proper censorship channels and have the work presented directly to Khrushchev by his trusted assistant Vladimir Lebedev. Khrushchev instantly saw the story's political value and threw his even more considerable weight behind it, bending his colleagues in the Presidium and officials at *Glavlit* (the state censorship body) to his will as he did so. This whole process reflected one of the key political differences between the Khrushchev and Brezhnev eras. The workings of the system did not necessarily become a great deal more conservative after Khrushchev, since the bureaucracy was already hide-bound during his time in power, but those few individuals who had both the will and power to effect dramatic

---

[64] For an excellent account of Aleksandr Esenin-Volpin's personal and political development see Ben Nathans, 'The Dictatorship of Reason'. Interestingly, Boris Vail' noted that when Ernst Orlovskii – also a mathematician by training – was arrested and interrogated in 1957, he, too, proved adept at deploying Soviet law against his interrogators long before this became commonplace among dissenters. B. Vail', *Osobo opasnyi*, London: Overseas Publications Interchange, 1980, p. 192.

[65] As Michael Scammell points out: '*Shch* is the twenty-sixth letter of the Russian alphabet. If each preceding letter stands for 999 prisoners in the camp, then [Ivan Denisovich] Shukov is the 25,829th prisoner, a vivid indication to Soviet readers of how big the camps were.' M. Scammell, *Solzhenitsyn: A Biography*, New York: W.W. Norton, 1984, p. 384.

[66] On the subsequent scandal that grew up around Solzhenitsyn's personal and professional criticism of Tvardovsky and his account of the publication process behind *Ivan Denisovich*, see E. Rogovin-Frankel, 'The Tvardovsky Controversy', *Soviet Studies*, Vol. 34, No. 4 (October 1982), 601–15.

steps like this (such as Tvardovsky at *Novy mir* and Khrushchev within the Central Committee Presidium) were gone. Since the prospects for deStalinization largely hung on a few such individuals (and Khrushchev in particular) it would first prove spasmodic up until the mid 1960s, and could then be easily killed off thereafter.

The story *Shch-854* was to become Solzhenitsyn's seminal debut novella, *One Day in the Life of Ivan Denisovich*. It was published in the November 1962 edition of *Novy mir* and immediately caused a huge sensation, finally bringing the issue of Stalin's labour camps into the public domain in conditions of complete openness.[67] In terms of subject-matter, this was the most daring literary publication to come out of the entire post-Stalin period, and one that the First Secretary let it be known that he had pushed through against the resistance of practically all his colleagues.[68] The fact that *Ivan Denisovich* broached one of the key taboos of the time yet was officially sanctioned – and therefore available on open sale and in public libraries – granted it a truly massive audience across the Soviet Union and beyond.[69] According to the *New York Times*, the initial print-run sold out in only a few hours and copies were quickly changing hands for as much as $10 each.[70] With total Soviet print-runs eventually topping a million copies, and many of those being passed from person to person until they fell apart, one can safely say that *Ivan Denisovich* was popular well beyond the liberal intelligentsia, in a way that much of the previous 'thaw literature' had not always been.[71]

As well as bringing the crimes of the Stalin era back to the fore, and making a global star of a man who would go on to become one of

[67] As Bohdan Nahaylo and Viktor Swoboda point out, a number of important anti-Stalin works were published in some of the non-Russian languages of the USSR and consequently did not receive the widespread attention or acclaim that those of Russian authors enjoyed. It was, for example, in Latvia that the first depiction of Siberian exile was published, back in December 1956. See B. Nahaylo and V. Swoboda, *Soviet Disunion: A History of the Nationalities Problem in the USSR*, New York: The Free Press, 1990, p. 124.

[68] There are numerous accounts of Khrushchev's personal involvement in the publication of *Ivan Denisovich*. Aside from Solzhenitsyn's own memoirs, some of the most informative and revealing works are V. Lakshin, *Solzhenitsyn, Tvardovsky and Novy Mir*, Cambridge, MA: MIT Press, 1980, and P. Johnson, *Khrushchev and the Arts: The Politics of Soviet Culture, 1962–1964*, Cambridge, MA: MIT Press, 1965.

[69] *Ivan Denisovich* was also very well received in Western Europe and the US, where competing translations (one Soviet-endorsed and one unofficial) resulted in a court battle which attracted even greater publicity for Solzhenitsyn's novella.

[70] RGANI, f. 5, op. 55, d. 44, ll. 39–51, in V. Afiani et al. eds., *Kul'tura i vlast'*.

[71] In addition to its usual print-run of around 140,000 copies, Tvardovsky had an extra 40,000 copies of *Novy mir* produced that month. In January 1963 *Roman-Gazeta* printed an additional 750,000 and *Sovetskii pisatel'* added a further 100,000 copies the following month. All sold out quickly. Zh. Medvedev, *Ten Years after Ivan Denisovich*, London: Macmillan, 1973, p. 31.

communism's most trenchant critics, the novella's publication raised expectations of further revelations and reforms and inspired many thousands of former inmates to write their own camp stories and memoirs. Vladimir Shlapentokh's claim that the subsequent explosion of Gulag literature 'had an enormous impact on Soviet society and, in fact, altered the ideological climate in the country' appears an entirely fair assessment. The volume of letters flowing in to *Novy mir* concerning political changes that had taken place since Stalin's death grew dramatically.[72] All the awkward questions arising from the mass repressions of the previous era hung in the air once more.

Soon enough, the authorities sensed the problems that this theme could present were it to dominate public discourse, as it seemingly threatened to do.[73] Chastened by their failure to do so in the wake of the Secret Speech, the leadership quickly moved to offer ideological guidance on *Ivan Denisovich*. When Leonid Il'ichev raised the subject at the Ideological Commission on 26 December 1962, he accepted that the story was about 'painful matters' but insisted its positive message rejecting the Cult of Personality helped to educate and inspire people.[74] Not long after the meeting in question, though, the leadership decided to rein in the growth of this potentially dangerous new subject-matter before it gained further momentum. In typically earthy fashion, Khrushchev warned that the 'camp theme' would 'provide ammunition for our enemies and huge, fat flies will fall on such materials like dung'.[75] Sure enough, the wave of camp literature that *Ivan Denisovich* had inspired was not to be published. However, many of those manuscripts that would be rejected officially – such as Evgeniya Ginzburg's *Into the Whirlwind* and Varlam Shalamov's *Kolyma Tales* – did not simply disappear, but instead went into *samizdat*, meaning that the authorities lost the power to control the content and dictate the meaning of such works.

Although the relationship between Khrushchev and the liberal intelligentsia had been through numerous ups and downs already by the early 1960s, almost immediately after the high point of *Ivan Denisovich*'s publication that relationship again began a steep downward trajectory. On

---

[72] M. Dobson, 'Contesting the Paradigms of De-Stalinization: Readers' Responses to "One Day in the Life of Ivan Denisovich"', *Slavic Review*, Vol. 64, No. 3 (Autumn 2005), 589. As Dobson points out, readers' responses to *Ivan Denisovich* were by no means uniformly positive in their assessment of Solzhenitsyn's work or their attitude toward former Gulag inmates.

[73] As Zhores Medvedev noted, articles about *One Day in the Life of Ivan Denisovich* soon began to appear all across the national and provincial media, in newspapers and learned journals. Zh. Medvedev, *Ten Years after Ivan Denisovich*, p. 30.

[74] RGANI, f. 72, op. 1, d. 3, ll. 185–213, in E. Afanas'eva and V. Afiani eds., *Ideologicheskie komissii*.

[75] M. Scammell ed., *The Solzhenitsyn Files*, Chicago, IL: Edition Q inc, 1995, p. 3.

visiting an exhibition of modern art at Moscow's Manezh gallery on
1 December 1962, Khrushchev quickly flew into a rage and began crudely
abusing the artists, firstly accusing the sculptor Ernst Neizvestnyi of being a
homosexual: this was more than simply machismo taunting since homo-
sexuality was a punishable offence under Soviet law.[76] He then said that the
work on display was 'dog shit' and threatened to despatch several of the
artists to logging camps in the far north until they had paid off the money
that the state had wasted on them.[77] It has since come to light that the
confrontation in question was engineered by conservatives in the cultural
and political apparatus, with Mikhail Suslov apparently playing a leading
role. Even so, Khrushchev's splenetic and vulgar fury was entirely genuine
and the whole episode earned him no credit whatsoever amongst the
intelligentsia.[78] That being said, there were undoubtedly plenty of Soviet
citizens who sympathised with Khrushchev's diatribe against modern art.

The more conservative elements within the cultural establishment were
clearly in the ascendancy by this stage. Later that same month, on 17
December, the First Secretary addressed a meeting of 400 leading cultural
figures and railed against non-conformists in his audience. After again
targeting Neizvestnyi, Khrushchev ominously declared that 'only the
grave can cure the hunchback', whereupon the poet Evgeny Evtushenko
retorted: 'Nikita Sergeevich, we live in a time when mistakes are corrected
not by graves but by words.' On that note, Khrushchev declared a break in
the meeting. A week later, the Ideological Commission met to force home
the narrowing of the country's cultural horizons, with 140 writers, painters,
composers and cinema workers in attendance. Most of them acquiesced
without complaint. Leonid Il'ichev reported that Evtushenko's speech –
unlike his remarks at the 17 December meeting – had been 'much more
correct and intelligent'. Most acknowledged serious errors in their work,
among them Ernst Neizvestnyi, and assured the Commission that they
would respond to the 'serious but justified criticism of their mistakes'.[79]

[76] Neizvestnyi's now-famous response was to insist that were Khrushchev to find him a woman he would happily prove his sexuality to the First Secretary. See Yu. Gerchuk, *Krovoizliyanie v MOSKh, ili Khrushcheve v Manezhe 1 dekabrya 1962 goda*, Moskva: NLO, 2008.

[77] This scatological theme was also present in Vladimir Semichastnyi's attack on Boris Pasternak, in which the author was branded worse than a pig, since 'a pig does not foul where it eats and sleeps'. Semichastnyi later insisted that Khrushchev had ordered the then Komsomol first secretary to make exactly these remarks. V. Semichastnyi, *Bespokoinoe serdtse*, Moskva: Vagrius, 2002.

[78] On the way that the confrontation was provoked, see L. Rabichev, 'Manezh 1962, do i posle', *Znamya*, No. 9 (2001), 121–52. See also Yu. Aksyutin, *Khrushchevskaya 'ottepel' i obshchestvennye nastroenniya v SSSR v 1953 – 1964*, Moskva: Rosspen, 2004, pp. 397–8.

[79] RGANI, f. 72, op. 1, d. 3, ll. 214–15 in E. Afanas'eva and V. Afiani eds., *Ideologicheskie komissii*.

Only a few proved to be more stubborn, and refused to accept reproach. Bella Akhmadulina and Bulat Okudzhava in particular were singled out by Il'ichev for insisting that divisions and tensions within the cultural establishment were not a matter of ideological conflict but one of talentless dogmatists domineering over the talented.[80] In another meeting with leading cultural figures, at the Kremlin's House of the Unions in March 1963, the First Secretary again grew particularly animated and tore into members of his audience, particularly the poet Andrei Voznesensky, and declared that 'The thaw is over. This is not even a light morning frost. For you and your likes it will be the arctic frost. We are not those who belonged to the Petöfi Club. We are those who helped smash the Hungarians.'[81] On this last point, he was, of course, telling the truth. Had he remained in power for longer, there may well have been further spells of liberalisation in the future, but this was by no means clear in the spring of 1963.

A number of sources cite the fact that Solzhenitsyn was denied the 1964 Lenin Prize for Literature – for which he had been an obvious and deserved front-runner – as proof that the tide was also turning against the recently celebrated author.[82] Actually, there had already been signs that Solzhenitsyn was falling out of favour some time prior to this. When the American filmmaker L. Cohen visited Moscow in 1963 and proposed to make a film of *One Day in the Life of Ivan Denisovich* he was immediately given short shrift. A note sent from Ekaterina Furtseva, the presiding head of the Ministry of Culture, to the Central Committee bluntly recommended that 'all possible measures' be taken to prevent the film from being made.[83] Whether or not any concrete steps in this direction were undertaken by the Central Committee remains unclear, though Cohen's proposed film did not emerge.[84] By the summer of 1964, when Tvardovsky attempted to have Solzhenitsyn's next major work, *The First Circle*, passed for publication it became clear that his official favour had just about ebbed away, with Vladimir Lebedev refusing to provide direct access to his boss again and warning Tvardovsky that Khrushchev regretted having ever intervened to help publish *Ivan Denisovich*. His advice was that Solzhenitsyn's latest work be kept well hidden.[85]

---

[80] RGANI, f. 72, op. 1, d. 3, ll. 214–15 in E. Afanas'eva and V. Afiani eds., *Ideologicheskie komissii*.
[81] V. Zubok, *Zhivago's Children*, p. 214.
[82] See, for example, M. Scammell, *Solzhenitsyn: A Biography*.
[83] RGANI, f. 5, op. 55, d. 52, l. 36, in V. Afiani et al. eds., *Kul'tura i vlast'*.
[84] A film version of *One Day in the Life of Ivan Denisovich* did come out in 1970; this was a joint British–Norwegian project which failed to arouse significant attention.
[85] See M. Scammell, *Solzhenitsyn: A Biography*, p. 506.

By this time, Solzhenitsyn's fellow giant of the subsequent dissident movement, the physicist Andrei Sakharov, had also begun to find his voice as a critic of the authorities, though not yet of the Soviet system as a whole. The incident that Sakharov considered his first foray into what he called 'civic activity' had come after he grew increasingly alarmed at the terrible environmental damage being caused by nuclear-weapons testing. In July 1961 he personally called on Khrushchev not to sanction any further explosions in the open air. Khrushchev, however, was unimpressed at this perceived impudence. The result was a public dressing-down from the First Secretary in which Sakharov was sharply upbraided and warned not to meddle in politics. As Khrushchev would recall in his memoirs, this disagreement 'left its mark on Sakharov'.[86]

The following year, Soviet atmospheric testing of thermo-nuclear weapons was resumed. This provoked a 'spiritual break' for Sakharov. As he later recounted: 'I had an awful sense of powerlessness. After that I was a different man. I broke with my surroundings ... The atomic question was always half science, half politics ... It was a natural path into political issues.'[87] Thereafter, Sakharov was to remain a persistent thorn in the side of the Soviet authorities until his sudden death in 1989, by which time he was known the world over for his dissident activity and had become one of the most widely respected and revered figures in the USSR. Sakharov was not the only one who struggled to accept the resumption of nuclear testing in spring 1962, however. Komsomol records show students at MGU also had particularly heated discussions on the issue among themselves.[88] As an avowed pacifist, Yuri Galanskov, too, was deeply opposed to the move and planned to release balloons on Red Square in protest, though he ultimately decided it was too dangerous. He also hoped to create a pacifist organisation that would join the global disarmament movement, though these plans did not get off the ground either.[89]

Two years after his 'internal break', in June 1964, Sakharov took another major step towards confrontation with the authorities when he waded into the growing schism within the scientific community over the continued official support for Stalin's 'charlatan biologist' Trofim Lysenko. When one

[86] S. Khrushchev ed., *Memoirs of Nikita Khrushchev*, Vol. 2: *Reformer: 1945–1964*, University Park, PA: Pennsylvania State University Press, 2006, p. 493.

[87] J. Rubenstein and A. Gribanov eds., *The KGB File of Andrei Sakharov*, New Haven, CT: Yale University Press, 2005, p. 14.

[88] See TsAODM (Tsentral'nyi arkhiv obshchestvennykh dvizhenii Moskvy), f. 4, op. 135, ed. khr. 18, ll. 39–41, in L. Polikovskaya, *'My predchuvstvie ... predtecha'*.

[89] See G. Kaganovskii ed., *Khronika kazni Yuriya Galanskova v ego pis'makh iz zony ZhKh-385, svidetel' stvakh i dokumentakh*, Moskva: Agraf, 2006, pp. 23–5.

of Lysenko's associates, Nikolai Nuzhdin, was proposed for election as a full member of the prestigious USSR Academy of Sciences, Sakharov used his own status as a member of that body in an attempt to arouse opposition to the move. At the meeting where Nuzhdin was expected to be elected, Sakharov took to the rostrum and rounded on him, stating that '. . . together with academician Lysenko, he is responsible for the shameful backwardness of Soviet biology . . ., for the adventurism, for the degradation of learning and for the firing, arrest, and even death of many genuine scientists'.[90] This was an act that he later recalled as a significant early landmark on his personal path from 'father of the Soviet nuclear bomb' to winner of the 1975 Nobel Peace Prize.[91] The anti-Lysenko sentiment within Soviet science may have been fundamentally rooted in professional rather than political concerns, but continuing government support for Lysenko ensured that the two could never remain entirely distinct from one another.

It was not only members of the Soviet scientific community who showed resentment at unfulfilled professional expectations. In March 1964, the sentencing of the twenty-three-year-old Leningrad poet Joseph Brodsky on charges of parasitism signalled a further degradation of the relationship between the liberal intelligentsia and the political authorities. Brodsky's was a case that would begin to galvanise those seeking to resist both the narrowing of acceptable cultural bounds and a seeming return to repression in the cultural sphere. It would also advance important changes in the context of the confrontation between critics and authority in the USSR, pushing it toward the international stage. This was a process that had already begun when the likes of John Steinbeck, Graham Greene and Jawaharlal Nehru protested against the persecution of Boris Pasternak back in 1958, but one that would reach an entirely new level over the next few years.

The young poet Brodsky had already been temporarily detained by the authorities twice by this point: firstly, when his work appeared in Ginzburg's *Syntaxis* and, secondly, after the KGB found out about a long-aborted plot to escape the USSR by plane for Afghanistan. Brodsky later reasoned that by 1963, his KGB file had simply grown too big to ignore.[92]

---

[90] Unbeknownst to Sakharov, a number of other leading scientists, including Igor Tamm and Mikhail Leontovich, had already decided to speak out over Lysenko at this same meeting. See A. Sakharov, *Memoirs*, New York: Alfred A. Knopf, 1990, p. 234.

[91] See A. Sakharov, *Memoirs*, p. 235. Sakharov reported rumours to the effect that when Khrushchev found out about his attack on Lysenko he ordered KGB chief Semichastnyi to begin gathering compromising material on the physicist.

[92] S. Volkov, *Conversations with Joseph Brodsky*, p. 64.

Much like the moralistic attacks on non-conformist young people outlined in Chapter 7, his unkempt appearance and bohemian lifestyle formed the basis of a November 1963 piece in the newspaper *Vechernyi Leningrad* entitled 'A Quasi-Literary Drone', written by an apparently outraged citizen, and former KGB colonel, named Yakov Lerner. Brodsky, however, had little doubt that Lerner had been prompted to action by a higher power, his former employers in the security organs.[93] The media invective against the poet continued to focus on his supposedly immoral lifestyle and lack of 'Soviet' values until he was arrested and charged with parasitism in February 1964. A confidential KGB report from the time immediately disabused the notion that the case was genuinely about 'parasitism', especially since it began by referring to Brodsky as an 'author of ideologically harmful poetry'.[94] The trial took place over two sessions, on 18 February and 13 March 1964.[95] In court, Brodsky vigorously defended himself against the accusation that he was a social parasite and was ably supported by a number of defence witnesses who testified to his skill as a poet and translator and to his willingness to work. Of course, this was in itself significant, since the hostile attitude of the state was entirely apparent.[96] Prosecution experts and witnesses repeatedly stumbled over their lines and contradicted one another. Nonetheless, a sign on the courtroom door that read 'Trial of the parasite Brodsky' was commentary enough on the nature of the proceedings.[97] On 13 March he was duly convicted and exiled to work on a collective farm in the far north of Russia for five years.

The case did not quite end there, as the authorities doubtless expected it would. Where previously Pasternak had been defended primarily from abroad (and numerous Soviet cultural figures had been successfully corralled into joining the attacks on him), Brodsky found a number of heavyweight supporters within the Soviet cultural elite, especially after his friend Frida

---

[93] Brodsky was basically correct in this assumption, though the Leningrad Komsomol had also played a role in spurring the attack. Yakov Lerner was anyway a particularly vigorous pursuer of non-conformist young people, having already targeted three other Leningrad poets and a schoolteacher in much the same way. See M. Dobson, *Khrushchev's Cold Summer: Gulag Returnees, Crime and the Fate of Reform after Stalin*, Ithaca, NY: Cornell University Press, 2009, pp. 228–30.

[94] RGANI, f. 5, op. 30, d. 454, l. 98. On the anti-parasite campaign of the early 1960s, see S. Fitzpatrick, 'Social Parasites: How Tramps, Idle Youth and Busy Entrepreneurs Impeded the Soviet March to Communism', *Cahiers du Monde russe*, Vol. 47, No. 1–2 (janvier–juin 2006), 377–408.

[95] It was between these two dates that Brodsky was interned for psychiatric assessment at the Serbsky Institute (see previous chapter).

[96] As Dobson points out, several of those who defended Brodsky in court would subsequently be reprimanded by the Writers' Union.

[97] See R. Burford Jr, 'Getting the Bugs Out of Socialist Legality: The Case of Joseph Brodsky', *The American Journal of Comparative Law*, Vol. 22, No. 3 (Summer 1974), 464–508.

Vigdorova produced a transcript of the trial proceedings and released it into *samizdat*. Through widespread reproduction, there were soon thousands of copies in circulation, and its bare factual content was to be a major influence on the format of future materials produced by human-rights activists.[98]

An April 1964 KGB report to the Central Committee noted that Writers' Union members Lev Kopelev, Raisa Orlova and Lidiya Chukovskaya had stated that the Brodsky case represented a return to Stalinism. Evgeny Evtushenko wrote to Vigdorova, describing the trial as 'fascistic'. Numerous complaints centred upon breaches of proper legal procedure. Others, including the film director Samuil Marshak, the celebrated children's author and literary critic Kornei Chukovskii and the composer Dmitry Shostakovich, promised to petition in defence of Brodsky. All this prompted a number of European intellectuals, including the 1964 Nobel laureate Jean-Paul Sartre, as well as the British newspaper *The Guardian*, to speak out in Brodsky's defence.[99] Then, on 26 June 1964 the West German newspaper *Die Zeit* published a smuggled copy of Vigdorova's transcript of the court proceedings, showing the world just how deeply flawed and politicised the case against Brodsky had been, and in the process causing acute embarrassment for the authorities in Moscow.[100] This sense of embarrassment was all the more galling in view of the fact that the persecution of Brodsky appears to have been a local initiative, to which a series of high officials in Moscow responded negatively, criticising the amateurish way that the trial had been handled.[101] A commission was set up to review the case at the end of December 1964, and in July 1965 the poet's sentence was reduced from five years to eighteen months, and he was duly freed. This represented one of the first times that the combination of domestic and foreign pressure had been successfully brought to bear in such a case, providing a valuable precedent for future dissidents.

New evidence suggesting this was a local initiative necessarily casts doubt on the traditional view of the Brodsky affair as a kind of 'show trial' intended to intimidate non-conformist intellectuals. Nonetheless, the case was part of

---

[98] As Aleksandr Daniel points out, the subsequent trial of Andrei Sinyavsky and Yuli Daniel was similarly transcribed by attendees (most notably, the wives of the accused) and then appeared in Aleksandr Ginzburg's *The White Book*, one of the seminal documents of the Soviet human-rights movement. See A. Daniel, 'Istoki i smysl Sovetskogo samizdata', in M. Barbakadze and E Shvarts ed., *Antologiya samizdata*, pp. 17–33.

[99] RGANI, f. 5, op. 30, d. 454, ll. 98–100.   [100] See RGANI, f. 5, op. 55, d. 99, l. 118.

[101] Vladimir Kozlov lists KGB chairman Vladimir Semichastnyi, head of the Procuracy Roman Rudenko and chairman of the Supreme Court Alexander Gorkin as being among those who complained about the way the trial had been conducted. V. Kozlov, S. Fitzpatrick and S. Mironenko eds., *Sedition*, p. 55.

a general process of hardening responses toward the threat posed by cultural heterodoxy in the wake of the 1958 Pasternak scandal. The handling of the poetry readings at Mayakovsky Square, the 'arrest' of Vasily Grossman's *Life and Fate* in February 1961, the use of psychiatric imprisonment against Mikhail Naritsa, the parasitism case against Brodsky and later charges of anti-Soviet activity against Sinyavsky and Daniel all testified to the authorities' growing intransigence in this field.[102] Of course, there were also liberal works that received official sanction during this period, such as Evtushenko's *Stalin's Heirs* and Yuri Bondarev's *Silence*, as well as *Ivan Denisovich*, but those who attempted to operate outside of the system would find things increasingly dangerous, while those who worked within the rules found that scope for the expression of heterodox views narrowed considerably.

With this in mind, September 1965 represents something of a natural endpoint for the present study. On 8 September, the literary critic Andrei Sinyavsky was arrested, followed four days later by the writer and translator Yuli Daniel. Both would subsequently be tried and then jailed, providing the catalyst for a cycle of intelligentsia protest and government repression that would rumble on for years. As F.J.M. Feldbrugge rightly pointed out in regard to the events that followed: '... hundreds of lines could be drawn connecting individual acts of protest ... and most of them converge on the trial of Sinyavsky and Daniel'.[103] While the impact of the trial resonated among the liberal intelligentsia throughout much of the Brezhnev period, and has been widely cited as proof of an emerging post-Khrushchev conservative retrenchment, the roots of the Sinyavsky and Daniel case were unmistakably to be found in the Khrushchev years.

Apparently inspired by the way that Pasternak had published *Dr Zhivago* in Italy (both men had been sufficiently close to the author to serve as coffin-bearers at his funeral), Sinyavsky and Daniel began smuggling their texts abroad for publication under the pseudonyms Abram Tertz and Nikolai Arzhak in 1959 and 1961 respectively. Neither had written anything we might today recognise as outright subversive, though both had published works that were either sharply satirical or else critical of regime policy.[104] A KGB investigation into Tertz and Arzhak was initiated

---

[102] It is also interesting to note that each of these instances was handled in a different way by the authorities. One is tempted to speculate that there was another process of 'trial and error' under way in terms of policing the cultural sphere.

[103] F. Feldbrugge, *Samizdat and Political Dissent in the Soviet Union*, Leiden: A.W. Sijthoff, 1975, p. 2.

[104] For a more detailed discussion on their works and the legal case that ensued, see L. Labedz and M. Hayward eds., *On Trial: The Case of Sinyavsky (Tertz) and Daniel (Arzhak)*, London: Collins and Harvill Press, 1967.

in the early 1960s, but for a long time failed to establish whether the pair were actually Soviet authors writing from inside the USSR or were foreigners who had an excellent knowledge of contemporary Moscow and its people. Focusing on the capital, the KGB net gradually began to close in. Lists were drawn up of those who had access to the kinds of information contained in Tertz's and Arzhak's works, as well as the necessary contacts with foreigners who could smuggle the manuscripts abroad. Those lists were then whittled down as clandestine searches were conducted, foreigners' luggage rifled through at airports and on trains, suspects secretly observed and mail intercepted as the security organs continued to home in on the mysterious 'Tertz and Arzhak'.[105]

It was the true identity of Nikolai Arzhak that first came to the attention of the security organs, courtesy of a denunciation from one of his fellow writers. The name was, however, not a particularly well-kept secret within Moscow *kompaniya*, so it remains something of a mystery as to why the KGB made such slow progress on the matter.[106] Nonetheless, as Mitrokhin's notes on the case stated: 'by the beginning of 1964 we [the KGB] came to the conclusion that Tertz and Arzhak were Soviet writers and that Yuli Daniel was one of the two'. This consequently drew the security organs' attention to Daniel's friend, Andrei Sinyavsky, whom they noted had 'many contacts with foreigners'. In fact, the KGB had suspected since 1959 that 'Abram Tertz' was based at Moscow's Gorky Institute of World Literature – where Sinyavsky did indeed work. As of May 1964, the KGB initiated operation 'Epigony' (literally 'followers' or 'imitators') in which they began to build evidence against Sinyavsky and Daniel.

The pair were observed and listened in on for months. According to Mitrokhin's notes on the case, Sinyavsky proved particularly difficult to keep tabs on since he was extremely cautious and knew well how to cover his tracks after a stint collaborating with the KGB, though they did manage to listen in on him at home. In Daniel's case, investigators were continually frustrated by the fact that his apartment was perpetually occupied by friends and family, so had to content themselves with eavesdropping from a neighbouring flat until they managed to make a copy of the house key. They then created a diversion so as to ensure that the place was empty for long enough for them to conduct a search. Soon investigators had compiled

---

[105] See V. Mitrokhin, 'The Pathfinders (Sinyavsky and Daniel Show Trial)', Folder 14, Woodrow Wilson Center, Washington, DC, Cold War International History Project Virtual Archive, Mitrokhin Archive.

[106] See, for example, L. Alexeyeva and P. Goldberg, *The Thaw Generation*, p. 113.

a wealth of material on the pair – on their works, their contacts, their political views and their future publication plans.

Aware that Sinyavsky was planning to send a new text abroad, the KGB placed both writers under round-the-clock observation. An intercepted letter then revealed that Sinyavsky was to meet with an intermediary named Alfreda Okutyure who would pass his latest manuscript to Hélène Peltier, the daughter of the French naval attaché in Moscow and the individual responsible for smuggling the works of Tertz and Arzhak out to the West. After secretly observing two meetings between the pair, the KGB conducted a clandestine search of Okutyure's belongings as she left the country, but found nothing, effectively leaving the case 'on ice' until the start of September 1965 when a decision was taken to bring the matter to a conclusion. By that time, of course, Khrushchev was languishing in forced retirement.

Even before the case against the arrested writers proceeded to court, it sparked the USSR's first public demonstration in defence of human rights, at Pushkin Square in central Moscow, on the evening of 5 December 1965: this was just a few hundred metres down Gorky Street from where the poetry meetings had taken place at Mayakovsky Square. The demonstration was organised by Aleksandr Esenin-Volpin, with help from Vladimir Bukovsky and members of the student group SMOG.[107] Estimates of the number of participants vary, though they fall somewhere between 'a few dozen' and about 200.[108] On Esenin-Volpin's urging, the protestors demanded only *glasnost'* (literally, 'openness') in the forthcoming trial and 'respect for the Soviet constitution'. Both of these were to be the central themes of the human-rights movement for years to come.[109]

With the widespread and seemingly logical assumption that the new Brezhnev administration was about to launch a major crackdown on non-conformists, including rumours that the KGB had prepared lists of

[107] The most detailed material on the demonstration is found in N. Kostenko et al. eds., *Pyatoe dekabrya 1965 goda v vospominaniyakh uchastnikov sobytii, materialakh samizdata, dokumentakh partiinykh i komsomol'skikh organizatsii i v zapiskakh KGB v TsK KPSS*, Moskva: Obshchestvo 'Memorial', 1995. Many of those who had helped to arrange the demonstration, including Vladimir Bukovsky, were subjected to preventative detention and thus were not present on the actual day. The acronym 'SMOG' stood for either 'Youngest Society of Geniuses' or 'Daring, Thought, Image and Profundity'.

[108] See L. Alexeyeva, *Soviet Dissent: Contemporary Movements for National, Religious and Human Rights*, Middletown, CT: Wesleyan University Press, 1987, p. 276, and A. Komaromi, 'The Unofficial Field of Late Soviet Culture', *Slavic Review*, Vol. 66, No. 4 (Winter 2007), 621.

[109] The resonances with Gorbachev's later policy are obvious and have been raised by Alexeyeva in particular. However, this was also an era when the KGB repeatedly spoke of introducing a greater degree of *glasnost'* into its work. See J. Elkner, 'The Changing Face of Repression under Khrushchev', in M. Ilič and J. Smith eds., *Soviet State and Society under Nikita Khrushchev*, pp. 142–61.

troublesome intellectuals to be arrested, the trial quickly took on great significance for much of the liberal intelligentsia.[110] On-going protest and repression inside USSR, with human faces and stories included, now came to the world's attention on a major scale for the first time, as foreign radio stations and newspapers took an interest in Sinyavsky and Daniel. Supporters and friends of the accused gathered outside the courthouse, where they soon made the acquaintance of Western journalists reporting on the trial. This proved to be the start of an enduring, though at times difficult, relationship between Soviet dissidents and Western newspapermen that would radically alter the nature of the struggle between dissenters and authority. Over time, it made the names of previously anonymous critics of the regime known around the world, thereby offering them a degree of protection and a vital body of moral support to help nourish their aspirations for liberalisation.[111] This marked the start of a vitally important transition in dissenting behaviour, moving away from using the threat of domestic unrest as a means of influencing regime policy, and toward reliance on Western governments and publics to pressure the Soviet leadership for better observance of basic human rights. What had begun in earnest with the emergence of *kompaniya* in the mid 1950s, and with the readings at Mayakovsky Square in particular, now reached a crucially important stage as like-minded individuals increasingly came into each other's orbit and to the attention of the West at a time when signs of cracks in the Soviet monolith were being sought more keenly than ever before.

On 14 February 1966 Sinyavsky and Daniel were both jailed under article 70 for anti-Soviet agitation and propaganda, the former for seven years and the latter for five, prompting the emergence of what would become known as the Soviet human-rights movement. Bearing in mind the impact that the case against Sinyavsky and Daniel was to have on the mood of the liberal intelligentsia inside the USSR, and on foreign perceptions of post-Khrushchev reStalinization, it is interesting to ponder just how different the perspective on Khrushchev and the Khrushchev era might have been if the pair had been arrested – as they easily could have been – back when they were first identified by the KGB in early 1964.

---

[110] See A. Solzhenitsyn, *Invisible Allies*, London: Harvill Press, 1997, p. 18. Solzhenitsyn himself suffered the loss of some manuscripts when the family who had been entrusted to hide them panicked at the news of Khrushchev's ouster and burned them. The rumours were not entirely unrealistic. Within months a clampdown had begun in Ukraine, with around sixty members of the intelligentsia there jailed by the end of 1965.

[111] See, for example, D. Bonavia, *Fat Sasha and the Urban Guerrilla: Protest and Conformism in the Soviet Union*, London: Hamish Hamilton, 1973.

Conclusion

When the news of Khrushchev's forced retirement broke in the middle of October 1964, Lev Karpinsky met up with Yegor Yakovlev to share a celebratory glass of cognac. Neither of the two could be called dissenters but they were both keen supporters of deStalinization and were well acquainted with Soviet elite politics. Both were of the opinion that Khrushchev had become a brake on his own reform programme and reasoned that the new leadership under Leonid Brezhnev could more effectively lead the deStalinization process.[1] For a while the results were somewhat ambiguous, but by 1966 it was increasingly clear that the pair had badly misjudged the palace coup. In fact, after holding high-level posts in the Komsomol and at *Pravda* during the early 1960s, Karpinsky's blossoming political career soon headed for the rocks. Like a host of others who considered themselves 'Children of the XX Party Congress', he would find himself ostracised and banished to professional obscurity, not returning to public life until the onset of *glasnost'* two decades later.[2]

Although his handling of the deStalinization process was not among the charges explicitly levelled at Khrushchev in October 1964, there is little doubt that the issue was hanging in the air. Most of his usurpers within the Central Committee Presidium, of course, wanted the reform process halted rather than accelerated. By the XXIII CPSU Congress in spring 1966, speakers made it entirely apparent that they felt the former First Secretary responsible for 'allowing subversive ideas to gain a foothold in Soviet society'.[3] While the themes and forms of political criticism

---

[1] 'The Autobiography of a Half-Dissident', in S. Cohen and K. vanden Heuvel eds., *Voices of Glasnost: Interviews with Gorbachev's Reformers*, New York: W.W. Norton, 1989, p. 289.

[2] Yakovlev fared better in career terms, working within the Central Committee apparatus until the mid 1970s before being dispatched to Canada for ten years as ambassador, apparently as a form of political exile. He would subsequently go on to become one of the key architects of *glasnost'* in the second half of the 1980s.

[3] C. Linden, *Khrushchev and the Soviet Leadership*, Baltimore, MD: Johns Hopkins University Press, 1990, p. 227. See, for example, 'Doklad Pervogo sekretarya TsK tovarishcha L.I. Brezhneva', in *XXIII s"ezd kommunisticheskoi partii sovetskogo soyuza: stenograficheskii otchet*, Moskva: Izdatel'stvo politicheskoi literatury, 1966, pp. 18–110.

certainly had proliferated under Khrushchev's leadership, one is inclined to suggest that, overall, the period was more notable for the extent to which the regime proved able either to assuage or to stifle discontent. Although by no means perfect, the transition to a post-terror political system could have been handled much worse than it ultimately was: both protest and repression could quite conceivably have been far more extensive. In many ways, Khrushchev had actually conceded surprisingly little in terms of granting additional rights and freedoms as he reconfigured the system for the post-terror environment. An increasingly educated and diverse society with rising material aspirations was governed without recourse to mass violence, yet also without the kinds of concessions that might undermine the survival of the system, such as freedom of speech or democratisation. In abandoning large-scale repression as a key means of social control, the Soviet regime turned instead to a more materialist social order and greater intrusion into people's daily lives; it increasingly pulled its citizens into the work of the state and took ever greater care to monitor and shape public moods. This ultimately proved a fairly durable model in the medium term, and one that helped provide many years of social stability.

There were always a whole host of reasons why people engaged in dissenting activity: from offended ideological sensibilities through to despair at living standards, as well as more nebulous impulses such as desire for adventure, aping of one's political idols or a more general sense of spite toward officialdom. Important though they were, questions of liberalisation and deStalinization were not the only wellsprings of criticism. Among workers, protest was most likely to stem from anger at material difficulties, such as goods shortages, low wages and resentment at elite privileges, rather than demands for political liberalisation. Acts of dissent stemming from these themes were ultimately rather ephemeral in nature but could be particularly vociferous in tone. The sheer number of Soviet workers meant that working-class grievances could not be entirely ignored. Although often manifested in political language, such as branding Khrushchev an 'enemy of the people' or threatening to kill communists, this kind of dissenting behaviour was primarily about 'lashing out' at authority, or else demanding that the regime fulfil its end of the emerging social contract, and generally did not imply a deep-seated ideological rejection of the communist system. It did, however, reflect a society going through some profound turbulence as old certainties began to change, the Gulag emptied, popular aspirations rose and the fallibility of political leaders became common knowledge.

Less liable to result in volatile explosions of anger than was worker protest, intelligentsia dissent posed more fundamental questions of the authorities. Initially these questions were mostly in regard to the prevailing interpretation of Marxism-Leninism and the progress of post-Stalin liberalisation. In later years they increasingly took on a more systemic critique of the regime, though this is not to say they consistently rejected core 'Soviet' values, such as social equality and collectivism. Even among the intelligentsia, there was relatively little in the way of 'truly anti-Soviet' sentiment, at least not from the perspective of the dissenters in question. As with workers, the vast majority of the intelligentsia either did not speak out in any public sense or else quickly fell back into line once the boundaries of permissible and impermissible began to harden again. Those few who remained steadfastly defiant were to play a major role in shaping the subsequent dissident movement of the late 1960s and 1970s.

Under less authoritarian political systems many of the behaviours described herein would not have been merely acceptable but would have constituted regular and constructive political interchange. This was especially true of the intelligentsia dissent that had followed the Secret Speech. However, it is also important not to lose sight of the fact that this was not always the case. Numerous of the more radical underground groups of the era, for example, would most likely have attracted the interest of state security almost anywhere in the world. Even though underground activity was in large part a result of the regime allowing practically no legitimate avenues for input from discontented citizens, one hardly had to be an intransigent hardliner to view calls for revolution and threats of violence as subversive, even if they were not realistic in practice. Paranoid and deeply intolerant of political heterodoxy as the regime remained, it was not entirely detached from reality. It is worth noting, for example, that Soviet concerns about foreign powers conducting propaganda offensives aimed at undermining the regime in the eyes of its citizens were not wholly inaccurate. Indeed, the evidence suggests that in the long term growing interaction with the outside world in particular did help to undermine the univocal public sphere that the authorities prized so highly.[4]

An overview of the bigger picture tells us that measures aimed at reducing dissent were for the most part successful at stifling discordant voices, if not necessarily at tackling the underlying discontent that had generated them. While fear of repression may well have declined substantially following the

---

[4] See, for example, A. Johnson and E. Parta eds., *Cold War Broadcasting: Impact on the Soviet Union and Eastern Europe*, Budapest: Central European University Press, 2010.

exposure of Stalin, this would always remain a powerful impulse within the Soviet system. Even so, mass passivity was not achieved by fear alone. For material discontent at least, the authorities showed a degree of willingness to meet rising expectations, where possible. There was to be no accommodation with demands for thorough-going political reform, however, at least partly because domestic pressure for such liberalisation was not nearly so widespread or so dangerous as material discontent. The majority broadly accepted and engaged with the system as it stood, and a great many actively supported it. Whether they did so entirely of their own accord or not, huge numbers of people participated in duties such as volunteer policing, blurring the boundaries of 'state' and 'society' as they did so. Similarly, the statements, the forms of protest and the aims of dissenters often showed a fundamental acceptance of the Soviet meta-narrative, especially during the earlier part of the Khrushchev era.

The abandonment of massive and arbitrary repression was, of course, the key policy change from the Stalin era. In many ways it prompted the Soviet Union's transformation into a different type of dictatorship, becoming an insidious and modern police state rather than a despotic terror state. Furthermore, the question was not just one of ending entirely groundless repression. Had the authorities imprisoned even half of all those who were involved in dissenting activity under Khrushchev, the number of sentences would have certainly been in the tens of thousands. Still, the system essentially became much more predictable and pragmatic, rather than significantly more tolerant of political non-conformity. The reforms of the era were not intended to benefit people who wished to speak out: they were primarily aimed at improving things for those who 'toed the line'. Less draconian measures for dealing with dissent, such as hauling critics into their local KGB offices for a 'chat', were deployed because they tended to have the desired effect, not because the authorities had become more tolerant of criticism.

Dissenting behaviour did not threaten to bring the Khrushchev regime crashing down at any point – though it was certainly highly combustible at times – but it did both contribute to and reflect the evolution of the post-terror Soviet system. In regard to the former, perhaps the most notable way in which protest (or the threat of protest) shaped the post-Stalin USSR was by making plain that there was to be no reneging on promises of improving living standards. Just as the authorities made clear what had and had not changed since Stalin's death by their handling of criticism following the XX CPSU Congress, so they themselves learned during the summer of 1962 in particular that the hardships of old would no longer be meekly accepted by the masses.

The inherent tension between regime discourse that centred upon a reinvigoration of revolutionary ideology and the reality of deepening political conservatism was also laid bare at times.[5] The early part of the Khrushchev period in particular showed that, unless closely prescribed from above, notions of 'return to Leninism' and what we might call 'activist idealism' could soon become problematic. Loyalty to the ideals of October 1917 could prompt sharp attacks on the incumbent political leadership. Similarly, typically communist values, particularly in regard to expectations of social fairness, were sufficiently embedded that they could become a serious point of contention when breached. Even in more autonomous spaces like *kompaniya*, underground political groups and *samizdat* literature, dissenters' separation from the discourse, ideals and values propounded 'from above' was never anything like complete, and nor could it be. Unambiguous signs of a generalised decline in communist idealism are naturally difficult to pin down, especially on the basis of behaviours that were only ever undertaken openly by a minority of citizens. Much of the evidence, however, tends to suggest that intelligentsia critics in particular were moving further away from the ideological prescriptions of the Soviet project as the era progressed.

In the most immediate sense, the intelligentsia dissent of the Khrushchev era had a vital impact upon the way in which the struggle between dissidents and authorities played out over the course of the Brezhnev era. Many of that small rump of the intelligentsia who would go on to dominate the first stages of the Soviet human-rights movement, and indeed some who would remain among the most prominent critics until the very fall of the regime, had already begun their own individual cycle of on-going conflict with the authorities by October 1964. Crucial forms and themes of dissent had also emerged: from the appearance of *samizdat* literature and the rejection of underground activity, through to growing ideological heterodoxy and pro-liferating questions of individual morality. In short, earlier claims that the Brezhnev-era dissident movement sprang up in response to the ending of the relative liberality of the Khrushchev years no longer stand up to scrutiny.

The changes to policing that came into effect around the end of the 1950s, including greater intrusion into citizens' everyday lives, more concerted marshalling of social pressures and a willingness to distinguish between 'mistaken' and 'genuinely anti-Soviet' protest activity, lay at the heart of the regime's efforts to combat dissent for years to come. Many of the measures

[5] On this, see also J. Fürst, *Stalin's Last Generation: Soviet Post-War Youth and the Emergence of Mature Socialism*, Oxford University Press, 2010.

that would become central features of the Brezhnev-era struggle against dissidents, most notably punitive psychiatry and prophylaxis, were also well established by October 1964. Indeed, the critical juncture that ultimately brought the human-rights movement to life in January 1966 – the trial of Andrei Sinyavsky and Yuli Daniel – was already in train prior to Khrushchev's ouster.

Of course, dissenting activity and government responses to dissent were only a fairly small part of the Khrushchev-era Soviet system. Nonetheless, they do consistently present the end of the 1950s as a useful time at which to bisect the period in question.[6] We can conceptualise the changes taking place around the turn of the decade as indicating that both authorities and dissenters had just about come to terms with the most pressing fall-out from the end of full-blooded Stalinism. The mass amnesties, the Secret Speech, the resurgence of political idealism and dissenters' striving to 'mend' the Soviet project, and the regime's lurching from one course of action to the next as they strived to rule without terror all told of a system enduring an understandably difficult spell of transition. What we start to see as the 1950s turned into the 1960s is the emergence of a more recognisably long-term post-Stalin system, in which the authorities came to gain a surer grip on protest and discontent, while those dissenters that remained showed a growing degree of alienation from the Soviet system.

---

[6] Karl Aimermakher has also pointed to the late 1950s as a time when the administration of Soviet culture changed significantly. See K. Aimermakher, 'Partiinoe upravlenie kul'turoi i formy ee samoorganizatsii (1953–1964/7)', in E. Afanas'eva and V. Afiani eds., *Ideologicheskie komissii TsK KPSS, 1958–1964: dokumenty*, Moskva: Rosspen, 1998, pp. 5–22. It is also worth restating that the KGB used approximately the same point to bisect the Khrushchev era. See V. Chebrikov et al., *Istoriya sovetskikh organov gosudarstvennoi bezopasnosti: uchebnik*, Moskva: Vysshaya krasnoznamenskaya shkola komiteta gosudarstvennoi bezopasnosti pri sovete ministerov SSSR, 1977. William Taubman also points to the late 1950s as a time when Khrushchev's personality and leadership style became somewhat 'harder'. See W. Taubman, *Khrushchev: The Man and His Era*, London: The Free Press, 2003.

Glossary

aktiv	Communist Party and Komsomol activists
ASSR	Autonomous Soviet Socialist Republic
CPSU	Communist Party of the Soviet Union
gorkom	city Party committee
KGB	State Security Committee
kolkhoz	collective farm
kolkhoznik/kolkhoznitsa	collective farm worker
Komsomol	Communist Youth League
militia	police force
MVD	Ministry of Internal Affairs
obkom	*oblast'* Party committee
oblast'	administrative division used in the USSR and present-day Russia, meaning 'province' or 'region'
raion	administrative division used in the USSR and present-day Russia, meaning 'area' or 'district'
raikom	*raion*-level Party committee
RSFSR	Russian Soviet Federative Socialist Republic
samizdat	self-published literature, printed and distributed by clandestine means
SSR	Soviet Socialist Republic

Bibliography

PRINCIPAL ARCHIVAL SOURCES

Budapest, Open Society Archive (OSA)
  HU OSA 299
  HU OSA 300-80-1 – The Red Archive
Leeds, Leeds Russian Archive
  Terlecka Collection
Moscow, GARF (Gosudarstvennyi arkhiv Rossiisskoi Federatsii)
  Fond 8131 – The Soviet Procuracy
  Fond 9401 – The Ministry of Internal Affairs
Moscow, RGANI (Rossiiskii gosudarstvennyi arkhiv noveishei istorii)
  Fond 5 – The General Department of the Central Committee
  Fond 6 – The Department of Party Organs
  Fond 72 – The Ideological Commission
  Fond 89 – Collection of Declassified Documents from the Trial of the Communist
    Party
Moscow, RGASPI (Rossiisskii gosudarstvennyi arkhiv sotsial'no-politicheskoi istorii)
  Fond 1 – The Department of Komsomol Organs
New York, Bakhmeteff Archive, Columbia University
Woodrow Wilson Center, Washington, DC, Cold War International History Project
  Mitrokhin Archive

MEMOIRS AND PUBLISHED ARCHIVAL COLLECTIONS

Adzhubei, A. *Te desyat' let*, Moskva: Sovetskaya Rossiya, 1989
Afanas'eva, E. and Afiani, V. eds. *Ideologicheskie komissii TsK KPSS 1958–1964: dokumenty*, Moskva: Rosspen, 1998
Afiani, V. and Tomilina, N. eds. *'A za mnoyu shum pogoni . . .': Boris Pasternak i vlast': dokumenty, 1956–1972*, Moskva: Rosspen, 2001
Afiani, V. et al. eds. *Kul'tura i vlast' ot Stalina do Gorbacheva: apparat TsK KPSS i kul'tura, 1958–1964*, Moskva: Rosspen, 2005
Aimermakher, K. et al. eds. *Doklad N.S. Khrushcheva o kul'te lichnosti Stalina na XX s"ezde KPSS: dokumenty*, Moskva: Rosspen, 2002
Alekseeva, L. and Goldberg, P. *Pokolenie ottepeli*, Moskva: Zakharov, 2006

Alexeyeva, L. and Goldberg, P. *The Thaw Generation: Coming of Age in the Post-Stalin Era*, Boston, MA: Little, Brown and Company, 1990

Amalrik, A. *An Involuntary Journey to Siberia*, Newton Abbot: Readers Union, 1971
Notes of a Revolutionary, New York: Alfred Knopf, 1982

Arbatov, G. et al. eds. *'Ochistim Rossiyu nadolgo . . .': repressii protiv inakomyslyashchikh, konets 1921 – nachalo 1923*, Moskva: Mezhdunarodnyi fond 'Demokratiya', 2008

Barbakadze, M. and Shvarts, E. eds. *Antologiya samizdata: nepodtsenzurnaya literatura v SSSR 1950–1980*, Tom 1: *Do 1966 goda*, Moskva: Mezhdunarodnyi institut gumanitarno-politicheskikh issledovanii, 2005

Bobkov, F. *KGB i vlast': 45 let v organakh gosudarstvennoi bezopasnosti*, Moskva: Veteran MP, 1995

Bonavia, D. *Fat Sasha and the Urban Guerrilla: Protest and Conformism in the Soviet Union*, London: Hamish Hamilton, 1973

Bukovskii, V. *I vozvrashchaetsya veter . . .*, Moskva: Zakharov, 2007
Pis'ma russkogo puteshestvennika, Sankt Peterburg: Nestor-Istoriya, 2008

Bukovsky, V. *To Build a Castle: My Life as a Dissenter*, London: Andre Deutsch, 1978

Burlatsky, F. *Khrushchev and the First Russian Spring: The Era of Khrushchev through the Eyes of his Adviser*, London: Weidenfeld & Nicolson, 1991

Chebrikov, V. et al. *Istoriya sovetskikh organov gosudarstvennoi bezopasnosti: uchebnik*, Moskva: Vysshaya krasnoznamenskaya shkola komiteta gosudarstvennoi bezopasnosti pri sovete ministrove SSSR, 1977

Cohen, S. ed. *An End to Silence: Uncensored Opinion in the Soviet Union, from Roy Medvedev's Magazine 'Political Diary'*, New York: W.W. Norton, 1982

Cohen, S. and vanden Heuvel, K. eds. *Voices of Glasnost: Interviews with Gorbachev's Reformers*, New York: W.W. Norton, 1989

Djilas, M. *The New Class: An Analysis of the Communist System*, London: Unwin, 1966

Esenin-Volpin, A. *A Leaf of Spring: A Free Philosophical Treatise*, New York: Praeger, 1961

Fursenko, A. et al. eds. *Prezidium TsK KPSS 1954–1964*, Tom 1: *Chernovye protokol'nye zapisi zasedanii stenogrammy*, Moskva: Rosspen, 2004
Prezidium TsK KPSS 1954–1964, Tom 2: *Postanovleniya 1954–1958*, Moskva: Rosspen, 2006
Prezidium TsK KPSS 1954–1964, Tom 3: *Postanovleniya 1959–1964*, Moskva: Rosspen, 2008

Gidoni, A. *Solntse idet s zapada: kniga vospominanii*, Toronto: Sovremennik, 1980

Gorbanevskaya, N. *Red Square at Noon*, Harmondsworth: Penguin Books, 1970
Polden': delo o demonstratsii na Krasnoi ploshchadi 25 avgusta 1968 goda, Moskva: Novoe Izdatel'stvo, 2007

Goryachev, Yu. *Tsentralnyi Komitet: istoriko-biograficheskii spravochnik*, Moskva: Parad, 2005

Grigorenko, P. *The Grigorenko Papers: Writings by P.G. Grigorenko and Documents on his Case*, New York: Westview Press, 1973
V podpol'e mozhno vstretit' tol'ko krys, New York: Letinets, 1981
Memoirs, New York: W.W. Norton, 1982

Hindus, M. *House without a Roof: Russia after Forty-Three Years of Revolution*, London: Victor Gollancz, 1962

Iofe, V. *Granitsy smysla: stat'i, vystupleniya, esse*, Sankt Peterburg: Nauchno-informatsionnyi tsentr 'Memorial', 2002

Kaganovskii, G. ed. *Khronika kazni Yuriya Galanskova v ego pis'makh iz zony ZhKh-385, svidetel'stvakh i dokumentakh*, Moskva: Agraf, 2006

Khlevnyuk, O. et al. eds. *Regional'naya politika N.S. Khrushcheva. TsK KPSS i mestnye partiinye komitety 1953–1964*, Moskva: Rosspen, 2009

Khrushchev, S. *Khrushchev on Khrushchev*, London: Little, Brown and Company, 1990

Khrushchev, S. ed. *Memoirs of Nikita Khrushchev*, Vol. 2: *Reformer: 1945–1964*, University Park, PA: Pennsylvania State University Press, 2006

Memoirs of Nikita Khrushchev, Vol. 3: *Statesman: 1953–1964*, University Park, PA: Pennsylvania State University Press, 2007

Kirk, I. *Profiles in Russian Resistance*, New York: Quadrangle, 1975

Kostenko, N. et al. eds. *Pyatoe dekabrya 1965 goda v vospominaniyakh uchastnikov sobytii, materialakh samizdata, dokumentakh partiinykh i komsomol'skikh organizatsii i v zapiskakh KGB v TsK KPSS*, Moskva: Obshchestvo 'Memorial', 1995

Kozlov, A. *Kozel na sakse: i tak vsyu zhizn*, Moskva: Vagrius, 1998

Kozlov, V. and Mironenko, S. eds. *58-10 Nadzornye proizvodstva prokuratury SSSR po delam ob antisovetskoi agitatsii i propaganda: annotirovannyi katalog Mart 1953–1991*, Moskva: Mezhdunarodnyi Fond 'Demokratiya', 1999

Kuzin, A. *Malyi srok: vospominaniya v forme esse so svobodnym syuzhetom*, Moskva: Rudomina, 1994

Kuznetsov, E. *Mordovskii marafon*, Ramat-Gan, Israel: Knigotovarishchestvo 'Moskva–Ierusalim', 1979

Lur'e, L. and Malyarova, I. *1956 god. Seredina veka*, Sankt Peterburg: Neva, 2007

Marchenko, A. *My Testimony*, Harmondsworth: Penguin Books, 1969

McClean, H. and Vickery, W. eds. *The Year of Protest: 1956*, New York: Vintage Books, 1961

Medvedev, R. *On Soviet Dissent: Interviews with Piero Ostellino*, New York: Columbia University Press, 1977

Mikoyan, A. *Tak bylo: razmyshleniya o minuvshem*. Moskva: Vagrius, 1999

Mukhitdinov, N. '12 let s Khrushchevym: vospominaniya byvshego chlena Prezidium TsK', *Argumenty i fakty*, No. 44 (1989), 4–6

Gody provedennye v Kremle, Tashkent: Izdatel'stvo narodnogo naslediya imeni Abdully Kadryi, 1994

Naiman, A. 'Picasso in Russia 2.0', *Moscow News*, 15 June 2010. On line at www.themoscownews.com/arts/20100615/187873959.html?id=

Orlov, Yu. *Dangerous Thoughts: Memoirs of a Russian Life*, New York: William Morrow and Company, 1991

Opsanye mysli: memuary iz russkoi zhizni, Moskva: Zakharov, 2008

Orlova, R. *An End to Silence: Memoirs*, New York: Random House, 1983

Pimenov, R. *Vospominaniya*, Moskva: informatsionno-ekspertnaya gruppa 'Panorama', 1996

Pimonov, V. ed. *Govoryat 'osobo opasnye'*, Moskva: Detektiv-Press, 1999

Plyushch, L. *History's Carnival: A Dissident's Autobiography*, London: Harvill Press, 1979

Polikovskaya, L. *'My predchuvstvie ... predtecha': ploshchad Mayakovskogo 1958–1965*, Moskva: Obshchestvo 'Memorial', 1997

Raleigh, D. ed. *Russia's Sputnik Generation: Soviet Baby Boomers Talk about their Lives*, Bloomington, IN: Indiana University Press, 2006

Reddaway, P. ed. *Uncensored Russia: Protest and Dissent in the Soviet Union*, New York: American Heritage Press, 1972

Romanov, S. *'"Ne etomu menya desyat' let v komsomole uchili!": interv'yu s M.S. Gol'dmanom'*, *Karta: rossiskii nezavisimyi istoricheskii i pravozashchitnyi zhurnal*, Nos. 17–18 (12.06.1997), 46–56. On line at http://ia601200.us.archive.org/13/items/Karta-RussianIndependetHistoricalAndHumanRights DefendingJournalN17-18/karta-17-18.pdf

Ronkin, V. *Na smenu dekabryam prikhodit yanvari ...*, Moskva: Obshchestvo 'Memorial', 2003

Rubenstein, J. and Gribanov, A. eds. *The KGB File of Andrei Sakharov*, New Haven, CT: Yale University Press, 2005

Sakharov, A. *Memoirs*, New York: Alfred A. Knopf, 1990

Schakovsky, Z. *The Privilege Was Mine*, London: Jonathan Cape, 1959

Semichastnyi, V. *Bespokoinoe serdtse*, Moskva: Vagrius, 2002

Shubin, A. *Dissidenty, neformaly i svoboda v SSSR*, Moskva: Veche, 2008

Solzhenitsyn, A. *The Oak and the Calf: A Literary Memoir*, London: Collins and Harvill Press, 1980

    Invisible Allies, London: Harvill Press, 1997

Sosin, G. *Sparks of Liberty: An Insider's Memoirs of Radio Liberty*, University Park, PA: Pennsylvania State University Press, 1999

Tarsis, V. *Ward 7: An Autobiographical Novel*, London: Collins and Harvill Press, 1965

Tertz, A. *A Voice from the Chorus*, London: Collins and Harvill Press, 1976

Tomilina, N. ed. *Nikita Sergeevich Khrushchev: dva tsveta vremeni: dokumenty iz lichnogo fonda N.S. Khrushcheva*, Tom 1, Moskva: Mezhdunarodnyi fond 'Demokratiya', 2009

    Nikita Sergeevich Khrushchev: dva tsveta vremeni: dokumenty iz lichnogo fonda N.S. Khrushcheva, Tom 2, Moskva: Mezhdunarodnyi fond 'Demokratiya', 2009

Tsentral'noe statisticheskoe upravlenie pri Sovete Ministrove SSSR. *Chislennost', sostav i razmeshchenie naseleniya SSSR: kratkie itogi vsesoyuznoi perepisi naseleniya 1959 goda*, Moskva: Gosstatizdat TsSU SSSR, 1961

US Congress, Senate, Committee on the Judiciary, *Abuse of Psychiatry for Political Repression in the Soviet Union: Hearings before the Subcommittee to Investigate the Administration of the Internal Security Act and Other Internal Security Laws*, 92nd Congress, 2nd Session, Washington, DC: US Government Printing Office, 1972

Vail', B. *Osobo opasnyi*, London: Overseas Publications Interchange, 1980

Voinovich, V. *The Anti-Soviet Soviet Union*, London: Harcourt, 1986

Volkov. S. *Conversations with Joseph Brodsky*, New York: The Free Press, 1998
Voprosy istorii, 'Vlast' i intelligentsiya: "delo" molodykh istorikov (1957–58.)',
   Voprosy istorii, No. 004 (1994), 106–35
'Studencheskoe brozhenie v SSSR (konets 1956g.)', *Voprosy istorii*, No. 0001
   (1997), 3–23
Voprosy partiinoi raboty, Moskva: Gosudarstvennoe izdatel'stvo politicheskoi
   literatury, 1957
XXIII s"ezd kommunisticheskoi partii sovetskogo soyuza: stenograficheskii otchet,
   Moskva: Izdatel'stvo politicheskoi literatury, 1966
Yakovlev, A. et al. eds. *Reabilitatsiya: kak eto bylo. Fevral' 1956 – nachalo 80-x godov*,
   Moskva: Mezhdunarodnyi fond 'Demokratiya', 2003
Zubkova, E. and Zhukova, T. eds. *Na 'krayu' Sovetskogo obshchestva: sotsial'nye margin-
   ally kak ob"ekt gosudarstvennoi politiki, 1945–1960-e gg.*, Moskva: Rosspen, 2010

NEWSPAPERS

Belgazeta
Istochnik
Izvestiya
Kazakhstanskaya pravda
Kommunist
Komsomolskaya pravda
Leningradskaya pravda
New York Times
Novoe vremya
Paris-Presse
Pravda
Trud
Vechernyaya Moskva
Washington Evening Star
Zarya vostoka

SECONDARY LITERATURE

Abramkin, V. and Chesnokova, V. *Tyurmennyi mir glazami politzaklyuchennykh*,
   Moskva: Sodeistvie, 1993
Adler, N. 'Life in the "Big Zone": The Fate of Returnees in the Aftermath of
   Stalinist Repression', *Europe–Asia Studies*, Vol. 51, No. 1 (January 1999), 5–19
   Trudnoe vozvrashchenie: sud'by sovetskikh politzaklyuchennykh v 1950–1990 gody,
   Moskva: Zven'ya, 2005
Aksyutin, Yu. *Khrushchevskaya 'ottepel' i obshchestvennye nastroenniya v SSSR v
   1953–1964*, Moskva: Rosspen, 2004
Albats, Ye. *KGB: State Within a State*, London: I.B. Tauris, 1995
Alekseeva, L. *Istoriya inakomysliya v SSSR: noveishii period*, Moskva: Zao Rits
   'Zatsepa', 2001

Alexeyeva, L. *US Broadcasting to the Soviet Union: A Helsinki Watch Report*, New York: Radio Free Europe/Radio Liberty, 1986
  Soviet Dissent: Contemporary Movements for National, Religious and Human Rights, Middletown, CT: Wesleyan University Press, 1987
Alexeyeva, L. and Chalidze, V. *Mass Unrest in the USSR*, Washington, DC: Department of Defense Office of Net Assessments, 1985
Andrew, C. and Mitrokhin, V. *The Sword and the Shield: The Mitrokhin Archive and the Secret History of the KGB*, New York: Basic Books, 1999
Applebaum, A. *Gulag: A History of the Soviet Camps*, London: Allen Lane, 2003
Axelbank, A. *Soviet Dissent: Intellectuals, Jews and Détente*, New York: Franklin Watts, 1975
Bahry, D. and Silver, B. 'Intimidation and the Symbolic Uses of Terror in the USSR', *American Political Science Review*, Vol. 81, No. 4 (December 1987), 1066–98
Barghoorn, F. 'Soviet Cultural Diplomacy since Stalin', *Russian Review*, Vol. 17, No. 1 (January 1958), 41–55
  'U.S.S.R. Revisited', *Russian Review*, Vol. 18, No. 2 (April 1959), 96–112
  Détente and the Democratic Movement in the USSR, London: Collier Macmillan, 1976
Baron, S. *Bloody Saturday in the Soviet Union: Novocherkassk, 1962*, Stanford University Press, 2001
Bergman, J. 'Soviet Dissidents on the Russian Intelligentsia, 1956–1985: The Search for a Usable Past', *Russian Review*, Vol. 51, No. 1 (January 1992), 16–35
  Meeting the Demands of Reason: The Life and Thought of Andrei Sakharov, Ithaca, NY: Cornell University Press, 2009
Berman, H. 'The Struggle of Soviet Jurists', *Slavic Review*, Vol. 22, No. 1 (June 1963), 314–20
  Soviet Criminal Law and Procedure, Cambridge, MA: Harvard University Press, 1972
Biddulph, H. 'Soviet Intellectual Dissent as a Political Counter-Culture', *Western Political Quarterly*, Vol. 25, No. 3 (September 1972), 522–33
Bittner, S. *The Many Lives of Khrushchev's Thaw: Experience and Memory in Moscow's Arbat*, London: Cornell University Press, 2008
Bloch, S. and Reddaway P. *Russia's Political Hospitals*, London: First Futura Publications, 1978
Boer, de S., Dreissen, E. and Verhaar, H. eds. *Biographical Dictionary of Dissidents in the Soviet Union, 1956–1975*, The Hague: Martinus Nijhoff Publishers, 1982
Boiter, A. 'When the Kettle Boils Over', *Problems of Communism*, No. 1 (1964), 33–43
Boobbyer, P. 'Truth-Telling, Conscience and Dissent in Late Soviet Russia: Evidence from Oral Histories', *European History Quarterly*, Vol. 30, No. 4 (2000), 553–85
  Conscience, Dissent and Reform in Soviet Russia, London: Routledge, 2005
  'Vladimir Bukovskii and Soviet Communism', *Slavonic and East European Review*, Vol. 87, No. 3 (July 2009), 452–87

Breslauer, G. *Khrushchev and Brezhnev as Leaders: Building Authority in Soviet Politics*, London: Allen & Unwin, 1982

Breyfogle, N., Schrader, A. and Sunderland, W. eds. *Peopling the Russian Periphery: Borderland Colonisation in Eurasian History*, London: Routledge, 2007

Brooks, J. *Thank You Comrade Stalin: Soviet Public Culture from Revolution to Cold War*, Princeton University Press, 1999

Brumberg, A. ed. *Russia under Khrushchev: An Anthology from 'Problems of Communism'*, New York: Praeger, 1962

In Quest of Justice: Protest and Dissent in the Soviet Union Today, London: Pall Mall Press, 1970

Burford Jr, R. 'Getting the Bugs Out of Socialist Legality: The Case of Joseph Brodsky', *The American Journal of Comparative Law*, Vol. 22, No. 3 (Summer 1974), 464–508

Bursa, G. R. F. 'Political Changes of Names of Soviet Towns', *Slavonic and East European Review*, Vol. 63, No. 2 (April 1985), 161–93

Casstevens, T. 'The Soviet Central Committee Since Stalin: A Longitudinal View', *American Journal of Political Science*, Vol. 18, No. 3 (August 1974), 559–68

Chamberlain, W. 'Émigré Anti-Soviet Enterprises and Splits', *Russian Review*, Vol. 13, No. 2 (April 1954), 91–8

'Khrushchev's War with Stalin's Ghost', *Russian Review*, Vol. 21, No. 1 (January 1962), 3–10

'USSR: How Much Change Since Stalin?', *Russian Review*, Vol. 22, No. 3 (July 1963), 225–35

Chatterjee, C. and Petrone, K. 'Models of Selfhood and Subjectivity: the Soviet Case in Historical Perspective', *Slavic Review*, Vol. 67, No. 4 (Winter 2008), 967–86

Cohen, S., Rabinowitch, A. and Sharlet, R. eds. *The Soviet Union since Stalin*, Bloomington, IN: Indiana University Press, 1980

Connor, W. 'The Soviet Criminal Correction System: Change and Stability', *Law and Society Review*, Vol. 6, No. 3 (February 1972), 368–90

Cullen, F. and Cullen, J. 'The Soviet Model of Soviet Deviance', *Pacific Sociological Review*, Vol. 20, No. 3 (July 1977), 389–410

Cutler, R. 'Soviet Dissent under Khrushchev: An Analytical Study', *Comparative Politics*, Vol. 13, No. 1 (October 1980), 15–35

David-Fox, M., Holquist, P. and Poe, M. eds. *The Resistance Debate in Russian and Soviet History: Kritika Historical Studies 1*, Bloomington, IN: Slavica, 2003

Davies, S. *Popular Opinion in Stalin's Russia: Terror, Propaganda and Dissent 1934–1941*, Cambridge University Press, 1997

Delaney-Grossman, J. 'Khrushchev's Anti-Religious Policy and the Campaign of 1954', *Soviet Studies*, Vol. 24, No. 3 (January 1973), 374–86

Dobson, M. 'Contesting the Paradigms of De-Stalinization: Readers' Responses to "One Day in the Life of Ivan Denisovich"', *Slavic Review*, Vol. 64, No. 3 (Autumn 2005), 580–600

'POWs and Purge Victims: Attitudes towards Party Rehabilitation, 1956–57', *Slavonic and East European Review*, Vol. 86, No. 2 (2008), 328–45

Khrushchev's Cold Summer: Gulag Returnees, Crime and the Fate of Reform after Stalin, Ithaca, NY: Cornell University Press, 2009

Dunlop, J. *The New Russian Revolutionaries*, London: Nordland Publishing, 1976

Durham Hollander, G. 'Recent Developments in Soviet Radio and Television News Reporting', *The Public Opinion Quarterly*, Vol. 31, No. 3 (Autumn 1967), 359–65

Eremina, L. and Zhemkova, E. eds. *Korni travy: sbornik statei molodykh istorikov*, Moskva: Zven'ya, 1996

Fainsod, M. 'Soviet Youth and the Problem of Generations', *Proceedings of the American Philosophical Society*, Vol. 108, No. 5 (October 1964), 429–36

Fedor, J. *Russia and the Cult of State Security: The Chekist Tradition, from Lenin to Putin*, London: Routledge, 2011

Feldbrugge, F. 'Soviet Criminal Law: The Last Six Years', *The Journal of Criminal Law, Criminology and Police Science*, Vol. 54, No. 3 (September 1963), 249–66

Samizdat and Political Dissent in the Soviet Union, Leiden: A.W. Sijthoff, 1975

Field, D. 'Irreconcilable Differences: Divorce and Conceptions of Private Life in the Khrushchev Era', *Russian Review*, Vol. 57, No. 4 (October 1998), 599–613

Private Life and Communist Morality in Khrushchev's Russia, New York: Peter Lang, 2007

Filtzer, D. *The Khrushchev Era: DeStalinization and the Limits of Reform in the USSR*, Basingstoke: Macmillan, 1993

Finkel, S. *On the Ideological Front: The Russian Intelligentsia and the Making of the Soviet Public Sphere*, New Haven, CT: Yale University Press, 2007

Fireside, H. *Soviet Psychoprisons*, London: W.W. Norton, 1979

'The Conceptualization of Dissent: Soviet Behavior in Comparative Perspective', *Universal Human Rights*, Vol. 2, No. 1 (January 1980), 31–45

Firsov, B. *Raznomyslie v SSSR 1940–1960 gody: istoriya, teoriya i praktika*, Sankt Peterburg: Izdatel'stvo Evropeiskogo universiteta v Sankt Peterburge, 2008

Fitzpatrick, S. 'Social Parasites: How Tramps, Idle Youth and Busy Entrepreneurs Impeded the Soviet March to Communism', *Cahiers du Monde russe*, Vol. 47, No. 1–2 (janvier–juin 2006), 377–408

Franks, C. E. S. ed. *Dissent and the State*, Toronto: Oxford University Press, 1989

Friedburg, M. *A Decade of Euphoria: Western Literature in Post-Stalin Russia, 1954–1964*, Bloomington, IN: Indiana University Press, 1977

Friedrich, C. and Brzezinski, Z. *Totalitarian Dictatorship and Autocracy*, Cambridge, MA: Harvard University Press, 1965

Fursenko, A. and Naftali, T. *Khrushchev's Cold War: The Inside Story of an American Adversary*, New York: W.W. Norton, 2006

Fürst, J. 'Prisoners of the Soviet Self?: Political Youth Opposition in Late Stalinism', *Europe–Asia Studies*, Vol. 54, No. 3 (May 2002), 353–75

'Re-Examining Opposition under Stalin: Evidence and Context: A Reply to Kuromiya', *Europe–Asia Studies*, Vol. 55, No. 5 (July 2003), 789–802

Stalin's Last Generation: Soviet Post-War Youth and the Emergence of Mature Socialism, Oxford University Press, 2010

Gati, C. *Failed Illusions: Moscow, Washington, Budapest, and the 1956 Hungarian Revolt*, Stanford University Press, 2006

Gerchuk, Yu. *Krovoizliyanie v MOSKh, ili Khrushcheve v Manezhe 1 dekabrya 1962 goda*, Moskva: NLO, 2008

Gerstenmaier, C. *The Voices of the Silent*, New York: Hart Publishing Company, 1972

Gessen, M. *Dead Again: The Russian Intelligentsia after Communism*, London: Verso, 1997

Gilburd, E. 'Picasso in Thaw Culture', *Cahiers du Monde russe*, Vol. 47, No. 1–2 (janvier–juin 2006), 65–108

Gilison, J. 'Soviet Elections as a Measure of Dissent: The Missing One Percent', *The American Political Science Review*, Vol. 62, No. 3 (September 1968), 814–26

Gilligan, E. *Defending Human Rights in Russia: Sergei Kovalyov, Dissident and Human Rights Commissioner, 1969–2003*, London: RoutledgeCurzon, 2004

Glazov, Yu. *The Russian Mind since Stalin's Death*, Boston, MA: D. Reidel, 1985

Golitsyn, A. *New Lies for Old: The Communist Strategy of Deception and Disinformation*, London: The Bodley Head, 1975

Gorelik, G. *The World of Andrei Sakharov: A Russian Physicist's Path to Freedom*, Oxford University Press, 2005

Gorlizki, Y. 'Delegalization in Russia: Soviet Comrades' Courts in Retrospect', *American Journal of Comparative Law*, Vol. 46, No. 3 (Summer 1998), 403–25

'Policing Post-Stalin Society: The Militsiia and Public Order under Khrushchev', *Cahiers du Monde russe*, Vol. 44, Nos. 2–3 (avril–septembre 2003), 465–80

Gorlizki, Y. and Khlevniuk, O. *Cold Peace: Stalin and the Soviet Ruling Circle, 1945–1953*, Oxford University Press, 2004

Grix, J. *The Role of the Masses in the Collapse of the GDR*, Basingstoke: Macmillan, 2000

Gross Solomon, S. ed. *Pluralism in the Soviet Union: Essays in Honour of H. Gordon Skilling*, London: Macmillan, 1983

Grushin, B. *Chetyre zhizni Rossii v zerkale oprosov obshchestvennogo mneniya: epokha Khrushcheva*, Moskva: Progress-Traditsiya, 2001

Grzybowski, K. 'The Extraterritorial Effect of Soviet Criminal Law after the Reform of 1958', *The American Journal of Comparative Law*, Vol. 8, No. 4 (Autumn 1959), 515–18

Gsovski, V. 'Reform of Criminal Law in the Soviet Union', *Social Problems, Symposium on Social Problems in the Soviet Union* (Spring 1960), 315–28

Hamburg, G. 'Writing History and the End of the Soviet Era: The Secret Lives of Natan Eidel'man', *Kritika: Explorations in Russian and Eurasian History*, Vol. 7, No. 1 (Winter 2006), 71–109

Hammer, D. 'Vladimir Osipov and the Veche Group (1971–1974): A Page from the History of Political Dissent', *Russian Review*, Vol. 43, No. 4 (October 1984), 355–75

Hardy, J. 'Gulag Tourism: Khrushchev's "Show" Prisons in the Cold War Context, 1954–59', *Russian Review*, Vol. 70, No. 1 (January 2011), 49–78

Hellbeck, J. *Revolution on my Mind: Writing a Diary under Stalin*, London: Harvard University Press, 2006

Hirschman, A. *Exit, Voice and Loyalty: Responses to Decline in Firms, Organizations and States*, London: Harvard University Press, 1970

Holquist, P. '"Information is the Alpha and Omega of Our Work": Bolshevik Surveillance in its Pan-European Context', *The Journal of Modern History*, Vol. 69, No. 3 (September 1997), 415–50

Hooper, C. 'What Can and Cannot Be Said: Between the Stalinist Past and New Soviet Future', *Slavonic and East European Review*, Vol. 86, No. 2 (April 2008), 306–27

Horvath, R. *The Legacy of Soviet Dissent: Dissidents, Democratisation and Radical Nationalism in Russia*, London: Routledge, 2005

Hosking, G. *The First Socialist Society: A History of the Soviet Union from Within*, Cambridge, MA: Harvard University Press, 1992

   Rulers and Victims: The Russians in the Soviet Union, Cambridge, MA: The Belknap Press of Harvard University Press, 2006

Hough, J. 'The Soviet Concept of the Relationship between the Lower Party Organs and the State Administration', *Slavic Review*, Vol. 24, No. 2 (June 1965), 215–40

Ilič, M., Reid, S. and Attwood, L. eds. *Women in the Khrushchev Era*, Basingstoke: Palgrave Macmillan, 2004

Ilič, M. and Smith, J. eds. *Soviet State and Society under Nikita Khrushchev*, London: Routledge, 2009

Il'ina, L. *Mezhdu dvumya ottepelyami 1954–1982*, Sankt Peterburg: Nestor-Istoriya, 2007

Inkeles, A. *Social Change in Soviet Russia*, Cambridge, MA: Harvard University Press, 1968

Inkeles, A. and Bauer, R. *The Soviet Citizen: Daily Life in a Totalitarian Society*, Cambridge, MA: Harvard University Press, 1961

Inkeles, A. and Geiger, K. *Soviet Society: A Book of Readings*, London: Constable & Company, 1961

Johnson, A. and Parta, E. eds. *Cold War Broadcasting: Impact on the Soviet Union and Eastern Europe*, Budapest: Central European University Press, 2010

Johnson, P. *Khrushchev and the Arts: The Politics of Soviet Culture, 1962–1964*, Cambridge, MA: MIT Press, 1965

Jones, P. 'Memories of Terror or Terrorizing Memories? Terror, Trauma and Survival in Soviet Culture of the Thaw', *Slavonic and East European Review*, Vol. 86, No. 2 (April 2008), 346–71

Jones, P. ed. *The Dilemmas of De-Stalinization: Negotiating Cultural and Social Change in the Khrushchev Era*, London: Routledge, 2006

Joo, Hyung-Min, 'Voices of Freedom: Samizdat', *Europe–Asia Studies*, Vol. 56, No. 4 (June 2004), 571–94

Kagarlitsky, B. *The Thinking Reed: Intellectuals and the Soviet State from 1917 to the Present*, London: Verso, 1989

Karklins, R. 'The Organisation of Power in Soviet Labour Camps', *Soviet Studies*, Vol. 41, No. 2 (April 1989), 276–97

Katz, Z. *Soviet Dissenters and Social Structures in the USSR*, Cambridge, MA: Center for International Studies, 1971

Kenney, C. 'The Twentieth CPSU Congress and the "New" Soviet Union', *The Western Political Quarterly*, Vol. 9, No. 3 (September 1956), 570–606

Kershaw, I. *Popular Opinion and Political Dissent in the Third Reich: Bavaria 1933–1945*, Oxford University Press, 2002

Kharkhordin, O. *The Collective and the Individual in Russia: A Study of Practices*, Berkeley, CA: University of California Press, 1999

Komaromi, A. 'The Material Existence of Soviet Samizdat', *Slavic Review*, Vol. 63, No. 3 (Autumn 2004), 597–618

'The Unofficial Field of Late Soviet Culture', *Slavic Review*, Vol. 66, No. 4 (Winter 2007), 605–29

Koppers, A. ed. *A Biographical Dictionary on the Political Abuse of Psychiatry in the USSR*, Amsterdam: International Association on the Political Use of Psychiatry, 1990

Kostyushev, V. ed. *Sotsiologiya obshchestvennikh dvizhenii: empiricheskie issledovaniya*, Moskva: Institut sotsiologii RAN, 1992

Kozlov, V. *Massovye besporyadki v SSSR pri Khrushcheve i Brezhneve, 1953–1980gg*, Novosibirsk: Sibirskii khronograf, 1999

Mass Uprisings in the USSR: Protest and Rebellion in the Post-Stalin Years, London: M.E. Sharpe, 2002

Neizvestnyi SSSR: protivostoyanie naroda i vlasti 1953–1985, Moskva: Olma-Press, 2006

Kozlov, V., Fitzpatrick, S. and Mironenko, S. eds. *Sedition: Everyday Resistance in the Soviet Union under Khrushchev and Brezhnev*, New Haven, CT: Yale University Press, 2011

Kozlov, V. and Mironenko, S. eds. *Kramola: inakomyslie v SSSR pri Khrushcheve i Brezhneve 1953–1982*, Moskva: Materik, 2005

Kramer, M. 'The Soviet Union and the 1956 Crises in Hungary and Poland: Reassessments and New Findings', *Journal of Contemporary History*, Vol. 33, No. 2 (April 1998), 164–206

Krylova, A. 'The Tenacious Liberal Subject in Soviet Studies', *Kritika: Explorations in Russian and Eurasian History*, Vol. 1, No. 1 (Winter 2000), 119–46

Kulavig, E. *Dissent in the Years of Khrushchev: Nine Stories about Disobedient Russians*, Basingstoke: Palgrave Macmillan, 2002

Kuromiya, H. 'Re-Examining Opposition under Stalin: Further Thoughts', *Europe–Asia Studies*, Vol. 56, No. 2 (March 2004), 309–14

The Voices of the Dead: Stalin's Terror in the 1930s, London: Yale University Press, 2007

Kydyralina, Zh. 'Politicheskie nastroeniya v Kazakhstane v 1945–1985', *Voprosy istorii*, No. 8 (August 2008), 64–72

Lapenna, I. 'The New Russian Criminal Code and Code of Criminal Procedure', *The International and Comparative Law Quarterly*, Vol. 10, No. 3 (July 1961), 412–53

LaPierre, B. 'Making Hooliganism on a Mass Scale: The Campaign against Petty Hooliganism in the Soviet Union, 1953–64', *Cahiers du Monde russe*, Vol. 47, No. 1–2 (janvier–juin 2006), 349–75

Leonard, W. *The Kremlin since Stalin*, London: Oxford University Press, 1962

Levitsky, S. 'The Ideology of NTS', *Russian Review*, Vol. 31, No. 4 (October 1972), 398–405

Lewin, M. *The Soviet Century*, London: Verso, 2005

Lewis, B. *Hammer and Tickle*, London: Weidenfeld & Nicolson, 2008

Linden, C. *Khrushchev and the Soviet Leadership*, Baltimore, MD: Johns Hopkins University Press, 1990

Litvinov, P. *The Demonstration on Pushkin Square*, London: Harvill Press, 1969

Loewenstein, K. 'Re-Emergence of Public Opinion in the Soviet Union: Khrushchev and Responses to the Secret Speech', *Europe–Asia Studies*, Vol. 58, No. 8 (December 2006), 1329–45

Lourie, R. *Sakharov: A Biography*, Hanover, NH: Brandeis University Press, 2002

Maravall, J. *Dictatorship and Political Dissent: Workers and Students in Franco's Spain*, London: Palgrave Macmillan, 1979

Matthews, M. *Class and Society in Soviet Russia*, London: Allen Lane, 1972

McCauley, M. *Khrushchev and Khrushchevism*, Bloomington, IN: Indiana University Press, 1987

McDermott, K. and Stibbe, M. *Revolution and Resistance in Eastern Europe: Challenges to Communist Rule*, Oxford: Berg, 2006

Medvedev, R. and Medvedev, Zh. *Khrushchev: The Years in Power*, New York: Columbia University Press, 1976

  Nikita Khrushchev: otets ili otchim sovetskoi 'ottepeli', Moskva: Yauza, 2006

Medvedev, Zh. *Ten Years after Ivan Denisovich*, London: Macmillan, 1973

Mee, C. *The Internment of Soviet Dissenters in Mental Hospitals*, Cambridge: John Arliss, 1971

Meissner, B. ed. *Social Change in the Soviet Union: Russia's Path toward an Industrial Society*, University of Notre Dame Press, 1972

Mickiewicz, E. 'The Modernization of Party Propaganda in the USSR', *Slavic Review*, Vol. 30, No. 2 (June 1971), 257–76

Mikkonen, S. 'Stealing the Monopoly of Knowledge? Soviet Reactions to Cold War Broadcasting', *Kritika*, Vol. 11, No. 4 (Fall 2010), 771–805

Millar, J. ed. *Politics, Work, and Daily Life in the USSR: A Survey of Former Soviet Citizens*, Cambridge University Press, 1987

Mitrokhin, N. *Russkaya partiya: dvizhenie russkikh natsionalistov v SSSR, 1953–1985*, Moskva: Novoe literaturnoe obozrenie, 2003

Mitrokhin, V. *KGB Lexicon: The Soviet Intelligence Officer's Handbook*, London: Frank Cass, 2002

Nahaylo, B. and Swoboda, V. *Soviet Disunion: A History of the Nationalities Problem in the USSR*, New York: The Free Press, 1990

Naiman, E. 'On Soviet Subjects and Scholars Who Make Them', *Russian Review*, Vol. 60, No. 3 (July 2001), 307–15

Nathans, B. 'The Dictatorship of Reason: Aleksandr Vol'pin and the Idea of Rights under "Developed Socialism"', *Slavic Review*, Vol. 66, No. 4 (Winter 2007), 630–63

Nordlander, D. 'Khrushchev's Image in the Light of Glasnost and Perestroika', *Russian Review*, Vol. 52, No. 2 (April 1993), 248–64

Oushakine, S. 'The Terrifying Mimicry of Samizdat', *Public Culture*, Vol. 13, No. 2 (Spring 2001), 191–214

Oznobkina, E. et al. eds. *KGB: Vchera, segondya i vchera*, Moskva: Obshchestvennyi fond 'Glasnost'', 1994

Pakulski, J. 'Legitimacy and Mass Compliance: Reflections on Max Weber and Soviet-Type Societies', *British Journal of Political Science*, Vol. 16, No. 1 (January 1986), 35–56

Parry, A. 'The Twentieth Party Congress: Stalin's "Second Funeral"', *American Slavic and East European Review*, Vol. 15, No. 4 (December 1956), 463–76

Petroff, S. *The Red Eminence: A Biography of Mikhail A. Suslov*, Cliffton, NJ: Kingston Press, 1988

Petrov, N. *Ivan Serov: pervyi predsedatel' KGB*, Moskva: Materik, 2005

Petrov, V. 'Radio Liberation', *Russian Review*, Vol. 17, No. 2 (April 1958), 104–14

Pfaff, S. *Exit-Voice Dynamics and the Collapse of East Germany: The Crisis of Leninism and the Revolution of 1989*, London: Duke University Press, 2006

Pikhoya, R. *Sovetskii soyuz: istoriya vlasti, 1945–1991*, Moskva: Rossisskaya akademiya gos. sluzhby pri Prezidente Rossiiskoi Federatsii, 1998

Pollack, D. and Wielgohs, J. *Dissent and Opposition in Communist Eastern Europe: Origins of Civil Society and Democratic Transition*, Burlington, VT: Ashgate, 2004

Pozharov, A. 'KGB SSSR v 1950–1960 gody: problemy istoriografii', *Otechestvennaya istoriya*, No. 3 (2001), 141–8

Prishchepa, A. *Inakomyslie na Urale*, Surgut: Surgutskii gosudarstvennyi universitet, 1998

Pyzhikov, A. *Opyt modernizatsii sovetskogo obshchestva v 1953–1964 godakh: obshchestvenno-politicheskii aspekt*, Moskva: Izdatel'skii dom 'Gamma', 1998
'XX s"ezd i obshchestvennoe mnenie', *Svobodnaya mysl'*, No. 8 (2000), 76–85
Khrushchevskaya ottepel', Moskva: Olma-Press, 2002
'Istoki dissidenstva', *Svobodnaya mysl'*, No. 12 (2003), 77–85

Rabichev, L. 'Manezh 1962, do i posle', *Znamya*, No. 9 (2001), 121–52

Rapoport, A. 'The Russian Broadcasts of the Voice of America', *Russian Review*, Vol. 16, No. 3 (July 1957), 3–14

Reid, S. 'Cold War in the Kitchen: Gender and the De-Stalinization of Consumer Taste in the Soviet Union under Khrushchev', *Slavic Review*, Vol. 60, No. 2 (Summer 2002), 211–52

Rigby, T. *Communist Party Membership in the USSR: 1917–1967*, Princeton University Press, 1968
'The Soviet Politburo: A Comparative Profile, 1951–1971', *Soviet Studies*, Vol. 24, No. 1 (July 1972), 3–23

Rittersporn, G., Behrends, J. and Rolf, M. eds. *Public Spheres in Soviet-Type Societies: Between the Great Show of the Party-State and Religious Counter-Cultures*, Frankfurt-am-Main: Peter Lang, 2003

Rogovin-Frankel, E. *Novy Mir: A Case Study in the Politics of Literature, 1952–1958*, Cambridge University Press, 1981

Rossman, J. *Worker Resistance under Stalin: Class and Revolution on the Shop Floor*, London: Harvard University Press, 2005

Roth-Ey, K. 'Finding a Home for Television in the USSR, 1950–70', *Slavic Review*, Vol. 66, No. 2 (2007), 278–306

   Moscow Prime Time: How the Soviet Union Built the Media Empire that Lost the Cultural Cold War, London: Cornell University Press, 2011

Rothberg, A. *The Heirs of Stalin: Dissidence and the Soviet Regime 1953–1970*, Ithaca, NY: Cornell University Press, 1972

Rubenstein, J. *Soviet Dissidents: Their Struggle for Human Rights*, Boston, MA: Beacon Press, 1980

Scammell, M. *Solzhenitsyn: A Biography*, New York: W.W. Norton, 1984

Scammell, M. ed. *The Solzhenitsyn Files*, Chicago, IL: Edition Q, 1995

Schapiro, L. *The Communist Party of the Soviet Union*, London: Methuen, 1970

   Political Opposition in One-Party States, London: Macmillan, 1972

   Totalitarianism, London: Pall Mall Press, 1972

Schlesinger, R. 'The CPSU Programme: Historical and International Aspects', *Soviet Studies*, Vol. 13, No. 3 (January 1962), 303–20

Scott, J. *Domination and the Arts of Resistance: Hidden Transcripts*, New Haven, CT: Yale University Press, 1990

Sebestyen, V. *Twelve Days: Revolution 1956*, London: Weidenfeld & Nicolson, 2006

Service, R. *A History of Modern Russia from Nicholas II to Putin*, Harmondsworth: Penguin Books, 2003

Sharlet, R. *Soviet Constitutional Crisis: From DeStalinization to Disintegration*, London: M.E. Sharpe, 1992

Shatz, M. *Soviet Dissent in Historical Perspective*, Cambridge University Press, 1980

Shelley, L. *Policing Soviet Society: The Evolution of State Control*, London: Routledge, 1996

Shlapentokh, V. 'Two Levels of Public Opinion: The Soviet Case', *The Public Opinion Quarterly*, Vol. 49, No. 4 (Winter 1985), 443–59

   Public and Private Life of the Soviet People: Changing Values in Post-Stalin Russia, Oxford University Press, 1989

   Soviet Intellectuals and Political Power: The Post-Stalin Era, Princeton University Press, 1990

   A Normal Totalitarian Society: How the Soviet Union Functioned and How it Collapsed, New York: Oxford University Press, 2001

Shtromas, A. *Political Change and Social Development: The Case of the Soviet Union*, Frankfurt-am-Main: Peter Lang, 1981

Siegelbaum, L. ed. *Borders of Socialism: Private Spheres of Soviet Russia*, Basingstoke: Palgrave Macmillan, 2006

Silina, L. *Nastroeniya sovetskogo studenchestva 1945–1964*, Moskva: Russkii mir, 2004

Simes, D. 'Human Rights and Détente', *Proceedings of the Academy of Political Science*, Vol. 33, No. 1 (1978), 135–47

Smith, K. 'A New Generation of Political Prisoners: "Anti-Soviet" Students, 1956–1957', *The Soviet and Post-Soviet Review*, Vol. 32, Nos. 2–3 (2005), 191–208

Smith, M. *Property of Communists: The Urban Housing Programme from Stalin to Khrushchev*, DeKalb, IL: Northern Illinois University Press, 2010

Smith, T. and Oleszczuk, T. *No Asylum: State Psychiatric Repression in the Former USSR*, London: Macmillan, 1996

Snyder, S. *Human Rights Activism and the End of the Cold War: A Transnational History of the Helsinki Network*, Cambridge University Press, 2011

Solovyov, V. and Klepikova, E. *Yuri Andropov: A Secret Passage into the Kremlin*, London: Macmillan, 1983

Solzhenitsyn, A. *The Gulag Archipelago*, Vol. 3, London: Collins/Fontana, 1978

Solzhenitsyn, A. ed. *From under the Rubble*, London: Harper Collins, 1975

Sorlin, P. *The Soviet People and Their Society: From 1917 to the Present*, London: Pall Mall Press, 1968

Spechler, D. *Permitted Dissent in the USSR: Novy Mir and the Soviet Regime*, New York: Praeger, 1982

Sushkov, A. *Prezidium TsK KPSS v 1957–1964gg.: lichnosti i vlast'*, Ekaterinburg: Institut istorii i arkheologii UrO RAN, 2009

Swearer, H. 'Changing Roles of the CPSU under First Secretary Khrushchev', *World Politics*, Vol. 15, No. 1 (October 1962), 20–43

Taubman, W. *Khrushchev: The Man and His Era*, London: The Free Press, 2003

Taubman, W., Khrushchev, S. and Gleason, A. eds. *Nikita Khrushchev*, London: Yale University Press, 2000

Taylor, P. 'Treason, Espionage and Other Soviet State Crimes', *Russian Review*, Vol. 23, No. 3 (July 1964), 247–58

'Underground Broadcasting in the Soviet Union', *Russian Review*, Vol. 31, No. 2 (April 1972), 173–4

Tökes, R. ed. *Dissent in the USSR: Politics, Ideology, and People*, Baltimore, MD: Johns Hopkins University Press, 1975

Tompson, W. 'The Fall of Nikita Khrushchev', *Soviet Studies*, Vol. 43, No. 6 (1991), 1101–21

'Khrushchev and Gorbachev as Reformers: A Comparison', *British Journal of Political Science*, Vol. 23, No. 1 (January 1993), 77–105

Khrushchev: A Political Life, New York: St. Martin's Press, 1995

Tromly, B. 'An Unlikely National Revival: Soviet Higher Learning and the Ukrainian "Sixtiers", 1953–65', *Russian Review*, Vol. 68, No. 4 (October 2009), 607–22

Vail', P. and Genis, A. *60-e: mir sovetskogo cheloveka*, Ann Arbor, MI: Ardis Publishers, 1989

van Voren, R. *On Dissidents and Madness: From the Soviet Union of Leonid Brezhnev to the 'Soviet Union' of Vladimir Putin*, Amsterdam: Rodopi, 2009

Vatulescu, C. 'Arresting Biographies: The Secret Police File in the Soviet Union and Romania', *Comparative Literature*, Vol. 56, No. 3 (Summer 2004), 243–61

Viola, L. ed. *Contending with Stalinism: Soviet Power and Popular Resistance in the 1930s*, London: Cornell University Press, 2002

Volkov, S. *The Magic Chorus: A History of Russian Culture from Tolstoy to Solzhenitsyn*, New York: Alfred Knopf, 2008

von Nostitz, S. 'Dictatorship and Resistance: The Problem of How to Resist', *The Western Political Quarterly*, Vol. 20, No. 1 (March 1967), 161–71

Watson, D. *Molotov: A Biography*, Basingstoke: Palgrave Macmillan, 2005

Wedgwood Benn, D. 'New Thinking in Soviet Propaganda', *Soviet Studies*, Vol. 21, No. 1 (July 1969), 52–63

Weiner, A. 'Déjà Vu All Over Again: Prague Spring, Romanian Summer and Soviet Autumn on the Soviet Western Frontier', *Contemporary European History*, Vol. 15, No. 2 (2006), 159–94

'The Empires Pay a Visit: Gulag Returnees, East European Rebellions, and Soviet Frontier Politics', *The Journal of Modern History*, Vol. 78, No. 2 (June 2006), 333–76

Wheatcroft, S. ed. *Challenging Traditional Views of Russian History*, Basingstoke: Palgrave Macmillan, 2002

White, S. 'Rethinking the CPSU', *Soviet Studies*, Vol. 43, No. 3 (1991), 405–28

Wolfe, B. *Communist Totalitarianism: Keys to the Soviet System*, Boston, MA: Beacon Press, 1956

Wolfe, T. *Governing Soviet Journalism: The Press and the Socialist Person after Stalin*, Bloomington, IN: Indiana University Press, 2005

Yanov, A. *The New Russian Right: Right-Wing Ideologies in the Contemporary USSR*, Berkeley, CA: Institute of International Studies, 1978

Yarska-Smirnova, E. and Romanova, P. eds. *Sovetskaya sotsial'naya politika: tseny i deistvuyushchie litsa, 1940–1985*, Moskva: Tsentr sotsial'noi politiki i gender-nykh issledovanii, 2008

Yurchak, A. 'Soviet Hegemony of Form: Everything Was Forever Until It Was No More', *Comparative Studies in Society and History*, Vol. 45, No. 3 (July 2003), 480–510

Everything Was Forever Until it Was No More: The Last Soviet Generation, Oxford: Princeton University Press, 2006

Zaslavskaya, O. 'From Dispersed to Distributed Archives: The Past and Present of Samizdat Material', *Poetics Today*, Vol. 29, No. 4 (Winter 2009), 669–712

Zezina, M. *Sovetskaya khudozhestvennaya intelligentsiya i vlast' v 1950–60e gody*, Moskva: Dialog MGU, 1999

Zhuk, S. *Rock and Roll in the Rocket City: The West, Identity, and Ideology in Soviet Dnepropetrovsk, 1960–1985*, Washington, DC: Woodrow Wilson Center Press, 2010

Ziegler, C. 'Worker Participation and Worker Discontent in the Soviet Union', *Political Science Quarterly*, Vol. 98, No. 2 (Summer 1983), 235–53

Zinov'ev, A. *Homo Sovieticus*, London: Gollancz, 1985

Zubkova, E. *Obshchestvo i reformy 1945–1964*, Moskva: Izdatel'skii tsentr 'Rossiya molodaya', 1993

Russia after the War: Hopes, Illusions and Disappointments, 1945–1957, New York: M.E. Sharpe, 1998

'Na "krayu" sovetskogo obshchestva. Marginal'nye gruppy naseleniya i gosu-darstvennaya politika. 1940–1960e gody', *Rossiiskaya istoriya*, No. 5 (2009), 101–18

Zubok, V. *Zhivago's Children: The Last Russian Intelligentsia*, Cambridge, MA: Harvard University Press, 2009

UNPUBLISHED DISSERTATIONS

Cohn, E. 'Disciplining the Party: The Expulsion and Censure of Communists in the Post-War Soviet Union, 1945–1961', Ph.D. Dissertation, University of Chicago, 2007

Hardy, J. 'Khrushchev's Gulag: The Evolution of Punishment in the Post-Stalin Soviet Union, 1953–1964', Ph.D. Dissertation, Princeton University, 2011

LaPierre, B. 'Redefining Deviance: Hooliganism in Khrushchev's Russia, 1953–64', Ph.D. Dissertation, University of Chicago, 2006

Spencer. I. 'An Investigation of the Relationship of Soviet Psychiatry to the State', Ph.D. Dissertation, University of Glasgow, 1997

Tromly, B. 'Re-Imagining the Soviet Intelligentsia: Student Politics and University Life, 1948–1964', Ph.D. Dissertation, Harvard University, 2007

Tsipursky, G. 'Pleasure, Power and the Pursuit of Communism: Soviet Youth and State-Sponsored Popular Culture during the Early Cold War Period, 1945–1968', Ph.D. Dissertation, University of North Carolina at Chapel Hill, 2011

Index